Ken, I
friendship and value
your wise counsel.
I wish you the best.
—Li

The Battle for Hearts and Minds

Uncovering the Wars of Ideas and Images Behind the Global War on Terror

A Study of Media Performance and Influence, Propaganda, and Strategic Communication

Timothy S. McWilliams

Published at:

Quantico, Virginia
United States of America

ISBN-13: 978-1460961544

ISBN-10: 1460961544

LCCN: 2011905050

To Julie,

My blessing—my joy—my guiding star,

with love,

Tim

CONTENTS

PREFACE

The media, in all of its forms, plays an important role in a democratic society. Accuracy and objectivity in reporting are essential to keep the both the public informed and its government accountable. Misinformation, whether it be inaccurate, incomplete, or misleading journalism, is detrimental to the democratic system. Likewise, shaping news to effect public opinion and policy, or sensationalizing news to attract audiences undermines the democratic process and misleads the electorate. However, despite the meaningful contributions of several exceptional journalists, the Western media, for a variety of reasons, failed to provide a complete or accurate picture of events and U.S. efforts on the two major fronts in the Global War on Terror. This deficiency had profound adverse effects in the wars of ideas that accompanied these conflicts. In the case of the Iraq War, Michael R. Gordon and General Bernard E. Trainor astutely observed that the Iraq War "was one of the most covered but least understood episodes in recent history. ...Many of the key battles are only dimly understood."* With both the Western and Arab media devoting so much attention to the Iraq War at the outset, how could this be so?

The purpose of this study is to examine the media's coverage of the Global War on Terror, focusing mainly on key events in Iraq from 2003 to 2009, to understand the effects of that media coverage on public opinion and policy as it pertains to the media's role in the wars of ideas that accompanied the conflict. This includes analyzing the multiple factors contributing to media performance and influence, such as journalism trends and techniques, developments in the media industry, and the challenges of reporting war. While integrating the important research of leading communication, journalism, and political science scholars, this study also examines the development of U.S. policy and strategic communication, propaganda, and belligerent use of the media.

This study will demonstrate that war is more than combat. It is also a war of ideas where the media, in all of its forms, plays a critical role in influencing public sentiment and public policy, and ultimately the course of events. As a result, the media is not only an independent political actor and a catalyst in historical events, but is also a weapon in wars of ideas that is subject to

---

* Michael R. Gordon and General Bernard Trainor, Cobra II: The Inside Story of the Invasion and Occupation of Iraq, (New York: Pantheon Books, 2006), xxxi.

manipulation by various competing political interests, to include the belligerents themselves. In regards to the Iraq War, this study will show how the United States lost the information initiative after ousting Saddam Hussein, then later regained it, and how Iraq's guerrillas and terrorists used the media to achieve their political objectives in Iraq. In doing so, this study will provide an early revision of the journalist's so-called "first draft of history" pertaining to key events in the Iraq War to put the examination of the media's coverage in context.

This study does not attempt to be a definitive account of the Global War on Terror. Nor does it attempt to judge the policy decisions that initiated and conducted the war. However, it will highlight key points in the policy debate to demonstrate the media's role in shaping U.S. foreign policy as it relates to this case study. The value of this contemporary history is that it will not only provide a timely, relevant, and useful analysis of media influence in U.S. foreign policy during crisis and conflict, but also examine the issues and challenges pertaining to reporting conflict as well as the challenges of U.S. strategic, operational, and tactical communication during war. It will also help the pubic, as both news consumers and the electorate, understand how the media attempted to shape their views on important issues during the war. Moreover, this examination will help historians better understand the role the media plays in historical events, and contribute to political science, communication, and journalism studies.

Like Thucydides, I endeavored to write about a war of which I had been a part and explain a phenomenon I witnessed firsthand. As a media analyst and historian, I followed events after the terrorists' attacks of September 11, 2001 carefully. However, while serving in Iraq in 2004, I witnessed a great disparity between actual events in Iraq and what journalists reported to the world. I then began to study the media's coverage of events in Iraq and its effects of that coverage on public opinion and policy, especially during subsequent trips to Iraq and Afghanistan.

ACKNOWLEDGEMENTS

Working on a contemporary history of the Iraq War that is yet to be decided has many challenges, among which is cutting through the political partisanship and the incomplete, erroneous, or misleading media accounts of events in Iraq to get an accurate picture of events. Another challenge is getting candid insight from people still employed in a conflict that is yet to be decided. The largest challenge, however, is in narrowing the range of topics to examine that such fresh, new historical events afford. I recognize and deeply appreciate the valuable guidance and inspiration of Dr. Jeffery Livingston, who worked closely with me to focus and refine my work. Likewise, I am grateful for Dr. Kenneth Rose for his advice, encouragement, and feedback on this study. I credit him with helping to define the aspect of the Iraq War to examine. I also greatly appreciate the counsel of Dr. James Matray, who not only taught me volumes about the history profession, but also challenged me to perfect my scholarship. Additionally, I am indebted to my colleagues at the U.S. Marine Corps History Division for their peer review and feedback in preparing my final draft. Moreover, I acknowledge and respect the seminal work of Peter Braestrup and Don Oberdorfer. They succeeded in describing and explaining a phenomenon that would not be fully understood until communication and political scholars examined media influence on public opinion and policy in more detail and validated their important contributions to history and media study.

I also give credit and thanks to the numerous scholars mentioned throughout this book, along with the seminal work of Harvard University's Belfer Center for Science and International Affairs, the American Enterprise Institute, and the PEW Research Center's Project for Journalism Excellence. While much of this examination is critical of the media as a whole, I acknowledge the quality reporting of those journalists who sought to provide both an accurate and comprehensive account of events in Iraq. Without the risks, hardships, and efforts of these exceptional journalists, this study would not have been possible. There was excellent reporting on the Iraq War, but much of it was buried by an abundance of incomplete, erroneous, or misleading accounts of events and the U.S. efforts. Finally, and most importantly, I recognize the valiant efforts of U.S. service men and women, who serve not for presidents, but for the American people and the U.S. Constitution they are sworn to defend.

DEFINITIONS

This book is about the wars of ideas and images that accompany military conflicts, focusing mainly on the Iraq War as part of a broader Global War on Terror. In doing this book crosses disciplines and touches on a variety of topics, to include: strategic communication, public diplomacy, information operations, propaganda, public relations, political communication, psychology, military-media relations, wartime journalism, media ethics, and media influence. Therefore, this section intends to provide a common framework for understanding the terms and phrases used through this examination. Whereas wars of ideas represent differing values and beliefs, Antulio J. Echevarria astutely describes wars of ideas as:

> . . a clash of visions, concepts, and images, and-especially-the interpretation of them. They are, indeed, genuine wars, even though the physical violence might be minimal, because they

> serve a political, socio-cultural, or economic purpose, and they involve hostile intentions or hostile acts.*

Like Carl von Clausewitz's definition of war, the goal of any war of ideas is to prevail over the opposing values, beliefs, and visions.** Therefore, the weapons in wars of ideas include all forms of media, rhetoric, and propaganda, and include the common media conventions of priming, framing, and agenda setting/gatekeeping. Importantly, it also includes the selective use of sources and facts, as well as clever misinformation and fiction.

The term "media" is broadly used because many journalists representing a wide spectrum of mediums either congregated in the same locations or relied on the same sources for information, reflective of the media as a whole—even when satellite television is the dominant medium. When possible, I offer specific examples to explain the role of a specific medium and its effect on a public sphere or multiple public spheres. Most often, these differences are expressed in Western versus Arab media, embedded versus non-embedded journalists, and investigative journalists who cover events over a significant period versus "parachute" journalists who are only on scene for a short time. Throughout this study, I use the phrase Vietnam Syndrome. While the definitions for the phrase may vary per source, I refer to Vietnam Syndrome as the fear of costly, protracted endeavor where the perceived risk and costs outweigh the perceived benefits. This applies to the perceptions many journalists have had of U.S. intervention and foreign policy after the Vietnam War. Likewise, through the Vietnam Syndrome lens, quagmire implies that the United States cannot succeed in foreign endeavors.

By definition, the phrase "guerrilla war" refers to the continuation of an armed conflict when conventional means have failed, whereas the term "insurgency" implies that conflict arose anew against an existing government. Because of the complexity of Iraq's conflict after the fall of Saddam Hussein, most analysts would argue that the post-Saddam conflict contained elements of both because many guerrilla elements continued fighting after Iraq's military dissolved, whereas other elements joined the fighting after Coalition forces expelled Saddam Hussein and established an interim government. Throughout this study, I will use both terms interchangeably with no differentiation, though the term "insurgency" is the more common in conventional use.

Since there are different English spellings or punctuations for certain Arab terms depending on the nationality of the source, this study will use one spelling except when another spelling is used by a source in a direct quote.

---

* Echevarria, Antulio Joseph, *Wars of Ideas and the War of Ideas*, (Carlisle, PA: Strategic Studies Institute, U.S. Army War College, 2008), v.

** Clausewitz, Carl von, Michael Howard, and Peter Paret, *On War*, Princeton, N.J.: Princeton University Press, 1976.

The Arabic word "jihad," has several meanings; in this study it refers to an Islamic "holy war." Likewise, the term "mujahedeen" refers to holy warriors. The terms Salafi and Wahhibi are largely used interchangeably; however, Salafi Islam refers to an Islamic fundamentalists movement that began in the 17th century in response to increasing Western influence, whereas Wahhabi Islam refers to a specific Salafi movement led by Salafi cleric Muhammad ibn 'Abd al-Wahhab. Because of their relation to modern fundamental Islam, at least as it pertains to this study, the terms are used without distinction.

INTRODUCTION

Journalists have long claimed to record the first draft of history. During the Global War on Terror, however, journalists have often provided incomplete, inaccurate, or misleading accounts of the wars in Afghanistan and Iraq. This had tremendous implications for both current and future conflicts, especially as U.S. forces operate in Afghanistan to face a renewed threat there. While examples of incomplete, inaccurate, or misleading news coverage during the Global War on Terror abound, the sequence of events following the fall of Baghdad on April 9, 2003 poignantly illustrates how the media's deficient and often erroneous coverage of the conflict in Iraq not only adversely influenced U.S. public opinion and policy in important ways, but also emboldened the enemy while discouraging cooperation with potential U.S. allies in Iraq. While various Western and Arab media establishments bear much responsibility through their framing and agenda setting conventions, a great deal of this also has to do with how various political interests, including both the U.S. government and Iraq's insurgents, attempted to use or manipulate the media to influence public opinion and policy in the wars of ideas that accompanied the military conflict. These wars of ideas not only played out on the geopolitical, strategic, operational, and tactical levels, but also played out on the domestic U.S. political landscape.

To fully understand the media influence in Iraq War, one must look back in history to another event in another war—the 1968 Tet Offensive in Vietnam. As the battle raged, journalists trying to keep up with the fast pace of events hastily rushed reports to editors and producers who presented them to the public without critical analysis. Many of these reports, created from scant facts amid surprise and confusion, were wrong or misleading. Therefore, because the news reached the public with such immediacy, the first reports, though inconclusive, shaped perceptions and opinions of both the American public and its decision makers, and in doing so influenced the events and conflicts themselves. Seldom did journalists have time to correct earlier reports; when they did, editors and producers already predisposed by the first reports were often unwilling to present corrected reports to the public. As a result, the media led the American public to believe that the United States was losing the war, which ultimately led to a loss of both public and political support, and the humiliating withdrawal of U.S. forces.

Later, historians and journalists alike reexamined the battles. Sifting through official reports and eyewitness accounts, they discovered not only that the reports and conclusions of field journalists were wrong, but that conclusions drawn from the media's coverage of Tet greatly influenced the course of the war after the battle. Despite these revelations, however, the media's erroneous first impressions of Tet still prevail in public memory. While the media shortcomings are worth thorough consideration, it is important to note that the rapid escalation and conduct of the war under the Johnson Administration, coupled with the prevalent spirit of optimism that the Johnson Administration encouraged through both his public relations campaign and misleading or exaggerated government progress reports, helped lay the foundation for the media's reaction to the Tet Offensive. This is important because the media's coverage of Tet created a Vietnam War mythology, a cynical view of U.S. involvement in foreign crisis, and a style of coverage that would manifest itself in the media's coverage of the Global War on Terror.

Almost forty years after Tet, journalists flocked to Iraq as they did in Vietnam. Yet unlike Vietnam, an unprecedented number of journalists backed by huge media budgets covered the Iraq war from every front with the assistance and protection of Coalition forces. However, when major combat operations ended, only a handful of journalists remained. Like their predecessors in Vietnam, these journalists no longer reported close to the front because of the threat that Baathist and Islamic guerillas posed, who hoped to take Western hostages such as Nicholas Berg or Jill Carroll. As a result, most journalists reported from the safety of military installations or the protection of Baghdad offices in the "Green Zone," and often did not witness events they reported on. Instead, they relied on partisan Arab journalists and the Arab media for information. Editors and producers then presented these reports to the public uncritically, giving the American public a very narrow and misleading view of what had transpired that again shaped perceptions of the situation. The competitive nature of journalism combined with the fast pace of activities caused journalists to file hasty, incomplete reports filled with speculation and unqualified analysis in the absence of facts, and discouraged journalists from filing corrections. Moreover, as products of their professional training and experiences, many reported the war through the lens of Vietnam Syndrome, and provided a pessimistic picture of events while overlooking positive events and developments—writing a gloomy, "quagmire" narrative of U.S. involvement. Also like Vietnam, pre-war skepticism coupled with the U.S. government's inflated optimism and belief in a short war influenced the media's perception of the conflict. The U.S. government's denial that an insurgency existed, the failure to find significant amounts of special weapons in the weeks after Coalition forced secured Baghdad, policy errors and battlefield mistakes during the conduct of the war, and exaggerated or misleading reports of progress also served to discredit the U.S. government in the eyes of the media.

However, unlike Vietnam and Tet, an abundance of published first-hand accounts combined with greatly improved access to official reports and timely studies on media performance and influence during the Iraq War allow historians to sort out information and provide timely revisions of the journalists' first draft of history. Importantly, they also contribute to a better understanding of both media influence in the Iraq War and the wars of ideas and images that accompanied the conflict. Just like the 1968 Tet offensive in Vietnam, there are numerous examples of media influence in the Iraq War, however, events in al-Anbar Province, Iraq between 2003 and 2010, especially in 2004 Fallujah and 2006 Ramadi, provide an ideal case histories for studying both media performance in wartime and influence because events were historically significant and occurred in a clearly delimited area and timeframe.

CHAPTER ONE

MEDIA INFLUENCE IN U.S. HISTORY

In the war of ideas that accompanied the Global War on Terror, the collective media played an important role as both an independent political actor and a tool for belligerents. Because the collective Western media's portrayal of events in Iraq was often different than the reality on the ground, it resulted in a misunderstanding that was not only not only amplified through the numerous media outlets that share material, but also produced an Iraq War mythology and adversely influenced public opinion and U.S. policy while emboldening enemies and discouraging potential allies. However, media influence in such historical events is not a new phenomenon. History demonstrates a long precedent for media influence on public opinion and behavior, and in doing so reveals that the media, in all of its forms, is more than a chronicler of historical events, but also a catalyst in them. A succinct examination of the history, nature, and dynamics of the modern media is useful in understanding the media's role in framing the issues and events before and during the Global War on Terror. Central to this investigation is an understanding of how the media has been a weapon in a long war of ideas over the political and social direction of the United States and how the media has served as an advocate for social and political change amid turbulent social, economic, and political times. It is also important to understand the seminal research on the media's influence on public opinion and behavior, as well as understanding U.S. government's efforts at state communication and media control during war.

The U.S. Government, the American Public, and the Free Press

Throughout history, ideas have both united and divided people. Representing differing sets of values and beliefs, the intrinsic elements of culture, ideas have been both the catalyst for moving public spheres to action and the seeds of conflict. Since ancient times, the conflict of ideas has often spurred vigorous debates, and leaders have often used persuasive language to influence, win support, and defeat others in the wars of ideas. As a result, ancient Greeks and Romans, and later intellectuals of the Renaissance, practiced both written and oral persuasion, rhetoric, as an art form. Ever since Johann Gutenberg's printing press provided the first means of mass communication in 1450, both sides of an issue or conflict have sought to use, manipulate, or control the media to influence the public sphere.* From the Protestant Reformation and the religious wars that followed to the English Civil War, pamphlets and a few small newspapers were the primary political weapons in the wars of ideas the accompanied these conflicts. For these reasons, both states and religious institutions attempted to censor all printed material.[1]

By the late seventeenth century, Britain had ended political and religious censorship after nearly three hundred years, and the free exchange of ideas that followed spurred intellectual and philosophical development across Europe in what became known as the Enlightenment. Meanwhile, the Protestant Reformation had dramatically improved public literacy and reading became a popular pastime as the public developed an appetite for news, information, and literature. In their efforts to meet this need, publishers found that books, pamphlets, and small newsletters could be profitable commodities, and some writers found they could earn enough to make writing a career. Importantly, improvements in roads and transportation helped printed materials reach broader audiences, which expanded public spheres and brought them into closer intellectual contact, while improvements in printing allowed publishers to add graphics, which became powerful additions to the printed word. Despite intellectual freedom and a growing free press, many publications remained highly partisan. In English politics, for example, Whigs and Tories alike continued to shape public opinion with their own pamphlets and newspapers.[2]

The American colonies were the beneficiaries of this revolution in intellectual freedom and expression, and by the American Revolution, the printed word had shaped the intellectual beliefs of the founding fathers and forged a national consciousness for more than a decade. As in England, Whigs and Tories each had their own representative publications that permeated the colonies, shaping opinions and fostering public debates leading to the important decisions that ultimately resulted in the landmark declaration proclaiming independence. During the American Revolution, these publications continued to provide partisan coverage of issues and events, including the coverage of the war itself. Importantly, the American Revolution demonstrated not only how carefully selected words and well crafted prose could define a problem, propose a solution, and move a public sphere to action, but also how the free press functioned as a catalyst in

* The term public sphere refers to a body connected through a common language and identity.

historical events.[3] John Adams describes this in an 1815 letter to Thomas Jefferson:

> What do we mean by the Revolution? The war? That was no part of the Revolution; it was only an effect and consequence of it. The revolution was in the minds of the people, and this was effected, from 1760 to 1775, in the course of 15 years before a drop of blood was drawn at Lexington. The records of thirteen legislatures, the pamphlets, newspapers in all the colonies, ought to be consulted during that period to ascertain the steps by which public opinion was enlightened and informed concerning the authority of Parliament over the colonies.[4]

This telling statements underscores the fact the American Revolution was more a war of ideas than just a military conflict.

Although the American founding fathers believed that freedom of the press was essential to a democracy by keeping the public sphere informed of events and the debates on important issues, they also believed that a free press was a political weapon in the young nation's politics. Therefore, in the early national period, partisan newspapers shaped the nation's political views, and both Federalists and Democrat-Republicans alike created newspapers as platforms for making their cases. Alexander Hamilton, for example, founded the Federalist newspaper the *New York Evening Post* in 1801 to counter the support the leading Democrat-Republican newspapers, the *National Intelligencer* and Philadelphia's *Aurora*, were giving Thomas Jefferson. However, as in England, newspapers remained independent political actors, and, the collective American media recognized its influence and adopted the term "Fourth Estate," a term that Edmond Burke had originally used to criticize the English press for its self-importance.[5] Even the famous French historian Alexis de Tocqueville observed the press' influence in early American politics writing, "I am far from denying that newspapers in democratic countries lead citizens to do very ill-considered things in common; but without newspapers there would be hardly any common action at all."[6]

Intended to be influential, the emerging American media would find itself caught between its own business and political interests, the public's right to know, and competing political interests attempting to use or manipulate it. Meanwhile, the government's need to communicate would find itself dependent on the free media as it attempted to balance the public's right to know with achieving national policy objectives amid competing political interests. This would be more complicated during wartime as the government attempted to balance national security and transparency. The American public would be left to judge the merits of arguments. Consequently, these early relationships between newspapers, political parties, the U.S. government, and the American public would become enduring part of the American political landscape.

During the nineteenth century, improvements in printing technology coupled with the American public's growing appetite for news and information fostered an abundance of new newspapers. This created a demand for writers, and as a mass media emerged, journalism became a growing profession. However, as more newspapers entered the marketplace, competing publishers featured sensational stories and images combined with aggressive marketing tactics to attract readers and sell newspapers. Importantly, advertising agencies came on the scene and would begin to professionalize and perfect persuasive techniques used not only by commercial advertisers, but also any entity hoping to influence the public sphere. Meanwhile, the telegraph increased the speed that news traveled from distant places, while the still photograph gave audiences a more powerful visual impression of what had occurred. Steam ship and rail travel took these popular new publications to places far beyond the American frontier, and with them important ideas and arguments that forged the public's political opinions and thus expanded the public sphere. Each advance in technology increased the speed, visual impact, and reach of news and information—which increased both the size of the public sphere and the press ability to influence it.[7]

As the United States expanded across the continent, growing newspapers, under infamous names like John O'Sullivan and Duff Green, would both forge national sentiment and frame the arguments justifying expansion as *Manifest Destiny*—a phenomenon that overpowered all opposition. Without such a powerful media force, President James K. Polk could not have won over the broad public and recruited the volunteers needed to sustain a long, protracted war needed to defeat Mexico. Again, like the American Revolution, the American media was clearly a catalyst in an important historical event, illustrating that the power of one word, label, phrase, or headline could influence the public sphere to action in arena of ideas.

By the American Civil War, new newspapers such as the New York *Tribune* and *New York Times* had become powerful forces in the U.S. political landscape. Newspapers like the *New York Tribune*, the *New York Herald*, and *The Charleston Mercury* took sides over issues of slavery and abolition, framing the important political issues that led to Southern secession and the Civil War.[8] However, in addition to the intense partisanship, competitive forces compelled newspaper editors to publish controversial information to "outscoop" competitors—such as when the "*New York Times* published the Order of Battle and the battle plan of the Union Army" during the Civil War.[9] Likewise, competing journalists, hoping to be the first to report breaking news, hurried reports to editors without fully synthesizing all the details, facts, or events while renowned photographers such as Mathew Brady,

Alexander Gardner, and Timothy O'Sullivan brought thousands of graphic war images showing the grim aftermath of battles into American homes. These powerful photographs and illustrations made strong impressions on the American public during the war, however, quite often these images told only part of the story. Edwin Forbes, an artist working for *Frank Leslie's Illustrated Newspaper*, recalled in his memoir that artists and journalists could not see all of the action the Civil War depicted. Forbes explained that often they arrived after a battle only to see the death and destruction and did not understand what had occurred, and then had to piece together the details afterwards, sometimes relying on rumors and camp-gossip.[10]

The effects of partisanship, competition, and hasty and incomplete journalism combined with powerful images that told only part of the story elicited strong emotional responses that conspired to mislead the public and decision makers far removed from the scene during the American Civil War. Moreover, they also threatened both the Union and Confederate war efforts by making sensitive military information public. This posed a problem for military officials, who imposed restrictions on the press to protect operational security and maintain public support amid gains and losses indicative of war. General William Tecumseh Sherman, for example, had a difficult relationship with the press and believed that press censorship was important for military victory. He once said "I hate newspapermen. They come into camp and pick up their camp rumors and print them as facts. I regard them as spies, which, in truth, they are."[11] In one case he was so dismayed with press coverage that he court-martialed *New York Herald* reporter Thomas W. Knox after the Battle of Vicksburg. However, this widened the gap between the military and the press.[12]

Despite the controversies, newspapers were both a popular and powerful force and a mainstay of American life. According to the creators of *The Time of the Lincolns*:

> America had the largest per capita newspaper circulation in the world at the time of the South's secession, and the war made the nation even hungrier for news. Correspondents headed for the battlefields, along with newsboys, who did a brisk trade selling papers to the soldiers. Even in the trenches, some soldiers obtained and debated the editorials from the latest journals. Civilians gathered at newspaper offices, anxious for news from the front. And editors unabashedly took up partisan positions, embarking on campaigns of their own to inform and persuade their readers.[13]

Therefore, the media's relationship with the U.S. government during the Civil War, particularly with the U.S. military, coupled with its own partisan political and business interests and limitations in battlefield reporting demonstrated that the American public did not always get an accurate representation of what had actually occurred.

Following the Civil War, the newspapers continued to flourish and expand with both the nation's population and its expansion across the continent. Near the end of the nineteenth century, competing publishers, such as William Randolph Hearst, publisher of *The New York Journal*, and Joseph Pulitzer, publisher of *The New York World*, not only used sensational means to attract readers, but also used their presses to influence public opinion and policy. In what became called " yellow journalism," both Hearst and Pulitzer recognized the power of the press to move a broad public and influence U.S. policy and used their newspapers to argue for war with Spain much the same way John O'Sullivan and Duff Green successfully framed the arguments justifying expansion as *Manifest Destiny* fifty years earlier.[14] Unlike the American Civil War, however, the U.S. military's more open media policy allowed the media to provide the American public with a tremendous amount of coverage of the Spanish-American War. According to Professor Michael S. Sweeney, the U.S. Army allowed each press agency up to seven journalists and photographers, and "as many as 500 reporters and photographers covered the war."[15]

The Media as a Catalyst for Social and Political Change

Just a year after the Spanish-American War, U.S. involvement in the Philippine-American War and Philippine Civil War would receive neither the pubic support nor the extensive media coverage because America was in a period of severe social and economic turmoil and was undergoing a changing social and political landscape that brought new ideological challenges to U.S. foreign and domestic policy. During the last quarter of the nineteenth century, the United States received a flood of immigrants, most from eastern and southern Europe escaping economic hardships in their native countries. Although these immigrants provided the labor to fuel U.S. industry, by the end of the nineteenth century the United States was in severe economic crisis with high unemployment, harsh working conditions, labor disputes, and crowed cities. This led to tremendous social unrest and public protests, which received considerable media attention. Importantly, these immigrants brought with them new ideas that began to spread and make their way into U.S. political debates and challenge traditional U.S. political philosophy. The fusion of the Marxists and Anarchist ideas with the hardships of the Industrial Revolution and the severe economic depression of the late 19th century was profound effect on the American political landscape as Anarchists and Marxists movements that had taken root in Europe during the nineteenth century began to emerge in the United States. In opposition to capitalism, these movements opposed U.S. foreign intervention imperialistic and oppressive, and launched alternative newspapers to advance their ideas. Influential and charismatic anarchists such as Emma Goldman and Alexander Berkman called for radical political activism and encouraged public protests and incited riots. This included political violence and murder to advance their beliefs, and sought to undermine U.S. society, government, and economic systems.[16] This would adversely affect the free media's coverage of the war in two important ways.

First, a much smaller number of journalists traveled a far greater distance to cover the U.S. effort because the press devoted much of its resources and focus to domestic issues and events amid the social and political turmoil taking place. Many of those journalists who did travel to the Philippines did not accompany U.S. soldiers into the field for long periods to endure hardships of tropical jungle guerrilla warfare, but instead congregated near the amenities of Manila where they were close to lines of communication to file their stories. As a result, most journalists succeeded only in bringing to the American public a limited and often disjointed portrayal of events that, like the coverage of the American Civil War, was often filled with journalists' interpretations of events they had not witnessed firsthand. Unaccustomed to the hardships and physical demands of conflict in foreign lands coupled with limited access and understanding, journalists had a difficult time recording events and often arrived after battles where they saw only the death and destruction. Sensational reports often filled with journalist's commentary combined with compelling photographs and silent movies shaped American opinions about the conflict and the U.S. effort. Importantly, as described in more detail below, journalists would view U.S. involvement in the Philippines through the lens of the changing political landscape in the United States.

Second, many Americans were skeptical of U.S. foreign involvement in distant lands while the United States endured a severe domestic crisis. This significantly affected both how some journalists reported the conflict and how many Americans interpreted it. Influential mainstream socialist writers such as Samuel Clemens and Helen Keller, strongly opposed and criticized U.S. involvement in the Philippines, and many impressionable journalists became advocates for political and social change, giving sympathetic media coverage to radical domestic movements.[17] Clemens influential commentary, and that of other like-minded journalists, combined with sensational and exaggerated news reports of the Philippine-American War, graphic photographs showing death, destruction, and the aftermath of combat, and new imagery in motion pictures often presented without full context, helped influence the American public against the war and fuel anarchist and socialist movements and activity. Writing as Mark Twain just a few months into the war, Clemens asserted that:

> We have got into a mess, a quagmire from which each fresh step renders the difficulty of extrication immensely greater. I'm sure I wish I could see what we were getting out of it, and all it means to us as a nation.[18]

In doing so, Clemens introduced to the "quagmire narrative" into U.S. politics, that is, premature pessimistic criticism of U.S. involvement in foreign affairs that implied that such intervention was doomed. Such coverage drew both public and government criticisms about the press' ability to report objectively, and continued to adversely influence the relationship between the press and the U.S. government. Importantly, a cynical view of U.S. involvement in foreign affairs became firmly established in the U.S. political landscape.

Following, anarchist Leon Frank Czolgosz's assassination of President William McKinley's in 1901, there was considerable public outrage and media condemnation of anarchists, and the U.S. Congress passed the Anarchist Exclusion Act to prevent anarchist from entering the country. In response, many American Anarchists went underground, joining emerging socialist and Marxist groups, and continued to spread their beliefs and cultivate a following through underground and alternative newspapers, including Emma Goldman's *Mother Earth* and Alexander Berkman's *The Blast*, for the next two decades.[19]

Vying for Influence: U.S. Government versus the Free Media

By World War I, anarchists and Marxist movements had gained a substantial international followings and began to affect international affairs in significant and dramatic ways. They opposed the Great War as an example of capitalist, imperialist aggression and social injustice to advance their cause, and engaged in anti-war demonstrations across Europe and in the United States while producing numerous anti-war films and literature.[20] This caused great concern to the allied powers which heavily restricted press access and not only engaged in press censorship, but also mounted substantial public relations efforts to win and maintain public support. According to Sweeney, the allied powers justified such censorship to support the concept of "total war," explaining that "too much was at stake they reasoned, to allow the press any degree of freedom."[21] When the United States entered the war, President Woodrow Wilson was not only concerned about maintaining public support and operational security, but also about the media's ability to report objectively. He recruited investigative journalist George Creel to encourage media self-censorship, provide the nation news of the war, and lead the government's effort to gain public support—a milestone in U.S. strategic communication and public diplomacy.[22] The Committee on Public

Information, also known as the "Creel Committee," also included Walter Lippmann, a socialist propagandists turned progressive who became an ardent supporter of Woodrow Wilson and the Democratic Party, and Edward Bernays, a progressive journalist who also supported Wilson's progressive agenda. Lippmann would later become a renowned expert in the use of propaganda to shape public opinion and believed that the manipulation of public opinion was necessary to achieve political goals. He described the process as the "manufacture of consent" in his enduring work *Public Opinion.*[23] Likewise, Edward Bernays considered one of the fathers of public relations, later popularized and employed the psychoanalytical techniques of his uncle, Sigmund Freud, to appeal to the subconscious in shaping public opinion and influencing behavior. He believed that the manipulation of public opinion was a necessary part of democracy, writing:

> If we understand the mechanism and motives of the group mind, is it not possible to control and regiment the masses according to our will without their knowing about it? The recent practice of propaganda has proved that it is possible, at least up to a certain point and within certain limits.[24]

This team would not only make an indelible mark on political communication, but also influence generations of journalists, political scientists, advertisers, public relations agents, and propagandists around the world. Even though Wilson's use propaganda and public relations to manage public opinion during the war was highly controversial, the fusion of progressive politics with the rise of public relations would be an enduring theme in the U.S. social and political landscape.*

After the Bolshevik Revolution in Russia, however, Marxist and anarchist groups in Europe and the United States answered Vladimir Lenis' call for world revolution, threatening international peace and security by engaging in espionage, riots, and political violence. In response, the U.S. Congress passed the Espionage Act of 1917 and the Sedition Act of 1918 to combat growing Marxist and anarchist subversion while the U.S. Department of Justice arrested and deported hundreds of suspected Communists in the Palmer Raids.* To counter the spread of Marxists propaganda, Wilson expanded the Creel Committee on Public Information functions to promoting Wilson's vision of democracy and the U.S. role in world politics both domestically and

---

* The term propaganda did not have the negative connotations in the early Twentieth century as is does today—which today suggests highly subjective misleading or untruthful information. It was used to describe any organization's public or promotional communication intended to shape public opinion and behavior.

* Goldman and Berkman were arrested in 1917 for violating the Espionage Act, and later deported under the 1918 Exclusion Act.

abroad—another milestone in U.S. strategic communication and public diplomacy.[25]

Following World War I, there were two significant media developments that increased the speed, impact, and reach of the media. First, radio was changing the way public spheres receive news, information, and entertainment and gaining large audiences. During the 1930s, radio became a powerful force, and President Franklin D. Roosevelt used radio broadcasts, known as "fireside chats," to gain public support for his agenda and policies. Perhaps the most striking example of radio's power to influence a broad public was the 1938 broadcast of H.G. Wells *War of the Worlds*, in which Mercury Theater's Orsen Welles portrayed the fictional Martian invasion in a sensational news bulletin format that caused fear and panic among tens of thousands of listeners, in which nearly a third believed the report was true.[26] Second, motion pictures, which had barely begun to come on the scene at the turn of the century and were in limited used during the war, began to emerge as a form of mass information and entertainment, especially after the effective incorporation of sound in the late 1920s, and newsreels had become effective visual means of bringing news and information into American communities. Played in local theaters, reports such as the Hindenburg disaster in 1937 combined powerful imagery with sensational narration and music to convey sensational news to the American public. In addition to his radio broadcasts, Roosevelt used these newsreels as edited versions of his fireside chats as part of his public relations effort. On the eve of World War II, radio had replaced newspapers as America's preferred medium, and eighty-three percent of U.S. households had a radio. Although the first television sets were available, they were not yet widely used, and newsreels would remain the most influential visual medium of the war.[27]

In addition to innovations in technology, advertisers, publishers, and political scientists began to better understand the media's influence on the public and how to affect its behavior during the 1920s. Although commercial advertising has always been a part of newspapers, commercial advertising agencies had been little more than middlemen between advertisers and newspapers until it evolved into a major industry by the early 1900s. By the 1920s, however, commercial advertising agencies integrated the new science of psychology, hiring psychologist and behavioral experts like Harvard University's John Watson to understand how the mass media influenced consumer preferences and decision making, along with public attitudes and behavior to develop influential communication strategies.[28] This important research not only had a profound effect on more effectively advertising consumer products, but also influenced journalism and all forms of government and organizational communication.

As technology and communications research conspired to make the media more powerful and influential, dramatic ideological and political changes were taking place on the international level. First, during the 1920s, the emerging Soviet Union began to supervise, finance, train, and otherwise support Communist parties' around the world through *Communist International* in Moscow.[29] This included subversive acts aimed to undermine governments, infiltrating social and political organizations, and expanding propaganda and recruiting efforts internationally. In the United States, the Communist Party of the United States of America (CPUSA) and the Socialists Party of America, backed by Communist International, engaged in bomb attacks on court buildings, police stations, churches, homes, and government officials. Facing U.S. government crackdowns, the CPUSA and other American Marxists groups went underground, infiltrating and often directing the U.S. labor movement through organizations such as International Workers of the World and the Worker's Party of America, and engaged in organized domestic propaganda efforts in support of political violence and domestic terror.[30] Indicative of these efforts, the Worker's Party of America, controlled by CPUSA, republished Leon Tolstoy's book *Terrorism and Communism* in 1920 as *Dictatorship versus Democracy*.[31] In response, the U.S. government continued to target suspected Communist agents and entered the first Cold War with the Soviet Union.[32] Joseph Stalin had build on the propaganda machine established by Vladimir Lenin, similarly exalting Communist values, denouncing Capitalism, and creating an enormous personality cult.

Second, the Nazi Party developed a sophisticated propaganda machine that masked the fanatical views and ambitions of the Nazi Party to appeal to all levels of German society to unite them against common enemies—primarily Jews—and motivate them for war. This included aggrandizing Nazi beliefs, reinventing German history, developing a personality cult around Adolph Hitler, and demonizing Jews, Gypsies, and others. Much of this propaganda effort involved fabricating history and evidence against Jews, and then very creatively propagating the misinformation and lies through every available medium in a very compelling manner that stirred emotional responses and compelled Germans to act. According to historian and media scholar Stuart Ewen, the Nazis used Bernay's 1929 book *Crystallizing Public Opinion* as a basis for their propaganda efforts.[33]

The success of Nazi and Soviet propaganda efforts and the threat they posed forced U.S. officials to take notice and examine them. Political science and communication scholars, such as renowned political scientist and communications theorist Harold Lasswell and Clyde R. Miller, the Colombia University professor and publicist who founded the Institute for Propaganda Analysis in 1937, began to understand the effects of mass media's influence in political communication as both Nazi and Soviet propaganda efforts influenced world politics. Miller studied how emotion based propaganda could sway public opinion over reason, whereas Lasswell studied propaganda and its influence to predict behavior, and was later involved in dissecting Nazi propaganda efforts in World War II.[34] Importantly, both Walter Lippmann and Edward Bernays remained influential in both the growing propaganda and public relations fields and in U.S. politics.

As the United States entered World War II, Roosevelt was both concerned about both the media's ability to report objectively and about the threat Nazi propaganda posed to the war effort. He sought to both counter Nazi propaganda while protecting operational security and maintaining public support for the war. Importantly, the U.S. government still had deep suspicions about the media's ability to report objectively. For these reasons, the U.S. government sought to manage the media during World War II to protect operational security and maintain public support, creating the Office of War Information in 1942. Roosevelt understood the First Amendment criticisms of Wilson's Creel Commission and sought a less overt the policy to achieve the same ends. According to Professor Sweeney, "Roosevelt decided to split the war-information into three pieces: a voluntary domestic news censorship program, run by civilians; a mandatory censorship operation for news originating in combat zones; and a global propaganda and publicity campaign aimed at wartime morale."[35] However, Roosevelt's information agencies were much more decentralized than Creel's Commission in World War I, and war correspondents were given considerably more latitude in reporting the war.[36] Although most wartime correspondents respected national and operational security needs and engaged in self-censorship, many, such as Ernie Pyle, still succeeded providing vivid stories and images from the front lines, reporting both the good and bad of war from a soldier's perspective while considering national interests and the sensitivities of Americans at home.[37]

Once government control and censorship faded, new stories about the war sought to describe the conflict in greater detail. A year after World War II ended, *The New Yorker* published a lengthy and compelling examination the Atom bomb's effects on Hiroshima by John Hersey titled "Hiroshima." In an effort to be influential, *The New Yorker* devoted its entire editorial space to Hersey's article for the purpose of causing people to consider the "incredible destructive power of this weapon, and that everyone might well take time to consider the terrible implications of its use."[38]

Wars of Ideas: The Media and the Cold War

After World War II, the U.S. government discovered the extent of Soviet infiltration, influence, and espionage during the war when it broke the code on thousands of messages intercepted between Moscow and Soviet agents in the United States from 1942-1946 through the VENONA Project. As many 349 Soviets infiltrated key U.S. institutions and agencies where their agents were successful in affecting U.S. policy favorable to the Soviet Union, including President Roosevelt's office, the Office of Strategic Services (the forerunner of the Central Intelligence Agency), and the second highest position in the U.S. Treasury. Equally significant, the Soviet Union enlisted some of its best journalists from its Soviet state controlled Tass News agency to penetrate the American media and not only influence American journalism, but also gain information from government sources and influence news reports. In response to the Soviet infiltration and espionage efforts, the U.S. government successfully arrested and prosecuted several Soviet spies, including U.S. high-ranking State Department official Alger Hiss. Meanwhile, facing both the government's crackdown on Communists agents and the social stigma that came with the term "Communists," many American Communists again went underground, while others recast themselves as members of the "new left" and "progressive" movements." This did not stop subversive Communist's activities in the United States. Moscow continued to finance subversive activities aimed at undermining world governments.[39]

Afterward, the U.S. government began to look at the media with suspicion during the Cold War believing that leaks and Communists spies threatened national security and knowing Soviet agents had infiltrated the American media.[40] However, facing the pre-World War II criticisms and U.S. government concerns about the media's ability to report objectively, the media established professional and ethical standards in 1947 centering on the "social responsibility" of journalists to be objective and provide a clear, accurate picture of events, validating facts and using credible sources while still adhering to its watchdog role.[41] This succeeded in winning public trust and confidence for the next two decades.

During the Cold War, the American media generally accepted the new U.S. Cold War policy, which carried over into the Korean War. However, there were relatively few journalists covering the Korean War, which received substantially less media attention than the Second World War a decade before. While some journalists reported that the U.S. military was not handling the war correctly in the early part of the war, most journalists, like Marguerite Higgins, largely exercised self-censorship. When the Korean War ended in a costly stalemate after China entered and committed tens of thousands of troops, criticisms of how the U.S. government handled the war began to surface and make their way into public memory. Meanwhile, U.S. Government sought to engage in public diplomacy as part of its strategic communication strategy to counter the global Communists propaganda efforts following the Korean War, creating the U.S. Information Agency in 1953.[42]

Television was still in its infancy during the Korean War, with only a few thousand television sets in use throughout the United States, but the medium matured rapidly during the 1950s. As the United States began deploying advisors and troops in Vietnam, however, the age of television was emerging. By September 26, 1960, television had not only matured, but had begun to thrust itself into political area when 70 million U.S. viewers tuned in to watch the first-ever televised presidential debate between Vice President Richard Nixon and Senator John Kennedy. Unlike early U.S. involvement on the Vietnam War, the Civil Rights Movement received considerable media attention and sympathetic coverage, bringing the dramatic visual social changes and turmoil into American homes every night and shaping the perceptions and beliefs of a nation. Amid this environment, a new generation of journalists arrived on the scene and incorporated their perception of reality based on their life's experiences, background, education, and perceptions. Influenced by the Civil Rights Movement, journalists became, advocates for political and social change by shaping news based on their selection and use of sources and information to reflect a desired perspective. These factors not only contributed to a decline in objectivity, but coupled with the increasing popularity of television also shaped public opinion in more profound ways.[43]

Return of the Advocacy Media

Like the Korean War a decade before, the mainstream media and American public generally supported early U.S. involvement Vietnam because incidents such as the Soviet invasion of Hungary, Soviet involvement in the Suez Crisis, and the Cuban Missile Crisis provided compelling visible evidence of Communists influence and aggression in Europe, Asia, the Middle East, and Latin America. Nonetheless, criticisms of U.S. involvement in Vietnam had began to surface in underground newspapers and "new left" circles, they began to emerge more frequently in college campus newspapers and organized campus meetings called "teach-ins." In 1962, Tom Hayden, student editor of the University of Michigan newspaper *Michigan Daily* and the socialist founder of the Students for a Democratic Society (SDS), published a manifesto titled the "Port Huron Statement" in the *Michigan Daily*, the University of Michigan's daily student newspaper, which fused together the tenants of the Civil Rights Movement with the antiwar and antiestablishment principles of the new left's platform.[44]

Early U.S. involvement in Vietnam did not receive much media attention, and the small number of journalists in Vietnam had great difficulty covering a complex, new form of conflict. Although journalists did raise some valid concerns about the Johnson Administrations' conduct of the Vietnam War, they often provided deficient and erroneous coverage. Respected Korean War correspondent Marguerite Higgins described the new generation of advocacy journalists, such as David Halberstam, as "typewriter strategists" who attempted to shape the narrative of the war according to their own aims.[45] Like Samuel Clemens a half century before him, Halberstam returned to the

United States and released a hasty, premature assessment of early U.S. involvement in Vietnam in his 1964 book *The Making of a Quagmire*, released the year before President Lyndon Johnson escalated U.S. involvement.[46] This assessment would influence many journalists' perceptions of the war thereafter.[47]

As U.S. forces increased under President Lyndon B. Johnson, however, so did its coverage. Importantly, these journalists would be allowed significant access to the battlefield without the previous constrains of censorship and continued to provide valid criticisms of the U.S. conduct of the war while also providing incomplete or inaccurate reports. Like Korea, the U.S. Military did not engage in a censorship policy, but instead encouraged voluntary restraints. When journalists began to discover exaggerated, misleading, or false government reports about U.S. progress in Vietnam, however, the U.S. government and President Lyndon Johnson's administration began to lose credibility, and the collective media began to report the war based on the perception that the government did not tell the truth. This not only strained the relationship between the media and the U.S. military, but also had profound effect on U.S. public opinion.[48]

By 1967, the media, particularly television, had become a powerful force in U.S. politics and society, and was a catalysts in dramatically changing the U.S. political and social landscape to that point. The Civil Rights and antiwar moments became strongly intertwined. Haden's SDS had evolved into a leading antiwar movement and other organizations such as the Blank Panthers emerged to promote the Civil Rights and anti-war causes. Political protests and violence became common as the Young Socialists Alliance and the Socialist Workers Party joined the SDS in antiwar and anti-government protests intended to be media spectacles, which provided the media with an abundance of sensational images and politically charged anti-United States rhetoric that appeared in headlines, sound bites, and quotes. The antiwar groups Vietnam Veterans Against the War (VVAW) and Veterans for Peace (VFP) also came on the scene that year and seemed to legitimize the antiwar movement, but unlike other antiwar organizations, the VVAW criticized the U.S. conduct of the war. At the same time, hundreds of "underground" or "alternative" newspapers supporting the antiwar movement, including many high school, college, and prison newspapers, took the antiwar and socialist platform to millions of Americans. Importantly, these young high school and college journalists would later enter the mainstream media.[49]

As 1967 ended, radical opposition to the U.S. government became more open, widespread, and violent. Although the increasingly violent and radical antiwar movement alienated much of the American population, it still gained considerable sympathy and coverage in the news, and the coverage of the Vietnam War would soon reflect these changes.[50] According to historian Alan Axelrod, only a year before the Tet Offensive the anti-war movement was largely perceived as a fringe movement, however, increasing media attention made it seem more "mainstream" and "legitimate."[51] However, "by 1968," he explains, "it had become commonplace for newspaper and television news commentators to write or speak of 'the war in Vietnam' and the parallel 'war at home'."[52] Meanwhile, academic elites along with anti-war politicians in the U.S. Congress became more open and outspoken about U.S. involvement in Vietnam, which provided the media with compelling sources for conveying the anti-war message.[53] Adding to the social discontent, the U.S. economy had began to decline after two decades of post-World War II prosperity.[54]

The Media, Popular Culture, and Public Memory

Since ancient times, music has always been both a reflection of society at a given time and an influential force. From the American Revolution, through the Civil War and beyond, some songs sought to evoke strong emotional patriotic feelings during difficult times. Both Adolf Hitler and Joseph Stalin understood the power of music, and powerful songs of nationalism were an integral part of their propaganda and indoctrination efforts. Even in the era of silent film, bands played compelling scores during the film to evoke the desired emotional response, and no major film in the modern era is without its own musical score and theme to enhance the experience. Likewise, successful advertisers understood the power of music, and developed creative, memorable jingles to help them sell their products. The 1960s would bring a new revolution of music that would be extremely influential in moving a new generation of Americans, and the major media outlets, with their coverage of the Civil Rights Movement, anti-war protests, and the Vietnam War would not only be a powerful force on popular culture, but also leave and indelible mark on public memory.[55]

While the collective major media outlets would serve to shape public opinion, music would serve to reinforce and even amplify certain themes during the 1960s, such as questioning both the nation's justification for the war and the execution of the war. [56] Importantly, anti-war music would become an integral part of the growing anti-war movement, as well as the numerous protests and events. According to music professor James E. Perone, "music was simply always there: one could not escape the presence of songs...[which] served to reinforce already held beliefs and to reflect what was happening in American society at large than anything else."[57] Like the anti-war movement itself, music would influence both journalists and their perceptions of the war.

In 1961, the first commercially successful anti-war song appeared. While most anti-war songs of the early 1960s came in response to the Cold War and the possibility of nuclear annihilation, as reflected in the Korean War, and by 1963 the first Vietnam protest songs began to appear, though these songs were mostly played at concerts, protests, and "singouts," and were not commercial successes. In 1968, however, parallel to the media's abundant and pessimistic coverage of Vietnam, there was a surge in anti-war songs, many becoming commercial success and finding spots on *Billboard*'s annual top 100 list. Importantly, many of these popular anti-war songs would continue to be popular well into the 1970s. As described more in the next chapter, the number of anti-war songs, the strength of the sentiments, and their popularity would only increase.[58]

Examining the Conventions of Media Influence

By 1968, however, the U.S. political and social landscape would make a dramatic turn in which the power of the media, especially television, would have a profound effect on both U.S. public opinion and policy that would have resounding effects on U.S. politics and society—and on journalism itself. Although some historians contend that the media did not influence public opinion or policy during the period, it is important to note that political science and communications scholars argue differently, contending that news is a manufactured commodity intended to be influential. Making this point, political science and communications professor Matthew A. Baum argues that "contemporary scholars have challenged [the traditional] perspective, finding that the media does influence public opinion in important ways—through priming, framing and agenda setting."[59] Professor of political communication Steven Livingston supports Baum's argument, concluding that research proves the global media has "a substantial, if not profound," impact on U.S. diplomacy and foreign policy.[60] The work of these contemporary scholars, and others, builds on the work of early 20th century scholars and researchers (such as Creel, Lippman, Bernays, Watson, Lasswell, and Miller) who both studied and understood media influence and sought to perfect its use to influence public opinion and behavior.

Communication scholars have identified three common media conventions to shape news, priming, framing, and agenda setting. "Priming" involves presenting a wealth of information on one particular issue over others, which leads the public to believe that those issues are more important. "Framing" entails carefully selected terms that evoke a collective group of interconnected ideas and emotions and shape public opinion.[61] These are often carried in carefully crafted headlines. According to the *Project for Excellence in Journalism*, journalists construct news stories around one of thirteen common framing devices.[62] "Agenda setting," also known as "gatekeeping," occurs through the media's subjective selection and placement of news stories, which supports the framing strategy by conveying "greater news value."[63] Agenda setting/gatekeeping determines both which information is selected, the content and context of information provided, and the placement within the publication or broadcast. However, international relations scholar B.A. Taleb explains, these media conventions "negate the notion of objectivity."[64]

Chapter Conclusion

The free media plays an important role in a democratic society by informing the electorate about important issues and events. However, history demonstrates that the media, in all of its forms, is never completely objective. Since the founding of the nation, various media establishments have always taken a side in American politics and have thrust themselves into important political and social issues, and in doing so have been catalysts in important historical events. Considering themselves the "Watchdog of Democracy" and the "Forth Estate" of government, the various media establishments are independent political actors intended to be influential in shaping public opinion and policy, and moving a public, or government, to action through carefully chosen words, phrases, or images.[65] Aware of their power to influence public opinion and policy, all levels of the media establishment, from journalists to editors and producers, act as "gatekeepers" determining what information the public should receive. Through conventions of priming, framing, and agenda setting, these gatekeepers define, prioritize, and draw conclusions on issues from a particular point of view. Often smaller media establishments follow the lead of the major elite media establishment in framing issues. As a result of this manipulation, news is a subjective, manufactured commodity—shaped by the values, beliefs, and experiences of journalists, editors, and producers, which naturally colors their perceptions and influences their reporting and selection of news.

History also shows that, above all else, media establishments are first commercial enterprises. Driven by profit and self-interests, the free market media uses marketing techniques and sensational means to attract audiences and build market share in a highly competitive industry. These marketing conventions not only further influence the selection and packaging of news, but also further negate objective reporting. Moreover, to succeed in a highly competitive environment, journalists, along with their editors and producers, rush to report breaking news, and in doing so provide pieces of a story that is yet to be played, and often fail to validate the information they report. History also demonstrates that from the first printing press to network television, each improvement in technology increased the media's speed, impact, and reach, and with it its power to influence the public sphere and ultimately public policy. By the mid-Vietnam War, television had become a powerful force on the American social and political landscape, which combined the speed and reach of electronic transmission through antennae and satellite relays with the impact of motion pictures.

Since the late 19th century, the free media has been an advocate for social and political change in the United States amid periods of social, economic, and political turmoil. Though tempered through the Second World War and Cold War, the Civil Rights Movement coupled with public anxiety over escalation in Vietnam spurred a new generation of journalists who encouraged social and political change. Aided by the new power of television, these journalists began to have a dramatic effect on the American public as a result of both their sensational coverage of the Civil Rights and anti-war movements and their coverage and interpretation of U.S. involvement in Vietnam. This advocacy journalism began to not only influence public attitudes, but also public behavior.

Because of its power to influence public opinion and compel a public body to action, various internal and external political interests attempt to use the media as a vehicle for persuading the masses to action, or to embrace an ideological position. In U.S. history, various political interests, from political parties and political action organizations to labor unions, have sought to influence U.S. society and politics to achieve their political aims using all forms of media to do so. This includes influencing and manipulating the mainstream free media. Importantly, for much of the 20th century, external foreign interests, including the Soviet Union's Communist International, have supported various domestic Marxist and Communist groups attempting to influence U.S. society and politics in a monumental, high stakes war of ideas. This influence has had a significant effect on the U.S. social and political landscape, where the media, in all of its forms, has been the lead weapon for all sides in this war of ideas. Therefore, because the U.S. government relied on the free press for state communication, the efforts of domestic and external agents attempting to influence the free media along with the free media's active and often adversarial involvement in political issues posed a challenge for the U.S. government. In response, the U.S. government, at times, has sought to understand, control, and use the media to achieve its political aims.

From the Wilson Administration's Creel Commission and commercial advertising and public relations firms of the early 20th century, to the modern scholars, advertising executives, political organizations of today, many have studied the techniques of media influence to understand, counter, and even perfect their use to influence public opinion and behavior. These efforts have provided tremendous insight into the media's power to influence a public sphere. However, these efforts have only succeeded in perfecting the techniques of media use in various wars of ideas that play out in numerous areas around the globe. With so many political and commercial actors attempting to influence attitudes and behavior, this not only also poses a dilemma for the American electorate who requires timely and accurate information for making political decisions, but also for the American public at large who requires honest, objective information to make important social and consumer decisions, leaving the American public to judge the information and arguments themselves.

CHAPTER TWO

THE LESSONS OF TET

War poses special challenges to journalists. In Iraq, much like Afghanistan, most Western journalists had a difficult time getting access to events during the post-Saddam insurgency, and often reported on things they did not witness first-hand. They also had difficulty understanding the conflict's numerous complexities. In a rush to be the first to report breaking news, they not only provided fragments of news produced in haste and confusion before all of details were known, but also filled the void in facts and details with hasty analysis and speculation. Moreover, journalists did not validate the information they presented to the public. This phenomenon, however, was not a unique. Because of its striking similarity to the media's coverage during the Iraq war, and examination of the 1968 Tet Offensive in Vietnam provides an excellent foundation for understanding media performance in the Global War on Terror. It is also useful in understanding media performance in times of conflict, as well as in understanding key issues such as the challenges of reporting combat, the relationships between the media and both the U.S. government and military, and the power of the media, especially television, to influence public opinion and policy.

The Media and the 1968 Tet Offensive

By 1968, television had become a significant force in American society. Television's coverage of both the Civil Rights movement and the global protests and political violence had a profound effect on the nation and its politics. According to veteran journalist and Vietnam historian Don Oberdorfer, by the height of the Vietnam War, television emerged as the dominant medium for the American public with "nearly a hundred million [television] sets...reaching sixteen of every seventeen homes and a potential audience of 96 percent of the population."[1] Compelling personalities such as Walter Cronkite not only reported the news during prime time, but also helped interpret it for American audiences. Oberdorfer, a senior correspondent for *Washington Post* in Vietnam during the war, explains that "Vietnam was America's first television war and the Tet Offensive was America's first super battle," and the media's coverage of Tet, "was to have a powerful impact on the emotions, opinions, and convictions of millions of Americans and the futures of their political leaders."[2] Ron Steinman, *NBC* television's news bureau chief in Vietnam agrees, observing that the "Tet Offensive changed the war...Nothing in Vietnam, including life in the bureau or our coverage of the war, would ever be the same again."[3]

As both an eyewitness to journalists' coverage of the battle and the effect of that coverage in the United States, Oberdorfer describes with a certain degree of astonishment, how the power of the media, particularly satellite television, adversely influenced "American public attitudes and governmental decision making."[4] In describing the contradiction between the actual events of the Tet offensive and the way journalists reported them, Oberdorfer explains the startling media phenomenon he witnessed as a correspondent during the Tet Offensive:

> As in the case of the Tet Offensive, the greatest media attention and public impact concentrates during the early hours of a Big Event when its novelty is greatest and when its true significance may be unclear. Tet is a lesson that there is a danger in the rush to judgment before important pieces of the puzzle can be identified or put together.[5]

The result of incomplete, inaccurate, and misleading reporting at the outset of Tet, these early incomplete, erroneous, and misleading judgments would shape subsequent reporting in Vietnam, and embed themselves in public memory for decades to follow.

Peter Braestrup covered the Vietnam War and Tet Offensive as chief of the *Washington Post's* Saigon bureau and expressed similar criticism. Shocked by the disparity between the events he witnessed and the way his peers portrayed them, Braestrup describes the adverse impact writing:

> Events in Vietnam in February 1968 was for a time obscure. But commentators and many reporters did not wait. ...By the time the fog of war began to lift later that month, the collective emanations of the major media were producing a kind of continuous black fog of their own, a vague conventional 'disaster' image, which few newsmen attempted to reexamine and which few news managers at home sought to question.[6]

Echoing Oberdorfer, Braestrup offers a troubling conclusion:

> The generalized effect of the news media's contemporary coverage of Tet in February-March 1968 was a distortion of reality—through sins of omission and commission—on a scale

> that helped spur major repercussions in U.S. domestic politics, if not in foreign policy.[7]

Much of this was the result of incomplete, erroneous, and misleading reports of events in Vietnam—reports that were often filled with speculation in the absence of facts.

The phenomenon Oberdorfer and Braestrup describe began months before the Tet Offensive when, as Oberdorfer observes, Communist leaders in Hanoi realized that despite the U.S. military continually beating their forces, they were not ready to surrender. Hanoi began looking for a humiliating American defeat as a way to rally its troops while undermining U.S. public support, hoping to replicate the significant victory it had won fourteen years earlier against the French at Dien Bien Phu. Meanwhile, growing public criticism about the Vietnam War coupled with an organized antiwar movement that received considerable media attention began to turn public support. President Johnson's administration, suffering politically in opinion polls, undertook a public relations campaign in the fall of 1967 aimed at calming the growing public pessimism about the war and reviving public confidence, especially after North Korea captured the a U.S. Navy intelligence ship, the U.S.S. *Pueblo*, in January 1968, which caused a considerable amount of national anxiety and embarrassment.[8] Historians Peter R. Young and Peter Jesser contend that Johnson's public relations campaign succeeded in deceiving the American public at all levels about the realities of Vietnam, from the White House to military public affairs officers in Vietnam.[9]

In daily military briefings, officials proclaimed success in Vietnam and indicated the war's end was near. Although General William C. Westmoreland, the commander of U.S. forces in Vietnam, became aware of a pending large enemy offensive, he was confident in the U.S. military's ability to defeat any attack. President Johnson did not disclose this information to the public for political reasons during the election year. The prevalent spirit of optimism in the American media and public about eventual victory in Vietnam is important in understanding the immediate reaction of the press and the public to the Tet Offensive. However, Oberdorfer explains that the media originally supported the war, but after some journalists discovered false or exaggerated battlefield reports during the early years of the war they became increasingly "disillusioned and pessimistic," creating a credibility gap between the press and the U.S. military.[10] According to Braestrup, journalists "became increasingly skeptical of the official rationales and 'progress' reports...[which] became part of U.S. journalism's conventional wisdom."[11] The suspicious press began referring to the daily military briefings sarcastically as the "Five O'clock Follies," which exacerbated the credibility gap between the military and the press as many journalists began to completely dismiss military reports of events.[12] While many journalists "ridiculed" the military's daily briefings and often dismissed government reports, veteran Associated Press reporter Richard Pyle argued that they provided some of the best information on the situation and events in Vietnam, writing:

> For all their failings, the Follies were not the pack of lies that some critics suggested. The best reporters and news organizations recognized the value of an on-the-record, official version of events to compare with information from field reporters and other sources.[13]

Nonetheless, Braestrup laments that these newly arriving American journalists inherited this conventional wisdom and sought to correct the *official* story. Using carefully selected words, phrases, and images, coupled with an abundance of "bad news" stories, the Western media continued to frame U.S. involvement as an immoral and failed endeavor, a "quagmire," which adversely influenced public opinion in significant ways. This in turn caused U.S. government officials to view the media's coverage as a media conspiracy to influence national policy, which fostered a growing animosity between the media and the government that played through the remainder of the war and beyond.[14]

On January 30, 1968, during the Lunar New Year cease-fire between North and South Vietnam, the Tet Offensive began as a simultaneous surprise assault on the major cities, towns, and military installations of South Vietnam. This unprecedented event took both the American media and the American public by surprise. More important, it contradicted everything the U.S. government had told them during the previous months. While a few places like Hue and Khe Sanh endured fierce, protracted fighting, U.S. forces quickly defeated the Communists attacks before they achieved their military objectives. "Many of the [Communist] units," writes Oberdorfer, "had been unable to reach their designed objectives, others had held them briefly but were forced to let them go."[15] By February 4, only five days later, fighting was reduced to the remote Marine outpost at Khe Sanh, and the cities of Saigon, Hue, Da Lat, and Phan Thiet. In Saigon, the fighting occurred largely in the suburbs of Cholon. With the exception of Khe Sanh, the Tet offensive ended February 25, 1968 with the recapture of Hue. On March 1, Marines repelled the last Communist assault on Khe Sanh, and by mid-March drove the enemy into Cambodia, Laos, and North Vietnam.[16]

"There is fairly broad agreement among historians today," Braestrup observes, "that Hanoi suffered a military setback during the 1968 Tet Offensive. The North Vietnamese and Viet Cong committed substantial numbers of troops to urban combat with "little effect," which resulted in "heavy losses."[17] In fact, Oberdorfer contends Communist forces lost 58,373 soldiers between January 29 and March 31, 1968—about the same number of troops the United States lost during its entire involvement in Vietnam.[18] While their surprise attacks had given them some early advantages, the Communists failed to maintain momentum and lost any military gains.[19] They failed to cause mass desertion of South Vietnamese troops, or cause a general uprising among the South Vietnamese.[20] Instead, the Communist offensive "caused resentment" across South Vietnam for attacking during the Tet holiday.[21] An official dispatch from North Vietnamese leaders acknowledged that "we failed to seize a number of primary objectives and to completely destroy mobile and defensive units of the enemy."[22] Oberdorfer concludes "there was a pervasive air of sorrow and disappointment;" because the North Vietnamese officials believed "the Tet Offensive had not been considered a success."[23]

Nonetheless, the American public, along with influential politicians, wrongly believed the Tet Offensive was both a psychological and political victory for North Vietnam and both a military and political defeat for South Vietnam and the United States. They also believed that as the South Vietnamese government neared collapse, Communist forces occupied the countryside unchallenged because South Vietnamese forces fled. The media led Americans to believe that U.S. troops used excessive force that brought widespread death and destruction. It also portrayed the fighting at Khe Sanh as an "impending disaster" on a scale of Dien Bien Phu.[24] None of this was to true. Despite the facts about the Tet offensive, few journalists pursued any evidence that contradicted their earlier reports and prevailing view.[25] Johnson's leading political opponents, Republicans George Romney and Richard Nixon, normally supportive of Johnson's war policy, changed their positions and exacerbated the situation by using Tet to attack Johnson.[26]

According to Oberdorfer, "Westmoreland thought the attacks had produced no significant military results," but wanted to exploit the Communist retreat with an offensive into North Vietnam and perhaps end the war with a U.S. victory.[27] However, Westmoreland's request for more troops during the Communists offensive caused a "national uproar" after it was leaked to the press and made public. [28] This caused President Johnson to deny General Westmoreland's request, which some historians and analysts contend resulted in a missed opportunity that allowed the North Vietnamese to recover and regroup. Until then, Westmoreland had received the troops he requested. Instead of pursuing a decisive military victory, Johnson, and later President Richard Nixon, pursued peace negotiations with Hanoi and the continual draw down of U.S. forces under a program of Vietnamization. Oberdorfer explains that "by the middle of February it was evident to Westmoreland and others in Saigon that official Washington as well as the American public had been shaken to an unprecedented degree by the Tet Offensive—to a far greater degree, in fact, than most Americans in Vietnam."[29] *How could this be so?*

The Fog of War: Erroneous First Reports and Hasty Conclusions

According to Peter Braestrup, a relatively small group of journalists covered the Vietnam War until the Tet offensive. As the number of U.S. troops increased, so did the number of "accredited" journalist reporting the war—but not to the extent that most people believe because many journalists only made temporary visits to Vietnam, and accompanying administrative personnel and family members were all counted on the rolls as "media."[30] Therefore, Braestrup contends that there were an insufficient number of journalists in the first days of Tet to cover the simultaneous attacks across Vietnam. Ron Steinman, NBC's news bureau chief, agrees with Braestrup explaining that he had enough staff to cover Vietnam until the Tet Offensive, but not after it began. Steinman explains that Tet overwhelmed his staff and forced him to request more personnel.[31]

Unlike their younger contemporaries, both Peter Braestrup and Don Oberdorfer were veteran journalist who had both served in the U.S. military and were critical of the new generation of young, ambitious journalists who were all hoping to make names for themselves in Vietnam. Ron Steinman explained that reporting war required experience and special journalistic skills, but in Vietnam there were many inexperienced journalists who did not understand the customs, politics, or policies.[32] Vietnam War journalist William Prochnou describes the cadre of journalists he met and worked with as young, driven adventurists hoping to emulate Ernest Hemmingway.[33] Writing of Neil Sheehan, for example, Prochnou writes "At the beginning, like all the young newcomers, he suffered from the Hemmingway disease. War was great; war was grand. Get shot at; prove you're a man."[34] Like Peter Arnett who was only twenty-eight when he arrived in Vietnam, Prochnou himself was only in his twenties when he arrived. These journalists lived posh hotels like the posh Hotel Caravelle and enjoyed the city's numerous social opportunities. For this young generation of journalists, Saigon was an exotic city with an abundance of restaurants, nightclubs. On the eve of the Tet Offensive, Western journalists congregated in Saigon enjoyed the lull in fighting that came with the cease-fire Tet holiday, attending parties and celebrations, or congregating in their hotels. Peter Arnett had married a local woman named Nina Nguyen, and enjoyed the evening with his wife's family.[35]

The sudden and radical shift in media coverage arose during the first hours of the Tet offensive and established a pattern that lasted until the war ended. As the Tet offensive unfolded, the most visible of the Communists' strategic targets was the U.S. Embassy in Saigon, near where the majority of American journalist stayed. In the attack, nineteen Viet Cong commandos blew a hole in the embassy wall and fought with Marines through the morning of 31 January 1968 in an effort to take over the embassy. After six and a half hours, at 9:20 a.m., all of the commandos were dead and the officials declared the embassy secure.[36] Oberdorfer explains the military's perspective, writing:

> The commando raid at the American Embassy was more of a nuisance than a threat, a minor item blown out of proportion by the concentration of the American Press and the concern of the American government. The U.S. Command never doubted how this platoon sized fight would end. Sooner or later, the commandos would be wiped out.[37]

However, the reporters outside the embassy compound during the attack lacked this perspective. Isolated from the events inside the compound, they could only hear the fighting and could not observe the event. Likewise, the military policemen outside the compound could not provide an eyewitness account of the fighting, but their hasty, uninformed assessment provided the journalists only "official source."[38] Amid the "inevitable confusion and haste," explains Braestrup, "first reports made it seem that the foe had succeeded in seizing the U.S. chancery," though the Marines largely contained the commandos to the courtyard and did not allow them to penetrate the main building.[39] These early news accounts produced in haste and confusion established an incorrect "first truth," and encouraged reporters, editors, and producers to take a defeatist view that affected the media manager's selection of stories.[40] Many media personal concluded that U.S. government had again lied about success in Vietnam, and that the commando attack on the embassy was "the most embarrassing defeat the United States had suffered in Vietnam."[41] Many others concluded that the United States was losing the war.[42] Commenting on NBC' failure to provide an accurate picture of the embassy ordeal, Steinman explains that amid the rush, confusion, and fatigue his small staff flooded his producers with an abundance of news fragments in unpunctuated teletype memos and film footage. "There were mistakes made in stories that were written in haste," he writes, "and admittedly, proofread faster that I would have preferred."[43]

Hours later, when journalist were allowed into the embassy compound and view all nineteen dead VC commandos, journalist began filing updated accounts. Most journalists, including Braestrup, accepted General Westmoreland's account that commando attack was readily defeated and a minor skirmish. However, editors and producers ignored the corrected reports of their journalists in the field and continued to report the initial false accounts more than twelve hours later.[44] Other reporters, however, such as Peter Arnett, continued to dismiss Westmoreland's account and reported the initial hearsay of military policemen not involved in the fighting.[45] Braestrup contends "the [*New York*] *Times'* and [*Washington*] *Post's* sins were mostly those of omission. Each of the newspapers' deskmen at home failed to add the full version of Westmoreland's brief account of the embassy fight, as reported by Associated Press, to the truncated versions hastily supplied by their own Saigon staffers."[46] NBC and CBS broadcast exaggerated and sensationalized reports during prime time. NBC called their "thirty minute NBC Television News Special, *Viet-Cong Terror: A Guerrilla Offensive*," while CBS called their "thirty-minute special report, *Saigon Under Fire*."[47] These sensational reports had immediate adverse effect on U.S. public opinion. Oberdorfer explains that "most people were unprepared for this stunning evidence of Communist resourcefulness, determination, and power, the Tet Offensive shocked the [U.S.] citizenry which had been led to believe that success in Vietnam was just around the corner."[48]

The day after the embassy attack, the newspaper giants *New York Times* and the *Washington Post,* like many other newspapers across America, printed large pictures of South Vietnamese police chief Nguyen Ngoc Loan executing a Viet Cong suspect on a street in Saigon on their front pages.[49] NBC edited the execution footage for maximum effect on the *Huntley-Brinkley Report.*[50] "Roughly twenty-million people watched the *Huntley-Brinkley Report* that night," which Oberdorfer observes lead most to conclude that Vietnam "was a 'wrong war' on the 'wrong side'."[51] However, according to Eddie Adams, the photographer who took the picture that appeared on newspaper front pages and became an icon for anti-war activists, the image was taken out of context and did not tell the full story. In his own words, Adams explained:

> I won a Pulitzer Prize in 1969 for a photograph of one man shooting another. Two people died in that photograph: the recipient of the bullet and GENERAL NGUYEN NGOC LOAN. The general killed the Viet Cong; I killed the general with my camera. Still photographs are the most powerful weapon in the world. People believe them, but photographs do lie, even without manipulation. They are only half-truths. What the photograph didn't say was, "What would you do if you were the general at that time and place on that hot day, and you caught the so-called bad guy after he blew away one, two or three American soldiers?" General Loan was what you would call a real warrior, admired by his troops. I'm not saying what he did was right, but you have to put yourself in his position. The photograph also doesn't say that the general devoted much of his time trying to get hospitals built in Vietnam for war casualties. This picture really messed up his life. He never blamed me. He told me if I hadn't taken the picture, someone else would have, but I've felt bad for him and his family for a long time. I had kept in contact with him; the last time we spoke

> was about six months ago, when he was very ill. I sent flowers when I heard that he had died and wrote, "I'm sorry. There are tears in my eyes."[52]

Adams reflection on incident and its aftermath revealed the emotional toll of war and not the malice as the pundits alleged at the time.

Rush to Judgment

Stunned by scope and audacity of the North Vietnamese offensive, journalists exaggerated the Communists' gains and provided their own analysis and predictions. Exacerbating the situation, journalists exaggerated Communists' gains and awarded them a psychological victory, while pundits far removed from the scene provided their own analysis and prematurely predicted a Communist victory based on the hasty, misleading reports.[53]

Further amplifying journalists false assertions, journalists cited academic elites who could articulate similar views based on the hasty, inaccurate, and incomplete reports. "Deeply impressed by the evidence of the Communist military power and projecting what the Communists might do next," Oberdorfer explains, "some sophisticated and articulate Americans began to speak of the possibility of defeat."[54] They reflected admiration for the enemy, going so far as to praise their skill, resolve, and resourcefulness—as well as revering General Nygen 'Giap's genius'."[55] In a very convincing manner, these influential people began to sway the public with predictions of Communist victory.[56] However, Braestrup argues that "U.S. journalists were even less qualified to judge Hanoi's psychological victory or defeat in Vietnam than they were to assess the communists' military successes or failures."[57]He explains that initially:

> Hanoi did not claim a victory—psychological, symbolic, or otherwise...but American newsmen were quick to award Hanoi a major 'psychological' triumph there, if only because they—the newsmen—and Lyndon B. Johnson had been taken by surprise.[58]

Nonetheless, headlines such as "Hanoi Attacks and Scores a Major Psychological Blow," "Shaken Assumptions About the War," and "Why the U.S. Isn't Winning a 'Little War'," reflected these hasty, unqualified predictions.[59]

Suddenly, Oberdorfer explains, "the Tet Offensive had become a big story in the United States and throughout the world."[60] American journalists, with little understanding of the conflict and predisposed by both the first reports and a growing conventional wisdom that the government was not telling the truth, rushed to cover the events in Vietnam and tell a different story.[61] Braestrup contends that these new journalists came with little understanding of the Vietnam's history or geography, or "the U.S. effort in that country."[62] He explains:

> Most newsmen in Vietnam, in their late twenties and thirties, sought the opportunity to witness a prolonged life-and-death drama of major importance in America. But their time on the horizons were short. Their focus was narrow. By temperament they were not 'experts,' sympathetic researchers, writers skilled at synthesis; they were adventurers and, to some extent voyeurs...tellers of tales...and the media in Vietnam committed major sins of omission as time went on.[63]

This "influx of newsmen," writes Oberdorfer, "some of whom had never set foot in Vietnam before, put a further strain on the already crowded luxury hotels, the cable and telephone facilities and the press agents and officials."[64]

According to both Oberdorfer and Braestrup, by the time the flood of new journalist arrived, however, the fighting had settled to Saigon, Hue, Da Lat, Phan Thiet, and Khe Sanh, and most of these journalists arriving midstream had trouble finding the fighting.[65] To assist journalist in covering the war, military public affairs officers arranged transportation to get journalists out of the cities believing that they would see firsthand the success on the battlefield. Yet despite the availability of military transportation, many journalists did not venture out of the cities or base camps and congregated in Saigon, Hue, and Khe Sanh where Braestrup explains they "informally exchanged gossips, impressions, and rumors."[66]

Assessing Media Performance

In Saigon, after the embassy attack, journalists had difficulty getting out to witness the fighting. Oberdorfer explains, "after the first few days there was little action in the city during the daylight. Movement on the streets at night was forbidden by tight curfew and made dangerous by trigger happy government soldiers and National Police."[67] In this situation, many journalists reported from the safety and comfort of their Saigon hotels. Braestrup reports that journalists "could view the smoke of burning buildings from the Hotel Caravelle roof garden," and hearing the explosions and gunfire, they concluded that Saigon was under widespread attack, though the fighting was "limited to the suburbs of Cholon."[68]

According to Oberdorfer, Hanoi soon recognized how the American media portrayed the event as an American defeat, and Communists propagandists quickly began circulating greatly distorted and greatly exaggerated accounts of their "victory" at the U.S. Embassy in what he describes as "the most creative writing to grace the whole affair."[69] Vietnam journalist and media historian William V. Kennedy observes that Communists propagandists included Communist Western journalists, who worked diligently to spread Hanoi's propaganda, and some unsuspecting journalists used the Communists reports uncritically.[70] In one case, Kennedy reports that *New York Times* correspondent Harrison E. Salsbury, who had only been in Vietnam a day, released a report based solely on Communist propaganda that wrongfully claimed that the United States deliberately bombed North Vietnam's dike to flood the country.[71] Similarly, Braestrup observed that Western journalists confined to Saigon during the first few days of intensive fighting monitored foreign reports and broadcasts from Hanoi, and some Western journalists confined to Saigon used Hanoi's propaganda as a basis for their own reports.[72] Braestrup reports one example when, "NBC was reduced to deriving its 'insights' from a captured Vietcong propaganda film, run with a narration by Douglas Kiker, who had been in Vietnam less than two weeks."[73] In another, Braestrup observed "CBS told an exaggerated story about Hanoi's supply lines to Hue, implying that the North Vietnamese were running trucks down a superhighway right up to the wall of the Citadel in the heart of the city."[74]

Those journalists who did venture out found only the aftermath of combat and did not understand what had transpired.[75] According to Braestrup, many overlooked the death and destruction caused by Communists forces, particularly in Hue City, and instead blamed the U.S. military as "callously destroying all Vietnam," though the destruction was isolated to certain areas.[76] In Hue, contrary to the findings of historians Eric Hammel and Keith Nolan who reported that Marines fought with courage and discipline, American journalists provided discouraging portrayals of the U.S. effort at Hue.[77] For example, *Newsweek*, *Time*, and *Life* inflated the Communists' resolve while focusing on the heavy U.S. casualties and destruction, which minimalized the hard-fought U.S. victory and portrayed the war as unwinnable and hopeless.[78] Similarly, at Khe Sanh, the Communists' main effort was also representative of these pessimistic predictions. According to Oberdorfer, "roughly one fourth of all the film reports on the evening news programs about the war during the two-month period were devoted to portraying the plight of the U.S. Marines at Khe Sanh."[79] He adds that journalists who only made brief visits to the Khe Sanh portrayed the Marines as being in "grave danger, though the view was not shared by the Marines who defended the base."[80] Braestrup reports that contrary to actual events at Khe Sanh, pessimistic journalists predicted a major American defeat, and portrayed the Communists' main effort as an "impending disaster" on the scale Dien Bien Phu, which in the end "did not occur."[81]

In addition inaccurate assertions about U.S. military performance during Tet, journalists also made a number of incorrect conclusions about the war about the South Vietnamese government and military. First, journalist wrongly asserted that the South Vietnamese government and military collapsed, and that the Communists controlled the countryside. However, Braestrup explains that, contrary to the media's portrayal of South Vietnamese troops, "the troops did not buckle," and both "the army and government demonstrated great resilience" despite being at fifty percent strength due to holiday leaves.[82] American reporters did not accompany South Vietnamese troops in the field, because as Braestrup explains, there were "few incentives for newsmen to accompany even the elite ARVN units on operations or to study at firsthand the overall ARVN performance in the war...U.S. reporters (including this one) usually got their impressions about ARVN secondhand."[83] Second, journalist also wrongly concluded that the joint program between U.S. and South Vietnamese forces to protect the cities, towns, and villages throughout South Vietnam and maintain positive relations between the citizens and a democratic government, pacification, failed. According to Braestrup, however, the Tet Offensive dealt the pacification program "a setback but no mortal blow."[84] He argues that the shortage of journalists, combined with the media limited interest and understanding of pacification, contributed greatly to journalist "hasty, uninformed, and apocalyptic" reporting.[85]

In addition to incomplete and erroneous reporting filled with hasty, premature conclusions, the press ignored a number of positive events and evidence that showed that the Communists were being defeated, even ignoring the independent research of a foreign service officer, Douglas Pike, who successfully detailed North Vietnamese intentions and failures using captured documents and prisoner interrogations.[86] Oberdorfer observes that, "The Viet Cong were being beaten decisively in the Saigon cables, but they were scoring great feats on television and in the press. The cables were seen by only a few, and the news reports were seen by nearly everyone."[87] According to Vietnam Historian C. Dale Watson "Many [journalists] were simply skeptical of any kind of success; few were hostile to the military and sympathetic to the academicians and senators active in the peace movement."[88] According to Vietnam War journalist William W. Prochnau, the Pulitzer Prize-winning Korean War correspondent Marguerite Higgins argued that many journalists in Vietnam "were 'seldom at the scenes of battle.' She alleged that they had ulterior motives, claiming 'Reporters here would like to see us lose the war to prove they're right'."[89]

According to Braestrup, "Vietnam required a lot of stamina, a lot of man-hours per story."[90] NBC's news bureau chief, Ron Steinman, complained that the shortage of media personnel during the Tet Offensive caused tremendous fatigue that impaired his crew's ability to cover the fighting.[91] Braestrup observes that the small number of journalists "did not work 'collectively' in a systematic sense."[92] Instead "for competitive reasons, much of each bureau's scare manpower in Vietnam was devoted typically to 'matching' coverage, for the most part, of the *same* subject matter."[93] Since most journalists congregated in Saigon, Hue, and Khe Sanh, "eyewitness reporting of combat, including combat by U.S. forces, was limited, "and therefore journalists did not "insure broad geographic coverage.[94] He adds that technical limitations, such as deadlines and time zone differences gave reporters "little time to spend analyzing or evaluating stories...in swift moving events were sometimes in error."[95]

The fast pace of events, coupled with the shortage of reporters in the first weeks of the offensive, caused reports to be filled in hasty assembled fragments, or confusing, disorganized articles that needed extensive rewriting—all based upon "unverified reports, official announcements, and rusty translations in Vietnamese."[96] The shortage of journalists also resulted in limited geographic coverage. Therefore, "U.S. forces in action..."were not covered firsthand by many journalists, despite ease of access to the battlefield.[97] Adding to the problems, editors revised and rewrote field reports, which were rewritten again as scripts for "radio news announcers" and "TV anchormen."[98] Although facts and details about events on the battlefield did become available for journalists to write follow-up reports, Braestrup explains that because editors relegated "catch-up or corrective stories" to the "back pages," there was "little incentive to produce such stories." [99]

Braestrup contends that in the absence of a solid understanding, journalist filled the news void with "subjective responses," which compelled "editors to publish, and reporters (and pundits) to compose, 'analyses' of the crisis that would fill the vacuum. It proved a serious lapse of self discipline," which he contends were "the hasty reactions of the half-informed" and condemns as "sins of commission"[100] Braestrup observes that such hearsay was "further distorted by editors and others 12,000 miles away."[101] Braestrup explains, "The U.S. press was extremely short of competent, let alone expert, judges of either military affairs or the rapidly evolving complexities of the two Vietnams."[102] Furthermore, Braestrup explains the media's collective shortcoming in reporting the Vietnam War was being "quite narrow" because "the media's focus was on the American presence," and not on the "war's complexities and 'political' dimensions."[103] Moreover, the war was complicated and difficult to follow. "Understanding the war in Vietnam," Braestrup argues, "demanded a great deal more than had prior U.S. overseas conflicts,"[104] This misery, destruction, and casualties colored the journalist's perception of events. Combined with their limited understanding of events and operations in the field and their critical view of government reports, these perceptions led many journalists to perpetuate myths and wrongly conclude the war was "lost" or "unwinnable."[105]

The most famous of these hasty assessments came from Walter Cronkite who reported to American Audiences:

> To say that we are mired in stalemate seems the only realistic, yet unsatisfactory, conclusion. … It is increasingly clear to this reporter that the only rational way out, then, will be to negotiate, not as victors, but as an honorable people who lived up to their pledge to defend democracy, and did the best they could.[106]

However, historians Bill Laurie and R.J. Del Vecchio are critical of Cronkite's assessment, observing that:

> Cronkite was not an expert in military matters or international politics, and he began his address noting it was 'speculative, personal, subjective' commentary, so his remarks could and should have been received as what they were: one man's feelings and perceptions of a complex situation, heavily colored by the confusion and destruction he had just witnessed. His popularity and prestige were such that his words were taken by many as a definitive analysis of the situation, and the existing antiwar movement capitalized on the impact of his broadcast.[107]

Nonetheless, Cronkite's remarks led President Johnson to conclude, "If I've lost Cronkite, I've lost middle America."[108]

Journalists provided "a deficient picture" of U.S. troop performance because competing teams of journalists "flocked to the same places and watched the same events."[109] Nonetheless, Braestrup contends that despite the confusion and problems reporters had getting to the battlefields, "by March 1, it would have been possible to observe and report" the Communists were being defeated and had not gained a major psychological victory.[110] Braestrup contends that:

> In February-March 1968 the normal competitiveness of the media to attract audiences favored disaster stories, think-pieces, and prediction rather than painstaking reporting of a changing political and military situation. On TV, especially, pressures to hold the viewer and compress complexities into 90-second 'standupers' resulted in 'microcosmic' commentary on only isolated segments of the total story—often a sheer distortion of both large and small facts.[111]...What began as hasty initial reporting disaster in Vietnam became conventional wisdom

> when magnified in media commentary...the press 'rebroadcast' it all uncritically, even enthusiastically, although many in the news media should have known better.[112]

Don Oberdorfer agrees, writing that "for the American press, the combination of high drama and low national understanding created a monumental challenge in Vietnam—and the press, like the government, was ill-equipped to meet it."[113] Asserting that television reporting did not provide the full picture of the situation or events in Vietnam, Oberdorfer concludes:

> The selective reality of the television film reports was more depressing than living in the war zone would have been. In Vietnam, most places were quiet most of the time, a fact which tended to be obscured in the reporting of the dramatic conflict. Television recorded the high points of drama and tension, compressed them into two-minute or three-minute stories containing the most electrifying moments, transmitted them around the world and broadcast them nationwide to the American public. It is probable that a regular viewer of the Cronkite or Huntley-Brinkley shows saw more infantry action over a longer span of days than most American troops who were in Vietnam during the Tet Offensive.[114]

Supporting Oberdorfer's argument, Braestrup contends that "at Tet, the short managerial attention brought down the curtain while the play was still going on."[115] He concludes:

> "The U.S. major media rich as they were in the 1960s, devoted insufficient resources and insufficient critical attentions to the conflict. With their various technical and manpower limitations, editorial predilections, and journalistic biases, the media, and the offensive began, were overwhelmed."[116]

These telling conclusions illuminate the media's collective shortcomings in accurately reporting the Vietnam War, as well as the factors that adversely influenced U.S. public opinion and policy.

Cause and Effect: Tet's Media Coverage and Public Opinion

According to polls of public opinion in February 1968, the collective effect of the media's erroneous, inaccurate, and misleading coverage coupled with the Johnson administration's drastic loss of credibility caused a dramatic adverse change in public opinion during the Tet Offensive.[117] Historian C.

Dale Walton explains, "From March 1968 onward, however, the trend was very clear; Americans were tiring of the conflict that seemed to defy positive resolution."[118] On March 31, 1968, President Johnson announced that he would not seek reelection. Then he replaced General Westmoreland as commander in Vietnam with General Creighton Abrams on June 10, 1968.[119] However, these moves seemed to have little effect in restoring public confidence. According to Walton, "as disillusionment with the war increased, the anti-war and anti government bias in Vietnam intensified."[120]

On the domestic front, pessimistic coverage of the war also fueled the antiwar movement causing a surge in domestic political violence and activity. During the Democratic National Convention in Chicago in August 1968, for example, protests organized by Tom Hayden's socialist Students for a Democratic Society (SDS) turned to riots, which led to a violent clash with police that caused injuries and destruction. Amid the violence, police arrested eight people, including SDS activist Tom Hayden and Black Panther leader Bobby Seale. However, it was not the protests and violence committed by radical groups that began to alter U.S. policy in Vietnam, but the adverse effect the sensational coverage of these events coupled with incomplete, erroneous, and misleading had on U.S. public opinion, which led to political victories for anti-war candidates in the 1968 national elections.[121]

According to professor and Vietnam antiwar activist Melvin Small, "by 1969, there may have been as many as 17,000 national, regional, and local organizations that could be considered part of the [antiwar] movements."[122] Infused with Marxists ideals, some organizations, such as the Weather Underground, Symbionese Liberation Army, and Black Panthers, declared war on the United States. Some groups bombed government buildings, robbed banks and National Guard armories, murdered law enforcement and government officials, and incited riots. Indicative of these activities, members of the William Ayres's Weather Underground, many wearing motorcycle or football helmets, began rioting through an affluent Chicago neighborhood on October 8, 1969, smashing windows of businesses and cars, and injuring twenty-eight policemen in what became known as the "Days of Rage." Then, after the arrest of several of their members, the "Weathermen" resumed the violence and vandalism two days later. These events drew significant media coverage, and from the end of Tet to the end of the Vietnam War, tens of thousands of antiwar protesters received sympathetic coverage.[123]

This was not just an American phenomenon. Soviet backed organizations were becoming violent on an international scale. According to Historian Jeremy Varon, following the teaching of "Karl Marx, Mao Tse-Tung and Herbert Marcuse, and 'revolutionary' icons like Che Guevara and Ho Chi Minh," radical groups "attacked governments, militaries, [and] institutions," attempted to bring down governments and initiate worldwide revolution and violence.[124] At the same time, underground newspapers and radio stations, including the New York *Guardian*, and the *Liberation News Service*, distributed and abundance of leftist information and images of sensational demonstrations and political violence aimed to advance Marxists ideas and inspire worldwide revolution.[125]

Media Coverage of Vietnam After Tet

When Richard Nixon became president seven months later, January 20, 1969, General Abrams implemented Nixon's policy of Vietnamization, which was designed to dramatically decrease U.S. forces and transition responsibility for the war back to the South Vietnamese. In November 1969, however news of the My Lai massacre reached the American media, which occurred nearly more than a year and a half earlier on March 16, 1968, and cast a shadow over General Abram's command and the U.S. effort.[126]

In 1970, U.S. forces made incursions into Cambodia to attack Communists forces that used it as a safe haven from which to launch attacks on South Vietnam.[127] Although U.S. and South Vietnamese forces continued to make military gains after the Tet Offensive, these gains went largely unnoticed, and erroneous, incomplete, and misleading reporting after TET continued. What is more, the media's pessimistic "quagmire narrative," the assertion that the United States could not win, had become firmly established as the media's narrative on the Vietnam War for the rest of the war.

Like 1968 and the Tet Offensive, 1972 was a critical year for U.S. involvement in Vietnam. On March 30, 1972, the North Vietnamese launched a large conventional attack on South Vietnam called the "Nguyen Hue Offensive" or "Easter Offensive." U.S. and South Vietnamese forces halted the Communists advance and launched a counter attack that pushed the North Vietnamese back in North Vietnam and ended the offensive. U.S. airpower played a significant role in defeating the Communist advance. Part of the U.S. response included bombing Hanoi and Haiphong Harbor. Like Tet, the Easter Offensive and the U.S. response drew considerable media coverage. By 1972, the media had become highly critical of U.S. bombing campaigns, asserting that the U.S. government was intentionally targeting infrastructure and civilians, though the sources for these claims was the Communist government in Hanoi. In addition to the media's critical coverage of the bombing campaign, it continued to provide an abundance of "bad news" stories and images such as South Vietnamese photographer Nick Ut's famous June 8, 1972 photograph of a young naked girl burned by napalm—which conveyed the media's narrative of an unjust war and U.S. atrocities.[128]

Tom Hayden made several Communist sponsored trips to Cambodia and North Vietnam, but in July 1972 Hayden made his most famous trip to North Vietnam with future wife Jane Fonda where Fonda infamously posed with Communists soldiers wearing a helmet at an anti-aircraft gun. Although

Fonda's trip received little coverage in the mainstream media, it helped energize the antiwar movement through the 1972 U.S. elections, and its fallout would endure in American public memory after the war. In the end, the continued incomplete, erroneous, and misleading coverage of the Vietnam War and its adverse effect on U.S. public opinion led to the election of more anti-war candidates to U.S. Congress 1972.[129]

By the fall of 1972, the failure of North Vietnam's Nguyen Hue Offensive coupled with U.S. bombing campaigns had put tremendous pressure to enter a peace agreement during the October Paris Peace Accords. According to Martin Herz, the U.S. Ambassador to Vietnam during President Richard Nixon's administration, when the Communist leaders in Hanoi hardened their positions and caused the Paris peace negotiations to fail, President Nixon resumed U.S. bombing campaigns in December to force Hanoi back to negotiations.[130] Except for Christmas, U.S. forces bombed the Hanoi and Haiphong Harbor areas throughout the month, which Herz explains was the heaviest of the war. Herz observed that the Hanoi media was the first to report exaggerated and misleading accounts of the bombings. When leading U.S. newspapers and magazines, what Herz calls the "prestige press," finally learned of the bombings they began to report them with little understanding of what had occurred and used Hanoi's unvalidated reports as a basis for their own. According to Hertz, the *New York Times*, *Washington Post*, *Time*, and *Newsweek* similarly reported exaggerated and propagandized accounts of what had occurred incorrectly alleging the United States engaged in carpet bombing that deliberately targeted civilians, and that tens of thousands were killed on a scale of Hiroshima. Likewise, the three major networks, particularly CBS, also uncritically based their reports Hanoi's exaggerated accounts. Herz contends that by interjecting commentary and opinion into the reports, the "prestige press," condemned the bombing as "senseless," "merciless," and "terrorism."[131] Although Hanoi resumed peace negotiation on January 8, 1973, the erroneous and editorialized accounts of the Christmas bombing contributed to Vietnam mythology and like the media's incomplete, inaccurate, and misleading of Tet became ingrained in public memory. President Richard Nixon was well aware of the effects of Hanoi's propaganda had on the media and public opinion, but his administration was unable to counter the adverse effects.[132]

The Legacy of Vietnam War Reporting

North Vietnam finally entered the peace agreement in January 1973. However, as the United States withdrew its forces from Vietnam, the North Vietnamese gradually moved their military forces to the southern provinces over the next two years. Meanwhile, the antiwar U.S. Congress decided to suspend any further funding for the war. Then, when Communists forces again invaded South Vietnam, the United States did not come to South Vietnam's aid and Communists forces captured Saigon on April 30, 1975. South Vietnamese President Nguyen Van Thieu argued that if the United States has given him the financial support the Nixon Administration had promised him, then his forces could have stopped the North Vietnamese incursion. Soon thereafter, the Communists sent more than 200,000 South Vietnamese government officials, military officers, and soldiers to "reeducation camps" when many died of malnutrition, torture, and disease in an effort to purge South Vietnamese perceived as sympathy to the United States. Unchecked, the Communist government in neighboring Cambodia under Saloth Sar, also known as Pol-Pot, killed an estimate two million people in his effort to Communize the country.[133]

Reflecting on U.S. involvement in Vietnam, Vo Nygen Giap, Hanoi's senior general and strategist during the Vietnam War, told Morely Safer:

> We paid a high price but so did you...not only in lives and materiel...do not forget that the war was brought into the living rooms of the American people...the most important result of the Tet Offensive was it made you de-escalate the bombing, and it brought you to the negotiating table. It was therefore, a victory. ...The war was fought on many fronts. The most important [front] was on public opinion.[134]

This telling statement demonstrated the war of ideas that accompanied the military conflict in Vietnam, and would prove a valuable lesson to U.S. enemies in later conflicts.

Public Memory and the Myths of the Vietnam War

The Vietnam War is the subject of numerous myths, largely born in the media's erroneous reporting and unqualified analysis, and then amplified in popular culture through film, music, and literature and continue to resonate in popular memory. With the rapid growth of the antiwar-movement in 1968 following the Tet Offensive, there was a surge in anti-war music, followed by another surge in 1970. These anti-war songs became an integral part of the growing anti-war movement. Many of these songs achieved considerable popularity and even commercial success, and would serve to amplify the media's quagmire narrative. Importantly, these songs would not only proved influential in effecting the attitudes and opinions of popular culture at the time, but also remained popular long after the Vietnam War and helped define and ingrain popular views of the war in popular memory.[135]

By 1970, however, anti-war films such as *MASH*, joined anti-war songs in shaping public views and amplifying the quagmire narrative, though most did so more subtly.[136] Though the film was set in the Korean War, the film's message was aimed directly at Vietnam. Although there were many patriotic themed films during the Vietnam War, an abundance of films playing on the Vietnam Syndrome theme, if not overtly anti-war, propagated Vietnam War mythology based on incomplete, erroneous, and misleading news coverage. In Stanley Kubrick's film *Full Metal Jacket*, for example, Public Affairs Officer, lieutenant Lockhart, tells his combat correspondents at the outset of the Tet Offensive that "the United States Embassy had been overrun by suicide squads," a further exaggeration of the media's incorrect first reports, and then tells them "even Cronkite's going to say the war is now unwinnable," underscoring the quagmire narrative even though Cronkite did not make that statement until weeks later in the battle.[137] While a number of respected Vietnam historians such as C. Dale Walton, Bill Laurie, and R.J. Del Vecchio address a number of myths about the Vietnam War, it is important to note that such myths would influence future journalists perceptions of U.S. foreign involvement, especially in the Global War on Terror.[138]

Contrasting Perspectives and Recent Scholarship

It is important to note that some journalists, historians, and other disagree with Braestrup and Oberdorfer, contending that the media did not decide the outcome of the war through its influence on public opinion and policy. In fact, skeptical views are plentiful. Early views expressing this belief included the views of historians David F. Hallin and Chester Pach. Other historians, such as Michael S. Sweeney, Greg McLaughlin, and Clyde Thayer III, argue that the media's role and influence on public opinion during the Tet Offensive is overstated.[139] Clarence R. Wyatt, also diminishes the media's effects on public opinion during the war while defending journalists' performance explaining that journalists did report official government information, statements, and views, and that "from the beginning of U.S. involvement to the fall of Saigon in 1975, the U.S. government systematically manipulated the press to its own ends."[140] More recently, historians David F. Schmitz and Bingham Robert K. assert that the media did not affect the change in policy that led to the U.S. military and political defeat.[141]

Conversely, historians C. Dale. Walton and James H. Willbanks both agree with Braestrup's and Oberdorfer's arguments that while the Johnson Administration deserves its share of the blame for creating a false sense of optimism in the American public and providing exaggerated and misleading reports of battlefield progress, the media, through its incomplete, erroneous, or misleading reporting, did adversely influence U.S. public opinion and policy in Vietnam.[142] Willbanks concludes:

> In the end, part of the blame for the ultimate outcome of the Tet Offensive may lie in biased and erroneous reporting, but the earlier burst of optimism from the highest levels of government that told Americans that the United States was winning in Vietnam did not square well with the stunning surprise of the Communist attacks.[143]

This should have been an enduring lesson for future administrations; however, by the Global War on Terror it would be a forgotten one.

Admittedly, as this examination of contrasting scholarship illustrates, drawing conclusions on the true effects of media reporting on public opinion and policy during Vietnam is challenging as historians and analysts in other disciplines attempt to examine public opinion polling data from decades gone by. Two conflicting RAND studies, the first by Benjamin C. Schwartz in 1994, and the second by Eric V. Larson in 1996, demonstrate the problems this poses.[144] The first problem with previous studies of the media's influence on public opinion during the Vietnam War is the narrow focus on the tone of that coverage (i.e. pessimistic, biased), and not the full examination of media coverage and the factors that led to incomplete, misleading, and erroneous reporting. By making selective use of credible and detailed first-hand accounts of media coverage, such as those of Peter Braestrup, Don Oberdorfer, historians and analysts of the do not account for how news reports not only feed editorial and commentary, but also how they affect the selection and placement of news, are spread through and abundance of news and entertainment mediums that used that information, including books, songs, and films that permeated popular culture during the period.

Second, heavy reliance on public opinion data alone, and to a lesser extent the reliability of that polling data, provide only one gage in measuring media influence on public opinion. The cause and effect relationship between media coverage and historical landmarks such as elections, policy changes, or leadership decisions based on public opinion provide better metrics for gauging media influence. President Johnson's decision not to run for a second term, Richard M. Nixon's narrow election victory over anti-war candidate Hubert Humphrey (popular votes), and the election of anti-war candidates to the U.S. Congress in 1968, 1970, 1972, and 1974 all offer better measurements to compare the media's cause and effect relationship with U.S. public opinion. Nixon's campaign was critical of the Johnson administration's policies and campaigned to bring peace with honor in Vietnam through Vietnamization and the withdrawal of U.S. forces.

Third, they did not look outside their disciplines to understand what communication and political science scholars have long understood about the media's power to influence a public body, as described in the previous chapter. In doing so, they would have synthesized a broader range of scholarship and found other models of media influence to help better understand the effects of Vietnam's media coverage on public opinion. Moreover, they could have analyzed media influence on public opinion and policy using more recent events to develop a model for comparison. For the purpose of this study, direct observation on how the media reported events in the Global War on Terror and the effects of that reporting on public opinion helps understand the cause and effect relationship between media coverage and public opinion in Vietnam.

Chapter Conclusion

The Tet Offensive was a landmark event because the immediacy of reporting, coupled with the powerful, moving images of television, proved the media could influence decision makers far removed from the scene before events had played out. Because of its power, both belligerents and outside political interests attempted to use or manipulate the media to influence public opinion and policy in the wars of ideas and images that accompanied the military conflict. In the era of active, global Soviet subversion, these wars of ideas and images not only played out on the geopolitical, strategic, operational, and tactical levels, but also played out on the domestic U.S. social and political landscape.

Tet provides five lessons to consider in understanding media influence and media performance in combat. First, intense competition drives journalists and media outlets to be the first to report breaking news. In haste and confusion, journalists rush to provide fragments of breaking news without validating information, and compensate for the absence of facts with hasty speculation or unqualified analysis. As a result, journalists' initial reports of a breaking news story are always incomplete because not all details are known, and they are most often wrong because the journalists' limited understanding and observation leads them to draw the wrong conclusions. This media fog of war is problematic because first reports shape the public's initial opinions and perceptions of important events, establishing an incorrect first truth, and they are often amplify through a plethora of media outlets that share information of follow the lead of major media establishments. In Vietnam, the rush to publish and produce caused journalists to file numerous incomplete, erroneous, and misleading first reports of the Tet Offensive while news managers failed to vet field reports and released them uncritically. This not only predisposed millions of American's as to the war's situation and outcome, but also adversely affected further Vietnam War reporting because it colored the perceptions of editors and producers who selected what stories to report, as well as incoming journalists would build on the established narrative. As the battle progressed, media pressures compelled journalists to continue filing hasty, incomplete reports of developments on the battlefield, and they began citing so-called experts far from the scene that drew premature conclusions based on deficient reports. Amid the fast pace of several events taking place simultaneously, there was little time or incentive for either journalists to write corrections, or editors and producers to produce them.

Second, war, by nature, is complex and difficult to cover. Most journalists inherently lack broad historical, political, and cultural understanding of conflicts, and usually have a superficial understanding, at best, of the art and science of war or national strategy. They are a product of their own education and experiences, which shapes their perceptions of issues and events and affects their reporting. In Vietnam, the shortage of journalists during the first critical days provided limited geographical coverage as many journalists were confined to Saigon and had limited access to battlefield events. As a result, they could see only what was in front of them and not the larger picture. When they did get out to the battlefields, many congregated in the same areas and covered the same events, which provided a narrow view of a much larger event. Journalists often arrived after events and saw only the aftermath of combat. Therefore, they had difficulty explaining what had happened, and relied on second and third-hand accounts, which included rumor, hearsay, and gossip, as sources of information; and filled voids in information with hasty speculation. In some cases, journalists used Hanoi's propaganda as a basis for their reports. Moreover, like soldiers on the battlefield, journalists were affected by both the physical and emotional effects of violence, danger, hardship, physical stress, fatigue, and other environmental or wartime factors, which influenced their reporting.[145] Journalists arriving midstream during the Tet Offensive, a phenomenon called "parachute journalism," were often predisposed by first reports and provided the American public with what media scholar Pippa Norris calls "a more confusing, disjointed, and violent image of the world, rather than an informed and balanced understanding of international events."[146] Popular media personalities, such as Walter Cronkite, were not immune to this, and because of their credibility helped advance Vietnam misreporting.

Third, during times of conflict the media is often at odds with the military and government as the press attempts to cover the conflict and the military seeks to protect operational security and maintain public support. In Vietnam, the press was able to report without restrictions on battlefield visits and without censor. Even so, the Tet Offensive exacerbated an emerging credibility gap between the government and the media following Johnson's success campaign because it caught the press, public, and key officials by surprise. As a result, many journalists sought to provide a contradictory view of the U.S. military effort and situation in Vietnam according to a quagmire narrative, which became known as the "Vietnam Syndrome," that is, reporting the costs of war in terms of death, destruction, financial costs, and body count vice the gains.[147] This continued through the remained of the conflict and, like the Tet Offensive, was influential during the U.S. response to North Vietnam's Nguyen Hue Offensive in 1972. The pattern of cynical reporting caused U.S. military and government officials to respond with suspicion.

Forth, the media's narrow focus on U.S. policy and involvement amid a larger, more complex situation resulted in both a narrow understanding of the whole and a narrow criteria for evaluating U.S. performance. Much of this was because the American free media gave considerable coverage to the debates over the war in the United States, including considerable coverage to the antiwar protests and movements. Additionally, the media failed to provide adequate coverage of the full political situation in South Vietnam or South Vietnamese military performance. Instead, the media gave substantial coverage of the political debates over Vietnam in the United States, concentrating on the anti-war protests and political dissent in the U.S. congress, which supported the quagmire narrative.

Fifth, because the media plays a key role in the war of ideas that accompanies a military conflict, it is both an independent political actor intended to be influential in shaping public opinion and policy, and subject to manipulation by competing political interests, including the belligerents themselves. In Vietnam, Communists broadcasted propagandized reports from Hanoi while agents distributed propaganda and misinformation in Saigon that some journalists used uncritically in absence of real news and information. In the United States, Communists agent successfully infiltrated the labor and anti-war movements, as well as media, and were influential in framing issue and shaping public perception. It is important to stress, however, that the false optimism that the Johnson administration's success campaign created, the institutional distrust of government or "credibility gap" created by false or exaggerated battlefield reports, the U.S.S. *Pueblo* incident, the criticism of both elites and Johnson's political opponents, and waning support for the war all contributed.

The cumulative effects of these factors provided incomplete, erroneous, and often misleading accounts of events that had significant adverse effects on public opinion and policy. These deficient reports forged a quagmire narrative not only caused decision makers to alter U.S. policy that allowed the Communists to regroup, but also served Communist propaganda by discouraging the American public while emboldening their forces. The premature withdrawal and eventual removal of U.S. forces allowed the Communists to not only take over Vietnam, but also Cambodia and resulted in the murder of millions of people in both countries. In the end, the media's deficient coverage of the Vietnam War not only created Vietnam War mythology, but also created a cynical Vietnam Syndrome model for reporting future U.S. involvement in foreign affairs, that is, the fear of a costly, protracted conflict, or quagmire, and the assertion that the United States could not win. As described more in the following chapters, these factors and pessimistic reporting style would continue to influence public opinion and policy in other U.S. efforts between the Vietnam War and the Iraq War. However, it would fully replicate itself in the post-Saddam conflict.

CHAPTER THREE

THE EFFECTS OF A CHANGING MEDIA ENVIRONMENT

After Vietnam, Americans recognized the misleading and biased news coverage of Vietnam and the U.S. political scene and began to lose confidence in the print media's ability to report objectively while becoming even more reliant on the convenience of television and compelling news personalities for their news and information. This caused a shift in media use that resulted in a decline in newspaper and news magazine circulation that began in the mid-1970s and continued for more than three decades.[1] Between the Vietnam War and the Global War on Terror, major media changes significantly transformed the way the free media covered important events and radically altered the way the American public received information. By the 1991 Gulf War, satellite television's global, instantaneous, twenty-four hour programming would prove to have a profound effect on the geopolitical landscape. However, other important changes occurred in the media during the 1990s, including new trends in radio programming and listenership, the emergence of the Internet, and industry consolidation, which helped create a mixed-media environment that further adversely effected both the media's ability to cover news how the public received information. Understanding satellite television's coverage of important events and its power to influence public opinion and policy, as well as the effects of industry consolidation and a mixed-media environment, is important in understanding how the media shaped public attitudes in the decade before the Iraq War.

Satellite Television: Instantaneous Coverage and Global Reach

The emergence of cable and satellite television during the 1980s allowed broadcasters to transmit directly to audiences rather than through transmitters, which provided consumers with many more choices in channels and programs and broke the television news monopoly the three major networks (ABC, CBS, and NBC) held. The abundance of new satellite channels and programs significantly increased competition, fragmented the U.S. television audience, and shrank the market for network news because many consumers often chose entertainment over traditional news formats.[2] To remain competitive and retain audiences, news broadcasters began to combine entertainment with news to attract audiences, sacrificing objective journalism to maintain and build market share while providing the public with a limited selection of news.[3] The result gave birth to sensationalized "soft news" programs like *Inside Edition* and *Hard Copy*, along with programs such as *Oprah*, *Letterman*, *Regis and Kelly*, and others that spurred conversation and commentary, but provided only a narrow or superficial examination of issues.[4]

By the 1990s, the immediacy, global reach, and powerful imagery of satellite television's continuous twenty-four hour coverage of world events had a dramatic influence on public opinion and policy. This was evident during the 1991 Gulf War, where the combination of satellite television with the military's new media policy gave the American public unprecedented accounts of battlefield operations almost as they happened, using professional graphics, color video, satellite images, and actual targeting footage of air strikes. CNN dominated this news coverage with twenty-four hour programming that included a traditional news format, its own original soft news programs, (*Crossfire* and *Larry King Live*), scrolling text, and panels of retired military officers who provided instant analysis and commentary. According to historians Ava Briggs and Peter Burke, "when Saddam Hussein invaded Kuwait, CNN had fewer than one million viewers," but "by the time that Allied planes were bombing Baghdad each night in 1991, it had nearly seven million."[5] Satellite television's combination of speed, imagery, and reach turned the media into a powerful force, influencing a global audience and creating a vehicle for both Saddam Hussein and Washington to use for public diplomacy.[6] Although the U.S. government had used the commercial media for political communication to influence public opinion to build support for policy, the use of satellite television created a new phenomenon in which governments attempted to communicate and influence a global public audience to achieve multiple political aims.

CNN and other media establishments in the United States benefited and profited greatly from the military's more open media policy during the war, while the military maintained operational security and credibility. However, it is important to note that such media coverage of the 1991 Gulf War would not have been possible had the military and media not reconciled their differences after Vietnam, but this came only after the relationship had further deteriorated. After Vietnam, the relationship between the media and the government remained one of mutual distrust and suspicion. This became evident in 1983 when military officials excluded the American media from operations in Grenada in an unprecedented manner for the first two days. When American correspondents finally provided reports of the military operations in Grenada, their reports reflected the journalists' lack of understanding.[7] It was evident that U.S. military-media relations had become completely estranged, which and forced senior military and media leaders to reconcile differences and find a workable solution that allowed media access without endangering the U.S. mission or personnel, as reflected in the military's 1991 Gulf War media policy that allowed the U.S. media to broadcast of military briefings.[8]

What is more, the arrangement was not without critics. Contending the media served as an agent for the government, media critic Marvin Kalb argued that the media was seduced by General Colin Powell and engaged in an "upsurge of unchecked patriotism," that "robbed U.S. reporters of...the ability to think critically, act in a detached manner, ask questions, remain unemotional, and resist—always resist—the strong temptation during war to cheer for the American side and denounce the enemy."[9] Conversely, communication and political science professors Robert M. Entman and Benjamin I. Page contend this was not the case because journalists were free to ask questions and provided contrary information.[10] Nonetheless, these criticisms reinforced institutional distrust of government characteristic of the Vietnam Syndrome and would fester among journalists until the Iraq War.

Although the military-media relationship during the 1991 Gulf War largely overlooked front line accounts of combat, some journalists, such as Peter Arnett, were among forty foreign journalists who reported the war from the al-Rashid hotel in Baghdad under the strict control of the Iraqi Information Ministry, which operated a sophisticated propaganda network in the basement of the hotel. While most of these reporters later left Iraq, Arnett was among a few who remained, and gained an exclusive interview with Iraqi President Saddam Hussein. Like his erroneous reporting in Vietnam, Arnett wrongly reported that the United States was indiscriminately targeting civilians and using cluster bombs on Baghdad, bombed a Baby Milk Factory during the Gulf War simply because the Iraqi sign in front of the building, written in English, read "Baby Milk Plant Iraq."[11] U.S. officials believed the plant was producing biological weapons. Since most Iraqis cannot read English, and only seventy-four percent of Iraqis can read Arabic, most analysts believed that Arnett had been mislead by Iraqi Information Ministry officials.[12]

Following the 1991 Gulf War, new satellite channels sought to emulate CNN's success and challenged its market share. In 1996, MSNBC and Fox News entered the twenty-four hour cable news market, while in Qatar, al-Jazeera became the first of several Arab satellite stations to emerge amid loosening media restrictions in the Middle East. Modeled after CNN, al-Jazeera followed U.S. involvement in the Middle East, centering on Israel, Iraq, and U.S. involvement in the Middle East along with discussion of Arab perceptions of them. However, al-Jazeera's engaging yet sensational journalistic style and radical, ideological perspective challenged several Arab states, causing them to exclude the satellite station. This did not stop the station from reaching global Arab audiences in Europe and North America.[13]

The CNN Effect: Satellite Television and U.S. Foreign Policy

Following the 1991 Gulf War, the power of satellite television to influence U.S. public opinion and policy proved itself in a series of foreign crises because the constant flow of real-time news coverage in a twenty-four hour news cycle provoked emotional public and government responses that led to U.S. intervention.[14] This became evident soon after the Gulf War when the media's powerful images of displaced Kurds following Saddam's genocidal campaigns in 1991 caused policy makers to ignore commanders on the ground overseeing Operation Provide Comfort and order the wrong humanitarian aid.[15] According to General Anthony Zinni, "when the Kurds came into the camps, we had no problem warming them up and keeping the warm," but what was needed was food and medicine.[16] However, because the media showed Kurds shivering in the cold, decision makers ordered Zinni drop blankets instead of the food and medicine already prepared. "And predictably," Zinni explains, "when the bundles fell from the sky, the Kurds tore them open and threw away the blankets. They were looking for food and medicine."[17]

Dubbed "the CNN effect," political communication professor Steven Livingston explains that the global media acts as an "accelerant" in foreign policy decisions because it "shortens the decision making response time" while also acting as "an impediment to the achievement of desired foreign policy goals" because its instantaneous and powerful imagery could threaten operational security or could undermine progress.[18] Aiding this phenomenon, however, was the shift in global power following the end of the Cold War and the absence of an effective post-Cold War foreign policy under President Bill Clinton. Political science and communication professor Robert M. Entman explains that new power of satellite television allowed the media to assert itself in the nation's post-Cold War foreign policy by framing the issues and setting the agenda with an abundance of images and well-crafted articles filled with carefully chosen words. Therefore, soon after President Clinton took office, media elites effectively framed U.S. foreign policy for humanitarian intervention in Bosnia, Kosovo, and Somalia, and Haiti urging U.S. intervention, then, after the United States intervened framed the cases for withdrawal, emphasizing the Vietnam Syndrome narrative that the United States had entered a quagmire in each of these efforts that it could not win.[19]

Using a chronology of *Newsweek* headlines as an example, Entman persuasively demonstrates how the influential publication first posed the need for humanitarian intervention in Somalia by priming the public with a wealth of information on Somalia's oppressive warlords, rampant lawlessness, and the widespread shortage of food while simultaneously framing a case for U.S. intervention.[20] Providing an abundance of print and television evidence,

Jonathan Mermin supports Entman's conclusion writing, "Next to Vietnam, Somalia may be the most cited case of media influence on American foreign policy."[21] When U.S. forces did intervene, CNN and other major networks used spotlights to film U.S. Marines wading ashore during the night, which not only gave away the Marine's position on live television, but invited artillery and sniper fire, thereby not only endangering American lives, but also jeopardizing the U.S. mission.

Only ten months into the mission, however, satellite television showed the graphic images of a Somali mob dragging the mutilated bodies of Army Special Forces soldiers through the streets of Mogadishu following a raid on the warlords. Although the media painted the event as a defeat according the post-Vietnam quagmire narrative of U.S. foreign intervention, the media failed to portray that an estimated 1,800 Somali rebels were killed compared to 19 Americans. Indicative of the pessimistic media response and call for withdrawal, *Newsweek* criticized President Bill Clinton's Somalia policy framing a case for withdrawing U.S. forces following the incident with article titled "Trapped in Somalia."[22] In response, President Clinton withdrew U.S. forces leaving the humanitarian mission unfinished, allowing the killing of thousands from famine and civil strife. This not only sent a message to al-Qaeda that Americans were squeamish but also showed that the quagmire narrative that had emerged during the 1968 Tet Offensive had come to full fruition more than two decades later with a new generation of journalists as the United States became more involved in foreign humanitarian crisis. According to *The 9/11 Commission Report* evaluation of the Somali effort:

> Under pressure from Congress, President Clinton soon ordered the withdrawal of U.S. forces. 'Black Hawk Down' joined 'Desert One' as a symbol among Americans in uniform, code phrases used to evoke the risks of daring exploits without maximum preparation, overwhelming force, and a well-defined mission."[23]

While this statement addresses the underlying weakness of U.S. foreign policy during the period, the role of the media in framing the case for intervention and withdrawal cannot be overlooked. According to Vietnam, "Somalia may be the most often cited case of media influence on American policy."[24]

Also following the 1991 Gulf War, the United States had become reliant on the power of satellite television and the global media to communicate to the international community—a new paradigm in U.S. foreign policy. In a major policy change, the Clinton Administration and disbanded the U.S. Information Agency (USIA) in 1999—the lead agency responsible for U.S. public diplomacy for more than four decades. Although the U.S. Department of State assumed some of the USIA's public diplomacy responsibilities, it would be slow to implement a strategic communication plan, and the action to abolish the USIA would have profound adverse effects in the Global War on Terrorism.[25]

Manufactured News: The Effects of a Changing Media Industry

Between the 1991 Gulf War and the Iraq War the media continued to evolve and these media changes not only began to affect the way the public received information, but also significantly limited the media's ability to adequately cover the Iraq War. First, the growth of cable and satellite television in terms of new channels and programs continued to fracture the news audience, while at the same time the market for hard news continued to decline as the public continually relied on soft news programs for information.[26] Competition for the shrinking hard news market compelled news broadcasters to rely on a steady flow of fresh news, and captivating, if not sensational, video to attract and keep audiences in satellite television's twenty-four hour news cycle to keep ratings, which meant news broadcasters could change stories quickly if another provided more appealing video imagery, ultimately limiting giving the public a limited selection of news while only providing fragments of news.[27] Meanwhile, prime time network news programs, which suffered from a decline in public trust over their loss of objectivity in reporting, continued to lose audiences to 24-hour satellite and cable news stations.[28]

Second, ninety percent of Americans turned to radio as a primary news source during the 1980s and 1990s because many Americans began spending more time in their cars commuting. This brought a revival of the AM radio band, and the emergence of news talk radio programs such as Rush Limbaugh and Dr. Laura Schlessinger. The reliance on radio as a primary source of information continued to increase after 2000.[29] The influence of compelling radio personalities and their criticism of the "mainstream" media also contributed to the declining public trust in the media and in U.S. public opinion and polices leading to the Iraq War.

Third, the Internet matured quickly during the late 1990s and began to shape the way the public received news and information. Many new online news publications emerged, allowing average citizens to become both reporters and commentators with websites and blogs. These new online publications provided a both variety of news and in-depth coverage that not only challenged the position traditional newspapers and news magazines held in the American political landscape along with their market share, but also challenged their content and editorial positions.[30]

Forth, newspaper and news magazine circulation continued to decline as the news market shifted to other sources for news; however, declining public trust in the print media's ability to report objectively was also a factor. To offset declining circulation, many traditional newspapers and news magazines launched websites, which allowed small remote newspapers to become part of the new global media. Nonetheless, because of declining subscription and advertising revenues, traditional newspapers and news magazines continued to reduce staffs, leaving fewer journalists to cover news.[31]

Fifth, intense competition coupled with shifts in media use caused the media industry to diversify and consolidate in the mid-1990s, which lasted for more than a decade and led to media conglomerates with more power to influence and control content and programming. This industry consolidation, however, also led to significant layoffs and downsizing that left fewer journalists to gather and report news in a demanding twenty-four hour news cycle and became a major factor after the first few months of the Iraq War. This, according to *The Project of Excellence in Journalism*, gave the public only "raw elements as the end product," which forced the public to use more news outlets to get a full range of news, which in turn created a competitive, fast-paced, entertainment based, mixed-media environment where sound bites, headlines, and carefully selected and edited images conveyed the intended message.[32]

Sixth, objectivity in reporting continued to decline. According to senior media analysts with the PEW Research Center's Project for Excellence in Journalism, Bill Kovach and Tom Rosenstiel, journalists increasingly blended opinion, assertion, and unqualified analysis into new reports, and through the subjective selection of news often focused on auxiliary issues that had little bearing on the relevant central issues.[33] This trend became evident during the 2000 presidential elections when a *Project for Excellence in Journalism* and *Committee of Concerned Journalists* conducted four studies that demonstrated how reporters provided very little information on which American voters could make informed decisions about the candidates. According to Kovach and Rosenstiel, "the press provided only scant reporting on the candidates' backgrounds, records, or ideas...Instead reporters focused more than 80 percent of their stories on matters that affect the campaigns or the political parties (i.e., changes in tactics, fundraising strategies, and internal organizational problems)."[34]

Importantly, Kovach and Rosenstiel argue that, along with the decline in objectivity, the media also moved into a dangerous new form of journalism they describe as "journalism of assertion," where "facts are less important than speed and ratings success."[35] However, the subjective selection of content and news was not just the result of journalists compiling stories, but also the result of news managers, editors, and producers who subjectively selected and shaped news through the conventions of priming, framing, and agenda setting to support their political and business goals. Kovach and Rosenstiel were not the only media experts to notice the problems with selective journalism. Journalism and communication scholars have filled university bookshelves with empirical studies on journalism bias, ethics, and media performance that support Kovach's and Rosenstiel's conclusions. Moreover, media observers such as Noam Chomsky, who criticized the media for putting profit above objectivity, and Brent Bozell III, who criticized the media for liberal bias, reflected two contrasting perspectives on declining public trust in the media.[36]

However, the most important criticism of the media would come from the public. By 2000, however, the public backlash against subjective journalism became evident not only as print and prime time news lost readers and viewers, but as public criticism against such journalism practices from the public came from citizens themselves using the Internet, which allowed them to become both critics and journalists. Communication scholar Stephen D. Cooper contends that blogs emerged to counter the media with criticism challenging media's accuracy, framing, agenda setting/gatekeeping, and journalistic practices."[37] By the Iraq War, the *Project for Excellence in Journalism* reports that seventy percent of Americans were getting their news from the Internet, with more than 32 million Americans reading blogs.[38] Most important, all of these changes would later manifest themselves in coverage of the Iraq War.

The collective effects of these industry changes would not serve the interests of the broad public because fewer journalists would provide less coverage of important events, the collective media would provide manufactured news filled with subjective opinion or diluted with entertainment, and the public would be forced to use a variety of news sources to stay informed on important issues and events, relying mainly on the new media for information. Ultimately, the public would receive both a limited selection and limited coverage of hard news. Importantly, these changes within the media industry would play an important role in limiting both the quantity and quality of news coming from the battlefields in post-Saddam Iraq.

Importantly, in addition to these changes in the modern media, there are other factors to consider in assessing the modern media. One is the issue of media elitism and media leadership. Large established media outlets, such as *The New York Times*, tend to lead media's framing and agenda setting roles, leaving smaller news outlets to follow the ques of the media giants.[39] A perfect example of this is Vietnam correspondent David Halberstam, described in the previous chapter, whose coverage of early U.S. involvement in Vietnam made him a hero to the generations of journalists the followed him, including *New York Times* Iraq War correspondent Dexter Filkins who honored him in a tribute following Halberstams' death in 2007 writing the Halberstam "set a standard for skepticism of official war-time pronouncements that carries on to this day."[40] According to Filkins, Halberstam went to Vietnam a "believer in the American project," but witnessed a disparity between what he witnessed and what he was told in official press briefings.[41] Nonetheless, Halberstam's reputation, coupled with the prestige of reporting for *The New York Times*, would set an example for future generations of journalists, including Filkins.

Chapter Conclusion

As this chapter had shown, between the 1991 Gulf War and the Iraq War, three key factors conspired to shape the media's coverage of international events and in doing so shape public's perceptions and policies. First, the transformation of the media dramatically changed the way news outlets present the news and how the world received its information. The abundance of new satellite programs and channels coupled with news-talk radio format and the Internet created a mixed-media environment that fractured the public sphere, and diluted the news market. Amid the highly competitive environment, the media industry consolidated, which led to layoffs and left a few industry giants to oversee a plethora of smaller media outlets and left fewer journalists to report news. Competition also led broadcasters to move to entertainment-based soft news programs, which provided only superficial examination and often-editorialized analysis of issues. While hard news programs changed stories often to new "breaking news" stories to attract audiences, which left news consumers with both a narrow range of news and shallow coverage. The combined effects of media transformation forced the public to use several news sources to get a both a full range of news and in-depth coverage.

Second, the immediacy, powerful imagery, and global reach of continuous satellite television's twenty-four hour real-time coverage of major world events gave the media more power to influence U.S. public opinion and policy through carefully selected and edited images and sound bites that provoke emotional responses. Between the 1991 Gulf War and the 2003 Iraq War, U.S. presidents have sought to harness the power of satellite television by using it as a vehicle for state communication and public diplomacy. However, after the Clinton Administration dissolved the U.S. Information Agency in 1999, the government became reliant on the collective, private media to communicate its messages to a broad public sphere in lieu of a comprehensive national communication strategy, public diplomacy program, and post-Cold War foreign policy. This allowed the media to not only to influence public opinion on international crisis and events in the post-Cold War era, but also to frame the U.S. response. As shown in this chapter's examples, in the absence of U.S. policy the "CNN effect" framed international crisis' leading to U.S. intervention and later, through criticism of U.S. policy and efforts indicative of the Vietnam Syndrome's "quagmire narrative," framed the case for withdrawing U.S. involvement. This effect is dangerous to public opinion and policy because it provokes hasty, emotional judgments instead of thoughtful deliberation that ultimately lead to shortsighted policies that adversely effect the realization of U.S. foreign policy objectives.

Third, as communication scholars, journalists, and other media observers have described, journalists' increasing insertion of opinion, assertion, and unqualified analysis into news reports along with their focus on auxiliary issues that had little bearing on the relevant central issues provided very little real information to American public on important issues. This, coupled with the news managers, editors, and producers subjectively selecting and shaping news through the conventions of priming, framing, and agenda setting/gatekeeping, demonstrates that news is a manufactured commodity intended to influence public opinion toward a particular point of view. All of these factors will manifest themselves in both the media's coverage of events leading to the Iraq War, as well as the media's coverage of the war itself, and in doing so influence public opinion and policy.

CHAPTER FOUR

UNDERSTANDING THE BELLIGERENTS

The guerilla war and insurgency that ensued after the removal of the Baath Party regime on April 9, 2003 was far more complex than most media descriptions portrayed during the conflict. While some Iraqis continued fighting after conventional mean failed, others took up arms later for a variety of reasons, joining a number of insurgent groups, each with its own particular interests and aims. Although many of these groups sometimes cooperated with each other toward a common goal, they often fought each other for control of Iraq's political districts, provinces, and Iraq itself. Likewise, most media explanations for Iraq's "Awakening," or turn toward reconciliation with Coalition forces, fall of short of providing full historical insight. Some accounts give all credit to the Iraq's tribal leaders, whereas other accounts give credit to certain U.S. military leaders or certain U.S. policy decisions. However, to understand media performance in the Iraq War and the wars of ideas that accompanied the conflict, one must understand the complexities of Iraq's multi-faceted post-Saddam insurgency and the series of events and circumstances leading to the "Awakening" as a basis for evaluating media performance. Before this can be accomplished, however, an understanding of the Middle East's unique and volatile history in relation to the West, especially Iraq, is critical in understanding the post-Saddam insurgency and the Global War on Terror as a whole, and the wars of ideas that were an integral part of the conflict.

Iraq at the Crossroads of the Middle East and Islam

Iraq has always been an important region in both Middle Eastern and Islamic history, and central to Iraq are issues that the Middle East has long struggled. Considered the heart of Mesopotamia, the grain belt of the Middle East, and the "Cradle of Civilization," Iraq was once the crossroads between the East and the West, and is where the world's most advanced civilizations once ruled the region. Long before Alexander the Great laid waste to Darius III's Great Persian Army in the Battle of Gaugamela in 331 B.C., Iraq was a strategic prize for any empire. Iraq is where the Muslim army defeated the Persian Empire, and where the Shia split over the succession of Muhammad's leadership, creating the deepest and most enduring conflict within Islam. With a longstanding history of authoritarian leaders, Iraq emerged from the ashes of the Ottoman Empire following World War I to become a contested region during both World War II and the subsequent Cold War, while mirroring the changes that took place throughout the entire Middle East. These changes include the rise of Arab nationalism, pan-Arabism, and Islamic fundamentalism.[1]

For centuries before Islam, nomadic Arab tribes competed for resources as they had for centuries. Built around a tribal leader whose authority is passed to the next generation from one male blood relative to the next, tribal culture is built around family relationships and a system of shame and honor where they jealously respond to insults, offenses, and crimes with revenge. As religious scholar Karen Armstrong explains, "one tribe fought another, in a murderous cycle of vendetta and counter-vendetta."[2] Because they worshipped many gods they were at odds with Christians and Jews. When Muhammad ibn Abdallah founded Islam in 610 B.C., he sought to unite Arabs and others living in the region. However, despite the new religion's similarities to Judaism and Christianity, Muhammad's efforts to reconcile his new belief system with the Jews and Christians failed. Both faiths rejected his religion, which alienated Muslims and further exacerbated the preexisting differences between Arab converts and the other faiths. Muhammad responded by denouncing those who would not follow him and told his followers to no longer pray toward Jerusalem but toward Mecca, and in doing so led Islam on a different path. Muhammad also established a Muslim army to win converts and unify the Arab tribes against Arab pagans, Christians, and Jews through force. Within twenty years, Muslims controlled the Arabian Peninsula, captured the Persian Empire, and moved into North Africa; within thirty years, Muslims controlled much of the modern Middle East and North Africa, and threatened both Europe and Central Asia. Muslim conquest and aggression in Europe under the Seljuk Empire triggered a Western response in 1095 A.D. with the First Crusade, whereas subsequent Crusades deepened animosity between Muslims and the West.[3]

Despite Islam's success in spreading across the Middle East, competing interests had divided the faith following Muhammad's death in 632 A.D. Some followers believed that Ali ibn Abi Talib, Muhammed's closest male relative, should succeed Muhammad as the new *caliph*, or Muslim leader, in accordance with Arab custom, because blood ties are important in Arab culture. Instead, Muhammad's closest followers elected Abu Bakr to succeed him. Therefore, not all of Muhammad's followers accepted Bakr's leadership. Following Bakr's death and the murder of Muhammad's next two successors, Umar ibn al-Khattab and Uthman ibn Affan, Ali appointed himself the fourth caliph in 656 A.D. However, Muawiyah, a Syrian governor, claimed the right to the caliphate and took arms against Ali in the *First Fitnah*, civil war, which led to Ali's assassination 661 A.D. and the beginning of the Umayyad Dynasty. Ali's son, Ḥusayn ibn Ali ibn Abi Talib, led a short-lived revolt against Umayyads in an attempt to claim the caliphate, but he was defeated at the Battle of Karbala, in modern Iraq, along with his infant son. Ali became a symbolic Shia martyr of the Sunni-Shia conflict, which has divided Islam since. The mosque dedicated to Ali's memory is an important Shia landmark in Iraq. [4]

The Muslim empire remained a single entity under the Seljuks until the tenth century when competing interest divided the Seljuk Empire into smaller dynasties. Competing caliphates emerged, followed by esoteric movements within Islam. Among these esoteric movements were the Ismailis, an offshoot of the Shia sect that challenged the prevalent Sunni doctrine as their missionaries spread across the Seljuk Empire. During the eleventh century, a Persian Ismaili convert named Hassan-i Sabbah, established a network of assassins called *Hashishiyya* or *Hashishin*, hashish eaters, who called themselves *fidayeen*—meaning guerillas ready to sacrifice their lives for their cause. Also known as the *Cult of Assassins*, these fidayeen effectively organized religious violence and engaged in religious and political terrorism and murder, and sought to depose the Seljuks and destroy the Sunnis along with other Muslim leaders. The assassins remained a feared and influential political force through the Ayyibid Dynasty until the Mongol invasion under Genghis Khan's grandson, Hulagu Khan, brought widespread devastation and disruption to the Muslin world and ended the *Hashishin.*[5]

After more than a century of harsh Mongol rule, a new Muslim Empire emerged under the Ottomans with Baghdad as its capital. From 1299 A.D., the Ottomans maintained strict control over the regions hostile religious and ethnic factions, and kept them isolated from the West. Between the fifteenth and eighteenth centuries, the Ottomans exacted tribute from the weaker Western nations for protection and rights to trade with the Empire. Muslim corsairs enforced Muslim hegemony over sea trade while also engaging in piracy, preying on Western ships and villages throughout the Mediterranean and the English Channel, and taking thousands of European slaves in a flourishing commercial enterprise. European slaves were especially valuable because as unbelievers they were considered inferior. Men were pressed into hard labor and sea service. Many women and children were forced into prostitution. All were forced to convert to Islam or die.[6]

Colonialism and European Competition for the Middle East

During the decline of the Ottoman Empire, however, emerging powers took a great interest in trade with the Middle East, mainly as a gateway to the ancient trade routes to the orient. When Napoleon Bonaparte invaded Egypt in 1798, he introduced Muslims to new technology and European ways. After he withdrew his Army, Egypt's ruler, Muhammad Ali Pasha sought to emulate the French and pursued modernization and the benefits of science, technology, and medicine, along with improved education and legal systems.[7] By the early nineteenth century, the West had become militarily superior and forcefully ended the tribute system and slave trade in other Arab territories. In doing so, Western powers opened the region to further commercial expansion into Muslim land during the eighteenth and nineteenth centuries. European nations invested in improving infrastructure such as railroads and ports. In 1889, the Suez Canal began operation as a neutral, privately owned company under British protection, providing safe passage to all ships during peace and war. Unfortunately, competition between European powers would significantly shape the region in the next century.[8]

According to renowned cultural anthropologist and Middle East expert, Dr, Raphael Patai, while colonization brought freedom, reform, and modernization that many Muslims welcomed, many Arabs felt that Western values threatened Arab culture and family relationships.[9] Islamic fundamentalists, known as Salafis, rejected modernity and Western colonial occupation, believing that Western values conflicted with Islam. They sought to restrict Western literature and influence, engaging in a policy of isolation, while promoting a return to pure or "authentic Islam."[10] During the eighteenth century, a leading Salafi cleric named Muhammad ibn 'Abd al-Wahhab developed a doctrine aimed at making "Islamic law (Sharia) as the law of the land."[11] Al-Wahhab forged an alliance with an influential tribal leader named Muhammad ibn Saud around 1744. Together, they sought to spread Wahhabism through force, while attacking both outsiders and those whom they believed strayed from true Islam—the Shia. Saud's Wahhabi descendants succeeded in gaining control of the Arabian Peninsula through violence and terror.[12] Wahhabi raids on Shiite areas in Mesopotamia forced the Ottomans to suspend Saudi rule and Wahhabism in Arabia, though only temporarily.[13]

Although the Ottomans succeeded in reconquering the lands and keeping them for two centuries, Saud's descendant, Sheikh Abd al-Aziz Saud, kept his independence by supporting the British in World War I, allowing him to quickly conquer the Arabian Peninsula and the holy cities of Mecca and Medina at the end of the Ottoman Empire.[14] After proclaiming himself King of Arabia, Saud made Wahhabism the official, state-enforced doctrine of the kingdom. Meanwhile, Saud's Wahhabi Army made several incursions into Iraq hoping to bring it into the Arabian sphere, and in the process terrorized the Shia population while establishing a base forty miles west of Baghdad in Fallujah. The Saudis viewed Iraq as part of Arabia, separated artificially by the British mandate, and they wanted control of Baghdad because of its importance in Islam.[15] According to Islam scholar Bernard Lewis "if Arabia is the most symbolic location in the world of Islam, Baghdad, the seat of the caliphate for half a millennium and the scene of some of the most glorious chapters in Islamic history, is second."[16] Amid the turbulent events to follow, Fallujah would become an important center of Wahhabi thought and instruction in Iraq.[17]

The collapse of the six-hundred year-old Ottoman Empire after World War I was a tragedy for Muslims because it ended both a geopolitical state and the thirteen-century rule of the caliphs that had united Muslims. Iraq came into being through the French and British Mandates, which exacerbated this humiliation and divided the former empire into arbitrary nations without respect for religion, ethnicity, or culture, and thereby separating families and tribes while confining longstanding enemies to the same area. In Iraq, violent and costly rebellions against the British Mandate became common across Iraq. In Fallujah, the British forces suppressed a violent and bloody that claimed many Iraqi lives on both sides. Such clashes exacerbated anti-western sentiments. Finally, the British installed Faisal ibn Husayn, Faisal I, as the pro-British monarch to control the situation. The Shiites, a minority in the Muslim world but sixty percent of Iraq's total population, found themselves under Sunni control.[18]

Continued resentment toward the French and British Mandates fueled Arab nationalist and pan-Arab movements across the Middle East. It also gave rise to Islamic fundamentalism and became Salafi Islam's basis for the modern Jihad, or struggle, against the West. In Egypt, the Muslim Brotherhood, became the first major Salafi movement in the twentieth century.[19] According its founder, Hassan al-Banna:

> "It is the nature of Islam to dominate, not to be dominated, to impose its law [Sharia] on all nations and to extend its power to the entire planet."[20]

To al-Banna, this meant waging a jihad using both violent and non-violent means.[21] During World War II, the Middle East was a hotly contested region. German and Nazi influence after World War I coupled with Arab nationalist and pan-Arab movements caused many Arabs to side with Germany during World War II, and Iraq was again suffered from both the ravages of war and a second humiliating defeat to the Allied, Western powers.[22]

The Cold War Competition in the Middle East

Following Germany's defeat, the creation of Israel, and the Arabs' humiliating defeat during the 1948 Arab-Israeli War, many Arabs began siding with the Soviets against Israel and the West because the Soviets shared similar animosities.[23] This created an opening that allowed the Soviet Union to exploit the growing enmity between the Arab world and the West and expand its influence throughout the Middle East. Soviet influence in the Middle East caused alarm in the West because Europe (primarily Britain, France, and Germany) depended on Middle Eastern oil to rebuild their war-torn infrastructure and economy. They feared that if the Soviets gained control over Middle East oil they could ruin the West's economy. Although the United States did not rely on Middle Eastern oil in the 1950s, it had invested heavily in European reconstruction and had an interest in the free flow of oil. Therefore, because of Western Europe's weakened conditions, the United States became the leading Western power to check Soviet expansion and subversive activity, which was active in every hemisphere, and even in the Middle East, the Cold War dictated U.S. foreign policy.[24]

When Iranian Prime Minister Mohammed Mossadegh courted the Communist party in 1953, President Dwight D. Eisenhower covertly acted to bring the Shah of Iran back to power fearing that a failure to act in Iran would lead to more "Soviet opportunism."[25] He believed Moscow was engaging in subversive activities aimed at installing Communist dominated totalitarian governments in the already unstable Arab states, and also believed that emerging "encroaching Soviet opportunism" created much of the political instability in the Middle East.[26] When Egypt's President Gamal Nasser took office in 1956, he found the Soviets not only sympathetic in the cause of Arab nationalism, but also willing beat any offers from the United States or its allies for help funding major development and infrastructure improvements. This caused alarm. However, when Nasser nationalized the Suez Canal in 1956, Britain and France believed it threatened the free flow of oil to Europe, and after gaining the support of Israel seized the canal in a short military contests against U.S. wishes. Although the Soviet Union quickly came to Nasser's aid, only after Eisenhower put financial pressure on Britain and France did they withdraw their forces. The Suez Crisis was a significant turning point in the Middle East because Nasser emerged as the victor and became the leader of Arab Nationalist and pan-Arab movements that swept the Middle East. When he turned to the Soviets for help, much of the Arab world followed, which entangled the Middle East in the Cold War and allowed the Soviet Union to expand its influence throughout the Middle East.[27]

The Rise of Fundamental Islam

While most of the Middle East followed a secular path that embraced modernization, pan-Arabism, and Arab nationalism following World War II, Islamic fundamentalism simmered under the surface in the forms of Salafism and Wahhabism. In the late 1950s, Muslim scholar Sayyid Qutb visited the United States and observed American social behavior. He argued that the United States was a threat to Islam because of what he perceived as its Zionist bias toward Islam, its materialism, and its "sexual promiscuity."[28] When Qutb returned to Egypt and began speaking publicly about his anti-American views, Nasser expelled him from his post in the Ministry of Education. Afterward, Qutb joined the Muslim Brotherhood and began defining the role of Islamic fundamentalism in Muslim politics and society while articulating Muslim grievances against the West. In his book *Milestones*, Qutb sowed the seeds of a global pan-Islamic movement aimed at restoring authentic Islam, defeating Western powers that prevented the establishment of an Islamic state, restoring the caliphate, and establishing a new, global Muslim empire by waging a "Salafi jihad."[29] According to terrorism expert Marc Sageman, Qutb's disciple, Muhammad Abd al-Salam Faraj, turned Qutb's criticism into a call for action, arguing that "Islam was not defensive," but throughout its history "had been spread by the sword."[30] Faraj, who became head of Tanzim al-Jihad's Cairo division responsible for assassinating Egyptian President Anwar al-Sadat in 1981, advocated overthrowing Muslim governments that blocked the creation of "an Islamic state," and argued for *jihad*, or Holy War, against distant, non-Muslim governments.[31] Contending that it was an Islamic duty to defend and advance Muslim power and influence, Salafis advocated murder and terror to achieve their political goals.[32]

While Arab nationalism and pan-Arabism succeeded in overcoming colonization, the new Arab secular governments were often repressive governments that kept most Muslims impoverished, illiterate, and isolated from Western influence. Such oppression not only encouraged a return to fundamental Islam and fostered a Salafi, pan-Islamic movement, but also created a fertile recruiting ground for Salifis seeking to lure others to their cause through indoctrinated hatred for all who do not follow the "true" path of Islam.[33] Moreover, continuing resentment of Western colonial influence also contributed to the rise of Salafi Islam. Because of its economic dominance and position in world affairs, some Muslim fundamentalists and intellectuals blamed the United States for the economic exploitation of the Middle East.[34] Many similarly viewed the U.S. efforts to counter Soviet influence and keep the region's oil fields from Moscow a mask for unwanted colonial intrusion. This coupled with the perception that the United States was the leader of Christendom and ally of Israel reinforced Qutb's contention that the United States was Islam's enemy.[35]

To circumvent government-controlled media in Arab states, fundamentalists used underground newspapers, pamphlets, and video or audio recordings to disseminate their ideology.[36] However, it would be the oil-rich Saudi Kingdom that most effectively promoted the spread of Wahhabi Islam in the decades that followed World War II, financing Wahhabi schools, *Madrasas*, not only across the Middle East, but also around the world.[37] Following the tradition of Wahhab, Qutb, and Faraj, these Wahhabi schools provided a form of indoctrination that taught that Western values threaten Islam, and blamed modernization, globalization, and Western influence for problems in the Middle East.[38]

The Soviet invasion of Afghanistan in 1979 caused a resurgence of Wahhabism because Islamic fighters called *mujahedeen*, Holy Warriors, viewed the invasion as both a betrayal of trust and a violation of Muslim lands. They initiated a tenacious jihad against the Soviets to expel them from Afghanistan. When the Soviets withdrew from Afghanistan almost a decade later, these victorious *mujahedeen* helped establish an Islamic Sharia government in Afghanistan called the Taliban, then turned on other enemies of Islam, including the United States, using terror as its primary weapon.[39]

With the benefit of education and privilege, and influenced by the Muslim Brotherhood, Afghanistan veteran Osama bin Laden successfully articulated the modern Muslim cause in the tradition of Qutb and Faraj. Using selective use of Islamic teachings and Muslim history, bin laden made compelling statements condemning the United States and the West for the problems in the Middle East, and repeatedly defining his enemy as 'Crusaders,' contending that the First Crusade was the result of Western imperialist aggression and not the West's response to Muslim conquests. With the goals of defeating Western powers and advancing Muslim power and influence, bin Laden's compelling rhetoric struck a tone with many Muslins, and succeeded in fueling anti-Western sentiment while advancing Salafism across the existing pan-Arab and pan-Islamic movements. With his deputy Ayman al-Zawahiri, a former Muslim Brotherhood member, bin Laden became the leader, organizer, and spokesman for the new Salafi movement, and developed al-Qaeda—the most complex terrorist network in the world with terror and propaganda cells in many parts of the world, and non-governmental agencies to serve as front organizations.[40]

Osama bin Laden's emerging al-Qaeda network soon began thrusting itself onto the world stage. In 1990, bin Laden threatened to lead a jihad against Saddam Hussein for invading Kuwait and positioning his forces to invade the Muslim holy lands of Saudi Arabia. He then turned on the United States for keeping forces in the kingdom following the 1991 Gulf War, and in doing so set the conditions for what would be the Global War on Terror. Terrorism provided al-Qaeda with political strategy to advance Salafi based beliefs across a much larger moderate Muslim majority, either by eliciting sympathy and support by attacking Western targets, or coercing the majority by attacking those Muslim governments that would not readily go along. Bin Laden cited Sabbah's Cult of Assassins and Saladin's counter-crusade in retaking Jerusalem as historical examples of past wars infidels and apostates to justify his use of terror in his *jihad* against the West.[41] Like Wahhab, al-Banna, Qutb, and Farj before him, bin Laden argued that Muslins are obligated to fight against the enemies of Islam and in doing so will be rewarded with material fortune in this life and "paradise in the next."[42] In a stark departure from Islam, however, bin Laden also justified the murder of women and children in the cause of jihad.[43] However, terrorism alone was not enough for al-Qaeda to attain Salafi political goals. According to terrorism expert Cindy Combs, "Terrorism is a crime of theater. In order for terrorism to be effective, the terrorists need to communicate their actions and threats to their audience as quickly and dramatically as possible" to either seduce sympathy and support from audiences, or coerce and intimidate them.[44] In al-Qaeda's case, developed a sophisticated propaganda division aimed at recruiting and promoting its cause in the war of ideas while providing misinformation to discredit its enemies.[45] Al-Qaeda's propaganda cells work to both manipulate and infiltrate tradition media outlets to influence local and regional audiences while using new technologies such as satellite television and the Internet to reach broader audiences beyond their borders.[46]

In 1993, al-Qaeda aided Somali warlords in fighting U.S. forces providing humanitarian aid there, and played a role in the 1993 World Trade Center attack in New York City. In 1995, al-Qaeda related terrorists attacked a joint-U.S.-Saudi military facility. Then, in 1996, al-Qaeda successfully attacked a U.S. military facility in Saudi Arabia killing 19 American service men and women, and injuring 372. Yielding to political pressure, al-Qaeda then moved from its base in Sudan back to Afghanistan, allowing it to grow and prepare for even bigger, bolder attacks on the United States.[47] Despite al-Qaeda's prominence, however, the Muslim Brotherhood continued to be a significant factor in the global Salafi movement. Attempting to portray itself as a moderate organization, the Muslim Brotherhood plays a covert role in Salafi Islam's jihad against the West, overseeing political parties and organizations all over the world aimed at expanding Islamic interests. Even in the United States, Muslim Brotherhood supported organizations are active in U.S. politics, which includes using courts in the United States, to make it illegal to voice legitimate criticism of Islam as "Islamophobia."[48]

In Iran, fundamentalist Shia cleric Ayatollah Ruholla Khomeini articulated similar sentiments as Qutb's and Faraj's during the 1979 Iranian Revolution, which overthrew the pro-West government of Mohammad Reza Pahlavi, and established and Islamic state devoted to spreading Shia influence. During his rise to power, Khomeini claimed the United States the enemy of Islam and called it 'the Great Satan.' He perpetuated a false claim "that American troops had been involved in the clashes in Mecca," which combined with other anti-American rhetoric created both crisis and divide. This inspired militant Iranians into storming the U.S. embassy in Tehran and taking fifty-six Americans hostage for 444 days.[49]

Hezbollah became Iran's lead terrorist agency to promote fundamental Shiism and Iranian interests outside Iran, particularly in Lebanon, where Hezbollah contributed to the small nation's instability and attacked both the U.S. embassy and U.S. Marine barracks in 1983.[50] According to Islamic and

Middle East history professor Yitzhak Nakash, "Hizballah recasts itself as a national liberation movement confined to Lebanon and seeking to make it safe for Shi-is in their local environment."[51] Importantly, Khomeini's influence left an indelible mark on Iraq's Shia population because he had spent time in Iraq gaining a large following that included the very popular and influential Shia cleric, Grand Ayatollah Muhammad Baqir al-Sadr. Al-Sadr founded Iraq's Islamic Dawa Party and openly rebelled against the Baathists, for which Saddam Hussein had him assassinated. Following the collapse of Iraq's Baath Regime in 2003, Baqir al-Sadr's son, Muqtada al-Sadr would become the torchbearer for his father and Iran's proxy for advancing fundamental Shia Islam.

Iraq Under the Baath Party Regime

Following World War II, events in Iraq mirrored those sweeping the region. The Baath Party emerged in 1947 as a pan-Arab, socialist, and nationalist political party that spread from Syria across the Middle East and attracted many anti-Mandate Iraqis who had supported the German Nazi leader Adolph Hitler.[52] Baathists sought to restore Arab greatness under an egalitarian, socialist society by eliminating the artificial boundaries the French and British Mandates created and reuniting all Arabs in a single Arab state.[53] In 1958, Baathists helped Brigadier General Abdul Karim Qassem overthrow Iraq's pro-Western monarchy of King Faisal ibn Husayn, but later attempted to assassinate Qassem when he courted the Soviets.[54] In a bloody 1963 coup, General Ahmad Hassn al-Bakr overthrew Qassem and brought the Baath Party to power in Iraq.[55] When Bakr's Baathists overthrew Qassem in 1963, Saddam Hussein set up prisons and torture chambers, where he was personally involved with interrogation, torture, and the murder of thousands in the Baath purges of Communists and other party enemies.[56] Then, when Hussein's faction lost power, Hussein successfully established the *Jihaz Haneen*, a ruthless and much feared secret organization composed of terror cells that undermined President Abdul Saltn Arif's regime and served as Hussein's personal bodyguards and agents.[57]

Hussein played a key role in the 1968 coup that finally brought Bakr to power, becoming Bakr's vice-president and the Deputy of Revolutionary Command Council. Together, they modeled the Baathist regime after the Soviet Communist Party and attempted to indoctrinate Iraq's diverse population in Iraqi nationalism, Baath ideology, and hatred for the West, while purging or expelling those who resisted.[58] Using the *Jihaz Haneen* as a model, Hussein built a sophisticated and effective internal security network to protect his power from both internal and external threats, and was effective in suppressing both Kurdish and Shiite uprisings. Hussein became close allies with Yuri Andropov, the head of the Soviet KGB, who assisted him in improving Iraq's secret police.[59] This resulted in the Baath Party Militia, the KGB-like secret police, and a complex network of spy, terrorist, and security agencies, such as Amn Al-Amma, Mukhabarat, and Amn Al-Khass, which became his chief means of controlling the population, attaining his political goals, and protecting his power.[60] Under the title Special Operations Group, Hussein built his own international terror network that included the Istikhbarat and Unit 999.[61] These secret organizations penetrated all levels of Iraqi society and received the best training, equipment, and pay.[62] Meanwhile, Hussein backed Palestinian terrorists such as Abu Nidal, who led an organization bearing the same name, and Abu Abbas, known for leading the Palestinian Liberation Organization highjacking of the cruise ship *Achille Lauro* and the murder of Jewish-American Leon Klinghoffer.[63] Other organizations that came under Hussein's patronage included the expelled Iranian group Mujahedeen el-Khalq and its National Liberation Army.

Hussein strengthened Iraq's relationship with the Soviet Union in 1972 when he signed the Treaty of Cooperation, which created a mutually beneficial trade relationship and brought Soviet economic and military assistance.[64] Under this agreement, Hussein purchased the most advanced weapons systems the Soviets could provide, while both Soviet and East German military advisors trained Iraq's military and built new military facilities.[65] He also purchased weapons from several Western countries and pursued new weapons technologies.[66] Under the pretext of agriculture reform, Hussein built dual-use facilities that manufactured pesticides, fertilizer, and nerve and mustard gas, while creating biological weapons under the auspices of veterinary medicine.[67] In 1975, Hussein launched his nuclear weapons program, purchasing the materials, technology, and expertise from both the Soviets and French.[68]

By 1977, Hussein controlled all military and security organizations and had become Iraq's central decision maker. He consolidated his own power by appointing close friends, family members and trusted Baathists to important positions in the secret police and military while eliminating his political rivals.[69] In 1979, he forced Bakr to resign and became Iraq's president.[70] Then he quickly strengthened his position, executing one-third of the Republican Command Council and those he believed threatened his position or questioned his actions. He portrayed himself as a great leader in the tradition of Nebuchadnezzar, Hammurabi, and Saladin, creating an extensive, Stalinesque personality cult to increase his stature among Iraqis.[71]

In 1980, Hussein took his first step toward achieving regional hegemony, believing he could quickly and easily seize a disputed oil-rich strip of land with improved access to the Gulf of Arabia from Iran. Although his initial air strikes and ground campaign caught the Iranians by surprise, Iran's counterattacks combined with its relentless effort to overturn his regime and replace it with a Shia-dominated one drew him into a long war for survival, forcing him to defend himself with chemical weapons as he terrorized Iranian cities with Soviet Scud rockets.[72]

Importantly, because the Soviets also had interests in Iran, they did not provide arms to Iraq during the Iran-Iraq war. This forced Saddam to turn to the United States for support.[73] The United States tried to use the opportunity make Iraq an ally against Iran check the spread of its Islamic Revolution. But Saddam proved uncontrollable for the United States and Iraq's relationship with the United States was short-lived. Saddam soon reconciled his relationship with Moscow.[74]

Following the inconclusive end of the Iran-Iraq War, Hussein invaded Kuwait in 1990 and positioned his forces to invade Saudi Arabia. He hoped to attain regional hegemony by controlling Middle Eastern oil and the holy cities of Mecca and Medina. In indiscriminate attacks, he terrorized the civilian populations in Israel and Saudi Arabia with improved Soviet Scud missiles, while his terror cells attacked Coalition rear positions and attempted to kidnap General Norman Schwarzkopf.[75] However, Hussein underestimated the response his hostility had provoked. His largely conscripted, Soviet-modeled military proved no match for Coalition forces that not only expelled him from Kuwait, but also damaged his nuclear, chemical, and biological weapons programs and weakened his regime by imposing humiliating UN sanctions and inspections.[76]

Chapter Conclusion

Because Iraq is important to both Middle Eastern and Islamic history, it became the heart of Global War on Terror. As this chapter describes, Iraq is a volatile combination of Arab tribal culture, Islam, and strict Baath Party control under Saddam Hussein, which are important in understanding Iraq's recent history, its relationship with the international community, and the nature of conflict in the post-Saddam insurgency. Moreover, understanding this character is essential in understanding the wars of ideas played out during the Iraq War. First, centuries of isolation from the West helped to preserve the ancient tribal system in much of Iraq, which remains central to Iraqi politics, society, and economics. With many tribal territories extending beyond the arbitrary national borders set by the British and French mandates, tribal status and autonomy remained many Iraqi's first loyalty, maintaining self-interests and longstanding competitions and divisions between tribes. Amid this tribal competition, violence was still believed necessary for both tribal survival and settling differences, with the ancient Arab tribal code of honor that calls for revenge in face of an insult or offense remaining deeply ingrained in modern Arab culture. As described later, for some Iraqis, this would motivate them to join the post-Saddam insurgency.

Second, while Islam serves as a unifying force that brings Arabs together, it not only justifies aggressive and often violent expansion, but also guides Muslims in dealing with non-believers, which, as history demonstrates, has put Iraq and the Middle East in a longstanding conflict with West. In the modern era, Western colonial expansion led some Muslims to embrace Salafi Islam and its animosity toward the West. Centuries of isolation and indoctrination, mixed with modern German, Nazi, and later Soviet influence exacerbated this animosity. However, the humiliation of 20th century military defeats in both World Wars and against Israel, coupled with continued Western expansion, caused many Muslims to first embrace Arab nationalism and pan-Arab movements, and later to embrace pan-Islamic movements. Inspired by Salafi Islam, modern terrorists organizations like al-Qaeda hope to advance Salafi Islam and reestablish and Islamic Empire, using terrorism in concert with propaganda to achieve their political goals. Because of its importance to Islam, these Salafis would not only later go to Iraq to fight the enemies of Islam and keep Western influence and culture out of the region, but also take advantage of Iraq's instability to reestablish a new Islamic Empire in Iraq under Islamic (Sharia) law. Complicating the matter is the longstanding conflict within Islam between Sunni and Shia over what each considers "true" Islam as each sect competes violently for control of both Iraq and Islam. This is important because Iran, a predominantly Shia country, will become a formidable and influential belligerent in its own right to help advance Shia interests in Iraq.

Third, from 1968 to 2003, Iraq's Arab Socialist Baath Party dominated Iraq's politics and government—defining modern Iraq and providing its direction. Like the Ottomans and Mongols before him, Saddam Hussein learned to control this volatile mixture of religious, ethnic, and ideological factions with force, coercion, and systematic indoctrination. A complex network of secret police, intelligence, and terror organizations was the key to controlling the population, attaining his political goals, and protecting his power. As demonstrated in the following pages, these secret police, intelligence, and terror organizations would continue to fight when Iraq's conventional military crumbled, thus laying the foundation for Iraq's guerrilla war that began in 2003 following the fall of the Baath regime.

The Global War on Terror that began following the September 11, 2001 terrorists' attacks is more a war of ideas than it is a military conflict. As a result, most of the conflict is waged through all available media for the hearts and minds of multiples public spheres. While the preceding chapters laid a foundation for understanding media influence on shaping public opinion, attitudes, and behavior, the following chapters will not only illustrate the nature, dynamics, and effects of media influence public opinion and policy, but also on the behavior of belligerents.

CHAPTER FIVE

FRAMING THE GLOBAL WAR ON TERROR

The wars of ideas and images that would take place during the Global War on Terror began long before military action on the ground in Afghanistan and Iraq, and were a vital part of the issues, events, and debates leading to the conflict. They would later have significant operational and tactical consequences later as the Iraq War unfolded. Shaping these issues, events, and debates were a series of important developments that require examination. Following the Gulf War, the rise of al-Qaeda, Iraq's continued aggression and defiance, and post-Cold War competition in the Middle East caused significant instability in the region. This volatility brought major challenges for U.S. post-Cold War foreign policy. As tensions between Iraq and the international community increased, both the Western and Arab media sought to shape public attitudes and perceptions of issue and events leading to the war. Al-Jazeera in particular was highly influential in shaping the attitudes of the global Arab audience, providing sympathetic coverage of al-Qaeda, whereas in the United States the American free media was actively involved in forging U.S. attitudes toward al-Qaeda and Iraq in the years before the war. Following the terrorists' attacks of September 11, 2001, however, the wars of ideas intensified at the geopolitical and strategic levels as multiple political interests sought to solicit or deter international support for the conflict. Meanwhile, competition among political interests over U.S. public opinion and foreign policy began to create clear divisions on the American political landscape, which would adversely affect perceptions and media coverage of the conflict. Understanding the series of events and developments in the 12 years between the 1991 Gulf War and the Global War on Terror, as well as media's influence on U.S. policy during the period, is essential for understanding both the complexities of the Global War on Terror, especially Iraq's post-Saddam insurgency and the wars of ideas that would accompany the Iraq War.

Post-Cold War U.S. Foreign Policy in the Middle East

In the aftermath of the 1991 Gulf War, the core of U.S. post-Cold War foreign policy in the Middle East was aimed directly at Iran and Iraq. Middle East Scholar Bernard Lewis explains that the U.S. focus was "to prevent the emergence of a regional hegemony—of a single regional power that could dominate the area and thus establish monopolistic control of Middle Eastern oil."[1] While international efforts to contain Iraq were largely effective, Iraq's continued aggressive posture toward its neighbors and its open hostility toward Israel created regional instability. The United States engaged in a policy of containment toward Iraq following the Gulf War assuming that UN sanctions, UN inspections, and a strong military presence would keep Iraq from menacing his regional neighbors. U.S. officials believed that Saddam Hussein could be contained and marginalized, and developed a defensive plan on the presumption that Hussein would strike first. However, in the decade that followed, Saddam had proved not only uncooperative and incorrigible in dealing with the world body, obstructing UN weapons inspectors, but was increasing openly aggressive and hostile, continuing to shoot at coalition aircraft and engaging covert operations beyond its borders. This coupled with concerns that Iraq still possessed and/or manufactured chemical or biological weapons, or neared completion of a nuclear weapon troubled the international community.[2] Complicating the matter, however, was the competition for influence and commercial ventures in the Middle East from European, Japanese, Chinese, and later Russian, interests in the absence of Soviet influence, which added to regional violence and exacerbated violence instability.[3] In regard to Iraq, this competition undermined the UN effort to keep Iraq in compliance with UN sanctions, and caused a conflict of interest when it came UN Security Council resolutions regarding Iraq.

Al-Jazeera and the Rise of Al-Qaeda

The emergence of the first Arab Satellite television in 1996, al-Jazeera, amid the wave of pan-Islamic fervor sweeping the Middle East during the 1990s gave Osama bin Laden and al-Qaeda access to a global Arab audience.[*] Through select interviews and video recordings, bin Laden used al-Jazeera to galvanize anti-American support and justify his jihad against the West, while contributing to the spread of Salafi Islam. He asserted that the occupation and oppression of Palestine was the primary cause of hostility between Islam and the West, and denounced the United States for what he calls the crimes,

[*] This is not to imply that al-Qaeda and al-Jazeera worked in collusion or formed a de facto alliance, only that al-Qaeda recognized al-Jazeera's value in promoting its messages, and that al-Jazeera was willing to broadcast al-Qaeda's them.

sins, and continued U.S. influence and occupation in Muslim land.[4] This aided al-Qaeda's recruitment and support, which allowed bin Laden's terror organization both grow and launch more devastating and sensational attacks.

Meanwhile, he cemented his relationship with the Taliban in his new safe haven in Afghanistan and was planning even greater attacks against U.S. interests.[5] In 1998, following bin Laden's *fatwa*, or religious decree justifying jihad against the United States, and later a videotaped interview with ABC News, al-Qaeda launched massive attacks on two U.S. embassies in Africa killing 12 Americans and 11 Africans, and injuring more than 5000.[6] In a 1999 interview with *Time*, bin Laden admitted that the United States "knows I have attacked it, by the Grace of God, for more than 10 years now."[7] In 2000, al-Qaeda attempted an attack on the U.S.S. *Sullivans*, but later succeeded in an attack on the guided missile destroyer U.S.S. *Cole* as it refueled in Yemen killing seventeen U.S. sailors.[8]

By this time, al-Jazeera had developed a global Arab audience and was already impacting public opinion on the world stage. The station was not only helping spread al-Qaeda's message, but also gave bin Laden's cause sympathetic coverage after President Bill Clinton's 1998 retaliatory cruise missile attacks against al-Qaeda targets in Sudan and Afghanistan. However, the satellite station's sensational coverage of the second Intifada, or al-Aqsa Intifada, the violent September 2000 Palestinian uprising in Israel and its aftermath, inflamed Arab audiences around the world. This not only spurred more hostility against Israel from Arabs and the international community, but also against the United States as Israel's supporter for allowing Israel's perceived disproportionate response to Palestinian violence.[9] Described later, al-Jazeera's sympathetic and sensational coverage of the Palestinian cause was an indication of what was to come in a post-September 11, 2001 era.

By 2001, al-Jazeera had replaced the Western media as the primary Arab news source, not just in the Middle East, but also among Arabs living abroad. The fusion of popular Muslim sentiments with an influential, far-reaching Arab satellite television drastically changed the way Muslims saw themselves in the world, and forged an Arab public sphere that had never existed before.[10] Arab journalists Mohammed El-Nawawy and Abdel Iskandar contend that by "detecting and highlighting the links that connect Arabs worldwide, al-Jazeera has become part and parcel of the Arab world. It speaks to and for it."[11] The new War on Terror soon revealed both the significance of the new Arab media and the differences between Western and Arab media coverage of events. El-Nawawy and Iskandar explain that "when the hijacked airliners crashed into the World Trade Center in New York on September 11, 2001, al-Jazeera reporters were there, and they transmitted to Arab viewers live scenes of the twin towers crashing to the grounds."[12] However, al-Jazeera also broadcast the sensational images of Arabs celebrating the attacks and burning U.S. flags in support of bin Laden.[13] As Middle East expert Walid Phares observes:

> Particularly in the Arab Muslim Nations, the War of Ideas is raging. It had inflamed millions of readers, viewers, and listeners, transforming large numbers of them into militants and demonstrators, some into suicide bombers, and many into voters.[14]

Al-Jazeera, and al-Qaeda's use of the satellite station, would prove to be a formidable alliance in the Global War on terror.

A Decade of Deception and Defiance: The Road to the Iraq War*

With a devastated military following the 1991 Gulf War, opposition groups in Iraq quickly emerged and threatened Saddam Hussein's Baath Party regime with coups and outright rebellion. In response, Hussein purged those with questionable loyalty, used chemical weapons on Kurdish villages, and engaged in the wholesale slaughter of Shiites. To curb the threat Wahhabi-inspired Islamic fundamentalists in Fallujah posed, Hussein stationed many of his best Republican Guard troops on a cluster of bases outside the city, along with the Iranian division composed of defectors and expelled dissidents belonging to the Mujahedeen El-Kalq.[15] In an attempt to unify and galvanize Iraq's population, while reducing Salafi opposition to the secular regime, Hussein launched his *Return to Faith Campaign* in 1993 to capture the pan-Islamic fervor sweeping the Muslim world. Hussein claimed to be the protector of Islam and the leader of Jihad against the West, and added the Arabic phrase "God is Great" to the Iraqi flag.[16] Moreover, he gave more freedom to Sunni Imams in religious practices and expression, and initiated a war against the Shiites in an attempt to rally Wahhabi support. His secret police and terror agencies murdered or arrested tens of thousands of Shia, including senior Shia clerics, and desecrated Shia mosques and holy sites.[17] These agencies maintained a looming presence in Shiite cities, and would lay the foundation for Iraq's guerrilla war. Hussein's personal militia, the *Fedayeen*, or Men of Sacrifice, was born during this movement.

Importantly, UN sanctions brought severe hardship for many Iraqis, and organized crime flourished amid a black market economy, as did corruption in government agencies as bureaucrats and workers alike used their positions to supplement meager salaries through bribes, kickbacks, and theft. Many of

---

* Refers to a background paper titled "A Decade Of Deception And Defiance Saddam Hussein's Defiance Of The United Nations," September 12, 2002. Available online at http://www.c-span.org/Content/PDF/iraqdecade.pdf. (accessed November 26, 2009).

Iraq's tribes, especially those whose traditional territories crossed international borders, had profited from smuggling for centuries. Some Sunni tribes in al-Anbar Province profited by both exporting contraband products such as oil and importing a wide variety of consumer and luxury goods from neighboring Jordan and Syria.[18]

Like the Ottoman Empire, Iraq's tribes presented special challenges to the Baath Regime because tribal leaders (sheikhs) wielded significant control over their members. Hussein attempted to control tribes through special favors and paternalism, often exploiting ancient tribal rivalries. The Iran-Iraq War demonstrated that some of the Sunni tribes of western Iraq provided the best soldiers and leadership for his military, and they received special favors, including weapons, for their loyalty. However, in some cases, even in the Sunni west, Hussein used a combination of patronage, coercion, and force to control tribes. In some cases, he executed tribal sheikhs and appointed new sheikhs. Because tribal sheikhs can trace their ancestry back hundreds or thousands of years, these acts were devastating to the tribes.[19] Meanwhile, restricted by Coalition containment actions, Hussein used his Mukhabarat to attack or intimidate enemies, defectors, and dissidents living outside Iraq, including the 1993 attempt to assassinate former U.S. President George H. W. Bush during his visit to Kuwait.[20] Two years after Iraq's humiliating defeat in the Gulf War, Hussein provided refuge for an Iraqi named Abdul Rahman Yassin, one of the bomb makers involved in the February 26, 1993 attack on the New York City World Trade Center.[21] The next year he amassed troops along the Kuwait border in a threatening manner. In the years that followed, hostilities escalated as Hussein maintained a hostile and aggressive posture toward his neighbors, resisted Coalition containment and UN inspections, and continued to pursue special weapons. This escalation would peak in 1998, forcing the President Bill Clinton to both respond and formulate a new Iraq policy.

The Media and a Paradigm Shift in U.S. Foreign Policy

During the 1990s, the media chronicled the escalation of conflicts between the United States and Iraq and between the United States and al-Qaeda. By 1998, the media began to challenge U.S. efforts to contain Iraq in articles focusing on the ineffectiveness of U.S. policies, U.N. sanctions, and UNSCOM inspections.[22] At the same time, the media became increasingly critical of President Clinton's terrorism policy in the wake of al-Qaeda's 1998 U.S. Embassy bombings in Tanzania and Nigeria. This coverage was influential on U.S. public opinion, and the American public was beginning to believe that U.S. actions and policy had done little to stop Saddam Hussein or al-Qaeda and that more aggressive action against al-Qaeda and Iraq was necessary.[23] President Clinton responded to the embassy bombings with cruise missile attacks on suspected al-Qaeda facilities in Sudan and Afghanistan, but these had little or no effect on the organization and drew considerable media criticism not only for the ineffective response to the al-Qaeda threat, but also for alleged collateral damage at both locations.[24] President Clinton responded to the media and public criticism and call for stronger action against Iraq and al-Qaeda in 1998 by taking a firmer public stance and connecting state sponsors of terrorism to terrorists' pursuit of Nuclear, chemical, and biological weapons.[25]

In February 1998, after eight years of steady escalation of conflict and non-cooperation with UNSCOM, President Bill Clinton connected Saddam's use of and Saddam's admission that he still possessed chemical weapons to his support for terrorist organizations, making the first public case proposing Saddam's removal, arguing:

> Those who have questioned the United States in this moment, I would argue, are living only in the moment. They have neither remembered the past nor imagined the future...this is not a time free from peril, especially as a result of reckless acts of outlaw nations and an unholy axis of terrorists, drug traffickers and organized international criminals. We have to defend our future from these predators of the 21st century...they will be all the more lethal if we allow them to build arsenals of nuclear, chemical and biological weapons and the missiles to deliver them. We simply cannot allow that to happen. There is no more clear example of this threat than Saddam Hussein's Iraq. His regime threatens the safety of his people, the stability of his region and the security of all the rest of us...If we fail to respond today, Saddam and all those who would follow in his footsteps will be emboldened tomorrow by the knowledge that they can act with impunity.[26]

Most analysts concluded that the only way to stabilize the region and ensure Iraq no longer possessed WMD was to remove Saddam. On May 1, 1998, President Clinton took the first step in removing Saddam Hussein from power when he signed Public Law 105-174, which authorized $5 million to support Iraqi democratic oppositions groups, mainly those excelled from Iraq. Tensions escalated quickly over the summer.

In June 1998, UNSCOM weapons inspectors discovered that Saddam had loaded VX nerve gas into Iraqi missiles. Later, they discovered a large quantity of Soviet Scud missile fuel and confirmation Iraq still engaged in VX nerve gas production. On August 5, Iraq ceased all cooperation with UNSCOM and the International Atomic Energy Agency, which led to President Clinton signing Public Law 105-235 on August 14, which declared that "the Government of Iraq is in material and unacceptable breach of its international obligations."

Responding to increasing media criticism and public support for more aggressive action against Iraq, President Clinton Finally signed into law Public Law 105-338, on October 31, 1998, the Iraq Liberation Act of 1998, which outlined Iraq's eighteen-year history of aggression against its neighbors, its own people, and the United States, as well as its support for international terrorism and its failure to comply with terms of the cease-fire agreement that ended hostilities at the of the Gulf War. Importantly, the Act also authorized force to remove Saddam Hussein's Baath regime and replace it with a democratic government, proclaiming that:

> It should be the policy of the United States to support efforts to remove the regime headed by Saddam Hussein from power in Iraq and to promote the emergence of a democratic government to replace that regime.[27]

When Saddam continued to impede weapons inspectors, President Clinton finally responded by launching Operation Desert Fox on December 16, 1998, which aimed to destroy more than seventy-five suspected special weapons facilities before he could move them after UNSCOM left. Following Operation Desert Fox, Iraq cut all ties with the United Nations and ended any chance for cooperation with UNSCOM inspectors.[28] The media remained critical of the Clinton Administration, focusing on Iraq's continued aggression, efforts to rebuild its military capacity, and refusal to allow UN inspections.[29]

Meanwhile, in 1999 U.S. Central Command took the intentions of the Iraq Liberation Act seriously and conducted a series of war games called Operation Desert Crossing, which forced military planners to consider the complexities removing the Baath Party regime in Iraq. The After Action report for the exercise predicted that rival factions would compete for power and that a high number of troops were needed, not to defeat Saddam, but to maintain order through Iraq's transition time.[30]

By January 2001, as President Bill Clinton left office, Iraq had gone more than two years without any UNSCOM inspections, and al-Qaeda had successfully attacked another U.S. target—the guided missile destroyer U.S.S. Cole. The media deepened its criticism of the lack of U.S. responses to these situations and frequently called for stronger action citing foreign policy elites. This media criticism was influential on the U.S. public, which believed that U.S. actions and policy had done little to stop Saddam Hussein or al-Qaeda and that more aggressive action against al-Qaeda and Iraq was necessary—especially after the terrorists' attacks of September 11, 2001.[31]

During the first eight months of President George W. Bush's first term, U.S. Iraq and al-Qaeda policy generally followed the Clinton Administration's Iraq and al-Qaeda containment models. However, following the terrorists' attacks of September 11, 2001, the combination of the media's powerful imagery with President Bush's strong rhetoric evoked both strong patriotic emotions and ideological convictions, forging a unified national sentient that was highly effective in priming and framing the U.S. response for military action in Afghanistan and the Global War on Terror in general.[32] Some observers believed the coverage was overly jingoistic and advanced the case for war instead of challenging it.

Although much of this patriotic response continued during the war on al-Qaeda and the Taliban in Afghanistan, some prominent Western journalists provided hasty, uniformed commentary on operations from the safety of the United States. Among these was R.W. Apple of the influential *New York Times*, who concluded just one week after combat operations began in Afghanistan that the United Stated had entered a "quagmire."[33] This would be just the beginning of deficient reporting and hasty journalists' commentary on Afghanistan, which provided a highly cynical "Vietnam Syndrome" view of U.S. policy and decision making as the Bush Administration turned its attention to Iraq.

The Bush Administration was concerned about Iraq's WMD development and production well into the late 1990s and its ongoing support for international terrorist organizations. In addition to Iraq's almost daily attacks on U.S. jets patrolling the no- fly zones and its ongoing violations UN resolutions and the cease-fire agreement, military leaders believed that Saddam Hussein was planning for war. According to Lieutenant General Michael Delong, assistant commanding general U.S. Central Command (CentCom), not only did Hussein openly voice hostile criticism toward his Arab leaders for allowing the air strikes or Operation Desert Fox, military officials discovered Iraq's detailed military preparations included rebuilding its air defense system with secure fiber optic, underground cable, "openly testing L-29 unmanned aerial vehicles with chemical sprayers...testing maximum range scud missiles that exceeded the range set by United Nations Sanctions" that could deliver chemical or biological weapons to Israel or any other regional neighbor.[34] Saddam's continued aggression toward Israel, however, made most analysts suspicious and concerned. Though covert operations or missiles, Iraq could wreck major havoc on tiny Israel with any form of WMD before the existing containment plan could stop it. In the end, CentCom believed that containment was no longer working, and that within a year or two Saddam could wage a more effective war against his enemies and be much harder to defeat.[35]

In 2002, using language similar to President Clinton's 1998 speech to Pentagon personnel, President Bush launched the opening salvo in the wars of ideas that would accompany the Iraq War when identified Iraq as part of the "axis of evil," arguing in his State of the Union speech that the War on Terror could be expanded to state sponsors of terrorism, such as Iraq, contending that terrorists could serve as rogue covert agents of a state with WMD.[36] In the months that followed, the Bush administration used the international media to gain broad domestic and international support for talking public preemptive action to remove Saddam Hussein from power in Iraq—a paradigm shift from the previous policies of deterrence and containment.[*] Iraqi President Saddam Hussein responded, using both the Iraqi state media and al-Jazeera to refute the administration's claims and dissuade international support. In August 2002, Hussein responded, "If they come we are ready. We will fight them on the streets, from rooftops, from house to house. We will never surrender."[37]

Meanwhile, the media demonstrated its short memory by challenging the administration's case for preemptive action against Iraq.[38] This included using the arguments of intellectuals and policy elites. Reminiscent of Vietnam, some of these criticisms came from the president's political opponents, which, ironically, included members of the U.S. House of Representatives and U.S. Senate who had come to their positions in the 1968, 1970, and 1972 elections amid the public's declining support for the Vietnam War. Moreover, the media's challenge also included raising questions of a costly protracted involvement, or "quagmire anxieties" in Iraq characteristic of Vietnam Syndrome. Much of the media's basis for criticism against U.S. claims against Iraq came from the international community, largely from three permanent members of the UN Security Council that had a vested commercial interest in Iraq—China, France, and Russia.[39] Like Vietnam, an organized antiwar movement emerged in the months before the war, and a number of artists, authors, musicians, and actors became activists, in such organizations as *Artists United to Win Without War*, but received little public support or media coverage and were ineffective in gaining significant media attention.[40] The early anti-war movements mobilized for protests, but received little public support or media coverage. It is important to note, that some media professionals and observers believe that the media did not do enough to challenge the Bush Administration's case for war, and that some influential pundits, columnists, and media organizations actually argued for war much the way William Randolph Hearst had done more than a century before.[41]

Despite these criticisms, the Bush administration dominated the war of ideas in the domestic and international arenas of ideas. Therefore, after several months of intense international diplomatic efforts with no success,

[*] These arguments, largely main tenants of the Iraq Liberation Act of 1998, became the administration's new National Security Strategy in September 2002.

both the U.S. Congress and the UN Security Council concluded that Iraq had adequate time to demonstrate goodwill towards its regional and international neighbors and relieve international concerns about terrorism and weapons of mass destruction, passing resolution to use force to remove the Baath Party regime and bring Iraq into compliance should it be found in material breach of UN mandates once UN inspections resumed.* According to Professor Entman, despite the media's challenges the media struggled with the complexity of President Bush's new paradigm and failed to articulate an effective counterframe to prevent or further delay war, the Bush Administration ultimately prevailed.[42] This frustrated media elites who had enjoyed nearly a decade of influence in U.S. foreign policy, and did not deter journalists from continuing to challenge the administration's policy. Nonetheless, public diplomacy continued as UN inspections resumed. According to Professors Eugene Secunda and Terence P. Moran, the Bush administration successfully used the "fear card" to win support of the U.S. Congress, United Nations, and the American public in "selling" the war to the American public.[43] Expanding this view, professor Wojtek Mackiewicz Wolfe explains that President Bush presented this fear in the form of the "threat" (of harm) frame in his January 2002 State of the Union address, and by the fall of 2002 had expanded his thematic framing to include the "loss" frame, in terms of what American would gain from war with Iraq versus what American would lose, as well as the "terror" frame, which linked Iraq to the threat.[44]

As the public's focus turned toward the preparations for the impending war, criticism of the administration's war plans came immediately. Both journalists and military analysts, recalling the Powell Doctrine of overwhelming force in the 1991 Gulf War, developed a new counter frame in General Anthony Zinni's contention that that the military's force was too small and its planning for interim administration of post-Saddam Iraq was insufficient and conflicted with the equally lacking State Department's post-Saddam plan.[45] These criticisms, coupled with the media's frustration in failing to affect the outcome of U.S. policy, succeeded in further fueling quagmire concerns, which would resurface as the war unfolded and come into full force during the early post-Saddam administration of Iraq.[46]

---

* The United Nations passed UN Security Council Resolution 1441. The U.S. Congress passed U.S. Public law 107-243, 116 Stat. 1497-1502 (Authorization for Use of Military Force Against Iraq Resolution of 2002), which was signed into law by President Bush on October 16, 2002. (The U.S. House of Representatives passed Joint Resolution 114 (H.J.Res. 114) by a vote of 296-133 on October 10, 2002, and passed the U.S. Senate by a vote of 77-23 on October 11, 2002).

Afghanistan and the al-Jazeera Factor

When the Coalition launched its offensive against al-Qaeda and the Taliban in October 2001, the difference in reporting between the Western and Arab media was immediately apparent as a war of ideas took place on the airways, on the Internet, and in the pages of publications around the globe.[47] Because al-Jazeera had been in Afghanistan long before September 11, 2001 and had established a relationship with al-Qaeda and the Taliban, it dominated media coverage and proved its power to influence the Arab public against the war in Afghanistan and United States with shocking images of dead civilians.[48] Conversely, the Western media provided only inadequate and disjointed accounts of U.S. military operations because journalists did not accompany U.S. forces in combat operations and thus had limited access to the battlefield. CNN overcame this problem through a controversial arrangement with al-Jazeera; however, its rebroadcast of al-Jazeera's videotaped interview with Osama bin Laden on October 7, 2001 brought both criticism and condemnation over the arrangement, and cast al-Jazeera as a propaganda tool for the al-Qaeda and the Taliban.[49]

It soon became clear that al-Qaeda made full use of al-Jazeera. According to journalism, media, and cultural studies professor Ehab Y. Bessaiso, "the carefully staged video tapes suggested that, while totally outgunned by his opponents, bin Laden was fully aware of the importance of the propaganda battle that would accompany the military conflict—so much so that some observers think that the real battle took place on the air waves of al-Jazeera."[50] What the U.S. government would later learn was that al-Qaeda had already established a complex and highly sophisticated media and propaganda network that was very effective in soliciting support and recruiting operatives.[51] Referring to this network, al-Qaeda operations expert Saif al-Adel, a former Egyptian special forces officer, admits "The Islamic media efforts were represented in what was being broadcast by al-Jazeera and the mujahideen sites on the Net."[52] Noting what the 1991 Gulf War did to CNN, British journalist Hugh Miles observes that "history has taught us that wars made television channels." Such was the case with al-Jazeera when the U.S. military took swift action against al-Qaeda and its sponsor in Afghanistan, the Taliban.[53]

While the Western media followed the U.S. policy debates on Iraq, the Arab media similarly followed developments. According to political science and international affairs professor Marc Lynch, "September 11, the American war on terror, and then the move to war with Iraq brought the Arab Media firmly into the center of American foreign policy debate."[54] He contends that even before September 11, 2001, many Arabs believed the United States would attack Iraq, largely due to Saddam Hussein's 1998 decision to end cooperation with UNSCOM.[55] Following September 11, 2001, he explains that the Arab media portrayed the United States as "seeking a confrontation" over UNSCOM's inspections, even to the point of alleging "American manipulation of UNSCOM and the Security Council."[56]

Chapter Conclusion

The wars of ideas and images that would accompany the Global War on Terror was shaped by a series of developments between 1991 and 2003. Following the Cold War, three factors created major challenges for U.S. policy in the Middle East and set the conditions for both the war in Afghanistan and Iraq. First, the absence of Soviet influence in the Middle East significantly changed the political dynamics in the region because it allowed various factions that existed under the Cold War landscape in the Middle East, including Salafi Islam and pan-Islamic movements, to expand and fill the void left by secular Soviet influence. It also opened the door to outside European and Asian commercial and economic interests. In Afghanistan, the power vacuum following the Soviet withdrawal allowed al-Qaeda to grow unchecked. In Iraq, these external interests came in conflict with U.S. and international goals of neutralizing Iraq's hostility during the pre Iraq War U.N. debates because the same nations that had economic and political interests opposed military action during the deliberations. Second, Iraq's and Iran's hostile posture toward both each other, their regional neighbors, Israel, and the West, coupled with their competing ambitions for regional hegemony increased regional instability.

However, Iraq's more overt threats and actions in the years following the 1991 Gulf War demanded considerable UN and Coalition attention to keep Iraq's aggression contained, which became the catalyst for UN resolutions intended to force Iraq to comply with UN mandates, the Iraq Liberation Act of 1998, and ultimately the U.S. and international decisions to remove the Baath Party from power in Iraq. Third, the rise of al-Qaeda coupled with the emergence of al-Jazeera not only fueled pan-Islamic and Salafi movements while fostering anti-American and anti-Western sentiment following the, but also exacerbated regional instability and threatened Western interests and relations in the region. Al-Jazeera provided al-Qaeda and the Salafi cause with sympathetic coverage for six years before the Global War on Terror, and was influential in fueling animosity toward the United States and Israel. This sympathetic coverage, coupled with its innovative use of the Internet, not only helped al-Qaeda fundraising and recruiting, but also increased its stature among a global Arab population.

Amid the decade of international crisis and instability following the Cold War, U.S. post-Cold War foreign policy was heavily influenced by the media's ability to frame cases for U.S. intervention and withdrawal, especially satellite television's ability to provide continuous and instantaneous coverage with compelling images and commentary that moved public opinion and policy. While the media largely supported the Clinton Administration's initial policies of containing Iraq and treating al-Qaeda as a rouge criminal threat, it became more critical of these policies, which swayed U.S. public opinion and ultimately a more aggressive posture toward Al-Qaeda and Iraq. This resulted in the 1998 military strikes against both Iraq and al-Qaeda, and the Iraq Liberation Act of 1998, which was the foundation for U.S. policy against these belligerents when President George W. Bush came into office.

The monumental terrorists attacks in the United States on September 11, 2001 caused policy makers to reevaluate U.S. Iraq and terrorism policies. While the American media was largely supportive of an aggressive U.S. response, the al-Jazeera satellite television station provided starkly different views of the September 11, 2001 terrorist attacks and Arab celebrations of those attacks in the Middle East. However, as the Global War on Terror unfolded in Afghanistan, the lack of accurate Western media reporting allowed al-Jazeera to dominate media coverage while providing material to the Western media, and in doing so was successful in providing al-Qaeda and the Taliban with sympathetic coverage while conversely providing disparaging coverage of the Coalition effort. As a result, al-Jazeera proved to be a very influential weapon in the war of ideas that accompanied the battles on the ground. Importantly, al-Qaeda's successful use of propaganda and the Arab media created a pattern that would repeat itself in Iraq.

As U.S. policy turned to Iraq, the wars of ideas played out both domestically and internationally at the strategic level to influence U.S. policy toward Iraq. Both President Bush and Saddam Hussein used the media to influence public opinion and policy at the geopolitical and domestic levels. Despite the American and international media's collective attempts to frame the issues and public political debates, President Bush prevailed in the war of ideas. In response to its loss of influence, the quagmire narrative that emerged in the Western media's coverage of Afghanistan became part of the media's pre-war framing themes aggravated political partisanship, which became evident in the media's confrontational coverage of the pre-war debates. Exacerbating the media's adversarial position was the loss of the media's ability to successfully shape Iraq policy toward delaying or preventing war, which frustrated media elites who had enjoyed nearly a decade of influence in U.S. foreign policy. All of this opposition would carry over into the media's coverage of the war. As the impending war drew near, the media became critical of the U.S. war strategy, contending that that the military's force was too small and that its planning post-Saddam Iraq was insufficient. This criticism not only provided journalists, analysts, and observers with a gage to measure the effectiveness of the administration's conduct of the war, but also succeeded in further fueling quagmire concerns that would resurface as the war unfolded and come into full force as a Vietnam Syndrome quagmire narrative during the early post-Saddam administration of Iraq. The strategic level wars of idea would have significant operational and tactical level consequences once combat operations began.

CHAPTER SIX

THE IRAQ WAR: CONFLICTING MEDIA VIEWPOINTS

As previous chapters have shown, the war of ideas that would accompany the Iraq War began long before military action on the ground. Decades of isolation and indoctrination forged Arab perceptions of the west, particularly of Western involvement in Middle Eastern affairs, while a partisan new Arab media exacerbated Arab sentiments against the west in the years before the war, aiding terrorists' movements like al-Qaeda while providing sympathetic coverage of their war on the west. In Iraq, a decade of UN sanctions coupled with a corrupt regime robbed Iraqis of critical resources as the Iraqi state controlled media blamed the west, leaving the people embittered. On the domestic front, the legacies of Vietnam remained active in U.S. public memory as the western media provided more than two decades of cynical coverage of U.S. foreign involvement after the Vietnam War. As diplomatic efforts to bring Iraq into compliance with UN mandates intensified in the weeks before the military offensive, so did the U.S. government's efforts to build and maintain domestic and international support. However, it would remain dependent on the independent media for its communication at the same time the Western media was continuing its efforts to frame the impending conflict, laying the foundation for a Vietnam Syndrome quagmire narrative. At the same time, the Arab media continued to portray the United States as looking for a conflict with Iraq, and alleged that it fabricated its justification to mask its real ambitions of capturing territory and controlling Iraq's oil.[1] As the Iraq war unfolded, the wars of ideas over U.S. involvement in the domestic and geopolitical arenas would begin to influence perceptions and events at the operational and tactical levels.

Preparing for the Wars of Ideas Behind the Iraq War

As the United States began shipping troops and equipment to staging areas in Kuwait, Saddam Hussein similarly prepared for war. Recognizing the Coalition's superiority in conventional warfare,[*] Hussein began preparing for

---

[*] As demonstrated during the 1991 Gulf War.

a guerrilla war using a "popular" army of guerrilla and paramilitary fighters. In preparation for this guerrilla war, Saddam Hussein had met with foreign "Arabs" in the months before the war and invited them to come into Iraq and take part in fighting Coalition Forces.[2] Iraqi Mukhabarat operatives also recruited foreign fighters from Palestinian refugee camps and other location outside Iraq believing that they could be controlled.[3] As these foreign fighters came into Iraq via staging areas in Iran and Syria, Baathist moved them to Fedayeen cells around Iraq. According to Iraqi Intelligence officer Staff Brigadier General Nuri al-Din Abd al-Karim Mukhlif, this act would offend many within Iraq's military community, along with many Iraqi's as a whole. Hussein also gave amnesty to tens of thousands of criminals in Iraq's prisons, many of which became part of Iraq's new paramilitary militias, and Iraqi forces distributed weapons and ammunition into small weapons caches.[4]

As Saddam Hussein continued to use both the Arab and Iraq state media to counter the Bush Administration's public communication efforts and deter international support for military action against his country, Osama bin Laden similarly used al-Jazeera and the Arab media to call for Jihad in Iraq to fight what he called were the enemies of Islam.[5] Many of those foreign fighters who did not arrive in Afghanistan in time to fight the coalition were diverted to Iraq via staging areas in Iran and Syria, and to a lesser extent Jordan and Saudi Arabia. Among those foreign "Arabs" was Abu Musab al-Zarqawi, a career terrorist with connections across the Middle East and Europe and ties to al-Qaeda. Al-Zarqawi was a chemical and biological weapons specialist who fled to Iraq in 2002 to escape the Coalition attacks on the Taliban and al-Qaeda in Afghanistan. Sometime prior to the war, he began running the terror organization of Ansar al-Islam, which seized villages in Northern, Kurdish occupied Iraq and established an Islamic Sharia government there. Arab journalist Zaki Chehab, who accompanied Iraq's guerrillas in 2003 and 2004, credits al-Zarqawi with "recruiting hundreds, if not thousands, of Iraqi followers, together with several hundred fighters from other Arab countries such as Syria and Saudi Arabia, and Sudan and Yemen."[6] These foreign fighters came to not only fight the enemies of Islam, but to prevent the creation of a Western democracy, which they believe contradicts the teachings of the Koran.[7]

Learning from the Western media's ineffective treatment of combat operations in Afghanistan and recognizing the immense public and media interest in the impending conflict, the Pentagon enacted a new media policy of "embedding" reporters in combat units, which gave many journalists an opportunity to get a front line account of the fighting under the protection of the U.S. military for the first time since Vietnam.[8] With virtually unlimited access to military briefings and combat, the military only prohibited reporters from showing graphic depictions of death, especially U.S. troops, and from reporting any information that might be useful to the enemy. Importantly, the new program underscored the U.S. government's dependence on the independent free-media to for state communication. Despite the its battle for control of U.S. policy, the Western media recognized the public's interest in the impending war and sought to provide better coverage than it had in Afghanistan. Various media outlets embraced the embedding large numbers of journalists and media personnel. Investigative journalist Phillip Knightley contends that through the embedding program, military officials intended to manage what they believed to "be the most thoroughly reported war of modern times."[9] Writing of the enormous media effort, Knightly explains that with "nearly one thousand media personnel—on the ground, in the air, and at sea—would miss nothing. It would be the biggest news gathering operation in the history of television."[10] Journalists and their media outlets eagerly participated in the program, as NBC Middle East correspondent Richard Engle described, "It was supposed to be luck of the draw, but we were jostling for the best seats for the performance, front row center. War makes great TV. It's the sexiest fucking ugly thing in the world. Don't let anyone tell you different."[11]

However, as embedded reporters took positions with their assigned units massing in Kuwait, non-embedded reporters, or "unilaterals," similarly took their positions across Iraq. Many unilateral journalists positioned themselves in Baghdad, far removed from any coalition forces or where the battle would begin. Likewise, the Arab media also prepared for the impending conflict in a manner largely sympathetic to Iraq. Between the Coalition's opening gambit against al-Qaeda and the Taliban in Afghanistan and the Iraq War, new Arab satellite stations emerged and challenged al-Jazeera's dominance. Facing competition for the first time, al-Jazeera took a more radical approach in its pre-invasion coverage compared to other more moderate Arab satellite networks, and was highly critical of the U.S. policy and the impending invasion, and to ensure broad, unmatched coverage of Iraq, al-Jazeera hired several Iraqis, which later provoked suspicions that agents from Hussein's Mukhabarat penetrated al-Jazeera and influenced its coverage.[12]

From Conventional War to Guerrilla War

In the days before the Iraq War, Coalition forces engaged in a psychological and information operations campaign aimed at encouraging Iraq's military units to capitulate to Coalition forces.[*] These units, Coalition commanders believed, could help stabilize Iraq after Saddam and eliminate the need for a large occupation force.[13] Then, on 17 March, President George W. Bush announced that the time for diplomacy was over, which sent many

---

[*] This marked the beginning of the Coalition's operational and tactical level communication.

Iraqi boarding buildings and those with means to flee the country—clearly demonstrating the tactical effect of a strategic message. The following day, Saddam responded on state television, "We are ready to sacrifice our souls, our children and our families so as not to give up Iraq."[14]

On March 19, 2003, the Coalition preceded its ground attack with a massive bombing campaign aimed at destroying Iraq's senior leadership, while intimidating Iraqi forces to desert or surrender. The following day, March 20, Coalition forces broke through Iraqi defenses in Southern Iraq while simultaneously attacking Iraqi and Ansar al-Islam forces in Northern Iraq. Saddam Hussein's military met quick defeat, despite a few exceptions where Coalition forces met stiff resistance from guerrillas composed of Saddam Fedayeen, Iraqi nationalists, Baath Party Militia, the al-Quds Militia, and an estimated four thousand foreign fighters.[15] Although many Iraqi forces deserted, there was not the mass capitulation Coalition planners had hoped for because they overlooked how Hussein's secret police, intelligence, and security forces thoroughly permeated all levels of society.[16] Instead, many of these Iraqi troops either fled or joined emerging guerrilla factions.

As Iraq's military collapsed, the Fedayeen hid among the population while firing on Coalition forces and compelled civilians to fight by holding their children hostage.[17] Their goal was to inspire hatred toward the Coalition and illicit sympathy for Iraq's cause. This was evident in the city of an-Nasiriyah where a serial the U.S. Army's 507th Maintenance Company convoy mistakenly turned into an enemy portion of the city before U.S. Marines secured the city and were ambushed. This event emboldened Iraqi military and paramilitary forces in the city, who believed that they could stave off the Marine's attack. Marines not only found a well-organized defense and a larger conventional enemy force than they expected, but also found fanatical paramilitary forces who wore civilian clothes and fired on Marines from crowds of civilians, and drove civilians into oncoming Marines to block the their advance, Fedayeen killed fleeing and surrendering Iraqis.[18] Indicative of Hussein's strategy, Marines interdicted more than 120 military aged males during the battle who claimed they had surrendered at Basra and were on their way home. However, Marines discovered that they carrying large amounts of cash and were intending to fall in on weapons caches inside the city as part of a plan to continue fighting a guerrilla war.[19]

Meanwhile, Wahhabi groups Ansar al-Islam, Ansar al-Sunnah, and renown terrorist Abu Musab al-Zarqawi's Jamaat al-Tawhid wal-Jihad joined Saddam Fedayeen and other emerging guerrilla organizations in attacking the Shiites to prevent collaboration with Coalition forces.[20] According to Lieutenant General Delong, these guerrillas with little or no training, discipline, or coordination continued to fight using guerrilla tactics, and "did not respect the laws of war."[21] He explains that a common tactic "was Iraqi fighters dressing as civilians (sometimes even as women), or pretending to surrender, then firing on troops. They also entrenched themselves at hospitals, mosques, schools, and other civilian, religious, and archeological buildings they knew we didn't want to hit."[22] General Delong concludes the Fedayeen were "trained killers, ruthlessly murdering Iraqi civilians who fled the cities or surrendered to the coalition."[23] In response, Shiite militias formed to defend against the Fedayeen and Sunni attacks. Some sought revenge against the Baathists and Sunnis for the losses of close relatives, forcing them to flee to protect their families from Shia reprisals.[24]

As Coalition forces pushed through Southern Iraq toward Baghdad after defeating Fedayeen resistance, crowds of Iraqi Shi'a met them with smiles, waves and oftentimes cheers. Coalition forces began providing humanitarian aid, which largely included food and medical supplies. This would provide a stop gap until Coalition forces entered Phase IV, security and stability operations, followed by U.S. civilian agencies and non-governmental organizations that would provide longer-term aid, reconstruction, and governance programs. To the surprise of most Coalition commanders, however, the degraded state of Iraq's infrastructure was far worse than they had expected.[25] When Coalition Forces continued their advance after major sandstorms caused a three-day operational pause, they faced the combined threats of Fedayeen guerrillas and chemical weapons as they fought along the highways through al-Diwaniyah and past al-Kut and tightened their grip on Baghdad. On 9 April, Marines secured eastern Baghdad as the U.S. Army's V Corps secured the west, and brought down the statute of Saddam Hussein in Firdos Square amid cheering crowds.[*] In both sections of Baghdad, soldiers and Marines began security and stabilization operations to provide humanitarian aid and restore essential services.

Media Coverage of the Conventional War

As the Coalition advanced toward Baghdad, embedded reporters working for all major Western news outlets provided live and unedited report from many locations, which provided broad, but sometimes disjointed coverage of the war. Other journalists reported without consideration for safety or operational security. In one case, Geraldo Rivera drew a map of his location, which violated CentCom's media policy by divulging the troop's position, while *Christian Science Monitor* correspondent Phil Smucker, who traveled with U.S. forces as a unilateral correspondent, similarly gave away his position.[26] Most journalists focused on death and destruction, ignoring the massive humanitarian efforts that accompanied combat. Addressing this in her

---

* Marines fought over 808 kilometers in 17 days of sustained combat, which included nine bridge crossings over the Euphrates, Tigris, and Diyala Rivers and the Saddam Canal.

memoir, embedded journalist Katherine M. Skiba comments on this, observing that the media focused on reporting "the worst of war," leaving out the compassion U.S. troops displayed for each other, their loved ones, and even the Iraqi people.[27] Conversely, some journalists and observers complained that media outlets, such as Fox News, provided overly patriotic coverage reminiscent of the "yellow journalism" that plagued the media a century before.[28]

Although most reports were accurate, like Vietnam, some embedded reporters had difficulty with the fast pace of combat and provided hasty, unqualified analysis wrought with errors and speculation. In one case, reporters exaggerated logistical problems and incorrectly attributed the operational pause on day three of the ground offensive to strained logistic lines. General Delong complained that, "embedded reporters complained that we had to abandon tanks that didn't have enough gas (not true)."[29] While logistical challenges were a factor in the rapid assault, unexpected sandstorms slowed events but did not bring the attack to a complete halt as air operations continued.[30]

Just a few days into the war, some journalists began to assert that the war had become a quagmire. Indicative of such reports, CBS's Lesley Stahl advanced the quagmire narrative on the March 25th program *48 Hours*, focusing on Iraqi's "surprising resistance," asserting with a high level of subjectivity that "Americans at home are confronting the reality of this war: Not everything is going as expected," challenging Secretary of State Colin Power about alleged problems on the battlefield and asserting the whole world hates President George W. Bush.[31] In the same program, she made the quagmire connection to Vietnam asking author and future U.S. senator Jim Webb, "You fought in Vietnam. Are you getting any feelings of deja vu?"[32] Writing for *Editor and Publisher*, Greg Mitchell observed the emerging quagmire narrative, writing:

> It was last Wednesday morning, just as nearly everyone in America (except perhaps a few Fox News commentators) was awakening to the bone-chilling reality of a quick war that was threatening to turn into a quagmire. And there, splashed across a spread in *The New York Times*, was a picture of a smiling Donald Rumsfeld bending over to shake the hand of an equally buoyant Robert S. McNamara. Unfortunately, it did not look like McNamara was whispering, 'What part of the word Vietnam don't you understand?'[33]

Criticizing this reporting, Mitchell added, "Of course, it is absurd, on one level, to compare a war of less than two weeks with one that lasted decades."[34] Like Don Oberdorfer and Peter Braestrup in 1968 Vietnam, some journalists reporting from Iraq were surprised to see how different the war was being reported at home. Critical of this disparity, BBC reporter Paul Adams commented on his perception of the BBC's "one-sided" coverage writing, "I was gobsmacked to hear, in a set of headlines today, that the coalition was suffering 'significant casualties'. This is simply NOT TRUE."[35]

Much like Vietnam, some of the media's experts and analysts far removed from the scene amplified the non-embedded reporters' hasty speculation and analysis. However, Delong complains, these so-called experts and analysts were "armchair generals and retired generals...[who] were out of the loop—in some cases had been for many years—and succeeded only in misguiding American public opinion."[36] Retired U.S. Army Colonel Kenneth Allard, an MSNBC military analyst, disagreed, contending that he and his colleagues, representing the major satellite channels in what he calls the "Electronic Coliseum," were well-versed and informed. However, Allard admits that he and his fellow military analysts sometimes had difficulty separating what they "saw or know" from what they "suspect or believe," which he explains "often succeeded only in spreading dismay and alarm."[37]

Commenting on the erroneous reporting, *Time* Magazine reporter James Lacey observed:

> I was embedded at brigade headquarters and saw everything the brigade commander saw. All the other *Time* and *Newsweek* embeds were at lower levels.
>
> Just after the sandstorm-enforced halt in the assault on Baghdad, *Time* sent me the copy for that week's cover story entitled "Why Are We Losing" and asked me to find comments to feed into the story.
>
> That day I saw Colonel David Perkins of the 3rd Infantry Division and talked to many of his officers. Their reaction to the story was, "Tomorrow we laager up to refuel and rearm. The next day we move out to hit the Medina Division. It's beat up, facing the wrong way, and does not know we're coming. The day after that we ride onto Baghdad International Airport." After a few calculations, I figured out *Time* was going to declare the war lost on the same day we entered Baghdad. This was not good.
>
> I sent a note to *Time* telling them they were about to look very foolish. Unfortunately, I was alone in my estimation of the situation. All of the talking heads on TV were shouting about disaster. However, expert talking-head opinions on the threat Saddam's paramilitaries were posing to the 3rd's supply line were

> not in line with the reality I was witnessing. Battlefield commanders in Iraq, rather than being alarmed at attacks on the supply lines, were thankful, "Isn't it nice of them to come out of hiding in the cities and attack across open desert to be slaughtered." In addition to the talking heads, most of my fellow embeds were echoing the disaster sentiment. When you are living in the dirt with an infantry platoon, it is easy to miss the progress that becomes visible when you get the big picture at a brigade headquarters or higher. After a six-hour meeting, the compromise at *Time* was to rename the story "What Will It Take to Win."
>
> *Newsweek* went with the cover story "Quagmire" in big red letters, which allowed *Time* to claim a major journalistic coup by not looking as foolish as Newsweek.[38]

Lacey's account says volumes about the American free media's predisposed, "quagmire" coverage of the war—especially how some Western journalists were directed to write the stories their editor wanted and not about how the events actually occurred.

Reporting closest to this fighting, al-Jazeera provided a starkly different account than the Western media. Using inflammatory and misleading headlines such as "Baghdad is Burning," and punctuating its reports with powerful images of dead Iraqis and burning buildings, the station insinuated that all death and destruction was due to the Coalition attacks, rather than internal skirmishes or Fedayeen terror. More accurately, Delong asserts it was clear the Fedayeen were killing fleeing and surrendering Iraqis.[39] British journalist Hugh Miles observes that by choosing "invasion of Iraq" over "the liberation of Iraq," Al-Jazeera separated itself from both Western media and other Arab satellite stations that would later follow Al-Jazeera's lead.[40]

Arab newspapers and television stations throughout the Middle East, such as Cairo's *Al-Akhbar*, portrayed the Coalition effort against Iraq as an illegal invasion to take control of Iraq's oil fields.[41] Using sensational headlines and phrases like the "enemies of life" and "an Iraqi holocaust," accompanied by graphic photos of dead or injured civilians, Arab media outlets depicted Americans as "aggressors" intent on callously destroying Iraq and killing innocent Iraqis.[42] This sensationalized coverage inflamed Arab audiences across the Middle East to protest, which al-Jazeera covered with equal enthusiasm, and encouraged more foreign fighters to join Iraq's guerrillas.[43] Similar to Vietnam, and following a practice developed in Afghanistan over a year earlier, some news outlets dismissed the reports of embedded correspondents and instead used al-Jazeera's sensational material uncritically. In one instance, to the shock of American audiences, CBS rebroadcast al-Jazeera's images of dead U.S. soldiers on its 23 March 2003 airing of *Face the Nation.*[44]

Meanwhile, many other non-embedded reporters, like Peter Arnett in Baghdad, provided a very different narrative than actually occurred because Iraq's Ministry of Information controlled Western and Arab journalists, telling them what footage they could shoot, what to report, and what they could not, and provided armed escorts to all foreign correspondents to ensure media control.[45] Aymar Gahallah, the Baghdad correspondent for al-Arabia, explains that "you had to do what the regime said—otherwise you went to prison or were shot. I could not say that US tanks were here in Baghdad over the bridge. You could not pan the camera across."[46] Reminiscent of Vietnam reporting, some non-embedded journalists, blind to actual events on the battlefield, monitored Iraqi Information Ministry reports of combat and viewed the ministry's footage of captured or killed American soldiers.[47] Thus, when Coalition forces encountered pockets of Fedayeen resistance or hunkered down during sandstorms, many independent reporters accepted Saddam Hussein's contention that U.S. forces were caught in a cleverly planned "quagmire," or reflected similar hasty analysis and pessimism.[48] Like his reporting during the 1991 Gulf War, Peter Arnett used Iraq Information Ministry information uncritically in his own reports. However, some of his unsubstantiated reports did not go unchallenged. *Today* show's Katie Couric and Matt Lauer challenged Arnett's assertion that the United States used cluster bombs against civilians inside Baghdad.[49] According to a *Project for Excellence in Journalism* (PEJ) report, Arnett "famously crossed that line [between pundit and reporter] when he went on Iraqi state TV and offered his opinions on U.S. military strategy."[50] However, journalists in Baghdad later discovered what American audience had already seen when Iraqi Information minister Mohammed Sayid al-Sahaf, aka "Baghdad Bob," continued to deny that Coalition forces were in Baghdad when they could clearly see them from the rooftop of the Palestine Hotel.[51]

On April 1, Coalition forces closed on Baghdad and other key cities like Fallujah, tightening the noose on the key elements of Hussein's defense forces—the Republican Guard and Special Republican Guard. By April 9, Coalition forces secured most of Baghdad, effectively ending the Baath Party regime. By April 14, Delong reports, Coalition forces secured "Saddam's hometown and the last Iraqi holdout," Tikrit.[52] Discussions of "quagmire" soon disappeared, triggering criticism of those pessimistic predictions from observers like Paul Stanway who titled his editorial "All Quagmires Should Go this Well."[53]

As Baghdad fell to Coalition forces, the disparity between Western reporting and Arab reporting was very clear. Like other Western journalists, Andy Geller described the capture of Baghdad with words as television cameras did with images. "Jubilant Iraqis," he reported, "stomped on a toppled statue of Saddam Hussein and dragged its severed head through the streets of Baghdad yesterday as the despot's regime collapsed in an orgy of cheering, waving and looting."[54] Conversely, al-Jazeera portrayed the U.S. flag draped over Hussein's statue and its subsequent falling as a humiliation to the Iraqi people.[55] Arab journalist Noha Mellor explains that the same picture of an "elderly Iraqi woman raising her hand with a caption saying she was welcoming the American forces...had been interpreted differently by an Arab commentator...as a clear indication she was in fact cursing, not welcoming, the Americans."[56] She adds that to counter the West's powerful imagery, the Arab media accused American media of "twisting the facts to favorably represent the stance of their government."[57] Despite the enormous presence of the Western journalists, however, al-Jazeera dominated media coverage during the conflict as it had in Afghanistan, with its viewership equaling the six major U.S. networks, ABC, CBS, NBC, CNN, Fox News, and PBS combined.[58]

The Western Media Deserts

With the end of major combat operations, so came an end to the Western media's broad coverage. Most embedded reporters returned to the United States after Baghdad fell, allowing al-Jazeera and other Arab mediums to increase their media dominance. Those few Western journalists who remained joined their non-embedded counterparts to report from the safety of Baghdad's "Green Zone."[59] Like the journalist who reported from the Hotel Caravelle in Vietnam 35 years earlier, Western correspondents reported from Baghdad's luxury Palestine Hotel. They no longer focused on military operations, but rather concentrated on the unfolding political situation from Saddam Hussein's former palace in Baghdad where Jay Garner and then Paul Bremer established their offices.[60] While Western journalists shifted their focus from military operations to post-Saddam policy and Coalition efforts to rebuild Iraq, danger was also a leading contributor to the Western journalists' preference to report from Baghdad's Green Zone.

After guerrillas kidnapped *Christian Science Monitor* correspondent Jill Carroll, journalists soon discovered they were easy targets for criminals who could profit by holding them for random or selling them to Zarqawi in Fallujah because, as Westerners, they reported for the wrong side in the war of ideas.[61] Therefore, few Western journalists accompanied troops on patrols, and thus had difficultly covering the war and making sense of Iraq's complex situation. They became reliant on Arab journalists, such as Zaki Chehab, or local Iraqis called "stringers," who reported for both Arab media and as Arab correspondents for Western media.[62]

Importantly, Iraqis found themselves free of Baath media control for the first time, and part of a larger Arab public sphere. "Within weeks of the fall of the regime," British journalist Hugh Miles reported, "hundreds of newspapers were being published, Internet Cafes had sprung up in all the major cities and in a two-mile stretch in Baghdad there were more than fifty shops selling satellite receivers."[63] This brought a plethora of fresh programming into the new Iraqi public sphere. However, Iraqi journalists, lacking any other model for free speech, followed al-Jazeera's example, and in the end, al-Jazeera remained the dominant medium in Iraq as the increase in satellite dishes increased al-Jazeera's viewership.[64] Moreover, Iraqi historian Jassim Mohammed al-`Azawi observed that the hundreds of new daily and weekly newspapers that emerged professional journalistic standards, and largely served as propaganda for religious and political groups.[65]

This represented a stark contrast to that of U.S. media policy in occupied Germany following World War II where the United States maintained strict media control to block Nazi propaganda. Instead, the United States allowed the rapid propagation of new media outlets while replacing Iraqi state controlled media with the *Iraqi Media Network*, a collection of new media outlets overseen by a private Department of Defense contractor, which failed because these companies had no experience in information and psychological operations and Iraqis rejected them as being associated with the United States. [66] In describing the challenge, Iraq War analyst and historian Peter J. Munson keenly observed, "...the CPA [Coalition Provisional Authority] was at a serious disadvantage in its efforts to counter years of suspicion and pessimism."[67]

According to Dr. Cora Sol Goldstein, "As a result of this strategic error, the insurgency and other civilian movements opposed to the American presence have been able to control information and spread anti-American messages."[68] As the rest of this study will show, this will not only be detrimental to the U.S. effort in the war of ideas at the operational and tactical levels in post-Saddam Iraq, but also at the strategic level in affecting both international support and domestic public opinion.

Guerrilla War and Insurgency: A Complex War Emerges

In the lull in violence following the capture of Baghdad, U.S. soldiers and Marines similarly provided humanitarian aid, established local government and police, and worked to restore essential services; however, the approach taken by different units varied. They also engaged the population at all levels with the message that they were there to help them to gain their trust and cooperation in returning Iraqis to normalcy.[69] As they did, however, many poor Iraqis began looting in the absence of security, and soldiers and Marines soon found that they did not have enough troops to maintain an active presence in the neighborhoods to deter looting and crime while also providing a stabilization operations. Additionally, they found they found that

Baghdad's infrastructure for such service was far more degraded than anyone had imagined, and that many of the Iraqi technocrats and bureaucrats needed to restore essential services were not available. The combination of insufficient Phase IV planning and training and insufficient troops would soon become a tremendous oversight.[70]

As U.S. forces conducted civil military operations to Eastern Baghdad, U.S. Army and Marine units moved North to Samara and Tikrit to eliminate the last Baath Party stronghold and locate Saddam Hussein and his sons. In Tikrit, the U.S. Marines of Task Force Tripoli began to employ the same security and stabilization practices as their counterparts in Baghdad, engaging the population in dialog, establishing sheikh's councils and local government, and providing much needed humanitarian aid as they restored order. Their message was that they were not there to stay but were there to help them and then leave. Marines drew upon their experience and successes in previous insurgencies as the basis for their Phase IV approach. As a result, public officials, technocrats, and Iraqi police returned to work, and there were few incidents of violence.[71]

Almost two weeks later, Marines turned Tirik over to General Raymond T. Odierno's Fourth Infantry Division (4th ID). However, the 4th ID arrived in Iraq too late for major combat operations because they had been delayed getting in the country, and came eager for combat. As a result they took a much more aggressive approach to the population than Marines.[72] According to 1st Marine Division Historian, Lieutenant Colonel Michel S. Groen:

> The follow-on staff of the US 4th Infantry Division had a different perspective on the situation. The US 4th ID had missed the combat phase of OIF, and were determined to have a share in the 'fighting'. They characterized their recent road march to Tikrit (in trace of the Marines) as an 'attack', and remained convinced that the situation in Tikrit required a very stern military enforcement posture. The dichotomy between the two peacekeeping strategies was unsettling for the Marines, and many winced when Army Apache attack helicopters swooped in to the Division battlespace without coordination, and began to strafe seemingly indiscriminately on abandoned enemy armor directly between, and in close proximity to, 2d and 3d LAR's positions.[73]

This heavy-handed approach was taken by other units, and would soon cause problems for the Coalition effort in Iraq. Moreover, some units had difficulty transitioning from combat to a softer security and stabilization mission and were often heavy-handed in their use of firepower and/or were culturally insensitive, which caused animosity and fueled retribution that created new cycles of violence and localized insurgencies. According to Major

General John F. Kelly, then assistant division commander and the commander of Task Force Tripoli, this "heavy-handed military approach taken by some" was one of the leading reasons "that caused events to spiral out of control."[74] In Fallujah, U.S. Army soldiers fired into crowd on April 28, shooting 77 residents and killing 17 of them.[75]

By this time, the lull in violence was over. Criminal gangs flourished in the chaos, engaging in looting, kidnappings, while tribal and sectarian factions began attacking their enemies in retribution for past grievances.[76] In the absence of control, families, tribes, and clans settled old scores with their enemies according to the old vendetta custom of the Middle East, while Sunnis and Shiites did so on a larger scale. The presence of 30,000-50,000 most dangerous prisoners released during the early days of the war greatly exacerbated the situation, as did the fact that most Iraqis owned guns and possessed some military training.[77] These criminals not only engaged in looting and kidnappings, but also took revenge on Iraqi police and officials—murdering them where they found them.[78] According to international relations and Middle East analyst Toby Dodge, criminal gangs flourished in the chaos, contributing to "80% of all violence in Iraq."[79]

While most Sunnis "adopted a wait and see attitude" following the Coalition capture of Baghdad, many others immediately took to the streets in protest and "demanded an end to the US occupation and the emergence of an Islamic state."[80] Lieutenant Colonel R. Alan King, commander of the U.S. Army's 422nd Civil Affairs Battalion, describes these demonstrations as being carefully orchestrated events for the media's cameras: "Every thirty minutes, another set of buses would shuttle in new demonstrators, with new signs and new chants," a telling observation of the war of ideas unfolding in post-Saddam Iraq[81]

On April 21, 2003, retired U.S. Army General Jay Garner arrived in Iraq as head of the Office of Reconstruction and Humanitarian Assistance (ORHA) to oversee reconstruction and assemble an interim Iraqi government in preparation for democratic elections. However, Garner had only come into the position three months before the war, and in that time built the ORHA from scratch.[82] With the exception of the those Baathists with serious crimes, Garner hoped to retain the majority of the Baath Party and move quickly toward restoring Iraqi control, assuming that Iraq's military would capitulate to Coalition Forces, and that Iraq's police and other necessary public service personnel remained in service. However, because neither Iraq's military capitulated nor Iraq's police and other necessary public service personnel remained in service, he did not get the indigenous work force he needed and expected.[83] Those soldiers and police who returned to their posts were ill-equipped to handle the violence they faced.[84] Thus, looting, crime, and disorder went unchecked as essential public services went unprovided, frustrating the Iraqi people.[85] Making full use of General Anthony Zinni's pre-war criticism, headlines such as "The Quagmire that is Iraq" reflected what Lieutenant Colonel R. Alan King describes as "the media outrage over our failure to control the looters, who were everywhere."[86]

Although Marines and soldiers continued to engage guerrillas, President Bush on May 1 declared victory and an end to major combat operations in Iraq in a highly publicized event on the deck of the U.S.S. *Abraham Lincoln.* Reminiscent of President Johnson's success campaign preceding the Tet Offensive, however, this early pronouncement inflated the optimism and expectations of the American public, which soon had a profound effect on how the media reported the war.

After only three weeks, President Bush replaced Garner's ORHA with the Coalition Provisional Authority (CPA), under Ambassador L. Paul Bremer III's direction. This action caused Iraqi resentment toward the Coalition because they viewed it as a move toward long-term occupation. More important, however, Bremer's leadership and policies had an immediate effect on post-Saddam Iraq. On 16 May 2003, Bremer issued Coalition Provisional Authority Order Number 1, "De-Ba`athification of Iraqi Society."[1] On 23 May, Bremer Coalition Provisional Authority Order No. 2, "The Dissolution of Entities," which disbanded the army and other branches of the Iraqi armed services as well as Iraqi governmental ministries and other organizations related to the Baath Party. These two policies had immediate, adverse consequences.

Although most, but not all, of Hussein's police, military, and civil servants had quit their positions during the Coalition offensive, Bremer's action to abolish the Baath Party and disband Iraq's military made it impossible for Iraq's military, police, and civil servants to change their minds and return to their former positions. in that Sunnis took "de-Baathification" to mean "de-sunnification," convinced many Sunnis that they were the target of the invasion, stripping them of centuries of power, which caused widespread resentment. This action caused resentment among the Baathist, while prolonging Iraqi suffering and the restoration of vital services.[87] In making these decisions, Bremer had not coordinated these policies with either ORHA or CENTCOM. The decision not only left thousands of 400,000 officers and soldiers out of work and without pensions, along with thousand of Baath Party bureaucrats, but also removed the only force that could protect the province from foreign fighters. Importantly, it was but also was a humiliation to Iraqis because its military was their most respected institution.[88] Bremer's decisions not only caused a chasm between the CPA and military, but also left the military deal with the aftermath.

Sunni Baathists vowed revenge for losing their livelihoods, status, and privileges, and joined the Saddam Fedayeen or other guerrilla organizations.[89] Many former soldiers and officers who had not had a chance to fight against Coalition forces, or who were not yet ready to surrender, joined militia and guerrilla groups like the Popular Iraqi Liberation Front, Iraqi National Resistance Movement, and the Army of Muhammad, sometimes cooperating against the occupation despite competing interest and leadership.[90] These organizations collectively made up Iraq's nationalist resistance—by definition a guerilla movement because they continued fighting when conventional means failed. The nationalists would sometimes cooperate with the Salafi elements, but would later find themselves fighting for control of Iraq's future. Importantly, many senior Baathist successfully fled Iraq with a millions of dollars, in which they could both finance and direct a guerrilla war and insurgency from the safety of Syria.[91]

As attacks against Shiites and coalition forces escalated in May 2003, the U.S. military responded by conducting raids on suspected insurgent hideouts and with cordon and search operations around Baghdad and the Sunni controlled al-Anbar Province in the West. While most U.S. soldiers and Marines followed the rules of engagement, showing discipline and restraint in the performance of their duties and respecting local customs, others responded to the savagery of guerrilla and terrorist tactics with excessive force, or acted in a blatant culturally insensitive manner.[92] Like the April 28th incident in Fallujah, news of these incidents spread quickly and caused resentment among the population.[93] However, through the Arab satellite television and the plethora of new, highly partisan newspapers in Iraq, various insurgents groups circulated a number of false accounts of U.S. misconduct, which included desecrating mosques, killing civilians, and raping Iraqi women, most reported on al-Jazeera, which investigators determined were false.[94] Adding to real, exaggerated or alleged incidents of U.S. misconduct, guerrillas acquired U.S. desert uniforms in order to blame Americans attacked their enemies, which fueled more retaliation.[95] Moreover, Rumsfeld's and other U.S. officials repeated public claims that the Sunnis were "dead-enders" and "losers" were taken as insults by many Sunnis, which invited revenge and fueled the insurgency.[96]

In June, Lieutenant General Ricardo S. Sanchez took command of V Corps, which CJTF-7, and aggressive response toward Iraq's growing insurgency, launching a number of major combat operations intended to eliminate large concentrations of insurgent forces in specific cities believing it would end opposition.[97] These include a series of cordons and searches, raids, on suspected insurgent sites and follow-on stability operations conducted simultaneously in many parts of the country. According to Middle East expert Ahmed S. Hashim, a Professor of Strategic Studies at the U.S. Naval War College, this succeeded in capturing "many mid-level Ba'th operatives who had been providing command and control and funds for insurgents."[98] However, Salafis under the umbrella of al-Qaeda in Iraq began to fill the vacancies in insurgent leadership left by Baathists. While the U.S. Army viewed its work a success, many Iraqis perceived the U.S. Army's tactics and use of force as both excessive and insensitive to their culture, which inflamed the Iraqis and incited revenge. As the summer progressed, Coalition forces began to understand that their intrusive cordons and searches and other aggressive tactics were not building support for the Coalition, but instead fostered resentment among Sunnis. Admitting that these major operations caused problems, Lieutenant General Sanchez said "I started to get multiple indicators that maybe our iron-fisted approach to the conduct of [operations] was beginning to alienate Iraqis...."[99]

Meanwhile, in addition to Batthists and nationalists groups, Wahhabi groups like the Iraqi Islamic Party, modeled after the Muslim Brotherhood, and Jamaat al-Tawhid wal-Jihad, began trying to establish an Islamic State, attacking Shiites, Coalition forces, Iraqis with an education of in a position of authority, and those Iraqis perceived to be cooperating with the Coalition.[100] Importantly, Salafi clerics harbored foreign fighters filtering into Iraq through staging areas both just within and just across Iraq's borders, where guerrilla leaders outfitted them with clothes, money, weapons, and other necessary supplies before being sent to Salafi cells either in or around Baghdad.[101] Emerging groups such as Saad bin Abi Waqas Brigades, Islamic Army in Iraq, and Jaish al-Taifa al-Mansoura joined Abu Musab al-Zarqawi in attacking Shiites to a fuel civil war as a strategy to preoccupy U.S. forces.[102] These various elements formed a loose confederation that made up Iraq's Salafi insurgency that would fall under the umbrella of al-Qaeda in Iraq. As these organizations began to fall under the umbrella of al-Qaeda in Iraq, they also attacked police stations, government employees and offices, recruiting stations and other public infrastructure to deter collaboration with the Coalition. Moreover, they "deliberately targeted international institutions, specifically foreign embassies, the United Nations and the Red Cross, signaling that they would try and make any multilateralisation of the occupation both costly and unworkable."[103] Guerrillas also attacked U.S. patrols with improvised explosive devises (IEDs), roadside bombs, car bombs, and suicide bombers, and engaged in hit-and-run skirmishes when they believed they had an advantage. According to "Sheik Saleh," guerrillas learned from history, proclaiming "with the help of God, we are going to win, and the resistance will succeed in forcing the Americans to withdraw—just like they did from Vietnam."[104] Importantly, with an abundance of outside financial support, the Salafi organizations began murdering educated Iraqis and those in positions of authority. This included Iraqi police, mayors, and tribal sheikhs. It also included doctors, teachers, engineers, university professors, and others.[105]

Meanwhile, fundamentalist Shiite cleric Moqtada al Sadr, leader of the Jaish al-Mahdi Militia, or *Mahdi Militia*, emerged in Southern Iraq and challenged Bremer's authority. Using harsh anti-American rhetoric reminiscent of Ayatollah Ruholla Khomeini, al-Sadr hoped to advance fundamentalists Shia interests in Iraq.[106] Conversely, the Shia's most respected leader, Grand Ayatollah ali Sistani, representing the Shia majority, urged the Shia not to join the violence against the Coalition, but work toward a peaceful resolution to the conflict.[107] Sistani's pragmatic leadership would help mollify the Shia majority. However, with support from Hezbollah and branches of Iran's Revolutionary Guard, particularly the Badr Army, al-Sadr and his Mahdi Militia would later become a dangerous force representing Iranian interests and fighting various Sunni groups for control of Iraq.[108] Behind the scenes, Iranian commandos and agents would begin assassinating key Iraqi leaders, especially military officers, and providing direct financial and material support to Iraq's guerrilla and insurgent elements, including al-Qaeda affiliated groups.[109]

As the U.S. Army took control of Baghdad and northern Iraq, the Marines had moved south and had taken over much of Southern Iraq, providing administrative control of Iraq's seven Southern Provinces and using the approach they had taken in Eastern Baghdad and Tikrit. Importantly, with the exception of Northern Babil Province, Southern Iraq remained largely peaceful under the U.S. Marines until they turned the area over to other Coalition and Multi-national forces. Because of its proximity to Baghdad, Northern Babil Province was becoming a location for insurgent groups to launch attacks on Baghdad, and was also becoming increasingly violent as insurgents groups asserted control over the area. Marines countered this with active, dismounted patrolling using Iraqi support, aggressive actions to eradicate insurgent groups, and exercising restraint during engagements when non-combatants were present. Meanwhile, they continued to engage the locals in dialog while conveying the consistent message that they were not there to stay, but were there to help them and leave. Their success in Northern Babil Province and Southern Iraq would provide an important foundation for the Marines' return to Iraq in 2004.[110]

However, as soldiers and Marines continued to engage Fedayeen, Baath loyalists, and other guerrillas, President Bush declared that 'major combat operations in Iraq had ended' in a dramatic media event on the deck of the U.S.S. Abraham Lincoln. [111] Reminiscent of the Johnson administration's infamous "success" publicity campaign preceding the Tet offensive in Vietnam, President Bush's dramatic "Mission Accomplished" speech inflated the optimism and expectations of the American public that the end of the war near.

Media Perspectives of Iraq's Insurgency

With much of the Western media confined to Baghdad's Green Zone, the Arab media, led by al-Jazeera, took the lead in defining the conflict from an anti-Coalition point of view. In stories with headlines like "US occupation forces kill 11 Iraqis," al-Jazeera sought to demonize Coalition forces while eliciting hatred and provoking violence through use of "indiscriminant" attacks.[112] Whereas numerous stories like "Resistance attacks continue in Iraq," "Resistance bomb adds to US deaths," "Resistance ambush kills US soldiers," and "Iraqis fighting US seen as 'martyrs'," provided sympathetic and emotional coverage of Iraq's insurgents and their glorious efforts while extolling them as heroes fulfilling their Islamic duty in fighting the "infidels" and "occupiers."[113] However, it was the graphic, gory video and photographs of dead children and grandparents the truly succeeded in fueling rage and vendetta violence, though the Arab media often used the same video segments and photographs for other events. Clever, misleading captions and sound bites often accompanied these images. In stories like "US troop morale in Iraq plummets," which sought to boost insurgent and sympathetic Iraqi morale, the presumptuous caption that came with a picture of U.S. Army soldiers read "US troops under siege and anxious to go home."[114] As described later, all of this coverage would embolden insurgents while aiding recruitment and gaining financial support. Importantly, it would send the message that Iraq's insurgency was larger and more widespread than it was.

Arab journalist Assad Taha tellingly illustrates the intensely partisan coverage the Arab media afforded Iraq's so-called "resistance" when he argues that "there is no such thing as a neutral journalist or a neutral media for that matter."[115] Zaki Chehab, Arab journalist and political editor of *al-Hayat*, describes this partisanship from another perspective, explaining that guerrillas often pressed him to cover their attacks and allow them to read statements for his broadcast. [116] Living among the Iraqi guerrillas, Chehab describes a form of Arab embedding writing:

> My hosts were fighters who were engaged in daily assaults against American troops...but I was deeply concerned that someone might discover what I learned from these militias. Not only had I been out and about during curfew hours with men whose intention was to kill military personnel of the coalition forces, but I also had information concerning their identity and whereabouts that would be extremely sensitive for the Americans.[117]

These telling accounts reveal a collusion where the Arab media reported information obtained from guerrillas uncritically, which influenced both the new Iraqi public spheres and Arab public spheres toward violence.

Reflecting media activism during the war, the same day that Coalition forces ended the reign of the Baath Party regime and toppled the statue of Saddam Hussein in Baghdad's Firdas Square, April 9, 2003, the British National Union of Journalist hosted a meeting in London in response to it inability to prevent the conflict and sought to "counter the lies and misinformation dominating most of the mainstream media and that the situation in Iraq was already a disaster human, social, political and military terms."[118] The meeting included several media organization such as the Media Workers Against the War, Stop the War Coalition, Campaign for Press and Broadcasting Freedom, and Campeace.[119] Such a concerted effort my media professionals not only highlights the intense partisanship displayed by some journalists and media organizations, but also offers troubling insight into the activist media's participation in the wars of ideas that came with the Iraq War and provided a glimpse into the reporting the would follow.

While the Arab media framed the conflict their way, the Western Media's few remaining journalists in Iraq forged a narrative far from the events they reported on, while journalists in the United States focused on criticisms of the Bush Administration's decision to go to war, reflecting deep partisanship in their reporting. Robert Entman points out that they "remained exquisitely sensitive to signs of policy failure and unacceptable costs" to justify their pre-war counter-framing strategy.[120] Adding to this suspicion was the failure of U.S. forces to find any significant amounts special weapons (weapons of mass destruction) and Secretary of Defense Donald Rumsfeld's inflated optimism and contention the U.S. forces were not fighting an insurgency.[121] This resulted in an abundance of pessimistic and bad news stories that overshadowed positive events on the ground. Commenting on the prevailing pessimism and reoccurring quagmire narrative, Entman explains:

> Representative of the ongoing media tone, *Time* magazine's lead story on July 7, 2003, was headlined 'THE WAR THAT NEVER ENDS,' and on its cover for July 14 appeared 'UNTRUTH AND CONSEQUENCES' over a picture of Bush giving the 2003 State of the Union address. The head of *Newsweek's* lead story for July 21, 2003 read 'STILL FIGHTING SADDAM,' and in a clear allusion to Vietnam quagmire—the issue pictured each soldier slain after May 1.[122]

This pattern continued through the end of 2003 in numerous articles like "Friendless: The U.S. is lost and alone in Iraq Quagmire, UN Members Unlikely to Agree to Help," continuing the assertion that the United States could not win in Iraq.[123] Yet again reminiscent of Vietnam, presidential hopefuls Senators John McCain and John Kerry referenced the media's popular tone and changing public attitude, drawing the parallel to "Vietnam" and "quagmire" to gain political advantage.[124] Moreover, other criticisms came from the president's political opponents in the U.S. House of Representatives and U.S. Senate who had come to their positions during the Vietnam War.

Critical of the media's quagmire reporting, Lieutenant Colonel Alan King complained, "Western media reports the Islamic Jihad to be everywhere and then group a billion Muslims into a single terrorist movement."[125] *Time* magazine reporter James Lacey, complained about his colleagues focusing on incidents of alleged U.S. misconduct and presenting them without context, writing:

> ...an article in *The Washington Post* screamed out about 91 cases of misconduct toward Iraqis being investigated by military authorities. U.S. soldiers and Marines were presented as marauding barbarians in tone if not in words.[126]

Lacey demonstrates that without context these incidents, as reported, appeared endemic of the U.S. military and not the aberrations that they were. Adding to the pessimistic coverage and the emerging quagmire narrative of U.S. involvement in Iraq, former U.S. diplomat Joe Wilson's assertion that the Bush Administration "twisted [intelligence] to exaggerate the Iraqi threat" became another emerging media frame that, like the Vietnam War, would fuel anti-war protests in the months that followed.[127]

Reminiscent of Vietnam, *The New York Times* reporter Dexter Filkins believed that military and Bush Administration representatives were not telling the truth in official press briefings, writing:

> In late 2003 and early 2004, as security around Iraq was deteriorating, reporters in Iraq were sometimes mystified by the rosy briefings they were given inside the Green Zone. In the streets where they lived and worked, they witnessed car bombings and assassinations, while the spokesmen for the Bush administration talked mostly about smiling Iraqis and freshly painted schools.[128]

Filkins also complained that as a result of their reporting:

> ...reporters who filed dispatches pointing out the pitfalls experienced by American troops sometimes found it difficult to secure an embed with an American military unit. Other reporters — including this one — were sometimes excluded from official briefings inside the Green Zone.[129]

Filkins' observations describe the conflict between the media and U.S. military and Bush Administration that occurred during the post-Saddam conflict. *Time* magazine reporter James Lacey, who had been a fan of the embedding program, similarly complained about getting access to units.[130]

It is important to note, however, that while focusing primarily on Baghdad, the collective media overlooked the relative calm in much of Iraq, especially Southern and Western Iraq, with the exception of Northern Babil Province and Fallujah because they were in Baghdad's immediate periphery, which demonstrated the Coalition's success in these areas. It also ignored gains in the Coalition's humanitarian efforts in these areas, efforts to restore Iraq's degraded essential service and infrastructure, and efforts to restore local government and security. Furthermore, the media also gave short life to evidence of Iraq's WMD programs discovered by Coalition Forces, and downplaying the discoveries through its news placement and framing conventions, which established unrealistic expectations that "stockpiles" of weapons would be found quickly in a nation roughly the size of California despite common knowledge that Iraqi forces distributed its weapons and supplies before combat operation began. The cumulative effects of the Arab media's continued dominance and the Western media's quagmire narrative and deficient reporting began to blur fact and fiction, which shaped perceptions that were often much different than the reality on the ground in Iraq.

Evaluation of Embedding

Military officials believed that embedding was a "qualified success" because journalists provided eyewitness accounts of Coalition combat.[131] *Time* magazine reporter James Lacey called the embedding program "a wonderful idea," adding:

> ...anytime you can get a journalist living in the sand and mud with real soldiers it is a major plus. It is impossible for anyone to be associated with U.S. soldiers in combat and not walk away impressed. As one CBS reporter told me, "I just had no idea our army was filled with such quality people."[132]

Even, Walter Cronkite approved of embedding commenting, "The principal advantage [of embedding] is that it is 180 degrees better than the blackout the military enforced during the first Gulf War."[133]

However, critics such as Phillip Knightley complained that embedding was a "sort of propaganda that would encourage a dubious American public to support the war."[134] Media critic Danny Schechter accused the U.S. government of "co-opting and orchestrating the media" through the embedding program as it had during the 1991 Gulf War. He further asserted that "hundreds of journalists were 'embedded' in order to sanitize war coverage."[135] Conversely, *American Journalism Review* writer Sherry Ricchiardi contends that embedded reports "were not really restrained but rather assisted in their work" by military public relations personnel. She describes the result she witnessed as "a far more complete mosaic of the fighting."[136] Journalism scholars Justin Lewis, Rod Brookes, Nick Mosdell, and Terry Threadgold agree, adding that embedded reporters kept their independence and reported without censor.[137] Finally, the *Project for Excellence in Journalism* used empirical research to conclude that embedded journalists provided valuable war coverage with 94% accuracy, but warned that the magnitude of "embedded coverage has made the war coverage richer, but also more difficult to absorb."[138] The next section will demonstrate the true value of embedding, where the few remaining western unilateral journalists would fail to accurately report both the events leading to the first Battle for Fallujah and the battle itself.

Chapter Conclusion

The guerrilla war that evolved after the collapse of Saddam's conventional military in 2003 bore Saddam's fingerprints in the form of secret police, intelligence, and terrorist organizations that continued fighting and attacked the Shia to prevent any new form of government that did not keep them in power. The U.S. decision to establish the CPA, which conveyed to the Iraqi that the United States was interested in long-term occupation, immediately followed by Bremer's actions abolish the Baath Party and disband Iraq's military was seen by many Sunni as "deSunnification" and was a tremendous humiliation. This, coupled with both real and fabricated reports of U.S. military heavy-handed tactics, cultural insensitivity, and alleged crimes, and repeated public insults by Rumsfeld and other U.S. officials that called the Sunnis "dead-enders" and "losers," helped trigger revenge and fuel the insurgency.

Adding to the volatility were the foreign fighters who came to Iraq from all over the Muslim world to fight against a common enemy. While some of these foreign fighters fought along Saddam loyalists at the outset of the guerrilla war, most came not as mercenaries for the Baath Party, but for their own religious and political interests. These Salafis sought to restore an Islamic Empire with Baghdad as its capital. With significant outside support, they used terrorism combined with a sophisticated propaganda effort to prevent Iraqi collaboration with the Coalition and coerce the Iraqi majority toward their political goals, while simultaneously eroding both international and domestic support for the United State's effort in Iraq. Conversely, the Shia, who originally took a defensive position against the Baath and Sunni attacks, became increasingly aggressive to prevent the Sunnis from destroying their new freedom and political autonomy. With help from Iran, Shia fundamentalists sought to increase their position in Iraq while also increasing Iranian influence in the region. Like the Wahhabists, the Shia fundamentalists hoped to instill an Islamic government, except in their image, and welcomed a devastating conflict, or apocalypse, that they believed would usher in the new caliphate.

These competing interests battled each other as they have for centuries, not only for dominance of Iraq, but for dominance in the Muslim world where Iraq was just one stage of a larger dramatic conflict. Because Baghdad is an important political and religious capital and where approximately one fifth of Iraq's 26 million people reside, it is a strategic target for Iraq's multiple factions and is where most of Iraq's fighting took place.[139] Whoever controlled Baghdad, each belligerent believed, controlled the Islamic Empire and the future of Islam. The wildcards in the struggle for Iraq were various rival factions vying for influence that were organized around various tribal, ethnic, economic, or political interests. Thus, the complex nature of hostilities in post-Saddam Iraq reflected a volatile mixture of ancient Arab culture, longstanding ethnic, religious, and ideological animosities, and Iraqi nationalism. However, while Iraq's sectarian violence affected many Iraqis, it did not embody a majority of Iraq's population or geography, and therefore defied any simple definition. This dynamic would characterize Anbar Province and the city of Fallujah in 2004.

The quick fall of Baghdad on April 19, 2003 quickly silenced media skepticism—but only for a while. Despite a few hasty "quagmire" conclusions in reports during the first six weeks of fighting, embedded reporters brought the public a rich, though sometimes disjointed, account of the campaign that brought down the Baath Party regime. However, the significant reduction of embedded journalists after major combat operations ended restricted the Western media's ability to cover the guerrilla war accurately and comprehensively. Given the special dangers and limited access to events in Iraq, those few Western journalists who remained reported from the safety of Baghdad's "Green Zone," focusing on the policies and efforts of U.S. diplomats and seldom covering U.S. troops in the field.[140] Reminiscent of Tet, journalists covered the same events, relied on rumor, hearsay, and gossip for information, and often compensated for a lack of details with impromptu analysis and predictions, which resulted in incomplete, inaccurate, and misleading stories that burred fact and fiction.[141] To compensate for their limitations, Western journalists became reliant on partisan Arab journalists or the partisan Arab media for material on events outside the Green Zone.[142] Thus, isolated from events outside their sphere, western journalists found themselves in their own fog of war. This phenomenon allowed the Arab media, primarily al-Jazeera, to retain its media dominance in Iraq, as Marc Lynch explains:

> The new Arab media arguably represented the single greatest strategic difference between 1991 [the Gulf War] and 2003...In

> 2003 the Americans proved unable to control the flow of information, images, or reporting from Iraq. Al-Jazeera, al-Arabia, and other Arab satellite stations reporting live from Iraq conveyed a picture of the war dramatically different from that emanating from the coalition, one that emphasized civilian suffering and American setbacks rather than bloodless and popular liberation.[143]

This not only supported the quagmire narrative, but also aided insurgent propaganda, which emboldened the enemy and fueled the insurgency.

Furthermore, reminiscent of President Johnson's pre-Tet success campaign, President Bush's "Mission Accomplished" proclamation before combat operations ended established a false sense of optimism. It encouraged the public to believe in a short war, which exacerbated the Vietnam Syndrome reporting that had emerged during the pre-war debates and initial Iraq campaign. Although the Coalition succeeded in quickly overthrowing Saddam, it never established full control over the population, leaving a security vacuum that regrouping Baathists, foreign fighters, and new militias quickly exploited. Ambassador Bremer's decision to abolish the Baath Party and disband its military coupled with heavy-handed and culturally insensitive tactics by some Coalition forces caused a ripple effect that fueled distain for and violence against the Coalition beyond Baghdad, which invited retribution that fueled the insurgency. This reality, coupled with Rumsfeld's insistence that no insurgency existed, the failure of U.S. forces to find special weapons in the weeks after Saddam's expulsion, and Joe Wilson's assertions that the Bush administration mislead the American public in his case for war, seemed to discredit the Bush Administration and validate the media's pre-war quagmire fears. Stories that emphasized death, destruction, and failure to control the crime and factional violence reflected the media's agenda setting and counter framing strategy.[144]

Thus, the quagmire narrative, that is, the assertion that the United States could not win, became the main media line following the significant reduction of embedded journalists in late April 2003, whereas positive news reflecting success and progress had a short life in the media.[145] Headlines, sound bites, and carefully selected and edited images conveyed the quagmire narrative, which was amplified in sheer volume of media outlets that shared material, while stories filled with opinion made assertions that were not accurate. The combined effects of al-Jazeera and new Arab media highly partisan reporting, few Western journalists in Iraq and their reliance on partisan Iraqi stringers, and the media's quagmire narrative and contention that the Bush administration mislead the American public, not only burred facts and fiction, altering perceptions of reality, but also revealed the nature of the wars of ideas behind the war in Iraq. All of these factors would lay the foundation for the Western media's inability to cover accurately events in 2004 Fallujah.

During hostilities, fours wars of ideas played out simultaneously as Western and Arab media outlets, each acting independently from the others, reported the war with varying degrees of objectivity and partisanship as belligerents sought to influence public opinion at all three levels of the war, strategic, operational, and tactical. First, at the strategic level, Iraq's emerging insurgent groups sought to erode international support for the war to break up the Coalition, to include eroding U.S. public support believing the United States could be convinced to abandon its efforts in Iraq. Second, also at the strategic level, some media outlets, as independent political actors themselves, attempted to assert themselves U.S. war policy by forging an early "quagmire" narrative or the war, that is, the assertion the United States could not win. Third, at the operational level, belligerents sought to influence both the mass Iraqi population and those of neighboring countries. While Iraq's emerging insurgent groups sought to inflame the population against the Coalition and recruit "resistance" fighters, the Coalition sought to "win the hearts and minds" of the population to bring peace and stability to Iraq in preparation for establishing a democratic government. Forth, at the tactical level, insurgents sought to provoke violence against the Coalition to deter local support, unravel the Coalition, and erode popular support. As Thomas Rid and Marc Hecker explain:

> Yet for all their conventional superiority, these forces soon discovered that they had two soft spots, one at home and one in the field. Both concern popular support. An insurgency first, is a competition for the trust and the support of the local civilian population. . . . The second vulnerability is domestic support.[146]

Although the United States began the war with an innovative embedding program, it did not have and effective strategic, operational, and tactic communication plan that either met the needs of the U.S. State Department or the U.S. military in Iraq or unified their efforts in post-Saddam Iraq. Instead, it continued to rely on the Western and Arab media outlets and a hastily assembled Iraqi Free Media network to communicate with the Iraqi population. Therefore, as a result of diminishing Western journalists, an active Arab media, and media savvy insurgents, the United States lost its information initiative.

CHAPTER SEVEN

THE MEDIA AND THE FIRST BATTLE FOR FALLUJAH

Iraq's insurgency did not begin in al-Anbar Province, but certain events coupled with pre-war conditions would quickly turn it into Iraq's most volatile region, threatening the security and stability of the whole nation in the post-Saddam period. Al-Anbar Province is the largest of Iraq's 18 provinces, with eight political districts, and it is dominated by Sunni Islam and ancient tribal culture. With the exception of the remote desert city of Rutbah, most its population is along the Western Euphrates River Valley, which includes the three key cities of al-Qaim on the Syrian border in the west, al-Anbar's capital ar-Ramadi in the east, and Fallujah on al-Anbar's eastern edge, with several notable towns and villages in between. Of the province's several tribes affiliated with the Dulaymi Confederation, the albu Mahal, albu Fahad, and albu Issa would play key roles in both Iraq's Sunni insurgency and its Awakening because of their relationship with these three key cities. With four official ports of entry, al-Anbar shares very porous borders with Syria, Jordan, and Saudi Arabia, and borders four other Iraqi provinces, and is where much of Iraq's imports and exports pass through. Anbar is where Saddam Hussein recruited much of his military's leadership and fiercest soldiers, and is where many retired Baath Party lived.[1]

Anbar's Arab tribes have a long and storied history in Iraqi affairs, and would play a major role in Iraq's growing post-Saddam insurgency. They survived for centuries under successive Muslim rulers, and maintained a degree of independence and autonomy under the Ottoman Empire because they were difficult to control. Tribes affiliated with the Dulaymi Confederation in the far west helped T. E. Lawrence fight the Ottomans in World War I, and they retained considerable status after the war. However, they also posed a problem for the British occupation during the British mandate period, and later they posed a problem for Baathist leaders until Saddam Hussein finally used a combination of patronage, bribery, intimidation, and interference to control the tribes, even removing true lineal sheikhs and appointing fake sheikhs.[2] However, Saddam Hussein found he needed the tribe to help fight the Iranians during the Iran-Iraq war, and many Anbari tribesmen not only answered his call to fight, but also became much of his fiercest soldiers. As a result, tribal status improved, and many continued to serve and rose to prominent positions in Iraq's military and Baath Party intelligence services.[3]

Mistrust and Misdeeds: Anbar's Sunni Insurgency

In the years before the Iraq War, U.S. intelligence operatives learned that al-Anbar's Sunni tribes were the key to gaining access to the both the province and Iraq. Although Saddam Hussein had recruited many of his best military leaders and soldiers from Anbar's tribes, his interference with tribal affairs had created enmity between many tribal leaders and the Baath Party regime. As a result of this enmity, some tribes had openly rebelled, and the suffered the harsh wrath of Baath Party justice. Following the Gulf War, many of these tribal leaders and Sunni expatriates living in Jordan were willing to help with U.S. intelligence operatives by providing intelligence, bringing intelligence and special operations forces into the country before the invasion, and helping prevent hostilities in al-Anbar Province during the invasion by convincing the population not to resist. These Iraqis included Ayad Allawi and Malik Abdul Karim al-Kharbit.[4] Most of these Sunni expatriates believed that they would remain in power after Hussein was expelled, because to not do so would upset the balance of power in the Middle East.[5]

During the Coalition's initial assault into Iraq, U.S. Special Forces largely bypassed al-Anbar's population centers and went on to and prevent Iraq's military from launching ballistic missiles and secure specific targets such as Haditha Dam to prevent Iraqi forces from flooding the Euphrates River basin and blocking the rapidly advancing Coalition forces from Baghdad.[6] As U.S. Special Forces attacked Iraqi targets in Anbar's desert they interdicted fleeing Baathists and key military members before they could flee into Syria. Aside from pockets of Fedayeen, they met virtually no resistance in al-Anbar. Four days after the collapse of the Baath regime in Baghdad, April 13, 2003, Anbar's leaders from Ramadi met with the Coalition forces to negotiate a peace treaty, and proposed that they would keep peace in the province not fight Coalition Forces if they out of the cities. Coalition Forces agreed, and for the next six months al-Anbar Province, with the exception of incidents in Fallujah, remained calm.[7]

Similar to the U.S. Marines in Southern Iraq, U.S. Army units operating in the area engaged tribal sheikhs, conducted census operations, provided humanitarian aid and reconstruction money, and began rebuilding the Iraqi Police in al-Anbar Province.[8] Like Iraq's Sunnis across Iraq, Anbar's Sunni's took a "wait and see" approach with the Coalition because they believed that, like the British did following World War I, it would support a new government that would leave the Sunnis in control, because not doing so would upset the balance of power in the Middle East between Shia Iran and the rest of the Sunni-dominated Middle East. However, not all Sunni's took this approach. After a Coalition bomb intended for Saddam Hussein killed 22 members of Malik Abdul Karim al-Kharbit's family, his family turned from being allies who helped the United Stated gain access Iraq to an insurgent intent on revenge.[9]

Importantly, Saddam Hussein had kept al-Anbar's borders open in the months before the war, allowing al-Qaeda and foreign fighters to enter and take residence in the province. His Fedayeen strategically placed many of these Salafi inspired foreign fighters around Iraq believing that they could be controlled. These borders remained open after the Coalition invasion, allowing foreign fighters sympathetic to foreign fighters to continue entering the country, finding safe havens with Baathists and Fedayeen. Before long, however, these foreign fighters began agitating al-Anbar's population, leading to demonstrations against Coalition's occupation and attacks on Coalition Forces. Small numbers of foreign fighters sought to bait coalition troops into firing into crowds to illicit hatred toward Coalition Forces and sympathy for Iraq's small "resistance," thereby driving a wedge between the Coalition and the population and undermining the Coalition's efforts to "win the hearts and minds" of Iraqis. In some cases, the tactic worked successfully.[10] However, the foreign Arabs soon proved to be incorrigible, and began to insert their will over Baathists and nationalists insurgent groups. This caused resistance to form against the foreign Arabs, including the "Eagle cell" in Fallujah; but this early opposition to al-Qaeda and the Salafis would prove to no match for the growing insurgency that continued to recruit from the large pool of emotionally charged and unemployed young men.[11]

At the same time, insurgent cells began attacking Coalition forces. In response, Coalition forces began entering the cities and in some cases responded with excessive force and in a culturally insensitive manner. Anbari leaders perceived this as a violation to their treaty, and many Anbaris began to question the Coalition's motives.[12] It also created enemies intent on revenge, which fueled a new cycle of violence. When Ambassador L. Paul Bremer abolished the Baath Party and disbanded Iraq's military, it not only left thousands of bureaucrats and soldiers out of work and without pensions, but removed the only force that could protect the province from foreign fighters.[13] To the Iraqis, debaathification meant "de-Sunnification," which fostered widespread resentment among a large segment of the population.[14] Importantly, the Bremer's Coalition Provisional Authority (CPA) abandoned efforts to work with the tribes, believing that "the tribes are a vestige of the past...they have no place in the new democratic Iraq."[15] In addition to alienating Anbar's population through Coalition heavy-handedness, debaathification, and disbanding Iraq's military, this act would be another critical mistake because in the absence of social structure that the Baath Party and the civil institutions that it controlled provided, Anbaris turned to their tribes an mosques for that structure and stability.[16] Adding to the friction, the

CPA prohibited many Coalition units from training police, and would not provided funding for weapons, equipment, and pay.[17]

Fallujah: The Epicenter of Iraq's Insurgency

Even before Saddam Hussein came to power, Iraqis considered Fallujah a dangerous and unfriendly place—a way station for merchants, smugglers, and thieves crossing the desert. Its location between Baghdad and both Syria and Jordan made it a crossroads for illicit trade and the Iraqi Baath Party maintained considerable commercial interests there. Tribal culture and Sunni Islam dominated Fallujah's dense population of 250,000 to 300,000 people.[*] Fallujah, nicknamed "City of Mosques," boasted seventy-two mosques and is the home of three Muslim colleges—making it a recognized center for militant Wahhabi fundamentalism.[18] The convergence of Arab tribal culture, crime, and Wahhabi Islam conspired to make Fallujah a rebellious, independent city, and a potential threat to Baath interests. For this reason, Saddam kept elements of his Republican Guard and Iranian Division, Mujahedeen El-Kalq, on the large cluster of bases outside the city. Adding to the city's volatility, Fallujans still harbored deep anti-West resentment from their rebellion against British occupation nearly a century earlier, exacerbated by an errant bomb during the 1991 Gulf War and a decade of UN sanctions. The convergence of fundamental Islam, Baath indoctrination, and Arab culture made Fallujah a microcosm of Iraq's guerrilla war and representative of a broader War on Terror. Most important, however, its proximity to Baghdad made it an ideal location for Baathists and foreign fighters to launch attacks on Baghdad following the absence of Baath Party control.

Following the Baath Party's fall from power, Fallujah's larger tribes began vying for control of the city's government, businesses, people, and crime.[19] While the tribal Sheiks, influential Baathists, and city elders held some power, the some of the Sunni Imams, or religious leaders, claimed a share of it for themselves, and used their abilities to influence large groups of followers.[20] Amid this factional climate, some groups began attacking and terrorizing their enemies, which invited retaliation and the full fury of vendetta and counter-vendetta custom, as Salafis began purging both Shiites and secular Iraqis.

When U.S. forces captured Fallujah following Baghdad's fall, Fallujans, like other Sunnis, immediately took to the streets in protest. Both leading Baathists, who had enjoyed paternalistic privilege and protection under Saddam, and Fallujan smugglers lost significant revenue as a consequence of the U.S. occupation.[21] On April 28, 2003, Saddam's birthday and less than

---

[*] Population estimates vary based on sources and how Fallujah's boundaries are defined. The same applies to the number of Mosques in the city, and whether personal Mosques are counted.

three weeks after his fall, Sunni Imams and Baathists organized a protest that resulted in a deadly clash between the U.S. soldiers and Fallujans. Although the soldiers maintained that guerrillas fired on them first, Fallujans circulated the story that Americans fired on unarmed civilians. These assertions incited more anti-American hatred and violence, and the cycle of violence grew until a formidable guerrilla opposition took shape.[22] A number of leading Baathists, former generals and officers who held key positions in Saddam's military, continued to fight, along with around 40,000 troops they once commanded.[23] This formed the core of the guerrilla army. Because of the absence of Western journalists, the Western media failed to portray events accurately, leaving the Arab media, in sympathy for or collaborating with Fallujah's guerrillas, to report events and shape public opinion.

Following the April 28, 2003 incident, clashes between Fallujans and U.S. forces became common. Fallujah's guerrillas used civilians to mask their attacks and movements, and, ignoring the laws of war, attacked U.S. troops among large crowds baiting careless soldiers to return fire. U.S. forces could no longer move through Fallujah without incident, and Western contractors and journalists, fearing for their safety, avoided Fallujah.[24] As clashes between U.S. soldiers and Fallujans became common, Sunni Imams, guerrilla leaders, and al-Jazeera attributed any incidents resulting in civilian casualties, regardless of who caused them, to U.S. forces. Soldiers responded forcefully to guerrilla attacks and succeeded in capturing or killing many Baathist generals and other guerrilla leaders, thereby allowing terrorist like al-Zarqawi to assert leadership of the guerrilla war. Insurgent leaders murdered Iraqis working for the Coalition for their "collaboration."[25] While the U.S. Army viewed its work a success, many Iraqis perceived the U.S. Army's tactics and use of force as both excessive and insensitive to their culture. Over the next eleven months, confrontations between U.S. forces and Fallujans would become more frequent and intense.[26] U.S. soldiers often remained on their forward operating bases (FOBs) and avoided the city. When soldiers did go into the city, they would typically drive through Fallujah quickly in armored humvees without dismounting. In one such case, CentCom commanding general, General John P. Abizaid visited Fallujah and was nearly assassinated there. Insurgents attacked Coalition convoys on the two main routes coming from Baghdad through Fallujah to Syria and Jordan, and initiated regular rocket and mortar attacks on U.S. checkpoints and bases.[27]

With most U.S. forces remaining on their FOBs, Iraqi nationalist groups grew in strength in Fallujah, so did various Salifi groups coming together under Abu Musab al-Zarqawi's al-Qaeda in Iraq. Fallujah, like other cities on Baghdad's periphery, would become a final staging point for foreign fighters coming into the country. Despite some cooperation toward a common enemy, these foreign fighters would soon begin to clash with Iraqi nationalists who resented both foreign intervention and the social restrictions the Salafis sought to impose on the population. With considerable financing from outside Iraq, the Salafis recruited operatives from Iraq's large pool of criminals and unemployed. Over the course of the year, and much like they were doing in Baghdad and other communities, the Salafi terrorists would murder leading Iraqi's who could oppose them, from Baathists, tribal sheikhs, and Iraqi police, to city officials and moderate, nationalists leaning Imams. Many, like Iraqi police, were told to go to the Mosques, confess their "sins," and repent by declaring they were no longer police. Those who did not were murdered. In some cases, the Salafi terrorists killed Fallujah's educated—doctors, teachers, and engineers.[28]

As one U.S. Army unit turned over the area of responsibility to another, U.S. Army units began moving into the cities and as these forces moved through the cities, they pointed their weapons at vehicles and people, and demanded the right away. Moreover, through their interaction with locals, soldier were insensitive to Arab and Muslim culture. Actions angered the population and fueled the insurgency, causing anti-Coalition violence to spill over to other parts of al-Anbar Province. From the Coalition Force's point-of-view, however, increasing anti-Coalition violence and improvised explosive device (IED) attacks on convoys contributed to Coalition units entering the cities.[29] By this time, however, Coalition commanders believed that al-Anbar Province was untamable, and provided relatively few troops and resources in hopes of containing the area until Coalition forces stabilized the remainder of Iraq. These complexities are important in understanding the events that follow.

The Absent Western Media

By the time the First Marine Expeditionary Force (I MEF) took over security and stability operations in al-Anbar Province in late March 2004, Fallujah had earned a worldwide reputation for danger and violence. U.S. Marines understood from post-Saddam experience the year before that the Army's "heavy-handed" approach had caused problems, so for this reason Major General James N. Mattis, the Commanding General of the First Marine Division, told his Marines to "knock on doors...not kick down the door and put a boot on a man's neck."[30] According to former Assistant Secretary of Defense and military historian Bing West, who was on hand in Iraq during this period working alongside embedded journalists, Mattis added "Do no harm" to the Division's motto "No Better Friend. No Worst Enemy."[31]

Marines integrated their assessment of the situation in al-Anbar province with almost a century of experience in guerrilla war and insurgencies—particularly the Crisis Action Platoon Program used in Vietnam where teams of Marines lived in local villages training local militias and building lasting relationships.[32] They also based their security and stability (SASO) strategy on the lesson learned the previous year following the liberation of Baghdad when Marines successfully conducted SASO operations in eastern Baghdad, and later in the seven provinces of Southern Iraq. Central to the Marines' strategy was to display restraint and work to win the hearts and minds of the Iraqi people, provide money to rebuild infrastructure and foster economic growth, and treat the Iraqis with dignity and respect while defeating the guerrillas. This would include aggressively engaging the population with a consistent message that Marines only wanted to defeat terrorists, that they were not there for long term occupation, and that they wanted to help them rebuild their country. It also included rebuilding Iraq's security forces and aggressively pursuing terrorist networks.[33]

They learned the previous year that Iraq's guerrillas hoped to draw the Marines into a fight that put the greatest number of civilians at risk while killing as many Americans as possible. Therefore, General Mattis wanted to ensure that the Marines under his charge took every precaution not to harm civilians and told his Marines, as paraphrased by Thomas Ricks, that "the Iraqis aren't your enemy, don't let the insurgents make you think that. The people are the prize."[34] Although Fallujah was significant, Marines believed that Ramadi, the capital of al-Anbar Province, not Fallujah, was the center of gravity for winning the population. For this reason they stationed the 1st Marine Division Headquarters there, while locating the I MEF headquarters on the cluster of base outside Fallujah.

By this time, however, nearly two-dozen journalists had been killed in Iraq since the Coalition invasion, and few western journalists traveled to Fallujah because to the danger and violence there.[35] Most reported from the safety of Baghdad or the U.S. Marine base outside the city, sharing rumor, hearsay, and gossip through what journalists Larry Kaplow described as "an active email grapevine."[36]Kaplow explains that during "trips out of town, we have started taking detours around known trouble spots. ...But now, like many of my colleagues, I will not leave Baghdad until things ease up."[37] *New York Times* reporter Ian Fisher, agreed, writing; "most of us have been locked down in Baghdad for months," and admitting reporters did not know whether the situation was getting better or worse.[38] This deficiency would not only have a profound effect on how the world saw events in the city, but also how it saw events in all of Iraq. However, some journalists such as James Lacey complained that while he sought to work through military channels to get information he military officials treated him poorly, and concluded the military is losing the media war is because of "a mind-boggling degree of ineptitude," adding "I still found virtually my every attempt to get information from public affairs officers (PAOs) to be akin to getting water from a stone."[39]

As Marines mirrored their counterparts with U.S. Army's 82d Airborne in preparation for the Relief-in-Place and Transfer of Authority (RIP-TOA), soldiers and Marines came in daily contact with Fallujah's insurgents and terrorists, which continued following the 26 March RIP-TOA. By this time, however, al-Qaeda supported terrorists had made large gains in other communities across al-Anbar Province, particularly in al-Anbar's capital Ramadi, and in al-Qaim on the border of Syria.

As Marines took over in al-Anbar, violence spiked as insurgents tested Marines. On March 31, 2004, just five days after I MEF assumed responsibility for the region, four agents from the Blackwater Security Consulting Company entered Fallujah without the permission or knowledge of U.S. Marine officials, and guerrillas murdered them in an ambush. Next, an inflamed mob dragged the bodies out of the vehicle and set them on fire. Later, Iraqis tore the charred bodies apart and drug them through the streets of Fallujah before hanging them on a bridge crossing the Euphrates. Al-Jazeera captured both the gruesome images and the sensational aspects of cheering crowds. Citing al-Jazeera as its source, the BBC reported "Iraqi Police Say Four Foreigners Killed In Al-Fallujah Attack - Al-Jazeera."[40] Since Western journalists could not report from Fallujah safely without the protection of U.S. troops, a small number of journalists lingered in the safety of Camp Fallujah, filing fragments of hearsay as a developing story without any real knowledge of what had transpired.[41] Sensational headlines like "Falluja becomes Iraq's Mogadishu: Iraqi mob kills four Americans, hangs their bodies up like slaughtered sheep," or "Americans Are Jolted By Gruesome Reminders Of the Day in Mogadishu," filled newspapers around the globe the following day.[42] Hasty reports accompanied these misleading headlines, followed by hasty analysis and predictions reflected in headlines such as "Time for U.S. to Cut and Run."[43] In the wars of ideas, these headlines emboldened insurgents while discouraging support for the Coalition.

Intelligence operatives quickly identified those responsible for the murders and I MEF was content with letting covert operations capture the culprits while continuing with its original security and stabilization plan. To the Marines, the Blackwater murder was simply just another of several such incidents involving Fallujah. In fact, the same day insurgents killed five soldiers traveling through Ramadi in a humvee in an explosion so enormous that little more than a tailgate and boot were found afterwards.[44] According to sheikh Aifan Sadun al-Issawi, he called a meeting with Fallujah's Imams and tribal leaders to cooperate with Coalition forces against the terrorists, however, al-Qaeda began killing these leaders and forcing others to flee.[45] However, the incident evoked public outrage, and to some higher in the command chain, the widely publicized murder and mutilation was the last straw in a long series of events. In a sweeping change of policy, CentCom overruled the Marines and ordered an attack.[46] "In Iraq," reports *New York Times* correspondent Jeffrey Gettleman, "Brig. Gen. Mark Kimmitt, deputy operations director for the occupation forces, said: 'We will respond. It's going to be deliberate, it will be precise and it will be overwhelming'."[47] In the war of ideas that would accompany the battle, this message had disastrous results in that it told the Sunnis that the Coalition's response was not only going to in retribution for the murders, but also be disproportionate to the mob action. As a result, Iraq's Sunnis quickly rallied to join their brothers in arms in Fallujah against to occupiers.

It is worth noting that as U.S. Marines prepared to assault Fallujah, the U.S. Army was similarly preparing to end the Shi'a uprising in eastern Baghdad and other Shi'a cities. Since Hussein's expulsion a year earlier, Iranian infiltration and support had fuelled fundamentalist cleric Muqtada al-Sadr's status and capability, allowing him and his Mahdi Army to emerge as a major insurgent force. Given the timing of the Shi'a uprising with the increase in violence in Western Iraq, cooperation between Shi'a and Sunni insurgent groups is not only possible, as some scholars and analysts contend, but probable because some of Iraq's tribes are spread across broad portions of Iraq and include both Shi'a and Sunni members.

In response to the sudden new change in policy, Major General Mattis sealed off the city to prevent guerrillas from escaping while still allowing Fallujah's residents to evacuate as Regimental Combat Team -1 prepared to assault the city with two available battalions. On the night of April 4, 2004, two U.S. Marine battalions accompanied by special forces, two battalions of Iraqi Civil Defense Corps, and a company from the 36th Iraqi Battalion, encircled the city and moved into blocking positions within the city.[48] By this time, Intelligence estimated that only 10-15% of the population remained, and believed as many 1,500 insurgents representing different insurgent groups operated out of as many as two-dozen safe houses.[49]

On 6 April, the battalions moved into the city to eliminate preplanned and high value targets, they slowly tightened the noose on the city while establishing stability and security for the citizens of Fallujah.[50] As U.S. Marines and soldiers began clearing the city in a house-to-house assault, they offered money to remaining non-combatants, as incentive to convince them to pack up their belongings and leave. Rules of engagement prohibited U.S. Marines from firing into crowds or buildings civilians occupied, though Marines understood the possibility of civilian causalities since the guerrillas fought from occupied buildings. Using observation posts on rooftops with high power optics and thermal sights coupled with unmanned aerial vehicles (UAVs) and U.S Air Force Boeing AC 130H/U Specter gunships circling overhead, U.S. Marines enjoyed clear visual images of the battle space and confidently took out insurgents and enemy strongholds confirmed by covert operatives with coordinated assaults and precision bombs.[51] Describing the precision targeting, Lieutenant General James. T. Conway, I MEF's commanding general, explains:

> We had AC-130's up at night and this was the first time that they [insurgents] had learned to deal with that weapon system. In one instance we had a radio call back, 'We've got 50 guys loitering around a road block in the middle of town, do we take them out?' We said yeah, take them out. Another instance of we had 40 or 50 come out of a mosque headed towards positions again, and an F-16 saw them. Again, we put a precision weapon in the middle of them and hit large numbers.[52]

Meanwhile, Sunni Imams in Fallujah and around the province used Friday sermons and continuous broadcasts from the loudspeakers on their minarets to incite the population with passionate emotional appeals to join the jihad against the Americans.[53] Al-Jazeera had a strong presence during the battle and dominated coverage. Through sensational accounts al-Jazeera's coverage made it look like U.S. forces trapped Fallujah's population in the city and massacred them, directly contradicting official reports and eyewitness accounts.[54] Often using recycled gory video footage and photographs, they broadcasted uncritically sensational accusations of coalition atrocities and that included reports that Marines were killing hundreds of women, children, and elderly, and also cited doctors at the Fallujah General Hospital, who supported their cause, to bolster their claims that hundreds of civilian casualties resulted from coalition attacks.[55] Marines did not dismiss the possibility of civilian casualties, but believed that the exaggerated casualty figures reported by al-Jazeera and picked up by the Western press were most likely guerrillas, or civilians killed in guerrilla attacks, factional fighting, or murdered as collaborators.[56] Few of al-Jazeera's reports made the English version of their web site, but those reports that did, such as "US: Fierce Falluja fighting recalls Vietnam" and "Fighting resumes in Falluja" provided sensational accounts that demonized "US occupation forces" while extolling insurgents as "Iraqi resistance fighters."[57] U.S. Marine Colonel Gary W. Anderson observed that:

> ...insurgents also made skillful use of the dead and wounded for propaganda purposes. A dead teenager who picked up a rocket propelled grenade at the imam's bidding could be stripped of his weapon once dead and displayed at the local hospital as a child victim of the Americans.[58]

Like the gruesome images of the Blackwater contractors just a week before, such staged events were common.

The effects of the Arab media combined with the insurgent's continuous calls from the mosque loudspeaker not only caused the insurgent ranks to swell with local sympathizers, but also influenced members of the Iraqi national guard battalions serving with Marines to defect. Importantly, al-Jazeera took the insurgent's messages far beyond Fallujah, and its coverage inflamed Anbaris across the province to join insurgent groups in solidarity with their brothers in Fallujah and attack Coalition forces across the province with improvised explosive devices, rocket propelled grenades, and small arms. As Marines battled insurgents in Fallujah, insurgents launched massive assaults on Marines in both Ramadi and Husaybah.[59]

With only one television crew representing all five major U.S. television networks, few Western journalists accompanied troops into the city.[60] Many Western journalists visiting the U.S. Marine base outside the city never seemed to grasp what they reported, providing simple factual errors, blatant distortions of events, and incomplete reports in the heat of media competition without looking back to provide corrections. Reminiscent of Vietnam, some Western journalists monitored al-Jazeera and cited them uncritically in articles such as one titled "Al-Jazeera Reports 52 Killed in US Bombing of Iraq's Al-Fallujah."[61] And characteristic of Vietnam Syndrome reporting, most journalists dismissed government reports that outlined the efforts to evacuate civilians and insisted that targets were well marked, instead preferring al-Jazeera's wrong assertion that U.S. forces used "cluster bombs" on civilian targets.[62] Based on this, articles like one titled "Massacre in Fallujah: Over 600 Dead, 1,000 Injured, 60,000 Refugees," began to appear in print and across the Internet.[63] Journalists also reported, without validation, false or exaggerated guerrilla claims that they shot down five U.S. helicopters and destroyed two U.S. tanks and five humvees.[64]

At one point during the battle, insurgents used the prominent minaret of the Abdul-Aziz al-Samarai mosque as a sniper position, wounding five Marines with a rocket-propelled grenade (RPG), and were effective in keeping others pinned down for several hours. Marines tried unsuccessfully to gain access to the formidable mosques compound or neutralize the enemy in the minaret with small arms. When a Hellfire missile failed to bring down the minaret, Marines dropped two 500-pound bombs along the mosque compound's wall, which breached the wall but left the mosques, minaret, and other buildings intact. Marines then rushed in and secured the mosque, but found only empty shell casings. The insurgents had fled amid the smoke and dust of the explosion. Unmanned aerial vehicles (UAVs) recorded the event, and not only confirmed that the only damage done in the bombing was to the mosques' compound wall, but also there were no people around the compound during the explosions.[65]

Keenly aware of the influence of insurgent propaganda, U.S. Marine Major Ben Connable watched the entire event and then tracked the media's reporting of the attack. He noted that soon afterward Associated Press reporter Abdul-Qader Saadi not only reported that Marines killed forty Iraqis gathered for prayer, but provided a colorful, fictional description of dead and wounded at "the scene."[66] Connable explains that while Marines prepared a rebuttal to AP report, "the story had taken on a life of its own," citing a BBC report titled "U.S. Bombards Mosques Complex," and a second AP report titled "US Bombs Fallujah Mosque; More Than 40 Worshippers Killed," which cited an "unnamed" that Marines later determined did not exist.[67] Connable observed how the erroneous first reports spread through the Internet and appeared on several blogs, which invited uninformed speculation and condemnation.[68] However, embedded *Los Angeles Times* reporter Tony Perry discredited first reports during an interview with PBS reporter Gwen, explaining:

> Yeah, I'm with the unit right now. The first reports are a little misleading. What happened here ... there are several mosques that have been used by the insurgents as places to either gather or strategize or even to fire at Marines. One particular mosque had 30 to 40 insurgents in it. They had snipers. They wounded five Marines. There were ambulances that drove up and the Marines let them come in to take the insurgent wounded away. But instead, people with RPGs, rocket-propelled grenades, jumped out of the ambulances and started fighting with the Marines. Ultimately, what the Marines did is call in air power. A helicopter dropped a hellfire missile and then an F-16 dropped a laser-guided bomb on the outside of the mosque, put a huge crater outside the mosque. There's sort of a plaza outside the mosque. And suddenly, the firing inside stopped. But when the Marines examined the mosque and went in and went door-to-door in the mosque and floor-to-floor, they found no bodies, nor did they find the kind of blood and guts one would presume if people had died.[69]

Like Peter Braestrup's astute observations on the problems with erroneous first reports during the 1968 Tet Offensive, Perry's candid account similarly underscores how erroneous first reports can manifest themselves in subsequent reports and editorials, creating twisted perceptions and a misleading conventional wisdom about events.

Again, reminiscent of Tet's first reports, Western journalists also quickly made narrow, inaccurate reports of the situation and provided unqualified analysis. Journalist Pam Belluck, provides just one example: "The barrage of violence that has seized Iraq over the last few days has jolted many Americans, causing deep anxiety and prompting many people to re-examine their positions on how the United States is handling the war."[70] Belluck offered no evidence to support the assertion. Moreover, editors did not challenge Belluck's unsubstantiated claim that U.S. forces were not handling the Fallujah situation correctly, releasing the story to the public without validation. Although attacks on convoys did face challenges on Iraq's highways leading in and out of Fallujah, headlines like "Troops in Iraq Strain to Hold Lines of Supply" were misleading and greatly exaggerated.[71]

Monitoring media reports, West asserts that the Western media's reports had "a spurious quality of its own, resulting in an erroneous certitude based on the sheer volume of repetition."[72] "Between April 6 and 13," he explains, "the CPA [Coalition Provisional Authority] documented thirty-four stories on Al Jazeera that hyped, misreported, or distorted battlefield events."[73] However, contrary to the reports of al-Jazeera and non-embedded Western journalists, West contends "the reports filed by Western journalists embedded with the Marines did not support the allegations of widespread, indiscriminate carnage."[74] A few exceptional journalists, such as *Los Angeles Times* correspondent Tony Perry, continued to provide accurate coverage of the battle in light of the erroneous reports of those not present or embedded with Marines. Of those few embedded reporters, Washington Post correspondent Rajiv Chandrasekaran later recalled:

> I was with a Marine battalion in the city. We were camped out in an abandoned soda pop factory. We went out on patrol with these guys. We ate the MREs with them. We were taking incoming fire in the evenings with them. We were in the same degree of danger as them. I was just blown away by how a bunch of eighteen-, nineteen-, twenty-year-old kids, from often very broken homes, inner cities, you name it, how they had come together and were exhibiting what I felt to be very great discipline. We all know there are exceptions to this, but by and large I was just really impressed by their ability to exercise restraint, to have such a disciplined chain of command.[75]

By April 8, insurgents not only provided more accurate small arms fire, but demonstrated better organization, cohesion, and tactics. It was clear that many of those Iraqis who had started the battle with Marines had switched sides. Meanwhile, Iraqis represented by a new Interim Iraqi Parliament poised to take over Iraq's administration that summer, believing al-Jazeera's accounts of Fallujah, demanded an end to the fighting.[76] By April 9, U.S. Marines had taken a third of the city and were within days of securing Fallujah and decisively defeating Fallujah's guerrilla forces when higher command ordered them to end their assault.[77] For the second time in two weeks, the United States changed its position, ordering a unilateral cease-fire based on misleading or sensationalized media coverage that caused public outrage. Fallujans and Jihadists alike proclaimed victory and celebrated in front of al Jazeera's cameras. It was evident that the decision to attack Fallujah had significant and immediate adverse consequences, which would set the tone for the next two years.

Contrasting the western and Arab media covering the battle, Lieutenant General Conway described the erroneous reporting:

> I don't think we ever saw the number of embeds in OIF II [Operation Iraqi Freedom II] that we saw in OIF I [Operation Iraqi Freedom I]. And by embeds by the pure definition of the term, we had some people that came and lived with us for a couple of days and did what the troops would probably classify as "a drive by shooting" and then left. Caused us to say, "hey either you are an embed or you are not." If you're just here to do a story there's a difference between calling yourself an embed. An embed lives with, sleeps with, gets to know the troops over an extended period of time. I don't think even you can reach that status in a three- or four- day period, which was some of what we were seeing.
>
> Our concern, though, wasn't so much with the US press as it was with the Arab press. That was where we come to understand that some of these folks, not all, but some of these folks have absolutely no journalistic integrity and they were not the least bit hesitant to virtually be the enemy combat camera. ...And these guys are only too happy to go interview the doctor at the hospital, who by the way, was probably one of the biggest insurgents in the town. But the credibility associated with the doctor at the hospital, 'who says,' was obvious. ...It taught us that these bastards cannot be trusted...[78]

Moreover, in describing another incident where al-Jazeera spend a day with one of his battalion commander's during the battle, Conway also explained that they fabricated the commander's comments to convey the battle had been fought to a stalemate, which wasn't true. According to Conway, "All they got right was his name and his hometown," and emphasized "that this whole IO [information operations] aspect of the fight was indeed important and very well understood by our adversary."[79]

According to Marc Lynch, "Al-Jazeera's reporting from the besieged city of Fallujah in April 2004 contradicted the coalition's narrative so graphically and dramatically that it determined the outcome of the battle."[80] A *New York Times* editorial titled "The Story Line in Iraq," quickly compared the sudden change in support for the war following the series of incidents in Fallujah to what happened in the Tet Offensive during Vietnam where the media portrayed America's victory as a defeat.[81] West concurs with the *Time's* Op-

Ed comparison, writing that "the initial impression, created by Al Jazeera, of massive civilian causalities became the accepted storyline about Fallujah."[82] Author and retired U.S. Army Lieutenant Colonel Ralph Peters described the contradiction that Marines witnessed between the media reports and the actual events during the Spring of 2004:

> In Iraq last month, I learned a great deal about the future of combat. By watching TV.
>
> During the initial fighting in Fallujah, I tuned in al-Jazeera and the BBC. At the same time, I was getting insider reports from the battlefield, from a U.S. military source on the scene and through Kurdish intelligence. I saw two different battles. The media weren't reporting. They were taking sides. With our enemies. And our enemies won. Because, under media assault, we lost our will to fight on.
>
> During the combat operations, al-Jazeera constantly aired trumped-up footage and insisted that U.S. Marines were destroying Fallujah and purposely targeting women and children, causing hundreds of innocent casualties as part of an American crusade against Arabs.
>
> It was entirely untrue. But the truth didn't matter. Al-Jazeera told a receptive audience what it wanted to believe. Oh, and the 'Arab CNN' immediately followed the Fallujah clips with video of Israeli 'atrocities.' Connecting the dots was easy for those nurtured on hatred.
>
> The Marines in Fallujah weren't beaten by the terrorists and insurgents, who were being eliminated effectively and accurately. They were beaten by al-Jazeera. By lies.[83]

Peters' candid observation underscores Lynch's contention that al-Jazeera is the single strategic difference in the battle of ideas accompanying the conflict.

Adding to the media's negative view of Fallujah were graphic pictures of prisoner abuses at Abu Ghraib by a small group of poorly trained, undisciplined, and under-supervised National Guard soldiers. CBS's Sixty-Minutes II first aired the photos on April 28, 2004, which were then reprinted in numerous publications over the following weeks.[84] Seymour Hersh followed the Abu Ghraib story with a series of articles in the *New Yorker* and industry leader *New York Times* that alleged the Bush Administration's culpability in the event. MSNBC military analyst Colonel Kenneth Allard

(U.S. Army retired) describes Abu Ghraib as "the antithesis of everything we had taught our [military intelligence] trainees.[85] Speaking to Marines about the incident, General Mattis commented, "They were undisciplined, sorry-ass excuses for soldiers. We will not cost America one ounce of its moral authority."[86] Though most in the military condemned the actions of the soldiers, many journalists portrayed Abu Ghraib as Iraq's My Lai Massacre in Vietnam where the misdeeds of a few came to reflect on the character of the entire U.S. military.[87] Moreover, reminiscent of My Lai in Vietnam, Abu Ghraib came to represent the media's abuse frame and would overshadow the U.S. effort thereafter.

However, the sensationalized Abu Ghraib event became the media line for Iraq following the first battle for Fallujah, with the photos appearing for weeks after the event. A ProQuest search found 635 articles on Abu Ghraib in the month following Hersh's story. As an MSNBC insider, Allard describes the media frenzy over Abu Ghraib as "Pandering to the worst impulses in journalism and profoundly shocking a large international audience, Abu Ghraib was undeniably sensational."[88] The damage to U.S. efforts in Iraq was significant as the continuous sensational news coverage of Abu Ghraib rallied support for Iraq's guerrillas and contributed to insurgent recruitment in Fallujah.[89] In addition to inciting animosity against U.S. forces, many Iraqis believed the media's sensational and continuous Abu Ghraib coverage "was a conspiracy to embarrass and dishonor the entire country."[90] "The sheiks and average citizens I met," Lieutenant Colonel R. Alan King reports, "begged me to stop the pictures."[91] Thus, before the U.S. government's investigation and case against those responsible played out, the media had tried and convicted the United States in print and on the airwaves. In Iraq, Iraqis perceived this event and its sensationalized coverage as an insult and humiliation that further fueled the insurgency. Recounting the damage of abu Ghraib and sensational media coverage, Major General Richard Natonski observed:

> We talked about Abu Gharib and what a stain it was on the reputation of the United States and the effect it had in the Muslim world from an IO perspective, one of the second or third order effects of the Abu Gharib prison scandal was the fact that many of the insurgents had fought in the city had been brainwashed by films and photographs of the Iraqi prisoners being maltreated by American soldiers and they were told that if you are captured this is what's going to happen to you. So they did not want to get captured. They wanted to fight to the death. And they did that. Some were on drugs…speed, amphetamines. Others had tourniquets around their arms and legs so that if they got shot they could continue to fight. But they literally fought to the death. So the fact that we had that scandal in Abu Ghraib

> made the resistance that much tougher when we had to fight in Fallujah.[92]

On the U.S. home front, the Abu Ghraib scandal became an example to criticize U.S. policy and involvement in Iraq.

Chapter Conclusion

Because the events surrounding the first Battle for Fallujah were historically significant and occurred in a clearly delimited area and time, they provide an extraordinary opportunity to study both media influence on public opinion and policy, particularly the influence of instantaneous coverage and global reach of 24/7 satellite television. It is also extremely valuable in studying and media performance under extreme stress amid a dangerous, complex, and rapidly evolving battlefield. More importantly, however, the first Battle for Fallujah clearly demonstrates how belligerents used the media to influence public opinion and policy toward their desired military and political goals at the strategic, operational, and tactical levels simultaneously in the wars of ideas that accompanied the battle.

During the battle for Fallujah, as during Tet, few Western journalists were on hand to record events because only a handful of journalists remained in Iraq after Coalition forces overthrew the Baath regime. Because of the dangers to Western journalists, most reported from the safety of Baghdad or the U.S. Marine base outside the city, sharing rumor, hearsay, and gossip. The few remaining Western journalists relied on partisan local Iraqi reporters, or "stringers," and Arab journalists, who either in sympathy for the guerrillas or fear of them would not give an accurate depiction of events in Fallujah because guerrillas threatened the lives of anyone who took a pro-Coalition position or portrayed them as other than freedom fighters.

Al-Jazeera not only dominated media coverage during the first battle for Fallujah, but provided material for the Western media. When the United States ended the first battle for Fallujah with a unilateral cease-fire, Fallujans and Jihadists alike proclaimed victory and celebrated in front of al-Jazeera's cameras. While the shortage of Western journalists was part of the problem, the U.S. government's reliance on the free media to tell its story caused it to lose the information initiative and allowed Fallujah's insurgents to make full use of sensational images and compelling sound bites to influence local, regional, and international public opinion and achieve their tactical and political goals, and thus win the battle of ideas that accompanied the Fallujah battle. Journalist and author Charles Jones sums up the U.S. government's failure in the war of ideas writing:

> The ballet of Fallujah is one of the prime examples of the cataclysmic failure of America's political and military leaders in understanding the importance of 24/7 news on the battlefield. It's a place where Al Qaeda in Iraq scored major propaganda victories, and it should serve as a cautionary tale of how not to take the bait when an enemy uses the media to goad you into a fight.[93]

In the war of ideas that accompanied the first Battle for Fallujah, al-Jazeera maximized the propaganda value, underscoring both Osama Bin Laden's and Saddam Hussein's assertion that the American public has no stomach to fight and is easily swayed by clever propaganda.[94] Furthermore, continuous sensational coverage and partisan political commentary of the Abu Ghraib prison abuses exacerbated the situation by aiding insurgent recruiting and propaganda efforts while dissuading support for the U.S. effort in Iraq. Therefore, journalists did not provide direct observation of Fallujah's mood and events. In the absence of facts, journalists added speculative commentary and unqualified analysis, while making unfounded assertions of the U.S. military effort—fabricating a perspective of the battle much different from actual events. Likewise, editors and producers then presented these reports to the public uncritically, giving the American public a very narrow and misleading view of what had transpired that again shaped perceptions of the situation. Like Tet, without all of the facts and details journalists' erroneous first reports led reporters to provide unqualified analysis and draw hasty, incorrect conclusions that amplified through various media outlets and helped set the tone for further coverage. Furthermore, the mass distribution of these news stories, through the satellite television, wire service, and the Internet, caused repetition that overshadowed good journalism or any counter-perspective.

Moreover, in both policy changes, the Western media rejected the government's arguments, presenting instead a distorted portrayal of events that adversely swayed public opinion and policy. Journalist Robert D. Kaplan describes the shortcomings of his peers and their reluctance to pursue facts. "Journalists with little knowledge of military history or tactics and with various agendas to peddle," he writes, "can go directly to lieutenants and sergeants, yet the very spokesmen of these soldiers and Marines themselves -- even through their aides -- seem unable to do so."[95] Moreover, as illustrated by the examples covered in this chapter, journalists cited no evidence or sources and drew wrong conclusions in haste and confusion. Lost in their own fog of war, reporters never seemed to grasp what they reported, providing simple factual errors, blatant distortions of events, and incomplete reports in the heat of media competition without looking back to provide corrections. Importantly, they never challenged al-Jazeera's "wild lies."[96]

Like Tet in 1968, events in 2004 Fallujah demonstrate that the media, especially the immediate, powerful images of satellite television, can influence decision makers far from the scene before events played out, and ultimately influence the outcome of historical events. It also demonstrates that the real war in Iraq, as in the War on Terror, is a war of ideas taking place through various, print, broadcast, and online media outlets. Coverage of the murder and mutilation of four American civilians forced the U.S. Marine Corps to abandon its original security and stability plan in Fallujah and take aggressive action against Fallujah's guerrillas and those responsible for the murders. Then, only two to three days short of securing Fallujah, the media's coverage generated another turn in policy, resulting in a unilateral cease-fire that not only delayed a decisive battle, but allowed guerrilla forces to build up and operate with impunity. Regarding it as a "lost year," Professor Thomas R Mockaitis concluded that between the toppling of Saddam Hussein and the unilateral cease-fire, the United States had very little to show for its first year in Iraq."[97]

Bing West compares the Western media's reporting of an event near Fallujah to that during Tet:

> As during Tet of 1968, the initial press stories focused on the American casualties. "12 Marines Killed" was the headline policy makers and politicians read on the morning of April 7. The press coverage of the Ramadi battle repeated the number of lives lost, and not that insurgents had failed in their planned offensive.

Even the influential newspaper giant *New York Times* compared the sudden change in support for the war following the series of incidents in Fallujah to what happened during the Tet Offensive, citing the waning support for the war stemming from discouraging news accounts.[98]

More importantly, however, the Coalition's harsh public statement conveying the disproportionate use of force in response to a perceived mob action followed by the decision to assault Fallujah went against everything the Coalition was had been telling the Sunnis; that it was there to help them and go home; and that it was not it was not there to occupy them. The action, along with the Coalitions harsh public statements, not only discredited the United States, but also served to validated the insurgent's message that the United States was not only there to occupy the country, but to seize it oil and resources as well. This widened the gap between the Coalition and the Sunni's of Iraq, and drove many of them to join insurgent groups, thereby exacerbating the cycle of violence across al-Anbar Province and Sunni Iraq. Therefore, in the wars of ideas that accompanied the battle for Fallujah, al-Qaeda, not the Coalition, won the battle for Iraqi's hearts and minds.

CHAPTER EIGHT

THE MEDIA AND THE SECOND BATTLE FOR FALLUJAH

Faced with few options following the unilateral cease-fire, U.S. Marines of First Marine Expeditionary Force (I MEF), sought to resolve the Fallujah stalemate with an Iraqi solution. They hastily created the Fallujah Brigade from former Iraqi soldiers led by former Republican Guard generals. Within days, the Fallujah Brigade moved into the city as the U.S. Marines pulled back to the city's edge where they kept Fallujah sealed off. Those U.S. Marine units that had come from across al-Anbar province returned to their original areas of operation. Meanwhile, ar-Ramadi, the capital of al-Anbar Province, became the new center of hostilities. Despite the cease-fire and the presence of the Fallujah Brigade, guerrillas fired on U.S. Marine checkpoints and convoys, ambushed convoys with improvised explosive devises (IEDs) and small-scale attacks, and fired rockets and mortars at Marine camps and outposts. Moreover, guerrillas continued to move in small bands, strengthening their positions and resupplying.[1] These insurgents often used children to move ammunition or weapons knowing the U.S. Marines would not fire on a child.[2] As attacks on Coalition and Iraqi forces continued over several weeks, the Fallujah Brigade could neither keep peace nor meet the terms of its agreement, and Fallujah quickly became a guerrilla stronghold.[3] Meanwhile, the wars of ideas continued at the tactical and operational level for the hearts and minds of Iraqis, as well as at the strategic level for both domestic U.S. and international support.

Fallujah's Insurgents Regroup

Amid the vacuum left by captured or killed Baathists, competing groups of Islamic fundamentalist and nationalists insurgents consolidated power in violent, murderous clashes for control of the city. Among those competing for power were the trio of Abu Musab al-Zarqawi, Sheik Abdullah Janabi, and Omar Hadid, who emerged as the most feared and most wanted terrorist leaders in Fallujah. Al-Zarqawi represented the foreign jihadists and established al-Qaeda's Iraq headquarters in Fallujah, and used the city as the base of his operations in Iraq. Arab journalist Zaki Chehab explains that "Zarqawi rose through the ranks of al-Qaeda and was honored by Osama bin

Laden with the title 'Emir of al-Qaeda in the Country of Two Rivers'."[4] Janabi was an outspoken tribal leader, influential businessman, a professor at the Islamic Institute in Fallujah, and a radical Salafi Imam of the Sa'ad Ibn Abi Waqqas Mosque.[5] His association with Zarqawi gave him power over competing tribes and Imams, and his local influence was effective in controlling Fallujah. He became Zarqawi's key lieutenant and a mouthpiece for al-Qaeda operations in Fallujah, but the media treated him as a spokesman for Fallujah's people.[6] Conversely, Omar Hadid played a distinctly different role. He was a common laborer and criminal who soon earned a reputation as a brutal killer.[7] According to Sheikh Aifan Sadun al-Issawi, Hadid was sadistic homosexual who raped and murdered children.[8]

With an abundance of funding, insurgent leaders recruited from Iraq's abundance of criminals and unemployed, including members of the Fallujah Brigade, and paid locals to provide intelligence and plant IEDs. They also continued to sponsor foreign fighters coming into the city and some of Fallujah's tribes and insurgent groups used the foreign fighters for their gain against competing tribes and groups for control of the city.[9] However, these foreign jihadists, mostly aligned with al-Zarqawi, proved they had their own agenda and could not be controlled. What is more, in accordance with Arab custom many locals welcomed these foreign Arabs into local homes, but as their welcome wore out the foreign fighters would take over the homes, keeping the family hostage or murdering them. Sometimes they raped wives, daughters, and boys at will, or sadistically tortured them to death.[10]

As al-Zarqawi and his affiliates competed for power and worked to control Fallujah through intimidation and terror, they murdered sheikhs, imams, and community leaders who held competing views as they consolidated power among Fallujah's factions.[11] Labeling them "collaborators," insurgents also intimidated and attacked member of the Iraqi police and Iraqi National Guard. They imposed strict Islamic Sharia law on Fallujah, imposed curfews, and banned alcohol, cigarettes, and pornography, along with western style haircuts or western style dress. They even took over local businesses and closed the pool halls in Fallujah. The jihadists patrolled the streets and intimidated everyone, including the remaining Fallujah Brigade and Iraqi police and national guard units, to enforce their authority. Importantly, while the Islamification of Fallujah continued, the Western press reported the changing situation incorrectly with misleading headlines like "The Re-Baathification of Falluja."[12] A resistance against al-Qaeda and the foreign Islamists began to form, but al-Qaeda succeeded in murdering the leaders of such movements along with other collaborators.[13]As the summer progressed, insurgent attacks on coalition forces increased as insurgent groups in Fallujah solidified. From Fallujah, al-Zarqawi worked to establish cells through Anbar and Iraq, and launched attacks against the Shia and Coalition in Baghdad and elsewhere. Through loose associations with Islamists and other insurgent groups, Zarqawi's agents assassinated government employees and bombed marketplaces, government buildings, police stations, international aid stations to coerce the population and make both democracy and cooperation with the United States unworkable. Moreover, his agents murdered Shia and bombed Shiite mosques with the goal of initiating a civil war and disrupting the transfer of authority from Bremer's CPA to the Interim Iraqi Parliament.[14] In Fallujah, Janabi and Hadid lured a respected Iraqi National Guard Officer, Lieutenant Colonel Suleiman, into a trap where they captured him, tried him in an illegal Sharia court, and then beat him beyond recognition and beheaded him.[15] Suleiman represented the interests of mainstream Iraqis, mediating between the Coalition and various Iraqi factions. Importantly, the Islamification of Fallujah kept residents from receiving millions in humanitarian assistance and reconstruction money, which caused resentment toward the foreign fighters.[16] Some Fallujans attempted to resist al-Qaeda, but they were either killed or forced to flee.

In addition to establishing terror cells, al-Zarqawi succeeded in creating effective media cells in a combined effort to influence Iraq's population and a larger world body. According to the Christian Science Monitor, al-Qaeda's "command of the Internet, their use of television, their release and timing of material calculated to be picked up and used by Arab and Western TV outlets and news agencies, indicates a high degree of planning and professionalism."[17] Illustrating this effort, al-Zarqawi's sensational execution of Nicholas Berg in May,* broadcasted on al-Jazeera and the web, were highly effective in underscoring the U.S. inability to secure Fallujah while contributing to al-Qaeda's prestige among sympathizers. This success not only helped erode and deter U.S. support, but also emboldened Iraq's insurgents.[18]

On June 28, 2004, Ambassador L. Paul Bremer III, transferred the Coalition Provisional Authority's control of Iraq to an Interim Iraqi government headed by expatriate Ayad Allawi and included a number of Shia leaders. Many Sunnis perceived the transfer of control of Iraq from the CPA to the Shia dominated Interim Iraq Government as another affront, which

---

* In a video created solely for propaganda, a frightened Berg sat on a chair wearing an orange jumpsuit. His wrists were bound. As directed by the terrorists, Berg briefly identified himself on camera. Then, he was seen sitting on the floor of the room facing the camera with five terrorist in masks behind him. One of them, believed to be al-Zarqawi, read a lengthy statement in Arabic. Then, when Zarqawi was finished, al-Zarqawi began to slit Nicholas Berg's throat with a dull blade letting him bleed and suffer while having the rest of his head slowly sawed off. As Berg struggled and pleaded for his life, terrorists grabbed Berg and forced him to the ground to hold him still for Zarqawi. The dull blade cut slowly, painfully. Berg screamed in terror—then he went silent. A moment later Zarqawi finally finished the job and held up Berg's head for the cameras.

confirmed their fears of "desunnification."[19] They responded with more sympathy and support for Iraq's growing Sunni insurgency.

U.S. Marines take a Different Approach

While most of the world focused on the amount of violence taking place, U.S. Marines continued to engage Iraqis in dialog in hopes of bringing peace and stability to both Fallujah and al-Anbar Province as a whole, believing that if they could get the economy going again the insurgency would end. In June, I Marine Expeditionary Group (I MEF), under the direction Lieutenant General James T. Conway, organized a business meeting in Bahrain with Anbar Province's leading sheikhs and prominent former regime figures, some of which were living in Jordan or Syria. Organized by Conway's senior Civil Affairs officers, reservist officers with experience in business and investments, I MEF flew Anbar's prominent leaders and businessmen to Bahrain to discuss economic opportunities for Anbar, such as finding investment for commercial enterprises, as a solution to the military standoff. All Marines present, including Lieutenant General Conway, wore suits in place of uniforms. During the meeting, a Japanese investment banker told the Anbaris:

> You can trust the Americans. When they say they'll work with you, they mean they'll work with you. They don't lie. They helped rebuild my country. They said they were going to rebuild the country after the war. No one believed them. They did. We expected them to occupy our country and take everything we own, and leave us destroyed, and they didn't, and now they're one of our best friends.[20]

Those Iraqis who had traveled to Bahrain during the 1960s before the Baath Regime restricted travel, were astounded by what they found in Bahrain, because between their visits Bahrain had been transformed from a small, impoverished third-world country, to a modern, wealthy, and thriving nation. Some wondered how Iraq had missed out.[21]

While the meeting itself did not yield any immediate solutions, the meeting opened the door to further U.S. Marine engagement with the Iraqis, and those Anbari leaders and businessmen who attended the meeting Bahrain began to realize Anbar Province's potential. Over the summer of 2004 there were other meetings and efforts. In August, senior I MEF officers met with Anbari sheikhs, former regime officials, and business leaders who dispensed with the usual customary pleasantries and presented them with a proposal suggesting that they could end the insurgency if the United States was willing to meet its lofty terms. They believed that they negotiated from the position of strength in that the U.S. military would never conduct another assault like Fallujah because the political repercussions were too great. While some U.S. Marines and officials embraced the idea believing they had found the key to reconciliation and stabilization in al-Anbar Province, senior U.S. government officials did not believe, based on intelligence assessments, the Anbaris in Jordan could deliver because they knew that so-called insurgent leaders did not have the influence they claimed to have. This did not end U.S. engagement efforts in Jordan with those legitimate al-Anbar tribal leaders who did have influence in the province.[22] This greatly contradicts the popular assertions of journalists David Rose and Mark Perry who took the side of the U.S. Marines and officials and Iraqis who claimed the insurgency could have ended in August 2004, and asserted that the Bush administration missed a great opportunity.[23]

The Road to a New Dawn

As the summer of 2004 progressed, many Fallujah residents began fleeing the city to escape al-Qaeda's oppression and Salafi infighting, believing that another major siege on Fallujah was inevitable.[24] By midsummer 2004, the Fallujah Brigade proved inept and almost completely dissolved. Both the mood of the Interim Iraq Government and the residents of Fallujah had changed dramatically. The Interim Iraqi government, which had taken over from Bremer in later June, conceded that the Fallujah Brigade had failed. In articles with titles such as "Iraq Won't Allow Falluja to Remain in Insurgent Control," the media began to describe the situation and the change in attitude that would bring another change in policy.[25] However, in the true spirit of Vietnam Syndrome reporting, the media spotlighted U.S. fatalities reaching 1,000. The influential *New York Times*' September 9, 2004 featured two stories titled "For 1,000 Troops, There Is No Going Home," and "A grim milestone: 1000 U.S. Dead," which were emulated by numerous newspapers across the nation, setting a pattern of reporting for the rest of the war.[26] Meanwhile, outside Fallujah, insurgent intimidation and violence increased. In July, insurgents kidnapped Provincial governor Abdul Karim Burghis al-Rawi's three sons and burned his residence, forcing him to not only resign, but also make and anti-American video.[27]

By August, U.S. Marines began preparing to finish what they had started in April, using precision munitions to destroy guerrilla positions and safe houses. Most targets were in the abandoned industrial area where the majority of guerrillas congregated and a large number of the attacks took place. However, al-Jazeera, followed by the Western press, reported that these U.S. bombing raids killed innocent civilians.[28] In response, Iraq Prime Minister Iyad Allawi closed al-Jazeera for a month because he feared its inflammatory and malicious coverage of Fallujah would fuel more violence and conflict.[29]

Meanwhile, in an-Najaf, Muqtada al-Sadr and his Iranian-backed Mahdi Army's renewed their campaign against Coalition forces, which significantly contributed to making August the most violent month since June 2003.[30] This not only invited a decisive Coalition response, in which U.S. Marines from I Marine Expeditionary Force (I MEF) and the 11th Marine Expeditionary Unit (11th MEU) participated, but also put actions on hold in Fallujah. Like Zarqawi's al-Qaeda operations, the Mahdi Militia began to produce it own videos in an increasingly more sophisticated propaganda efforts to accompany its insurgent campaign.[31]

Although hostilities continued to simmer in Fallujah over the summer, a similar uprising and increase in violence against Coalition Forces in Samarra drew Coalition attention. Marines would have to wait for the Coalition to clear Samarra of insurgents and reinstate Iraqi Government, Operation Baton Rouge, before they could decisively defeat Fallujah's terrorists and insurgents. The U.S. Army's 1st Infantry Division (1st ID) had been working with Iraqi Security Forces to shape the battle space in Samarra over the late summer, and had already began to isolate the city and take action against insurgents as Najaf cooled. Although this further delayed decisive action in Fallujah, it allowed I MEF to not only engage in detailed, deliberate planning, a luxury not given them the previous April, but also allowed them to shape the battlefield in significant ways.[32]

In the mean time, by the end of August fresh Marines arrived with new leadership. Lieutenant General John F. Sattler assumed command of I MEF, and Major General Richard F. Natonski assumed command of the 1st Marine Division.[33] Many of these newly arriving Marines had fought the previous year to remove Saddam Hussein. With the Samarra operation underway, I MEF officially began Phase I operations, preparation and shaping, on September 1, though no date for the decisive operation, dubbed Operation Phantom Fury, had been set.[34] In a continuation of what I MEF had been doing during the summer, covert operations worked continuously to gain actionable intelligence on the ground as UAVs monitored the city from above twenty-four hours a day, often catching guerrillas as they reinforced fighting positions, set mines, or loaded weapons into cars, homes, and mosques for the impending battle.[35] Marines systematically shaped the battlefield by taking out defensive positions, weapons caches, and guerrilla safe houses with artillery, mortars, and precision, laser guided bombs. While U.S. bombs took out strategic targets and guerrilla defenses, U.S. Marines tested the enemy's defenses and responses to attacks by conducting various maneuvers and feints. They noticed the guerrillas no longer assembled in small groups of six to twelve people like they had in April, but were more organized and attempted tactics using larger forces as trained professionals.[36] Guerrillas probed Marine positions and periodically attacked them with rocket propelled grenades and sniper fire.[37]

While the U.S. Marines did not attempt to mislead the media during these critical shaping operations, many journalists putting the pieces together began to speculate that the second battle for Fallujah was coming soon. When Marines launched a major feint in early September, a Marine public affairs officer, 1st Lieutenant Lyle Gilbert, told both Fox News and CNN that there was a significant operation taking place in Fallujah, but that was all he could say. He could not say that it was a feint or the launch of the anticipated second battle. Col Jenny Holbert, I MEF's Senior Public Affairs Officer, observed that initially Fox News and CNN reported the event at face value as intended, but that the story was expanded over time with speculation that by both stations that the second battle had began. When the media finally learned that the operation had been a feint, some journalists accused the Marines of co-opting the media for their information operations purposes. However, it was nothing the Marines had done, but simply the speculation of media pundits in the United States.[38]

In Samarra, insurgents responded to Coalition efforts to resecure the city an increase in attacks on Coalition Forces, forcing the 1st ID to move faster and more aggressively against Samarra's insurgents. On October 1, 2004 Coalition forces in Samarra launched a swift sweeping two-day attack through the city, which cleared the city and allowed reconstruction and information operations intended to foster stabilization and prevent the return of the insurgents. Once completed, Coalition commanders then focused on Fallujah, putting the Coalition's full support behind the Marines.[39]

Importantly, Coalition commanders in Baghdad, along with Marine Commanders in al-Anbar, sought to regain the information initiative during the shaping phase and maintain it throughout the impending battle.[40] During the first battle for Fallujah, largely due to the inadequate time for planning, the entire Coalition learned the hard way the side that presents the first truth, where it was really true or not, wins the battle of ideas. They understood that the enemy had no problems fabricating stories or staging events, but that no matter what the U.S. military had to preserve its credibility and be factual. What is more they knew that any report or photograph at the lowest tactical level could have strategic implications.[41] To overcome this, Coalition planners at Multinational Forces-Iraq began planning the information operations IO portion of the fight reverse the insurgent media dominance as they had with Samarra.[42] However, U.S. Marines did not wait for IO guidance from higher headquarters and began planning own IO campaign.[43] I MEF developed a comprehensive information operations campaign that had two key features. First, Marines wanted to defeat al-Qaeda's information campaign, which had successfully derailed the April battle. Despite taking care to confirm their targets and minimize collateral damage, Marines knew that Fallujah's insurgents would claim that the Coalition's precision attacks against high-value targets only killed innocent non-combatants. Marines began telling the public after each attack who they went after and why. Lieutenant General Sattler explains:

> ...after about a week of us getting the first shot out, their IO campaign fell apart. ...we started to drive a wedge between the terrorists and the local residents and then we drove a wedge between [Omar] Hadeed, one thug lord; [Abu Musab al-] Zarqawi another thug lord; and Janabi, another thug lord. So, each one of our themes was set to open the gap, and once the gap was open, it continued to pile into it. ...[44]

Additionally, Marines supported this Information effort with synchronized senior leader engagements, military diplomacy, and public diplomacy activities.[45]

Second, Marines hoped to regain the information initiative, establishing an accurate first truth, by ensuring that this time plenty of embedded reporters would be on hand when U.S. Marines moved on the city.[46] This included bringing Western journalists like Martha Raddatz closer the operations to see both the entire targeting process and the actual precision strikes on targets in Fallujah. This not only improved transparency, but also dispelled insurgent's accusations that Marines were indiscriminately bombing Fallujah.[47] What is more, I MEF's public affairs officer, Col Jenny Holbert, understood that a journalist's view of urban combat is limited to one city block at best, and that the impending battle would require as many journalists and combat correspondents as she could muster. On the eve of battle, she embedded 52 western journalists with combat units. Twenty more journalists arrived later.[48]

As the day of the Fallujah battle neared, information operations campaigns helped convince the city's residents to leave.[49] Military planners believed that only about five hundred of the two hundred-fifty thousand residents remained in the city, substantially lower than in April, and estimated 4,500 guerrillas in the city of Fallujah.[50] As it would turn out, many of those who remained did so to protect their homes and property, or were held hostage by al-Qaeda terrorists in the city. As the exodus of population moved out of the city, U.S. Marines and soldiers occupied checkpoints looking for fleeing insurgents and weapons.[51]

The Shadow of Abu Ghraib

As the war unfolded, an organized antiwar movement gained momentum. A number of actors, artists, and musicians began to apply their trades in ending the war and turned their focus on gaining support for Democratic candidates in the 2004 and 2006 U.S. elections, participating in movements such as *Rock the Vote*.[52] Meanwhile, Abu Ghraib remained in the news and forefront of the media's abuse theme throughout 2004, and its continuous sensational coverage inspired retaliation and an increase in attacks against Coalition forces.[53] Punctuating the Abu Ghraib abuse theme, just weeks before the 2004 U.S. presidential election, journalist Seymour Hersh's book, released *Chain of Command: The Road from 9/11 to Abu Ghraib*, largely a hasty and disjointed compellation of his articles. Despite his problematic use unnamed sources, Hersh was not only quick to condemn the Bush administration for what he alleged was its culpability in the abuses, but his loose political commentary openly propagated the abuse theme and quagmire narrative. Journalist Lila Rajiva also provided another hurried political polemic before the election, titled *The Language of Empire: Abu Ghraib and the American Media*. Rajiva claimed U.S. and Iraqi forces killed a thousand civilians during the first battle for Fallujah and asserted that the Abu Ghraib abuses were typical of the character and conduct of the entire U.S. military when she wrote: "Fallujah is one face of the American occupation in Iraq; Abu Ghraib is the other."[54] In addition to books, films, such as Michael Moore's controversial film *Fahrenheit 9-11*, also attempted to add legitimacy to the quagmire narrative told in the news summer before the 2004 presidential elections, yet provided powerful visual message that appealed to much larger audience.

Like the 1968 elections following the Tet Offensive, the quagmire narrative was a key political theme in the November 2004 U.S. presidential elections. Although Abu Ghraib and other criticisms of U.S. policy did not weigh enough on the U.S. public to affect the outcome of the presidential race as President George W. Bush was elected to a second term; it did result in the election of anti-war candidates such Barrack Obama to the U.S. Congress.[55]

Operation al-Fajr (New Dawn)

During October, I MEF and Coalition planners finalized coordination and details for the decisive operation in Fallujah, and determined that it had to be after the U.S. presidential elections yet early enough before the planned January 2005 Iraqi elections to secure and stabilize the city and let its citizens back in. Following the U.S. Presidential elections, both U.S. president George W. Bush and interim Iraqi Prime-Minister Ayad Allawi authorized Marines to secure Fallujah guaranteeing that this time there would be no stopping until U.S. Marines, soldiers, and Iraqi Security forces had taken back the city from insurgents. At Prime Minister Allawi's request, Operation Phantom Fury was renamed Operation New Dawn.[56]

As the combined U.S. Marine and Army assault force conducted its final preparations, so did the western media, which had its own ideas on covering the battle, and the various independent media outlets decided to pool their coverage. This meant that any photographs, video, or interviews taken during the battle by any one agency became the property of all.[57] This would be important because during the battle different media outlets would put their own spin on the same events, sometimes sparking controversy with hasty, unsubstantiated claims.

On the eve of battle, a 12,000 strong joint assault force consisting of six Marine battalions, three U.S. Army battalions, three Iraqi battalions, and one British battalion sealed off the city and positioned themselves for battle. On the night of 7 November 2004, a task force of the Marines, soldier, and Iraqi troops fought through IEDs and insurgent positions as they swiftly secured the peninsula on the western flank formed by the meandering Euphrates River, blocking the bridge into the city. This act was significant because it captured the hospital, which served as both a control and propaganda center for the insurgents. Marines also shut down all power to the city and used Electronic Warfare to cause a blackout, which prohibited insurgents from broadcasting any messages or posting anything to the Internet. Meanwhile, part of what Coalition commanders called Phase II, enhanced shaping, coordinated air strikes destroyed defensive positions, command centers, and other strategic targets. Guerrillas believed this operation was the main attack and the Mosques' loud speakers called the guerrillas to their designated positions, forcing the insurgents to stay awake through the night and the day of November 8.[58] However, despite the efforts to prevent insurgents from using the hospital, Iraqi special forces soldiers and their American mentors were surprised to see themselves on al-Jazeera television which was playing as they assaulted the hospital. As it turned out, an al-Jazeera reporter in the hospital used his cell phone to record video of the event and sent it to his producers, which underscores the speed in which Iraq's insurgents could get their message out.[59]

On the night of November 8, two U.S. Marine Regimental Combat Teams with Iraqi infantrymen supported by the Army's heavy armor assaulted on line from the north beginning Phase III, the long awaited decisive operations. In a classic application of hammer and anvil tactics, these "twin hammers" drove insurgents into the anvil the Army's Black Jack and Stryker Brigades created, which left the guerrillas nowhere to escape. As the U.S. Army's tanks led the way down booby trapped streets, U.S. Marines cleared Fallujah, district by district, neighborhood by neighborhood, house by house, and room by room.[60] In the streets, the guerrillas' cohesion eroded as they attempted to maneuver in such a way as to maintain a mobile defense, their tactics reminiscent of Chechen rebels or Taliban militiamen, whereas others preferred to make a "last-ditch, suicidal stand."[61]

Both Regimental Combat Teams reached the highway that ran down the center of the city from east to west, much earlier than expected. Instead of wheeling the assault force to the east as planned, a move intended to drive insurgents into the Euphrates River, Marine commanders decided to continue assaulting straight through. As they did, Marines and soldiers continued to meet a determined enemy. From holes dug into the floors of homes called "spider holes," or in rooms called "panic rooms," guerrillas waited inside homes for U.S. Marines to come to them, while others used civilians as human shields to cover their attack. They disappeared into tunnels to rearm and resupply themselves, and emerged from other homes. Wounded guerrillas often played dead, only to come alive and suddenly kill or wound U.S. Marines with grenades and hidden weapons. Guerrillas also scurried from building to building, rooftop to rooftop, often sneaking back into areas already cleared by U.S. Marines in an attempt to attack from behind. Iraqi soldiers and U.S. Marines occupied secured areas and killed guerrillas who managed to squeeze through. Most guerrillas did not surrender, but fought to the death, sometimes requiring several bullets to kill them. U.S. Marines and soldiers later discovered that many guerrillas ingested or injected methamphetamines, heroin, cocaine, or adrenaline, boosting their courage and giving them almost superhuman powers. Meanwhile, U.S. Marines and soldiers, working with U.S. and international relief agencies, provided humanitarian assistance and reconstruction activities while combat operations continued just blocks away.[62]

By the evening of 12 November, days ahead of schedule, the regimental combat teams had reached the southern edge of Fallujah where the twin hammers met the anvil of blocking forces on the southern edge of the city. For the next several weeks, Marines continued to clear and reclear the city, hunting insurgents who stubbornly evaded direct confrontation with Marines and soldiers. As they did, Marines discovered tunnels and safe houses, torture rooms, and Abu Musab al-Zarqawi's headquarters where he beheaded Nicholas Berg, Jack Hensley, Eugene Armstrong, Kenneth Bigley, Kim Sun-Il, and Shosei Koda in front of his cameras. Marines also discovered two mutilated bodies of Arabs who had been tortured to death, along with the corpse of a woman in the street, whose mutilated body revealed the same horrific fate. However, U.S. Marines rescued the taxi driver who had transported the two French journalists that Zarqawi's cell had earlier captured. He had been chained behind a safe and left to die.[63] According to Lieutenant General John F. Sattler, U.S. Marines discovered "629 weapons caches...enough to equip a good sized army."[64] In all, the second Battle for Fallujah paved the way for elections and allowed Coalition forces to concentrate on securing Iraq's borders and other volatile areas.[65]

Media and the Second Battle for Fallujah

Unlike the previous April, the Western media was present and closely followed the battle, telling a more complete mosaic of the fierce combat. However, the media preceded the battle with a gloomy forecast of mass casualties and destruction and the quagmire narrative that the United States could not win. In an article titled, "In Falluja's Ruins, Big Plans and a Risk of Chaos," these views not only carried on into the battle itself, but also after the battle in articles like "No Victory in Falluja."[66]

According to Holbert, western journalists performed admirably, providing an abundance of accurate "straight reporting." Due to the intense violence, there were two experienced photographers who asked to be taken out of the fight. Fallujah was in the media spotlight for about two weeks, but as Holbert observed, both Yasir Arafat's death (November 11, 2004) and Scott Peterson's murder verdict (November 12, 2004) began to take the media's attention off Fallujah. In the case of Arafat, western journalists actually began to leave Fallujah to cover his funeral. After the battle reporters left, a few returned to cover the elections.[67]

While accuracy improved compared to the earlier battle, some stories still reflected the insurgent's unsubstantiated claims that not only contradicted the U.S. military's accounts, but also those of the Western media. One such report by Dahr Jamail that made it into the world media asserted that:

> The real face of the 'success' of the U.S. military assault in Fallujah is now beginning to present itself. Thousands of families remain trapped inside Fallujah with no food, clean water or medical assistance.
>
> No one can say how many of the 1,200 'rebels' U.S. forces claim to have killed inside Fallujah are civilians, or whether the death toll is higher. Very few bodies of insurgents have been found.[68]

Although some civilians did remain behind to protect family property and many insurgents were buried in hasty graves, Jamial's claims of "trapped" civilians were greatly overstated and his allegation that few insurgent's bodies were found was wrong. Jamail's claims echoed throughout the Internet on website and blogs in countless titles such as "Fallujah's Massacre," asserting that U.S. forces used chemical weapons (white phosphorous) and committed numerous indiscriminate crimes against civilians, again asserting that large numbers of civilians remained trapped in the city.* During the battle, U.S.

* Google searches of "Fallujah massacre" produced more than 133,000 articles and 24,000 images, representing both battles for Fallujah.

forces did use white phosphorous in seemingly deserted areas as a smoke screen for the assault battalions. Days later, some mistook bodies blackened by decay as being burned by white phosphorous, but this was not the case. Holbert also observed that Chinese newspaper *Xinhua*, showed a front page photograph of a pile of fresh rubble with a red baby carriage on top and insinuated that a baby had died in a U.S. bombing in Fallujah. However, already knowing that the story was not true, she noted that the baby carriage was in pristine condition as if had just been taken from the store.[69]

What is more, not all journalists understood the character of the fight or the rules of engagement. Kevin Sites, an embedded journalist, reported one account of U.S. Marines discovering a seemingly wounded guerrilla in a mosque and in a split-second shooting him without knowing whether the man was really injured or had a weapon. Site's footage implied that it was an unjust killing; however, the military soon cleared the Marine's action as a just act given the enemy's tactics of playing dead to kill Marines.[70] Sites was obligated to give the video to the reporter pool, but held off doing so held off doing so for 18 hours so the Marines could do an investigation.[71] When he finally released the video to the pool, other Western and Arab news outlets released it without its full context and provided unqualified commentary that aided pro-insurgent, anti-American propaganda.[72] As it turned out, Sites was not with the Marines during their assault on the mosque, but joined the unit as it was cleaning up and therefore had no knowledge of had transpired to put the incident in context. Moreover, Sites failed to mention that the Marine had been shot through the cheek by an insurgent playing dead and had returned to fight with his buddies.[73] Nonetheless, in articles such as "The Falluja tragedy," the media tried the Marine and the U.S. military on the front page of the world's newspapers and on prime time Western television.[74] What is more, like many of the articles concerning Iraq, the headline of this report told a different story than what followed in the accompanying article, which casually used the event out of context to make a blanket assertion about U.S. involvement in Iraq as a whole. As illustrated in the story "Newsman Who Taped Marine Shooting Captive Keeps Silent," many in the media had trouble getting the facts of the story correct, incorrectly describing the insurgents in the mosque as "prisoners," and "insinuating they were all "Iraqis."[75] Commenting on the media's coverage of the second battle, *Christian Science Monitor* correspondent Dan Murphy observed "Probably the way Fallujah was leveled [in November 2004] was not as well reported or understood as it could have been. But press had great access to that story. They were there. They were banging away with the Marines, so they saw a lot."[76] Murphy also noted that there was less coverage as time went on, particularly at a refugee camp, explaining, "...the people who ran that refugee camp took to kidnapping foreign reporters who wanted to talk about the situations those families found themselves in. So that story got a lot less coverage as time went on because they were shooting the messenger."[77]

Chapter Conclusion

Operation New Dawn was really a continuation of the first battle, which was both instigated and prematurely ended because of the effect that sensational Arab media coverage, and reiterations of it in the Western press, had on influencing public opinion and ultimately military policy. In the second battle, military commanders had significantly more time to plan and prepare the battlefield for decisive operations. Importantly, they learned from both the previous battle and recent operations in Najaf and Samarra. This included regaining and maintaining the information initiative, which incorporated public information programs that coincided with military actions and operations in Fallujah, and facilitating active Western media coverage. Equally important, military commanders sought to gain the commitment and resolve of both U.S. and Iraqi political leaders. Its success marked a turning point in Iraq's guerrilla war, helping to stabilize Western Iraq, al-Anbar Province, and reducing the number of attacks on Baghdad.

The two battles for Fallujah in 2004 hold special historical significance because they not only represent significant events in a larger military conflict, but also demonstrated that war is as much a battle of ideas as it is a military conflict. The first battle for Fallujah poignantly illustrates how the U.S. military's inability to construct and information plan yielded the information initiative to the enemy and how the media's deficient and often erroneous coverage of the conflict in Iraq adversely influenced public opinion and policy. In Iraq, insurgents could respond to events in hours, by the time information was vetted through various channels could take more than a week. Compared to how fast U.S. political campaigns could respond events, usually within 18 hours, the U.S. information effort in Iraq was unacceptable. Therefore, gaining the information initiative first required thinking and responding with the first truth faster than the enemy.

The second battle for Fallujah, conversely, demonstrates the importance of public communication and information dominance in the war of ideas that accompanies military conflict, as well as the importance of having journalists close to events. Recognizing the insurgent's media advantage and its affect on world public opinion, Coalition Forces developed a communication campaign to support the military effort, which included ensuring journalists were present to provide richer, more balanced accounts of the second battle. Despite this effort, many media outlets still favored stories that carried the quagmire narrative that were skeptical of U.S. success. Together, these historically significant events, within a delimited area and time, provide an ideal case study for examining press performance in conflict.

Providing a counterfactual history is not the purpose of this study; however, the results arguably would have been different had U.S. Marines not been order to make a hasty assault on Fallujah in April and instead been allowed to continue with their original plan in the city. First, both the public proclamations by U.S. officials outlining the U.S. response, which Iraqis perceived as disproportionate, coupled with the assault on the city never would have fuelled animosity toward the coalition that undermined the Coalition's overall efforts. This included giving al-Jazeera material for Zarqawi's propaganda effort. When the policy makers decided to end the assault without eliminating the guerrillas and foreign fighters, they created a sanctuary for terrorists to attack Shiites and cause political instability and social unrest in Baghdad during a critical time. Though U.S. Marines and soldiers secured Fallujah eight months later, a considerable amount of damage already had been done not only to the U.S. efforts in Iraq, but to public support in the United States. Second, General Mattis' battalions would have remained along the Syrian border during a critical time when foreign fighters were coming to Zarqawi's aid. Third, the lives of Nicholas Berg and other Western hostages might have been spared.

Despite the two significant 2004 battles in Fallujah, Marines would continue their efforts to engage local Iraqis in dialog and finding non-military solutions to peace and security, as well as continuing to rebuild Iraqi Security Forces and defeating nationalists and al-Qaeda related terrorists in Iraq in 2005. Central to this was a consistent message that Marines were there to help them defeat terrorists and rebuild their country, and were not there for long-term occupation. As described in the next chapter, this message would begin to take root with a year as U.S. Marines aggressively pursued terrorists in other key population centers along the Western Euphrates River Valley between Baghdad and Syria.

CHAPTER NINE

WAR UNCOVERED: THE EFFECTS OF ABSENT REPORTERS

Following successful military operations in Samarra, Najaf, and Fallujah, Coalition Forces, in cooperation with the Interim Iraqi Government, turned their focus to providing safe, secure national Provincial elections that afforded all Iraqis the opportunity to vote in January 2005. Despite setbacks, however, surviving elements of nationalist insurgents and al-Qaeda consolidated elsewhere and launched attacks attempting to disrupt the historic January 2005 elections, as reflected in headlines such as "More bombs as Iraq Voting Nears."[1] Although these pre-election attacks were largely insignificant, other headlines, such as "Can Iraq's Election Be Saved?" and "The Calm Before The Storm," conveyed prevailing media skepticism that the elections would take place at all or be legitimate because of al-Qaeda's increased attacks and promise of violence to prevent the elections would cause low voter turnout.[2] It was clear that though Iraq's insurgents had continued loosing militarily in al-Anbar Province, they had not yet surrendered the war of ideas. Although a few articles like "Iraqis Provide Lesson in Courage" described the historic significance of the record turnout and Coalition-Iraqi success, such positive election news and optimism received short media life as news of violence quickly returned.[3] Numerous headlines, such as "Optimism After Iraq Election, But Views on War Remain," conveyed the media's attempt to downplay the event and reassert the quagmire narrative.[4] Such reporting demonstrated that the media was still an independent political actor in the wars of ideas.

The second Battle for Fallujah was devastating to the insurgency, scattering survivors like Abu Musab al-Zarqawi who fled before the battle actually began. Many found refuge in other al-Anbar Province cities along the Western Euphrates River Valley, and others in Sunni strongholds outside al-Anbar on Baghdad's periphery. With the Fallujah battle finally behind them, U.S. Marines returned to their original counterinsurgency plans for al-Anbar, delayed by nearly a year. Unfortunately, even fewer Western journalists would be there to record their efforts, and many of those who did would not be able to provide a comprehensive account of U.S. efforts there.

The Shrinking Western Media Presence

With the exceptions of media spikes during the second battle for Fallujah and subsequent Iraqi Provincial elections in January 2005, the number of Western journalists in Iraq continued to decline, especially the number of journalists who embedded with Coalition forces. Importantly, most Western journalists remained in Baghdad and focused on casualties and sectarian violence in Iraq's capital and often reported far from the events they reported on. Those who did embed with Coalition usually only embedded for short durations. Compared to the 600 embedded reporters covering the initial war, by 2005 there were only forty-eight embedded reporters, and by October 2006, only twenty-six embedded reporters remained, though a larger number of unilateral journalists continued to report from the seclusion of Baghdad's Green Zone.[5] Typical of the disproportion between unilateral and embedded reporters, for example, of CNN's two-dozen journalists in Iraq during the period only one embedded with U.S. forces.[6]

As a result, al-Anbar Province and U.S. efforts there received little coverage. While some journalists such as Michael Yon complained that the "ineptly managed" embed media system and difficulties in moving around contributed greatly to the inability of the press gaining access to the battlefield, danger remained the primary deterrent that kept journalists from reporting on the front lines.[7]

Such hazards had adverse consequences for journalism. According to journalists P. Mitchell Prothero, journalists feared for their lives and developed a "bunker mentality," preferring the safety of reporting from their hotels.[8] Many hotel bound journalists continued to monitor al-Jazeera and the Arab media for material. Ralph Peters contends this caused a "'herd' mentality," where "reporters gave more credence to the claims of terrorists and insurgents than military briefings.[9] In a manner similar to Peter Braestrup during Tet, embedded journalist Franklin Raff offers sharp criticism of this approach to journalism writing:

> Our journalist, 'on the line' in his cushy suite, scrambles to the balcony. He sees a puff of dust on the horizon, shivers in the cool night air and the intensity of the moment, and turns down CNN on the television. He e-mails his editor about these explosive developments and then, with a cool beer in hand, begins writing about a great and desperate war. Brothers in the crosshairs. A rag-tag insurrection, gaining momentum in dramatic increments. A few historical references. A scribbled, out-of-context comment overheard in the mess hall. A line or two from some radical imam, if a desirable translation can be found. Bingo: It's a front-page story.[10]

Like Tet, this not only mislead the public, but also became the basis of Iraq war mythology.

To compensate, Western media outlets used Arab journalists and local Iraqi reporters to report news or gather information, but this too was an imperfect solution.[11] While these Iraqi reporters could move around more freely than Westerners, those such as Khalid Hassan also became targets for insurgent groups who sought to control the narrative of Iraq and neutralize opposing voices.[12] For this reason, many Iraqi journalists remained anonymous and most did not carry notebooks or cameras to identify themselves as journalists for fear of being murdered or kidnapped.[13] Importantly, these Iraqi journalists lacked training, and subject to personal bias and insurgent coercion, often provided a partisan perspective that aided the insurgents' political aims.[14]

Other Arab journalists worked for insurgent groups, including al-Qaeda's sophisticated propaganda cells and helped to get the insurgent's messages out.[15] According to embedded reporters David Danelo and Andrew Lubin, these journalists often reported fabricated pro-guerrilla and anti-Coalition reports, which made their way into mainstream circulation.[16] Many provided sensational pictures and video that demonstrated cooperation with terrorists, which the Western media used uncritically.[17] Citing an incident where Marines clearly defeated an insurgent attack but what was reported in the western media as a victory for the insurgents, communication professor John Hughes observed:

> Their command of the Internet, their use of television, their release and timing of material calculated to be picked up and used by Arab and Western TV outlets and news agencies, indicates a high degree of planning and professionalism.[18]

The success of these insurgent propaganda efforts continued to have a profound effect on world opinion supporting the quagmire narrative. As senior al-Qaeda leader Ayman al-Zawahiri explained in a letter to Abu Musab al-Zarqawi, "We are in a battle, and more than half of this battle is taking place in the battlefield of the media. And that we are in a media battle in a race for the hearts and minds of our people."[19] Underscoring the wars of ideas that accompanied the conflict, both al-Zawahiri and al-Zarqawi understood that to defeat a superior power, al-Qaeda had to defeat its will to fight. Thus, al-Qaeda sought to combine sensational acts of terrorism with sensational media coverage to achieve al-Qaeda's political goals in Iraq—inciting a civil war, or at least the illusion of it, to cause a decline in U.S. national resolve and ultimately the withdrawal of U.S. forces.[20]

In a telling statement al-Qaeda operative Mohammad al-Janabi describes the great lengths al-Qaeda and other insurgent groups will go to maximize propaganda value in their use of coordinated terrorism to affect U.S. public opinion and policy, stating:

> I can assure you that we will start pressuring Bush in a new way at the same time he is facing pressures from the Democrats and the American people. And there will be no problem to sacrifice 10 soldiers in order to abduct a single American soldier and get him on television screens begging for us to release him.[21]

Al-Janabi refers to an actual abduction of U.S. soldiers, described in the article titled "5 Die in Ambush of U.S. Patrol in Iraq: Massive Search Launched for 3 Missing After 'Coordinated' Attack'."[22]

However, it was not just partisan Arab and Iraqi stringers that contributed to advancing the insurgents view, but interpreters who interfaced with between Western journalists and their Iraqi sources. While the ability of the interpreter to accurately translate English into Arabic and Arabic into English posed considerable accuracy problems, Foreign Area Officers trained in Arabic often observed that some interpreters injected their own opinions and beliefs in translating interviews between western journalist and Iraqi subjects, which gave journalists an inaccurate portrayal of the conversation. In one instance during an important press conference, an interpreter provided journalists a significantly different account of what an Iraqi subject said, reflecting more the interpreter's views than the subject's.[23] Moreover, Marines also discovered that some interpreters were agents for insurgent groups.*

U.S. Marines Return to Counterinsurgency

Despite suppressing the democratic process in al-Anbar during the January 2005 elections, the nationwide success of the elections meant a further loss of power and prestige for Anbaris. Al-Anbar's insurgent groups responded with vengeful attacks on Coalition forces and the newly forming Iraqi government because it did not give the Sunnis fair representation in government.[24] At the same time, al-Anbar's tribes, insurgent groups, and other competing interests continued in their attempts to fill the power vacuum left by the absence of the Baath Regime. As they competed for business, power, and influence, they frequently murdered rivals under the guise of having collaborated with the Americans, and often conveniently blamed the Americans for the murders.[25] Sometimes they gave Coalition Forces the names of their rivals as insurgents to shift suspicion and blame, or

* The author uncovered these problems while interviewing Iraqis and Marines in Ramadi, Iraq in 2009.

to have their rivals arrested.[26] To U.S. Marines and soldiers, such competition and behavior between insurgent groups muddled the lines between friend and enemy.

Meanwhile, expelled from Fallujah, al-Qaeda began to reorganize and move into other cities along the Euphrates River Valley, absorbing the foreign fighters who continued to come into the province from Jordan, Syria, and Saudi Arabia. Still seen as allied against a common enemy, these foreign fighters often found hospitality in local homes according to Arab custom. As they did in the previous year in Fallujah, al-Qaeda recruited agents from the abundance of local criminals and unemployed in the province, paying them handsomely, and paid locals to provide intelligence on locals collaborating with the Coalition and to plant IEDs (improvised explosive devices). Although most of Anbar's military aged men had some form of military training, al-Qaeda's experienced foreign fighters provided leadership, money, and training.[27] According to insurgency expert David Kilcullen, key al-Qaeda operatives married into prominent tribes "creating a bond with the community, exploiting kinship-based alliances, and so "embedding" the AQ network into the society. Over time, this makes AQ part of the social landscape, allows them to manipulate local people and makes it harder for outsiders to pry the network apart from the population."[28] In some cases, al-Qaeda agents forced Iraqi couples to divorce so that they could marry the women of their choice.

As al-Qaeda grew, Ramadi became the new epicenter of the insurgency. They imposed Sharia, Islamic, law on the population, which included imposing strict codes on clothing and hairstyles, and banning alcohol, cigarettes, and pornography, while establishing Sharia courts to settle disputes and judge the enemies of Islam.[29] Meanwhile, al-Qaeda's agents took over hospitals, gas stations, and local businesses, and even attempted to control the extortion and smuggling operations of the local tribes. In doing so, they often disguised themselves as Iraqi police or soldiers and established false checkpoints on highways and roads to murder, extort money, and hijack shipments of products heading to Baghdad—often murdering drivers and passengers under the guise of being collaborator, or a Shi'a.[30] Even al-Jazeera reported these atrocities, describing one incident:

> Fighters have executed 15 Iraqis after ambushing their vehicle on a road north of the city of Falluja, police said. The armed men ordered the passengers out of the vehicle and lined them up before shooting them in daylight on Sunday afternoon, police on Monday quoted witnesses as saying.[31]

Such incidents were regular occurrences in al-Anbar Province.

Hoping to instill mass compliance and subservience through fear, al-Qaeda publicly beat and humiliated people who did not conform to their restrictions on clothing and behavior, such as those they caught smoking and women who did not cover. At the same time, they attempted to consolidate and control nationalist insurgent groups through murder and intimidation. They also engaged in public torture and beheadings, and murdered anyone who resisted or who had been working with Americans. This included murdering entire families, or torturing children to death in front of their parents to send the intended message or coerce people to carryout suicide attacks. They targeted authority figures such as the local police, sheikhs, or Imams who were not willing to follow them, along with the region's educated, such as doctors, teachers, and technocrats, to eliminate opposition. This forced those with means to flee the city to avoid persecution.[32] Al-Jazeera continued reporting such events in stories like "Corpses of slain Iraqi soldiers found" and "Iraqi troops find headless corpses."[33] In articles like "Many die in Samarra, Ramadi attacks," al-Jazeera reported how insurgents targeted Iraqi police and soldiers.[34] They even held hostage or murdered their host families as they took over their homes to use as safe houses. Many of these insurgents were not driven by ideology, but were simply criminals who were given wide latitude in their association with al-Qaeda to victimize the population. In doing so, they raped, robbed, and murdered at will.[35]

As al-Qaeda terrorized the population, they not only violated Islam's tenants to not attack women and children, but also prevented families from collecting the bodies of those murdered for proper burial.[36] These terrible acts, coupled with its infringement on local business, crime, and other self-interests, put al-Qaeda at odds with other insurgent groups and began to cause resentment and organized resistance against them.[37] In the al-Qaim region, local tribes had operated independently for centuries, and even under the Baath Party regime controlled the borders and the smuggling trade. Al-Qaeda's infringement on tribal business coupled with the atrocities they committed through their murder and intimidation caused residents in the border region to openly revolt. [38] Tribal leaders formed the Hamza Battalion to defend against al-Qaeda's violence and intrusion.[39] However, as they did in Fallujah, al-Qaeda met those who resisted their efforts with brutal force, and continued to murder those collaborating with either the Coalition or the new Iraqi government.[40] Peter J. Munson acutely described the situation, writing:

> ...in addition to al-Qaeda's quest for domination in Anbar, generated a deadly mix of violence driven by greed, ambition, and vengeance that burned on behind the veil of the insurgency. Beyond the vague dreams of an Islamic caliphate, many al-Qaeda foot soldiers were drawn from a peasantry that targeted land-owning sheikhs and educated classes that had oppressed them

> for ages. Sheikhs eager to protect themselves and their tribes' lucrative enterprises had little choice but to unite their tribesmen and ally themselves with their recent enemy, the Coalition, against the greater threat to their existence.[41]

Meanwhile, with the battle in Fallujah and provincial elections behind them, Marines continued to rebuild Fallujah while finally turning their focus outward and returning to their original counterinsurgency strategy for al-Anbar Province. With limited time before turning the area over to II Marine Expeditionary Force, Forward (II MEF), however, the core of I Marine Expeditionary Unit's (I MEF's) counterinsurgency focused on increasing security and disrupting insurgent forces while masking the relief-in-place and transfer-of-authority with II MEF.[*] In February, I MEF's Marines and Iraqi security forces conducted major operations in the Ramadi, Hit, Baghdadi, and Haditha to achieve these aims. Complementing the Marine's overt actions to neutralize insurgents, special operations worked diligently to identify and eliminate insurgent leadership through covert operations.[42]

After assuming control of the Province, II MEF Forces under Lieutenant General Stephen Johnson then began to build on the counterinsurgency foundation left by I MEF. First, they continued operations in the Western Euphrates River Valley to root out nationalists insurgent groups and al-Qaeda related terrorists' cells; and second, they began rebuilding the new Iraqi Army and the Iraqi police, which included the highway patrol, border enforcement units, and special police. In addition to pursuing security and rebuilding Iraqi security forces, II MEF initiated renewed efforts to promote local and provincial governance, foster economic opportunities, and cultivate cooperation and reconciliation through better communication with Anbaris. These five lines of operation all worked toward the goal of facilitating successful democratic elections in the October referendum and December national elections.[43] Like I MEF, two U.S. Marine Regimental Combat Teams (RCTs) would oversee the east and west areas of operation, and a U.S. Army Brigade Combat Team (BCT) with Marine Battalions and attachments would oversee the greater Ramadi area.[44] However, the heavy focus on aggressive combat operations would detract from essential non-combat engagement and influence operations.

Before II MEF could execute its campaign plan, however, insurgents launched another massive assault on the U.S. Marine garrison in Husaybah in an effort to overrun and eliminate U.S. presence, nearly a year after the first

---

[*] U.S. Marines would no longer have a three-star (Lietenant General) presence after I MEF left. Therefore, the assistant II MEF commanding general would be the senior Marine in al-Anbar and his command was designated "forward," indicating that it was not the full MEF. At the same time, the Marine MEF were redesignated "Multinational Forces-West."

major attack, but they were repelled after almost 24 hours of fighting.[45] At the same time, al-Qaeda responded to resistance in the Husaybah-al-Qaim region by massing its forces and attacking the abu Mahal Tribe, one the of the area's largest and most prominent tribes, to eliminate resistance. During a series of massive assaults, the tribe was in danger of being overrun and defeated. However, through connections made a year before in Bahrain and Jordan, tribal leaders called U.S. Marines for help. Marines quickly responded with Operation Matador and in a lengthy pitched battle succeeded in helping save the tribes and population around al-Qaim, but this did not cement relations with U.S. forces as they returned to their forward operating bases.[46]

Marines then followed up with a series of major operations aimed at driving insurgents out of population centers along the Western Euphrates River Valley, regaining control of the borders, and setting conditions for the Iraqi people to vote in the upcoming elections.[47] Meanwhile, to counter al-Qaeda's efforts to control Ramadi and reassert themselves in Fallujah, Marines also conducted major operations in and around Ramadi and greater Fallujah to eliminate insurgent sanctuaries as special operations units and other U.S. government agencies also worked throughout the province targeting insurgent cells and leadership.[48] Nonetheless, al-Anbar's insurgent groups fiercely resisted and waged pitched battles for hegemony over control of Anbar's population centers. In Ramadi, al-Qaeda sought to make the city their new base of operations and resolved to control the city despite U.S. efforts to expel it.

In June, al-Qaeda related insurgents launched a series of brazen attacks on U.S. forces in Ramadi and succeeded in kidnapping al-Anbar's governor, Raja Nawaf Mahalawi.[49] Mahalawi was the forth Provincial governor since U.S. Marines gained control of the province after insurgents drove his predecessors from office. Coalition Forces in Ramadi located the house in which Mahalawi was kept, but after killing the governor's kidnappers they found that he had been killed.[50] After Mahalawi's kidnapping and murder, al-Qaeda repeatedly attempted to murder his replacement, governor Mamoon Sami Rashid al-Awani and other members of al-Anbar's governing council while also continuing to murder or intimidate anyone perceived to be working with U.S. forces. U.S. Marines protecting the Provincial Government Center repelled daily assaults while enduring daily mortar and rocket attacks.[51]

Two important issues are worth noting. First, like its predecessor, II MEF had inadequate U.S. and Iraqi forces to both secure and hold the cities. This meant that Marines and Iraqi security forces could clear areas of insurgents, but would eventually have to move on. Secondly, General George W. Casey, Jr., commander of Multinational Forces - Iraq, believed that U.S. presence in the cities caused resentment and the insurgency and required that U.S. forces withdraw from the cities and largely remain on their bases. [52] This was a stark departure from I MEF which had sought to defeat the insurgency and "win hearts and minds" through active patrolling and engagement backed with humanitarian aid and money for reconstruction.[53] Therefore, once Marines and Iraqi security forces left an area they cleared, insurgent groups reinfiltrated the cities and reasserted control of the population, and continued to kill those they perceived to have worked with Americans. [54] As the numbers of trained and equipped Iraqi police and soldiers increased so did the ability for Marines to clear and hold the population centers.

Over the summer, al-Qaeda succeeded in forcing the cooperation of other tribes in the al-Qaim region and turning them against the abu Mahal. Marines again responded with Operation Iron Fist, intended to eradicate insurgents, clear routes, establish battle positions, and distract insurgents while Marines assembled for larger operation in the Haditha, Haqlaniyah, and Barwanah area.[55] Afterward, Marines stayed in the area and continued to partner with the abu Mahal Tribe to provide security and stability to the region, communicating that they were there to help them and were not for long-term occupation. Importantly, they brought humanitarian aid and money for reconstruction and economic improvements, which opened the door to further engagement and cooperation.[56]

By the fall of 2005, despite the shortage of U.S. and Iraqi forces, II MEF and special operations forces had began to make considerable gains in capturing or killing insurgent leadership. Nonetheless, as major operations against al-Qaeda continued to drive insurgents out of population centers elsewhere along the Western Euphrates River Valley, Marines implemented Operation Liberty Express, a product of extensive planning and coordination, to facilitate secure and successful October and December elections.[57] Although U.S. Marines and soldiers working with the Iraqi Army had undertaken a series of operations in Ramadi to eliminate al-Qaeda in the city, al-Qaeda remained a determined enemy that was difficult to dislodge. However, with the exception of Ramadi, al-Qaeda's efforts did not discourage wide voter turnout as 200,000 Anbaris voted.[58]

In al-Qaim, cooperation with abu Mahal Tribe led to the establishment of the Desert Protectors, a local anti-al-Qaeda unit that assisted in identifying al-Qaeda insurgents in the area.[59] Enabled by this cooperation, combined U.S. Marines with U.S. Army and Iraqi soldiers launched the largest offensive since the second Battle for Fallujah in November, Operation Steel Curtain, in Husaybah, Karabilah, and Ubaydi along the Syrian border.[60] This helped expel al-Qaeda from the area and reestablish the border under Iraqi control. [61]

Recognizing that al-Anbar's Sunnis were increasingly embracing democratic representation and joining the Iraqi Army and police, al-Qaeda increased its murder and intimidation campaign in Ramadi. Three days after the election, al-Qaeda succeed in killing Talib al-Dulaimi, Deputy Governor of the Anbar province, and his bodyguard in Ramadi.[62] Ramadi's tribal and political leaders found themselves in a difficult predicament. To the Marines, the success of the October 15 Iraqi Referendum elections represented success along all lines of operation and validated their campaign plan.[63] However, to Anbar leaders in and around Ramadi the substantial voter turnout meant that they not only faced extinction or complete loss of prestige and power at the hands of al-Qaeda, but also the threat of being left behind by the democratic process, which meant they would be what they perceived as the Iranian controlled Shia government. They also recognized that the Coalition's successful military operations against al-Qaeda showed U.S. strength and resolve while hurting al-Qaeda and helping secure Anbaris. Moreover, the Coalition's consistent message that it sought to work in cooperation with the Iraqis to provide peace and stability and did not want to be a long-term occupation force had struck a chord, and some Anbar leaders were willing to listen.[64]

With this realization, several sheikhs and notables around Ramadi, some of which were insurgent leaders, formed an organization to oppose al-Qaeda called the Anbar People's Committee and then approached the Coalition to discuss ending the violence.[65] These leaders held a series of meetings in Fallujah with Coalition Forces and representatives from the Iraqi government, and were also attended by religious leaders, former Iraqi military officers, other sheikhs, and many ordinary Iraqis. These meetings spawned new cooperation between Anbar's tribal leader and notables, many of which had been insurgent leaders. As a result of this new cooperation, these sheikhs went back to their tribes and encouraged their people to vote and join the Iraqi police and Army, and the influence of the sheikhs was soon apparent. Recruitment into the Iraqi Army and police increased, and in the December 15 National elections 500,000 Anbaris voted. Importantly, this success opened the door to further engagement, governance mentoring efforts at both the provincial and local levels, and allowed economic and reconstruction efforts.[66] Furthermore, Marines in Ramadi were ready to get back among the population.[67]

Though still critical of U.S. involvement, al-Jazeera reported the sudden changes throughout Ramadi in late 2005. In a report describing a turn against al-Qaeda, al-Jazeera reported:

> Iraqi and US forces have been witnessing increasing signs of citizens tipping-off al-Qaida members within Anbar governorate, which used to be al-Qaida's safe haven for the past 31 months. US troops detained a senior al-Qaida operative in Iraq on December 9 with the help of local citizens in Ramadi....[68]

In describing Sunnis efforts to participate in the December 2005 elections, al-Jazeera reported:

> In a move that would have been inconceivable only months earlier, former members of Saddam Hussein's Baath party are urging Sunnis to vote in Thursday's poll and warning al-Qaida fighters not to launch attacks.[69]

Although they did not attribute such incidents to al-Qaeda, al-Jazeera reported insurgent efforts to suppress Sunni participation in the fall 2005 Iraqi elections, in one example al-Jazeera reported:

> Armed attackers wearing Iraqi army uniforms have broken into the home of a senior Sunni leader and killed him, his three sons and his son-in-law on the outskirts of Baghdad. Khadim Sarhid Ali al-Batawi was the leader of the Sunni Batta tribe and the brother of a candidate in the 15 December election, Maj. Falah al-Mohammedawi said.[70]

As this example illustrates, much like the insurgents' murder of Iraqi police, soldiers, and other "collaborators," insurgents murdered families to send the indented message.

Media Coverage of U.S. Counterinsurgency Efforts in al-Anbar

As they had with the second battle of Fallujah in late 2004, Marines encouraged journalists to accompany them on operations against insurgents in 2005 to provide transparent coverage and counter insurgent propaganda. However, despite the temporary surges in journalists during Iraq's January, October, and December 2005 elections, most journalists still avoided al-Anbar Province because of the dangers there. As a result, most journalists reported from Baghdad and continued to focus on violence and U.S. casualties around the capital, and continued to rely on Iraqi stringers for information in the outlying provinces. Of those journalists who did venture to al-Anbar to cover operations, many provided fair, objective coverage. Unfortunately, many of their reports received poor placement, were given short life in the media cycle, or overshadowed by the abundant bad news coverage from Baghdad.

Nonetheless, other journalists provided a narrative very different than events on the ground, often overlooking the significance of these operations and their success, providing very superficial reporting based on the observations of junior Marines who were often not well informed, or presenting erroneous or misleading reports because of their reliance on Iraqi stringers or interpreters.[71] In one case, *Washington Post* reporter Ellen Knickmeyer, with *Washington Post* special correspondent Othman Mohammed, not only rushed to judgment in condemning U.S. forces, but also provided an incorrect account of the U.S. effort to rescue Governor Raja Nawaf Mahalawi, wrongly stating U.S. forces used tanks in their assault and implied without validation that the assault killed the governor.[72] In another case, during Operation Matador Knickmeyer violated embedding rules by identifying the squad and platoon designations for Marine causalities belonging to 3d Battalion, 25th Marines.[73] Colonel Stephen Davis, Commanding Officer of Regimental Combat Team 2, complained "...so you had a bunch of families probably sitting there in agony, not knowing whether their kid's dead or...That's unsat. Unsat."[74] In yet another case, Brigadier General James Williams, Deputy Commanding General for II MEF in 2005, observed that the *Washington Posts'* Ellen Knickmeyer's interpreter during the 2005 Anbar Security Council meetings that her interpreter provided greatly distorted translations in interviews with key Iraqis participating in the meeting.[75] Therefore, as clear signs of progress and success were emerging in al-Qaim and Ramadi, the American public would only get would only get fragments of news, of which many were inaccurate or misleading.

The Legacy of Abu Ghraib

While the U.S. Marines worked to defeat al-Qaeda in al-Anbar Province and gain the cooperation of Anbar's citizens, the Abu Ghraib prison abuse scandal continued to resonate as a leading media theme on the war throughout 2005. Keenly aware of this, insurgents marked the anniversary of the scandal, April 2, 2005, with launched a retaliatory attack on Abu Ghraib. The same day, Iranian supported Shia leader Moqtada al-Sadr used the anniversary to protest the U.S. occupation. Both events received considerable coverage and succeeded in adding fuel to the media's ongoing coverage of Abu Ghraib. In his article such as "Demonstrators in Iraq Demand That U.S. Leave," *New York Times* correspondent Dexter Filkins and Iraqi stringer Khalid al-Ansary reported "The marchers echoed the demands by Mr. Sadr and the Sunni clerics: a timetable for the withdrawal of American forces and the release of Iraqi detainees from American-supervised prisons."[76] Such reports provided little contributions to the media's coverage of the Iraq War and only served to fuel the political debates in the United States and amplify the quagmire narrative.

Importantly, by the scandal's anniversary Abu Ghraib became both a leading justification in the Iraq policy debate for withdrawing U.S. troops and a central theme of anti-war protests staged around the war's anniversary. As illustrated in the *New York Times* headline "Hundreds of Rallies Held Across U.S. to Protest Iraq War," and "Mother Who Lost Son in Iraq Continues Fight Against War," these protests also received considerable media attention.[77] The media built a sympathy frame around Cindy Sheehan, a mother who lost a son in Iraq, and gave considerable attention to her as an outspoken critic of U.S. policy and an anti-war protest leader. Reminiscent of Vietnam, Sheehan's demonstrations and exploits not only drew considerable primetime and front-page coverage, but also provided numerous value sound bites and images supporting the quagmire narrative and helped carry the anti-war movement well into the year.[78]

By this time, the media's ongoing coverage and commentary of the Abu Ghraib scandal not only continued to overshadow the U.S. effort in Iraq, but also kept a significant portions of the media's focus away off the U.S. effort in Iraq as a whole. When the U.S. Army's investigation and response to Abu Ghraib did come to a close in the spring of 2005, headlines like "Rank and File Have Taken Heat for Abu Ghraib" conveyed the media's dissatisfaction that the Army prosecuted only those directly responsible for the abuses at Abu Ghraib, and not those higher in the chain of command as Hersh, Rajiva, and other suggested should be done.[79] Punctuating the media's critical coverage, *The Torture Papers: The Road to Abu Ghraib* debuted in time for the scandal's one-year anniversary and the Iraq War's second anniversary. Similar to *Chain of Command* and *Language of Empire*, which were still active in the market, *The Torture Papers* not only passed a verdict on the soldiers at Abu Ghraib responsible for the pictures and abuses before the U.S. Army completed its investigations into the Abu Ghraib, but also on the Bush Administration's Iraq polices.[80] In addition to these books, picture books such as *Unembedded*, also began to appear, which added to the quagmire narrative through vivid imagery without context, much like Eddie Adams' famous picture of Nguyen Ngoc Loan in Vietnam. These books not only legitimized the media's criticism, but also helped keep the prisoner abuses at Abu Ghraib in the media spotlight.

Cause and Effect: Quagmire Narrative and the Absent Media

In May, *Newsweek*, presented its own variation of the Abu Ghraib abuse frame with what it presented as a breaking story of guards at the U.S. Detention facility at Guantanamo Bay (Gitmo), Cuba allegedly flushing a Koran down the toilet.[81] The story not only reinforced criticisms of U.S. policy in the United States, but sparked protests across the Muslim world—particularly in Pakistan and Afghanistan.[82] In this case, however, *Newsweek's* allegations and use of anonymous sources drew immediate criticism and controversy, which quickly discredited the story.[83] Although Newsweek retracted the story and offered an apology, it continued its critical coverage of Gitmo, including a story referring to it as the "Guantanamo gulag."[84]

Not related to the abuse theme, but garnering increasing media coverage through 2005, was coverage of the alleged Administration's wrong doing concerning Valerie Plame being outed as a CIA operative. Although the story had been out for more than a year since Robert Novak made the connection in a November 2003 column, *Vanity Fair*'s January 2004 article "Double Exposure" kindled considerable political interest that encouraged months of continuous media coverage in numerous stories like "America Turns On Bush As All The President's Staff Face Integrity Test" intended to discredit the Bush Administration.[85]

What is important about the media's coverage of Valerie Plame, the Abu Ghraib investigations, the U.S. Detention facility at Guantanamo Bay, and anti-war protests, however, is that in the absence of real news from Iraq, the media focused on a number of secondary issues surrounding the war that in one form or another supported the quagmire narrative in that they reflected criticisms of U.S. policy. As illustrated more in the next chapter, research from the PEW Research Center's *Project for Excellence in Journalism* (PEJ) would show that as media coverage of the war in Iraq waned, coverage of secondary issues, especially debate over U.S. involvement, surpassed coverage of the war.[86]

As it had the previous year, the prominent *New York Times* commemorated the 2,000th death in Iraq as a "grim milestone," in its October 26, 2005 headline "2,000 Dead: As Iraq Tours Stretch On, a Grim Mark."[87] Such abundant bad news stories focusing on violence and U.S. casualties were often accompanied by carefully selected and edited images that all conveyed the quagmire narrative. Moreover, with little actual media coverage coming from Iraq, the media focus in 2005 was increasing more on the Iraq policy debates in the United States and less on actual events in Iraq. As illustrated in the article "Democrats struggle to find one voice on Iraq," coverage of Abu Ghraib and the U.S. Detention facility at Guantanamo Bay remained key themes in the U.S. policy debates throughout 2005, underscoring quagmire assertions that Iraq was in "seemingly endless turmoil" and that U.S. forces should be withdrawn from Iraq.[88]

Despite the relatively limited press coverage over 2005, a survey of major polls taken after each of Iraq's three showed that Americans were still optimistic about Iraq and that progress was being made.[89] However, other indications showed that Americans were growing weary of the war, a sign that bad news and the quagmire narrative were taking its toll on the American public.[90] Headlines like "Poll: USA is losing patience on Iraq" and "Time for U.S. to withdraw," demonstrated the media's efforts to shape public opinion and influence U.S. policy.[91]

A 2005 Media Research Center (MRC) report on network news coverage of the Iraq War (ABC, CBS, and NBC) found that:

> More than half of all stories (848, or 61%) focused on negative topics or presented a pessimistic analysis of the situation, four times as many as featured U.S. or Iraqi achievements or offered an optimistic assessment (just 211 stories, or 15%). ...Just eight

> stories were devoted to recounting episodes of heroism or valor by U.S. troops, and another nine stories featured instances when soldiers reached out to help the Iraqi people. In contrast, 79 stories focused on allegations of combat mistakes or outright misconduct on the part of U.S. military personnel.[92]

The abundance of negative reporting, supporting the quagmire narrative that the U.S. effort in Iraq had failed, would quickly begin to erode public support the following year.

Chapter Conclusion

Over the course of 2005, U.S. Marines began to make significant gains in al-Anbar's security situation while ongoing U.S. Marine efforts to engage Iraqi leaders began to yield significant results, as demonstrated in Iraq's two democratic elections of late 2005. However, those efforts in al-Anbar Province were largely unreported because only a few journalists ventured to al-Anbar Province to cover them. Of those journalists who did, most provided only fragments of the much larger story, while others journalists provided incomplete, erroneous, or misleading reports because they often overlooked the importance of U.S. operations, used sources with little knowledge of events, or relied on Iraqi stringers or interpreters who provided inaccurate accounts.

Importantly, not only did the wars of ideas continue to play out in 2005, but they intensified as the stakes for all sides grew higher. As insurgents continued to target Western and Iraqi journalists alike, danger and difficulties getting around Iraq kept many journalists confined to the safety of Baghdad's Green Zone where they focused on Baghdad's violence and relied on local Iraqi and Arab stringers to gather news from outlying areas. This not only gave sympathetic coverage of the insurgency and allowed insurgent propaganda make its way into media, but the abundance of bad news stories and images continued to frame and support the quagmire narrative, which was amplified in sheer volume of media outlets that shared material. It also blended facts and fiction, altering perceptions of Iraq's reality. Moreover, with little real news coming from Iraq, the American public saw more coverage of the Iraq policy debates in the United States, anti-war protests, and other secondary issues such as the Abu Ghraib and Guantanamo Bay than actual events and operations in Iraq.

By the end of 2005, just one year after President George W. Bush's reelection victory, the cumulative result of the media's deficient coverage of the U.S. effort in Iraq, along with the media's coverage of ancillary issues and the Iraq policy debates in the United States, began to erode public support. This demonstrates the media's adverse influence at the strategic level.

However, the Western media's inability to accurately and comprehensively report U.S. efforts in Iraq and its focus on political debates in the United States with emphasis on withdrawing U.S. forces also had significant adverse consequences at the operational and tactical levels. First, the coverage conveyed a lack of U.S. resolve to the Iraqi people, which deterred them from joining the coalition because doing so meant risking abandonment and facing al-Qaeda's vengeance. Second, the quagmire narrative emboldened al-Qaeda and Iraq's insurgent groups to continue their attacks because they believed they were attaining their political aims. This would be important in understanding the events in 2006.

CHAPTER TEN

AL-ANBAR'S UNREPORTED AWAKENING

U.S. Marine and Army gains in al-Anbar Province would not go uncontested in 2006 as al-Qaeda and other insurgent groups increased their attacks on Coalition forces, the Iraqi government, and Iraq's Shia. Like the military conflict on the ground in Iraq, the war of ideas would become more contentious and complex as the stakes got higher and a larger segment of Iraq's population became involved. With few Western journalists covering Iraq, the collective Western media would continue to have challenges in accurately reporting the complex series of events that unfolded during the very critical year. At the strategic level in the wars for ideas, 2006 was an election year in the United States, which dramatically affected the overall nature and dynamics of Iraq War coverage in the United States, as well as journalists' perceptions of the conflict and their interpretations of events. Al-Qaeda and insurgent groups would continue to murder and intimidate journalists, produce sensational propaganda, and manipulate the media to support their goals. These insurgent efforts in the arena of ideas would continue to affect the geopolitical landscape as well as public attitudes at all three levels of war. At the operational and tactical levels, U.S. forces would begin to better counter insurgent propaganda while communicating with the Iraqi population.

The Quagmire Narrative Takes Hold

As 2006 dawned, al-Qaeda and other Sunni insurgent groups responded to the successful 2005 elections with widespread violence against Iraq's Shia, Coalition forces, and those Sunnis who began to embrace the democratic process.[1] Emboldened by the growing media call for troop withdrawal in the United States, Iraq's insurgents hoped to create the conditions for the United States to withdraw and they could regain power.[2] In headlines like "Iraq's Bloodiest Day in Months Includes 11 U.S. Deaths" and "Analysis: Iraq Violence Kills More Than 200 In A week," the media continued to focus on these events and provide an abundance of bad news stories and carefully selected and edited images focusing on violence and U.S. casualties that conveyed the media's quagmire narrative.[3] A review of articles in January and

February 2006 showed that most positive news stories of U.S. efforts and improvements on the ground were either unreported, or received limited space or airtime and short life in the media cycle.[4] Even in Baghdad, where the few remaining journalists congregated, the western media largely ignored the results of the recent successful elections in preference for stories of violence, as U.S. Army Lieutenant Colonel John M. Kanaley described:

> The silence was deafening and the seats were empty. The western press was nowhere to be found. The location was Baghdad and the event was a February 10th, 2006 press conference announcing the final verification of December's election results. Although the final allocation of parliamentary seats did not change from last month's tentative reports, the conference was nonetheless significant for American and Iraqi history. What was equally significant was the absence of members of the western press.[5]

Reminiscent of Vietnam, this telling observation described the relationship between the media and the military, and was a forecast for the Western media's reporting during 2006.

While the quagmire narrative had not significantly changed U.S. public opinion in 2005, two events in 2006 would not only serve to validate quagmire narrative, but also begin to change U.S. public opinion over the course of the year. First, on February 22, 2006, al-Qaeda in Iraq's bombing of the al-Askari "Golden Dome" Mosque in Samarra, Iraq showed the depths of the sectarian divide, and quickly became an accelerant for increased sectarian violence. Headlines like "From Iraq Shrine's Rubble, Civil War Threat Emerges," and "Sliding Toward an Uncivil War" appeared immediately following the event became the central framing convention justifying for the media's quagmire narrative, implying that the U.S. effort to keep peace and stabilize the nation had failed.[6] The media largely ignored reports showing how the Iraqi government and security forces in cooperation with Coalition forces had quelled sectarian violence in the aftermath of the bombing, instead augmenting civil war assertions with daily stories like "85 Bodies Found in Baghdad in Sectarian Strife," which reverberated across the media outlets that shared material.[7]

Second, *Time* magazine's March 19, 2006 online article titled "Collateral Damage or Civilian Massacre in Haditha?" (*Time's* print version was titled "One Morning in Haditha"), insinuated that Marines killed twenty-four civilians in Haditha as retaliation for the loss of a fellow Marine in an incident that had occurred on November 19, 2005.[8] The story also alleged the incident was covered-up, though Marines immediately launched an investigation.[9] However, when Pennsylvania representative John Murtha told *MSNBC*'s

Chris Mathews that the Marines committed "cold blooded murder" and then attempted to covered-up the incident, the Congressman not only legitimated the assertion but also became the media's authority on the matter—cited in numerous articles such as "Haditha Revives Memory of US Abuses."[10] As Haditha became the new frame on U.S. abuses, CNN's Tony Harris reported "Men, women and children, gunned down in cold blood. That's the allegation....U.S. Marines are suspected of killing two dozen unarmed civilians, accusations of a cover-up also a part of the mix. Democratic Congressman John Murtha has been briefed on what happened....Murtha calls the alleged atrocity as bad as the Abu Ghraib prison abuse scandal, if not worse."[11] When CNN's Wolf Blitzer asked Murtha what evidence he had to support the allegations, Murtha replied "Wolf, you read the 'Time' magazine articles. There are pictures, there are photos. You don't have to talk to the military about the proof."[12] MSNBC aired thirty-six stories on the unproven claims of U.S. misconduct and abuses at Haditha, while CNN aired 59; Fox News, by comparison, reported 12 stories pertaining to alleged abuses and misconduct.[13]

Despite the death of al-Qaeda leader Abu Musab al-Zarqawi in June 2006, sectarian violence increased significantly after the Gold Dome Mosque bombing, which forced many Iraqis to flee the country. Moreover, increases U.S. casualties caused by both al-Qaeda and Iranian-supported Shia factions, in what some analysts considered a proxy for war, underscored the assertions that the U.S. led effort was failing.[14] Meanwhile, hotel bound journalists exaggerated the scope of Iraq's sectarian violence, asserting that Iraq was engulfed in a widespread "civil war,"[*] though most of Iraq's violence remained restricted to multiple factions in localized areas, most of which around Baghdad, while much of the country was untouched.[15] Through carefully selected and edited images and headlines, most major media outlets contentiously defined the conflict as a widespread "civil war," which became the new media frame representing the quagmire narrative, amplified in sheer volume of media outlets that shared material. However, embedded journalist Franklin Raff offered a contradictory perspective of Iraq's "civil war" writing:

> I did not see a civil war. I did not see the beginnings of a civil war. But I did learn a thing or two about the "roots" of this civil war: Iraq's civil war has been engineered, in no small part, from the comfort of a Baghdad hotel room. It is catalyzed by minor exaggerations, partial facts, and propagandistic suppressions. It

---

[*] Assertions of "civil war" began as early as 2004, Independent journalist Michael Yon was certain that Iraq sectarian violence had become a civil war in 2005.

> will escalate, over time and across media, as minor mistruths beget outright lies, until the truth itself begins to change.[16]

While the civil war claim remained controversial, much of Iraq's violence was contained to Baghdad and a few Sunni strongholds, and did not represent the majority of Iraq's population or geography.

Importantly, as the media concentrated on the 2006 U.S. mid-term elections, it was not news from Iraq that dominated the Iraq coverage, but the public Iraq War debates in the United States, magnifying the quagmire narrative through headlines, quotes, and sound bites using commentaries and criticisms of U.S. policy based on incomplete or misleading news from Iraq that emphasized casualties and sectarian violence.[17] Based on the Western media's hasty conclusion and narrow view of events in Iraq, some influential politicians and intellectuals asserted that Iraq had indeed spun into a civil war, and called for withdrawing U.S. forces from Iraq.[18] In numerous articles such as "Rep. Cardin Calls For President To Submit Strategy To Withdraw U.S. Troops From Iraq" and "Capitol Hill Showdown on Iraq: GOP Crafts Resolution In Support Of War; Democrats Call For Timetable To Withdraw Troops," elevated the domestic political debate over U.S. involvement in Iraq.[19] Although the U.S. Senate defeated proposals in June calling for U.S. forces to withdraw from Iraq, the domestic political debate over U.S. involvement in Iraq continued into the second half of the year and became the central issue for many candidates going into the 2006 U.S. mid-term elections.[20]

The Battle for Ramadi and the Awakening

Al-Qaeda responded to the success of the October and December 2005 elections in al-Anbar Province with increased attacks on Coalition targets, the Iraqi government, and Iraq's Shia.[21] However, they also responded by increasing their brutal murder and intimidation campaigns in al-Anbar Province to reassert control of the population.[22] Indicative of these attacks, on January 5th insurgents succeeded in detonating a suicide bomb on an Iraqi Police recruitment drive, the largest turnout to date, killing several Iraqis.[23] Although many Iraqis got back in line, the devastating attack curtailed police recruitment for the next six months.[24] Al-Qaeda then went after the Anbar People's Committee and proceeded to take it apart methodically over the span of about two weeks, assassinating several principles, some in very cruel ways and leaving their bodies in the desert, and forcing one to flee to Syria.[25] Al-Qaeda recognized that if they could not control the tribes, then they could not control the people, and they viewed the Anbar People's Committee as a direct threat to their ability to continue to control the tribes and population. Representing both the competing loyalties and divisions within the tribes, some of the sheikhs were murdered by members of their own tribe. Although Governor Mamoon survived numerous assassination attempts, he remained confined to the Provincial Government Center in Ramadi under the protection of Marines and was therefore ineffective.[26] In the end, al-Qaeda had succeeded in crushing the movement, much the way it had most other Anbari efforts to organize resistance.[27] Following the Anbar People's Committee murders, Al-Qaeda then boldly proclaimed that Ramadi was the capital of the new Islamic empire.[28]

Despite the setback in indigenous anti-al-Qaeda efforts, the Anbar People's Committee murders did not change popular opinion. In fact, it not only increased public opinion against them, but also strengthened Anbari resolve. With their survival threatened, some Anbar tribes continued a covert war against al-Qaeda Anbar Revolutionaries in Ramadi, and some were increasingly cooperating with Coalition forces.[29] Despite al-Qaeda's assassination of several key Iraqi leaders, the Anbar Security Council continued to meet as an advisory group to Governor Mamoon.[30] What the Anbar People's Committee murders did do, however, is leave a number of armed groups leaderless, which allowed al-Qaeda to recruit from these groups or absorb them into their umbrella. This strengthened al-Qaeda, and began an increase in violence that would continue until Anbari resistance to al-Qaeda could reorganize.[31]

Importantly, the increase in sectarian violence following al-Qaeda's successful attack on the Golden Dome Mosque in Samarra, Iraq caused the Coalition to keep much of its attention and resources on Baghdad.[32] In al-Anbar, just six days after the Samarra Mosque bombing, on February 28, 2006, I Marine Expeditionary Force Forward (I MEF) relieved II Marine Expeditionary Force Forward (II MEF) as Multi National Force-West (MNF-W). Under the direction of Major General Richard C. Zilmer, MNF-W sought to renew the counterinsurgency efforts in al-Anbar Province after a year of heavy combat operations and focusing on Ramadi, seeking to build an effective police force and executing a comprehensive plan for securing the city with both Coalition and Iraqi forces.[33] In a complete change of direction from II MEF, who operated under General Casey's guidance, MNF-W developed a *clear, hold, build* counterinsurgency plan that concentrated on securing the population by isolating the city, clearing neighborhoods one at a time, and putting U.S. and Iraqi forces out among the population.[34] It also included engaging the population at all levels to nurture cooperation and reconciliation, and importantly, recruiting police.[35]

Marines hoped to accomplish this by overlapping a new U.S. Army Brigade with the existing U.S. Army's 2nd Brigade, 28th Infantry Division Brigade Combat Team (2/28 BCT), a Pennsylvania National Guard Unit, by a month, thus surging forces in Ramadi.[36] Despite the being part of the U.S. Marine's Area of Operations, Ramadi had been under control of a reinforced

U.S. Army Brigade with Marine Battalions and companies serving under the BCT. However, unlike the previous national guard units, the new brigade was the U.S. Army's 1st Brigade Combat Team, 1st Armored Division (1st BCT), an experienced active duty unit that had taken over successful counterinsurgency efforts in Tal Afar, but the 1st BCT would not arrive until late May.[37] In the meantime, the 2/28 BCT, with its U.S. Army Battalions operating out of two camps at opposite ends of the city, Camp Ramadi and Camp Corregidor, began encircling Ramadi to isolate it.[38] Importantly, 3rd Battalion, 8th Marines (3/8), which held Ramadi's most important district in western Ramadi, which included the government center, began a "green zone" campaign to secure one neighborhood at a time as other U.S. Army and Marine units worked in their sectors to accomplish the same.[39] In Eastern Ramadi, the U.S. Army's 2nd Battalion, 506th Infantry conducted similar operations.[40]

By this time, sectarian violence in Iraq had continued to increase following the Golden Dome Mosque bombing. Importantly, it also increased significantly in Ramadi as al-Qaeda became more ruthless in expanding its murder and intimidation campaign to the point where violence surpassed Baghdad. Al-Qaeda's atrocities and terror had so much alienated the population that the people were becoming increasingly desperate for an end. Al-Qaeda's extreme cruelty and indiscriminant attacks caused Anbaris to turn away from al-Qaeda's ideology and led to increasingly more organized resistance in the populated centers along the Euphrates River Valley in al-Anbar Province—resistance that was organized largely along tribal lines. In some cases, tribal members were divided between tribal loyalty and loyalty to al-Qaeda, which led to intra-tribe violence.[41] By June, both Ramadi's general population and tribal leaders were ready to side with the Coalition, and Marines continued to engage tribal leaders.[42]

In June, the 1/1 BCT assumed control of Ramadi and completed encircling the city and began operations to secure the population, clearing al-Qaeda strongholds and establishing new combat outposts within the city as the vital first tasks in the clear, hold, build, strategy.[43] However, even with a robust complement of five reinforced U.S. Marine and Army maneuver battalions, two additional Marine rifle companies, a Marine riverine patrol unit that patrolled the waterways, and two U.S. Navy SEAL Teams, 1/1 BCT still had insufficient forces and needed to increase Iraqi soldiers and police.[44] As 3rd Battalion, 8th Marines (3/8) expanded into their sector of the city from the north west from the fork in the Euphrates River, they secured select neighborhoods while providing humanitarian aid and reconstruction money, believing these footholds would spread like ink blots into other neighborhoods.[45] Meanwhile, the U.S. Army's 1st Battalion, 37th Armor attacked into southern Ramadi at the other U.S. Army maneuver battalions, 1st Battalion, 35th Armor, 1st Battalion, 6th Infantry, and 1st Battalion, 506th Infantry, spread out into their respective areas and similarly focused on protecting the population by establishing outposts, engaging tribal leaders, and defeating al-Qaeda.[46]

Al-Qaeda had been aware of the impending attack, and prepared by emplacing Improvised Explosive Devices (IEDs), establishing defenses, and staging weapons and ammunition. According to U.S. Army Colonel Anthony E. Deane, commander of the 1st Battalion, 35th Armor:

> ...civilians were leaving the city in droves, packing as many of their worldly possessions in their vehicles as they could. There was an overall feeling of apprehension among the populace.[47]

On July 24th, al-Qaeda responded with a series of assaults that escalated to a citywide battle, which left al-Qaeda severely diminished.[48] As combat operations sought reclaim the city and secure the population, soldiers and Marines continued to engage local sheikhs in an effort to increase recruitment into local security forces and to take a stand against al-Qaeda, telling them that they would help them defeat the insurgents and stay as long as necessary, and would then leave as soon as they had their own security.[49]

During the summer, U.S. soldiers and Marines had succeeded in weakening insurgent groups through continuous joint operations with the improving Iraqi Security Forces. These successful military operations against al-Qaeda, showed U.S. strength and resolve while hurting al-Qaeda and helping secure Anbaris. Moreover, the Coalition's consistent message, that it sought to work in cooperation with the Iraqis to provide peace and stability and did not want to be a long-term occupation force, succeeded in winning increasing Iraqi support and demonstrated that the Coalition in western Iraq could be both trusted by al-Anbar leaders.[50] Coalition officers engaged Sheikh Sattar abu Risha to provide tribesmen for the police and to build a police station in the Jazeera district north of the Euphrates River.[51] Abu Risha, an oil smuggler and a lesser Sheikh from a smaller tribe, had lost his father and three brothers to al-Qaeda's callous murder sprees and was willing to help.[52] In response to the new Jazeera police station, al-Qaeda detonated a massive bomb that killed several Iraqis and caused many severe burn injuries. Later that day, they murdered Sheikh Abu Ali Jassim, whose tribe comprised many of the Jazeera policemen, then desecrated and hid his body, which denied its burial for several days in violation of Islamic funeral law. This inflamed the population.[53]

Sheikh Sattar then hosted a meeting of several Sheikhs at his home in the Jazeera District of Ramadi and established the Emergency Council for the Rescue of al-Anbar (ECRA), also known as the Anbar Rescue Council, and then gained Coalition for support. Within weeks the movement grew, and on September 14, Sheikh Sattar hosted meeting of more than 50 sheikhs and notables from Ramadi the Sahwa al-Anbar, or al-Anbar Awakening publically proclaimed its opposition to al-Qaeda.[54] With protection from Coalition forces and the support of the Government of Iraq, Ramadi's tribes then realized that they could work with U.S. forces against a common enemy. Following Sattar's announcement, tribal militias engaged in a series of pitched battles over the fall of 2006 to expel al-Qaeda from the city. At the same time, Iraqi police and Army units grew and became a formidable force that worked alongside soldiers and Marines.[55]

In September, 1st Battalion, 6th Marines (1/6) replaced 3/8 in the heart of the city, and in what became a month of continuous combat operations, 1/6 continued operations to clear al-Qaeda strongholds in the city as U.S. Army Battalions similarly did so in their respective areas in and around the city.[56] As these units secured neighborhoods, they established new police stations and checkpoints that provided a continuous presence and protected the population. Meanwhile, U.S. Marine Civil Affairs teams and U.S. State Department Provincial Reconstruction Teams worked with soldiers and Marines to meet the needs of Ramadi's citizens while helping provide economic and social opportunities.[57] Between September and December 2006, a Sahwa, or Awakening, had occurred whereas. With tribal support, Iraqi army and police recruitment in al-Anbar grew, and U.S. and Iraqi forces secured the population and began to turn the tide in al-Anbar.[58]

As Iraqi security forces grew, tribal militias evolved into "concerned citizens" and "neighborhood watch" organizations called the Sons of Iraq.[59] Meanwhile, Marines, soldiers, and other U.S. agencies began providing humanitarian aid, restoring vital services, and rebuilding the region's infrastructure. They also helped establish new education, social, and economic development programs, and helped establish local democratic governments that had tribal support. Once Iraqis and Americans began working together, the cultural divide created by centuries of isolation and indoctrination quickly began to erode, and reconciliation based on mutual understanding and respect between the West and the Middle East developed.[60] Importantly, Sunnis in other areas were also beginning to recognize the need for cooperation with Coalition forces, even to the point of revering their previous demands that the United States leave Iraq and instead stay to protect them from increasing Iranian supported militias and death squads.[61]

However, al-Qaeda had not given up and heavily contested the Sahwa's effort to retake Ramadi. Using al-Jazeera, al-Qaeda reiterated its claim that it was part of the Islamic state in Iraq.[62] In November, al-Qaeda sought to eliminate Sheikh Jassim Muhammad Saleh al-Suwadawi, one of the Anbar Revolutionaries and Anbar Emergency Rescue Council Members. Jassim has already been fighting al-Qaeda and had established his own checkpoints to protect his people. Al-Qaeda responded by launching large assault against his tribal area in what became known as the Battle of Sofia (Sufiyah). Jassim rallied seventeen members of his tribe and made a stand against a larger force, but as the hours past Jassim and his men fell back. Unmanned Aerial Vehicles monitored the battle, but Coalition observers could not tell the difference between friend and foe. Eventually, U.S. Marine F-18 fighters identified vehicles fleeing the scene dragging a body as the enemy and began attacking, and by nightfall, U.S. Army soldiers of the 1st Battalion, 9th Infantry Regiment (1-9 INF) arrived to help. The battle was significant in Ramadi because it showed the people that they could throw off al-Qaeda.[63]

One important aspect of the Battle of Ramadi and the Awakening was the war of ideas that played out with military action. Through various media, such as radio, television, magazines, newspapers, and through the engagement efforts of soldiers and Marines on patrol to the senior Coalition commanders, U.S. forces consistently communicated that "we are not your enemy, al-Qaeda is," and that "We are here to help you and then leave. We are not here to occupy you or take your oil."[64] However, it was the Anbari tribal leadership, particularly Sheikh Sattar, who communicated this to the Iraqi people. Sattar was particularly media savvy, and effectively used the media to both discredit al-Qaeda and promote the Awakening in al-Anbar, in essence, defeating al-Qaeda and its ideology in war of ideas.[65]

In late 2006, as dramatic changes were taking place in al-Anbar Province, a new counterinsurgency strategy emerged under the direction of U.S. Army General David H. Petraeus and U.S. Marine Lieutenant General James N. Mattis, which outlined the necessary steps to win the population.[66] This was the same strategy already being employed in al-Anbar. At the same time, the Pentagon released a new Information Operations doctrine to overcome the U.S. military's shortcomings in operational and tactical communication and win the war of ideas on the battlefield.[67] Similarly, the U.S. Department of State, which faced the severe criticisms that the United States abandoned its public diplomacy program when President Bill Clinton dissolved the U.S. Information Agency, rededicated itself to both public diplomacy and a united strategic communication effort with the Department of Defense and other government agencies.[68] This more unified reorientation would soon bring significant changes not only at the geopolitical and strategic levels, but also on the battlefields in Iraq.

Media and the Awakening

By December 2006, violence in Iraq had reached its highest level in post-Saddam Iraq and some analysts and military officials were conceding that Iraq's sectarian violence had indeed evolved into a civil war, however, what went unreported in 2006, because Western journalist did not venture to Ramadi or Fallujah for fear of their lives, was not only that the situation was already beginning to change in al-Anbar Province, but also that the Awakening was beginning to spread beyond Ramadi.[69] Some observers, such as Thomas Ricks, believed that al-Anbar was a "lost cause."[70] However, Ricks assertion, based on selective used of a leaked classified report intended to paint a worst case scenario, which did not take into account current operations and developments, and was taken out of context would grossly misrepresent the situation in Anbar.[71] Nonetheless, Rick's assertion that al-Anbar was beyond repair was quickly echoed throughout the media, and went undisputed in the media because journalists were not in Anbar to report the rapid and dramatic changes taking place in the province. Meanwhile, other journalists confined to the Green Zone and Baghdad's wrongly claimed that al-Anbar was also engulfed in sectarian violence. [72] This reporting frustrated U.S. forces in the province. According to U.S. Army Colonel Sean B. MacFarland, Commander of the 1/1 BCT:

> It's amazing how little of our story gets out as far as Baghdad. Our higher headquarters in Baghdad, I think the commanders understand when they come out and they see it, but so much of what we're doing here is being filtered at the staff level that it gets lost. I had a reporter in here earlier today, and I was explaining to him how we're flipping these tribes one by one, and I said the thing people don't understand in the states, and you see it in the Baker-Hamilton Report, is this underlying assumption that Baghdad is Iraq and that the Sunnis [means Shia] are monolithic. Well, Baghdad is an important part of Iraq, but they are no more representative of the rest of Iraq than New York City is of the rest of New York State. You can have a totally different dynamic outside of Baghdad than you have in Baghdad. There's no sectarian violence here.[73]

Contrasting Western and Arab media's coverage of Iraq, Brigadier General Robert B. Neller, Deputy Commanding General of Multi-National Forces-West 2006-2007, explained:

> I guess that we suspect that the Western media is the most powerful information operations tool in the world, and they tell the story they want to tell. We try to get them to tell our story, but they choose. Whereas the insurgency, al-Qaeda, the Arab street, most of the media outlets that cater to that particular clientele tells their story rapidly, quickly, immediately. We timed it the other day. We had a tank attack with an IED and it caught on fire and an hour and 45 minutes later it was on al-Jazeera. ...We're trying to improve the life of the average Iraqi, trying to give the average Iraqi an opportunity for choice and for economic development. We're not going to be here forever. We

> are going to leave. We don't want your oil. We're here to help you. Why do you continue to persist in this fighting when all it does is delay the reconstruction of your country? They watch their TV, whether it's al-Iraqia or al-Arabiya or al-Jazeera, and all they see is IED strike after IED strike...The message is the insurgency is doing great things.[74]

Speaking on the Western Media, Brigadier General Neller explained:

> I had a reporter with me, and we went out and saw the police out west, talked to him about all the increase in police and how many there were and we went to a police station and obviously they had concerns. It's a young police force. And I thought it was a great story, and, hey, Al Anbar police are increasing by X thousand. All he wanted to talk about was one guy said he had a pay problem. That's all he wanted to talk about in the whole article. Very discouraging.[75]

The direct and measurable effects of few western journalists in Iraq and their focus on Baghdad's sectarian violence and suffering meant that Americans received both very little and very narrow coverage of the U.S. effort in Iraq. This allowed the bad news about Iraq's escalating sectarian violence to dominate coverage.

By April 2007, 100 journalists, many Iraqis, had died in Iraq since 2003—thirty-two in 2006 alone. A *Broadcasting & Cable* report underscores the Iraq's dangers:

> Since the beginning of the war in March 2003, more journalists have been killed in action covering Iraq than in Vietnam, the first Iraq war, Afghanistan, Kosovo and Somalia--combined.[76]

With journalists being targets of insurgents, this telling statement punctuates the fact that war is more than combat, but also a war of ideas where belligerents will murder the to control the narrative of the war. Importantly, with few journalists willing to travel to Ramadi and other al-Anbar towns, the Western media would fail to reports the dramatic transformation taking place in the province.

Meanwhile, in numerous reports such as "Fresh Iraq violence claims 135 lives," al-Jazeera and the Arab media provided an abundance of coverage of Iraq's sectarian violence, which tended to bring a more neutral and objective tone in report, though not in every case.[77] In reports like "Zarqawi video vows defeat for US," and "Transcript: Bin Laden accuses West" al-Jazeera continued to broadcast al-Qaeda's messages and inflammatory terms such as "crusader."[78] While the station had shown some sympathy in reporting the Sunni turn against al-Qaeda over the past eighteen months, al-Jazeera continued to promote al-Qaeda's related insurgents' aims in Ramadi in articles such as "Sunni fighters claim Ramadi."[79] Typical of Arab media coverage at the time, the article titled "Many killed in US raid on Ramadi" wrongly portrayed the nature of fighting in the U.S.-Sahwa cooperation against al-Qaeda, reporting:

> Residents, who declined to be named, said US tanks had fired into the area and that those who died were not fighting. They criticized the US forces and the Shia-led Iraqi government. Several said men who had gathered to play a traditional street game had been attacked. [80]

Articles like this often implied the U.S. fought unilaterally, omitting the fact the U.S. soldiers and Marines worked closely with local militias and police, using local intelligence, as well as with Iraqi soldiers. This played into the established notion that the United States was the "aggressor," "invader," and "occupier."

Cause and Effect: Public Opinion Turns

Though still controversial at the time, by mid-2006 the label "civil war," and all that the media implied by it, coupled with the alleged U.S. abuses at Haditha, became firmly established as the media's central themes in reinforcing the quagmire narrative. The underlying assertion that the U.S. effort had failed continued to fuel the domestic political debate over U.S. involvement in Iraq continued as the 2006 U.S. mid-term elections drew near. Although some journalists, such as Michael R. Gordon, cited analysts and observers who argued for more troops in Iraq, these calls were greatly overshadowed by the plethora of reports, like "Most in poll want plan for pullout from Iraq," amplified criticisms from influential figures as U.S. Senators Harry Reid and Barrack Obama calling for withdrawal.[81] Furthermore, because igniting a civil war in Iraq was an al-Qaeda's goal, the label "civil war" was a propaganda victory for both al-Qaeda's and Iran, who both hoped to force the U.S. withdrawal.

A December 2006 Media Research Center (MRC) report on satellite coverage of the Iraq war found that "60% of all CNN stories on the war emphasized setbacks, misdeeds or pessimism about progress in Iraq, compared to just 10 percent that reported on achievements or victories." Similarly, forty-eight percent of MSNBC's Iraq War coverage featured bad news stories while only 12% of good news stories.[82] "While all three networks presented news of Zarqawi's death as a victory for the U.S.

coalition," the MRC reported, "CNN chose that day to interview a Middle East journalist who complained, "There's no good news in Iraq. There's no corner that's been turned, there's no milestone....I just feel very depressed and hopeless." MSNBC ignored the breaking news of Zarqawi's death, instead featuring a positive story on U.S. military deserters.[83]

The cumulative effects of few western journalists in Iraq, the narrow focus on Baghdad's sectarian violence, and the quagmire narrative being the central feature of the U.S. domestic debates adversely affected U.S. public opinion in 2006. Adding to this was the media's domestic coverage of antiwar protests and Cindy Sheehan, aiding the antiwar movement. According to an American Enterprise Institute study, leading polls showed that U.S. public opinion had changed dramatically over the course of the year in response to the Iraq War coverage and debate.[84] The adverse change in public opinion had four important political implications. First, much like 1968 Vietnam, the Iraq War became the most significant campaign issue in the 2006 mid-term elections, where the cumulative effect of the media's quagmire narrative in adversely affected U.S. public opinion led a significant portion of the U.S. public to elect representatives that were committed to changing U.S. policy and withdrawing U.S. forces. This was reported in stories titled "The Impetus for Changes: Voters Display Frustrations and Dissatisfactions," and "Power Shift: Democrats Take Control of House; Divided Government Looms as Voters Seek Change."[85] Importantly, the antiwar movement continued to gain momentum following the elections. With recent election victories and mobilized support, the broad coalition of anti-war artists, authors, musicians, and actors, much of the Hollywood establishment, put their efforts behind the campaign Barack Obama.[86]

Second, this cumulative effect of the western media's post-Saddam coverage not only had a direct and measurable effect on U.S. public opinion and policy, but also had a direct and measurable effect on Iraq's insurgents. According to the research of the Belfer Center for Science and International Affairs at Harvard University, a 2008 project titled "Is There an 'Emboldenment' Effect?: Evidence from the Insurgency in Iraq" determined that "insurgent groups are strategic actors that respond to incentives created by the policies of the incumbent government and its external supporters."[87] Based on empirical data collected on insurgent attacks in relation to the variation in access to international news across Iraqi provinces, the number of anti-resolve statements in the U.S. media, and the release of U.S. public opinion polls, the study concluded that" in periods immediately after a spike in anti-resolve statements* the level of insurgent attacks increased in

* Anti-resolve" statements are any news highlighting the costs of the war reflected in casualties, any framing device indicating U.S. failure or quagmire, or any direct reference calling for withdrawing US forces.

provinces with greater access to U.S. news."[88] Thus, the media become a facilitator in a perpetuating cycle where violence inspires anti-resolve statements supporting the quagmire narrative, which in turn inspires more violence.

Third, anti-resolve statements, such as the continuous call for U.S. troop withdrawal, not only emboldened Coalition enemies in the Iraq War, but also discouraged many Iraqis from turning against al-Qaeda and joining U.S. forces in al-Anbar sooner. Iraqis were reluctant to side with U.S. forces and turn against al-Qaeda because the Western media, citing the cries of anti-war critics and politicians, signaled that the United States might not be there to support them.[89] This rendered the U.S. policy of Iraqization ineffective, which caused policy makers to reconsider their Iraq strategy.

Forth, the downturn in public support for the war coupled with the election of anti-war candidates forced the Bush Administration to succumb to more than two years of media amplified criticisms that there were not enough troops to adequately secure Iraq and the current strategy for contending with Iraq's insurgency was insufficient. In doing so, the administration accepted the resignation of Defense Secretary Donald Rumsfeld, which led to a new strategy and a surge in U.S. forces the following year.[90] This new strategy would come from a new counter insurgency doctrine developed between 2004 and 2006.

A Counter-Media Narrative Emerges

Facing a limited scope of reporting and an aggressive insurgent effort to control the media and get their message out, another voice emerged in the war of ideas—this time from the men and women on the front lines. Unlike previous conflicts, U.S. service men and women serving in Iraq received immediate, twenty-four hour news as they watched satellite television in recreation rooms and dining facilities, and read both major and hometown newspapers over the Internet. Many quickly saw that the media reported a war and situation far different than what they saw. General James T. Conway, U.S. Marine Corps commandant, makes this point well:

> There's a level of negativism in our press today that our young troops find a little bit disconcerting...I've talked to very few troops who have come back from theater who haven't had to go through about a two-week transition of saying, 'That's not what I saw taking place, but that's what the country's being shown every day'.[91]

Thomas E. Ricks punctuates General Conway's concern, writing: "Many military officers, meanwhile, grew deeply distrustful and resentful of the media, feeling that it focused on the negative—bombings and casualties—while neglecting the positive, such as political progress and reconstruction efforts."[92] General Michael Delong similarly complained, "It has been frustrating for me to have to watch the onslaught of inaccurate reporting, and it has been even more frustrating for me since, as I continue to travel frequently in an Iraq that bears slight resemblance to what appears in the newspapers and on television.[93]

However, the same technology that globalized news and made it instantaneously availably to a global public sphere also made possible a global, instantaneous counter-media narrative. In response to the media's deficient reporting and quagmire narrative, many U.S. service members complained about the media and began telling their stories in emails, letters, and telephone conversations to family and friends. Some would make their cases in local newspapers and radio or television shows. However, a large number would begin a counter-information crusade on online journals called blogs, a phenomenon Matthew Currier Burden's *The Blog of War: Front-Line Dispatches from Soldiers in Iraq and Afghanistan* documented.* Indicative of the popularity of blogging, *Mudville Gazette's Milblog* reported 460 members since its inception in 2003, while *Milblogging.com* reported "1,766 military blogs in 31 countries with 3,655 registered members."[94] A common theme among military bloggers is their criticism of the media's emphasis on casualties, or body count, and not on the heroic actions of U.S. service members. Indicative of this sentiment, Sergeant Tim Sumner contended in his blog titled "NY Times Names WOT's Dead; Tosses Their Heroism," that:

> Since 9/11, on all battlefields, more than 4,000 American soldiers, sailors, airmen, and Marines have earned and been awarded the top six medals for valor, the Bronze Star with 'V' device and higher. Conversely, the *Times* has written and published but four straight stories about the battlefield heroics of the War on Terror's most highly decorated troops — *and not one time has even their heroism made the Times' front page.*[95]

Yet while the *New York Times* and other major newspapers often overlooked reports of valor on the battlefield, they continued to give front page coverage to U.S. casualties. Sumner's sentiments and observations reverberate through the military blogs, especially after the *New York Times* made no mention of President Bush awarding the Medal of Honor posthumously to Navy

* Although the U.S. military has published a blog policy to protect operational security, it has not prevented U.S. service men and women, along with their family members, from telling their stories.

Lieutenant Michael P. Murphy on October 22, 2007, nor did it cover Navy Petty Officer 2nd Class Michael Monsoor's Medal of Honor ceremony on April 3, 2008.[96]

An Endemic Problem: The 2006 Israel-Hezbollah War

Importantly, media performance in Iraq during the Iraq War and insurgency, like media performance in Afghanistan during the initial fight against the Taliban and al-Qaeda, is part of a larger phenomenon. Therefore, it is worth examining media performance in other Middle-East conflicts during the same period as common themes and similarities relate to each other both in the regions and on the world stage. For example, as U.S. military forces battled insurgent groups across Iraq in 2006, Israel took action against Hezbollah in Lebanon. In a similar manner as al-Qaeda in Iraq manipulated Western journalists with staged events of casualties and destruction, sensational video of their attacks, and heavily scripted and well rehearsed "witnesses," Hezbollah's propaganda arm manipulated the Western media as it attempted to shape world opinion against Israel.[97]

CNN's Nic Robertson fell for Hezbollah's staged media event when he reported, uncritically and without validation, that "Tyre, the port city in the south of Lebanon, took a pounding from Israeli bombs Tuesday. Civilians were caught up in the carnage." But Roberson showed no evidence of civilians caught up in any "carnage." Then, in a taped report replayed during a late night live broadcast on July 18, 2006, Roberson followed a Hezbollah representative on a short and hurried tour through an alleged suburban area bombed by Israel where he filmed what the representative directed him to film and made no effort to either validate the man's claims or qualify the report with a disclaimer by describing the limitations and restrictions Hezbollah placed on him.[98] During the report, the Hezbollah representative forcefully directed Robertson, "Just look. Shoot. Look at this building. Is it a military base? Is it a military base, or just civilians living in this building?" Then, when Robertson asked the man a question about Hezbollah's intentions in accepting a cease-fire offer and in keeping or releasing captured Israeli soldiers, he replied with a statement "We always teach Israel a lesson. We always teach it a lesson. Now we will teach Israel a lesson again." Roberson then asked the press agent another pointed question about Israel's claim that Hezbollah is killing civilians the press agent does not answer, instead pointing to the sky replied, "Now there is jet fighters. We have to move." But there are no sounds or videos of jet fighters, and Roberston's hard questions go unanswered as Hezbollah succeeded in getting its message out through the western media. A few days later, Roberson admitted Hezbollah's media controls on CNN's Reliable Sources, telling host Howard Kurtz:

> Well, Howard, there's no doubt about it: Hezbollah has a very, very sophisticated and slick media operations. In fact, beyond that, it has very, very good control over its areas in the south of Beirut. They deny journalists access into those areas. They can turn on and off access to hospitals in those areas. They have a lot of power and influence. You don't get in there without their permission. And when I went we were given about 10 or 15 minutes, quite literally running through a number of neighborhoods that they directed and they took us to. ...But there's no doubt about it. They had control of the situation. They designated the places that we went to, and we certainly didn't have time to go into the houses or lift up the rubble to see what was underneath. ...There's no doubt that the [Israeli] bombs there are hitting Hezbollah facilities."[99]

This telling report underscores the media's culpability in aiding the enemy by reporting without validating Hezbollah's claims and eagerly believing that Israel was wrong.

Conversely, in another report titled "Inside Hezbollah," CNN's Anderson Cooper describes Hezbollah's manipulation of the western media his own similar incident:

> We'd come to get a look at the damage and had hoped to talk with a Hezbollah representative. Instead, we found ourselves with other foreign reporters taken on a guided tour by Hezbollah. Young men on motor scooters followed our every movement. They only allowed us to videotape certain streets, certain buildings. ...And while that may be true, what the Israelis will say is that Hezbollah has their offices, their leadership has offices and bunkers even in residential neighborhoods. And if you're trying to knock out the Hezbollah leadership with air strikes, it's very difficult to do that without killing civilians. ...As bad as this damage is, it certainly could have been much worse in terms of civilian casualties. Before they started heavily bombing this area, Israeli warplanes did drop leaflets in this area, telling people to get out. The civilian death toll, though, has angered many Lebanese. Even those who do not support Hezbollah are outraged by the pictures they've seen on television of civilian casualties....
>
> Civilian casualties are clearly what Hezbollah wants foreign reporters to focus on. It keeps the attention off them — and

> questions about why Hezbollah should still be allowed to have weapons when all the other militias in Lebanon have already disarmed. ...After letting us take pictures of a few damaged buildings, they take us to another location, where there are ambulances waiting. ...This is a heavily orchestrated Hezbollah media event. When we got here, all the ambulances were lined up. We were allowed a few minutes to talk to the ambulance drivers. Then one by one, they've been told to turn on their sirens and zoom off so that all the photographers here can get shots of ambulances rushing off to treat civilians. That's the story that Hezbollah wants people to know about. ...These ambulances aren't responding to any new bombings. The sirens are strictly for effect. ...Hezbollah may not be terribly subtle about spinning a story, but it is telling perhaps that they try. Even after all this bombing, Hezbollah is still organized enough to have a public relations strategy, still in control enough to try and get its message out.[100]

Lebanon, like Iraq, is another front in a larger conflict between the Middle East and the West, and as this example illustrates, the real battle is waged for public opinion, and such attempts to shape perceptions blurs the lines between fact and fiction, perceptions and reality.

Like al-Jazeera, both Hezbollah's satellite television station, *al-Manar* (the beacon), and Hamas' al-Aqsa TV, attempt to control the narrative on news coming from the Middle East while attempting to promote anti-Western hatred and radicalize Muslims outside the region.[101] In doing so, they have sought to use creative means of reaching young audience with such characters as "Farfur," a near perfect reproduction of Disney's famous Mickey Mouse to indoctrinate children into participating in murder and terrorism against the West.[102] According to Jonathan L. Snow, President of the Coalition Against Terrorist Media, "From the time that the al-Aqsa television station was launched, in January 2006, a major element of the programming has been geared toward children."[103]

Equally significant is an effort by some Muslim nations to criminalize legitimate criticism if Islam as "Islamophobia" while at the same time propagating hatred for Israel and the West.[104] Legitimate appearing front organizations for the Muslim Brotherhood, such as the Council of American-Islamic Relations (CAIR), seek to enforce this through court actions in the United States and other nations, even going so far as to shape how Islam and terrorism are defined.[105] Meanwhile, terrorists organizations such as the Muslim Brotherhood, Hamas, and Hezbollah use front organizations to purchase advertisements in Arab publications and on satellite television that used recycled graphic images of civilian casualties to fuel animosity toward Israel and the United States.[106]

Chapter Conclusion

By 2006, the abundance of bad news stories filled with hasty analysis and commentary focusing on violence and U.S. casualties, carefully selected sound bites, and graphic images of violence and destruction supported a quagmire narrative that emphasized U.S. misconduct, heavy-handedness, and the inability to end the insurgency in Iraq. At the same time, Iraq's insurgent groups continued to make effective use of the collective media to influence public opinion. At the strategic domestic level in the wars of ideas, this caused a marked turn in U.S. public support for the U.S. effort in Iraq as well as conveying a lack of U.S. resolve that discouraged many Iraqis from working with Coalition forces or taking a stand against al-Qaeda for fear that they would be abandoned and left to al-Qaeda's murderous retribution. Moreover, at the operational and tactical levels, the deficient and pessimistic coverage and high profile calls in the United States for withdrawing U.S. forces emboldened Iraq's insurgent groups who continued their sensational attacks in hopes of setting the conditions for restoring power to Sunnis and causing the withdrawal of Coalition forces. As demonstrated by the examples in the chapter, these insurgents and terrorists also skillfully used and manipulated Western journalists to spread propaganda.

The Samarra mosque bombing in February 2006 seemed to validate the media's quagmire assertions and immediately drew hasty conclusions from Western journalists that Iraq was engulfed in a civil war. Coverage of the bombing and the subsequent increase in sectarian violence included carefully selected images of death and destruction accompanied by gloomy assertions that the United States could not win. Over the course of 2006, as the U.S. election season came into full swing, the lack of Western journalists in Iraq continued to provide an abundance of bad news stories, which overshadowed positive news of U.S. efforts and improvements on the ground. This deficient and pessimistic coverage, coupled with an inordinate amount of media attention on the alleged Haditha massacre, fueled criticisms, protests, and more calls for U.S. withdrawal in the United States. In covering the campaigns, the American media gave more coverage to the political debates in the United States than to events in Iraq, magnifying the quagmire narrative and calls for withdrawing U.S. forces through headlines, quotes, and sound bites using commentaries and criticisms of U.S. policy. Reminiscent of the 1968 U.S. elections following the Tet Offensive, the narrow reporting of a few Western journalists confined to Baghdad's Green Zone amplified the quagmire narrative and adversely influenced American public opinion to the extent that it threatened a major change of U.S. policy—that is, the election of a number of anti-war candidates committed to prematurely withdrawing U.S. troops. Criticisms of the media's deficient Iraq War coverage became increasingly plentiful over the course of the war. NBC News correspondent Richard Engel defended criticisms, writing "...journalists in Baghdad certainly weren't just reporting from hotel balconies. We were dying and being kidnapped in record numbers."[107]

In response to inaccurate, incomplete, and misleading media coverage coming from Iraq, a counter-media movement, which had simmered under the surface, came to full fruition in 2006 and not only provided criticisms of mainstream American media's reporting of the war, but also began correcting the record and providing rich, alternative coverage of U.S. efforts in Iraq. Moreover, both the U.S. military and State Department sought to regain the information initiative through new doctrine and policies built around strategic communication, public diplomacy, and providing timey, relevant information on the battlefield. This was particularly effective at the tactical level in Ramadi, where both U.S. forces and Iraqis made effective use of the media to communicate with the local population and turn them from al-Qaeda during the Awakening. Meanwhile, as the counter-media narrative challenged the traditional media in the United States, the information operations doctrine and public diplomacy policy would have significant effects in Iraq. This set the stage for events in 2007 and beyond.

CHAPTER ELEVEN

Winning the War of Ideas and Images in Iraq

As the debate raged in the United States over the war in Iraq, President George W. Bush announced the nation's new counterinsurgency strategy for Iraq on January 10, 2007, and appointed General David Petraeus as the new commander of Multi-National Forces - Iraq responsible for carrying it out. Importantly, the President allocated the additional forces required to secure the population and carry it out, with the majority going to Baghdad. Once these additional surge forces arrived, General Petraeus' launched a series of major military operations to secure the population, with the first operation securing Baghdad and subsequent operations clearing al-Qaeda sanctuaries outside Baghdad and targeting both al-Qaeda in Iraq and rouge factions attempting to destabilize the country.[1] In an effort to counter al-Qaeda's highly effective propaganda efforts, Coalition forces targeted propaganda cells and implemented its new Information Operations doctrine. Because Coalition Forces working with the local population in al-Anbar Province was already securing the province, General Petraeus put these forces where he needed them the most, largely in Baghdad and other key cities on its periphery, and U.S. Marines would get few of these additional forces in al-Anbar.[2]

Al-Anbar's Awakening Spreads

In February 2007, I Marine Expeditionary Force, Forward (I MEF), operating as Multinational Forces-West, turned control of al-Anbar Province back to II Marine Expeditionary Force, Forward (II MEF), which continued pursue al-Qaeda in the other population centers and outlying areas while continuing to build Iraqi security forces and engage the population. Although al-Qaeda continued to attack Awakening members, including the desperate use of chorine bombs and suicide attacks that killed and wounded civilians, Iraqi and Coalition forces were successful in killing and capturing al-Qaeda members.[3] At the same time the rapidly growing and improving Iraqi Army and police began to take a greater role in protecting the Anbaris from al-Qaeda's murder and intimidation campaign and expelling the organization, the Sahwa spread across Western Iraq. By September 2007, these operations had significantly damaged al-Qaeda and other factions, and greatly reduced sectarian violence in much of Iraq. From al-Anbar Province, the Sahwa, Awakening, spread to other areas as the surge provided security and helped expel al-Qaeda and other insurgent groups. In a letter to the troops in Iraq, Gen Petraeus described the phenomenon:

> As the months passed in 2007, in fact, the tribal awakening that began in Al Anbar Province spread to other parts of the country. Emboldened by improving security and tired of indiscriminate violence, extremist ideology, oppressive practices, and criminal activity, Iraqis increasingly rejected Al Qaeda-Iraq and rogue militia elements.[4]

Thus, after four years of hostility, many Iraqis began to realize that through the Coalition's consistent actions and message that it was there to help, breaking through centuries of isolation and indoctrination. The U.S. led Coalition's progress had even broader implications in that it was a breakthrough in the "clash of cultures"—showing that reconciliation based on mutual understanding and respect could indeed occur between the West and the Middle East.

By the end of October 2007, both civilian and military deaths had fallen to late 2004 levels, and eight of Iraq's eighteen provinces were under Iraqi control.[5] By January 2008, al-Qaeda in Iraq was effectively defeated in al-Anbar Province and its ideology essentially rejected among the majority of the population. U.S. soldiers and Marines reduced their presence in the cities and began turning more responsibility over to the Iraqis. An al-Qaeda leader's captured diary described al-Qaeda's rapid decline at the hands of Sons of Iraq calling them "scoundrels, sectarians and nonbelievers."[6] Similarly, an intercepted letter from another al-Qaeda leader revealed that the Awakening movement and loss of al-Anbar:

> ...created weakness and psychological defeat. This also created panic, fear and the unwillingness to fight. The morale of the fighters went down...There was a total collapse in the security structure of the organisation [sic].[7]

Confirming military accounts, Independent journalists Michael Totten had these observations on the dramatic changes in Iraq during his fifth trip there:

> Baghdad, the most dangerous city in all of Iraq, is only half as violent as it was when I was there during the summer. And the fact that the capital is now the deadliest city is itself evidence of a tectonic shift on the ground. In the spring of 2007, Ramadi was the most violent place in Iraq. But the insurgency there has been

> finished. The Taji area north of Baghdad, which was a catastrophe when I paid a visit in July, is now going the way of Ramadi.[8]

Totten also spend some time in Fallujah, and commenting on the disparity between reality in Iraq and media created perceptions wrote:

> Almost everyone I know back home was sure I'd be shot at every day, that it's still a war zone out here. Based on the news reports - even the new, optimistic ones, could you blame them for thinking that? But attacks against coalition forces in Fallujah are down by more than 90% since March of this year...There hasn't been a single firefight in this city for months...There's a gigantic perception lag in America these days. The Iraq of the popular imagination and the Iraq of the real world are not the same country.[9]

Totten's telling observations dramatically contradicted the mainstream media, and soon caused other journalists to take notice.

Throughout 2008 and 2009, Iraqis increasingly took the lead in providing their own security. U.S. Marine trained Iraqi forces traveled outside the province and successfully defeated Sadr's Mahdi Militia in Basra, Baghdad and Mosul, along with defeating al-Qaeda holdouts in and Diyala Province.[10] By mid-2008, Iraqi forces had successfully defeated al-Qaeda in Mosul and remote desert regions, defeated Moqtada al-Sadr's Madi Militia in Basra and Sadr City, and al-Qaeda were leading operations against al-Qaeda's remaining strongholds. In fact, Iraq's security forces had reached 540,000 individuals, increasing by more than 100,000 during the surge.[11] Amid the new security environment, Coalition forces began transferring authority to Iraqi police and military units, and many Iraqis who had fled the country to escape the sectarian violence began returning in large numbers. By July 31, 2008, ten of Iraq's eighteen provinces were under Iraqi control, and U.S. casualties had the lowest monthly toll since the 2003 invasion.[12] Independent journalist Michael Yon, who asserted in 2005 the Iraq was in a civil war, began his July 20, 2008 report with "The war in Iraq is over. We won. Which means the Iraqi people won." [13] As perhaps the most embedded journalist in the Iraq War, at least since he began covering the post-Saddam conflict in 2005, Yon makes the following arguments to support his conclusion:

> So I will be very clear what I mean when I say we have won the war. A counterinsurgency is won when the government's legitimacy is no longer threatened by the insurgents, the government is able to protect its own people and the people are

> participating in the government. In Iraq, all three conditions apply.[14]

Yon also adds that "The Iraqi government has reached 15 of the 18 benchmarks set by the U.S. Congress to measure security, political and economic progress.[15] Even the Associated Press conceded, "The United States is now winning the war that two years ago seemed lost."[16]

This was just the beginning. On 1 September 2008, Major General John F. Kelly, commanding general of Multinational Forces –West (I Marine Expeditionary Force Forward) formally turned over the governance of al-Anbar Province to Mamoon Sami Rashid al-Awani, governor of al-Anbar Province, and turned over security to Major General Murthi Mush'hen Almhalawi, commanding general for all Iraqi Security Forces. Al-Anbar Province became the 11th of 18 provinces to be handed back to Iraqi control. On January 31, 2009 Iraq held its second provincial elections. What is most significant, unlike the three previous elections, was that Iraqi Security Forces provided the physical security for all polling places on election day, and that there was no surge in U.S. forces prior to an Iraqi election. There was minimal violence, and many Iraqis felt secure enough to take their children to polling places. What is also significant is that Iraqis overwhelmingly chose nationalist, secularist parties over religious parties, and chose Iraqi unity over referendums in some provinces to split Iraq.[17]

In al-Anbar Province, like the other Sunni Provinces, not only was voter turnout significant, but their diverse political parties won representation. According to military scholars Kimberly Kagan and Frederick W. Kagan, "The big loser in this election was Iran. Iranian agents spent a lot of money trying to influence the outcome of the elections in the south, and they largely failed."[18] In a *Washington Post* Op-ed, Iraq's ambassador to the United States, Samir Sumaida'ie, described the significance of the elections as:

> These elections have shown that, finally, those who refused to accept the new order and were determined to defeat it by rendering the country ungovernable through violence have come to realize that they have lost; that the political process is the only game in town and that it is in their best interest to play by the new rules. ...Furthermore, the elections have proved wrong those who had claimed that Iraqis could not comprehend democracy and therefore could not abide by its rules. The world watched as millions of ordinary Iraqis, proudly displaying their purple forefingers, declared their desire to choose their leaders, and the leaders themselves demonstrated their ability to make adjustments and compromises. ...At the most critical junctures of this transition, Iraqis have demonstrated their independence and

> unity. This has given them more confidence in their future. Those who thought that they could dominate Iraq from outside, directly or by proxy, surely have realized that their influence will always be limited.[19]

This telling statement not only shows progress in stabilizing Iraq, but also describes a breakthrough in the war of ideas in that Iraqis rejected violence and embraced political and social reform.

As 2009 progressed, Iraqis found new confidence and optimism in their security, government as violence declined and as their economic conditions and quality of life improved. One of the most notable signs, was in the Iraqis willingness to purchase new cars, which led to a surge of new auto dealerships and an new automobile boom in Iraq.[20] Based on an ABC/BBC/NHK National Survey of Iraq, the story titled "Dramatic Advances Sweep Iraq, Boosting Support for Democracy," described the progress and prevailing spirit of optimism.[21]

Between January 1 and April 1, 2009, U.S. forces transferred more than 40 bases, districts, and facilities to Iraqi control as Coalition forces reduced their numbers prepared to leave Iraq.[22] During the summer of 2009, American forces withdrew from Iraq's population centers, putting Iraqi security forces in the lead. A spike in terrorist violence in August and October 2009 did not reignite sectarian violence, and only served to both strengthen Iraqi resolve and force competing Iraqi security agencies to address problems.[23] On January 23, 2010, U.S. Marines ended their participation Iraq. Although small numbers of Marines would continue in advisory roles, the U.S. Marine Corps completed it withdrawal of force and equipment, ending the presence on any standing unit.[24]

The Media's Response to the New Strategy

By 2007, the media's focus remained on U.S. presence and policy, including the domestic debates in the United States, defined in terms of casualties and not on the full political, social, and cultural situation in Iraq that showed progress.[25] In fact, the media largely overlooked the rapid transformation of al-Anbar. Embedded journalists Charles Jones documented Major General Walt Gaskin's frustration with the abundant coverage Anna Nichole Smith and Paris Hilton received compared to the minimal coverage the media gave to al-Anbar's rapid progress.[26] Like the previous three years, much of this was due to the limited number of journalists covering Iraq. According to Jones, "At the time [2006], I was one of only four embed reporters in the province and thirty-nine in the entire country."[27]

A 2007 *Project for Excellence in Journalism* (PEJ) study found that the Iraq War received "three times the amount given to the next biggest story," but more than half of this coverage (55%) was on the Iraq policy debate in the United States and not on actual events in Iraq.[28] Only 1% of all Iraq coverage was on Iraq's reconstruction, whereas 15% was on U.S. casualties and 14% was on Iraq's domestic and humanitarian issues.[29] Since January 7, 2007, "when President Bush announced his troop surge...the question of troop strength remained the major subject discussed about the war. Debate surrounding added deployments or withdrawals accounted for 33% of all the Iraq policy debate stories."[30] Furthermore, despite the media's emphasis on the troop "surge" during this period, a Google search in the week following President Bush's announcement revealed that the word "'Quagmire' appeared 1,044 times."[31] Representative of this focus, the *New York Times*' began the year with a report titled "3,000 Deaths in Iraq, Countless Tears at Home."[32] *Time* magazine followed in similar fashion with an article titled "A Grim Milestone: 500 Amputees."[33]

The effects of these negative reports are clear. According to an American Enterprise Institute study on U.S. public opinion, polling data showed that during the same period, the quagmire narrative and deficient Iraq coverage had succeeded building fears of Vietnam Syndrome among the American population, explaining:

> The public is divided about whether or not they think the Iraq War has become like the Vietnam War. Initially, Americans were quite skeptical of this comparison. In the March 2007 PSRA/Pew Research Center poll, 46 percent said that Iraq will turn out to be another Vietnam while 37 percent said the U.S. would accomplish its goals there.[34]

This poignantly illustrates that absence of comprehensive reporting in Iraq and focus on the Iraq War debates in the United States adversely affected U.S. public opinion.

As U.S. troop surge and new counterinsurgency strategy began to improve Iraq's security situation, news from Iraq began a significant decline as the media lost interest in Iraq. According to a March 2008 PEJ study, news of Iraq began to decline in May 2007 as a result of the improved security situation and a reduction in violence.[35] Characteristic of this reporting, respected independent journalist Michael Yon explained that the media overlooked the successful handoff of Maysan Province security from a British regiment to the Iraqi military on April 18, 2007, in a series of such events, instead reported the day's violence in several articles.[36] In al-Anbar, where U.S. Marines and soldiers were already making huge gains in conjunction with the Awakening movement taking place, journalist were largely absent, and those who did travel to the area failed to report the scope and significance of what was taking place.* However, the news that did come from Iraq continued to concentrate on the negative, as illustrated in articles like those titled "Anti-U.S. March Marks Fourth Anniversary of Iraq Occupation" and "Students Mark War's Anniversary: Protests Across Nation Recall 1960s" characterized media coverage in the Spring of 2007.[37] A ProQuest search of articles between March 1 and April 30 2007 found 166 stories on Iraq War anniversary protests, a significant number from the nation's second largest newspaper corporation McClatchy/Knight Ridder. Adding fuel to the media's forth anniversary coverage were Senate Majority leader Harry Reid's contention that the war was "lost," and Senator Ted Kennedy's quagmire analogy to Vietnam, "We cannot repeat the mistake of Vietnam."[38] By the fall of 2007, nearly seven months after President Bush announced the "surge," two leading analysts and critics often cited by the media to substantiate the quagmire narrative, Michael E. O'Hanlon and Kenneth M. Pollack, reported both the progress and improvements in Iraq's situation. This report supported General Petraeus' testimony to Congress on September 10-11, 2007 that outlined Iraq's gains.[39] A few leading media correspondents reporting from Iraq, such as CBS's Katie Couric, reported progress.[40]

However, such reports were short lived, and were also overshadowed by a wealth of negative coverage focusing on the debates over U.S. policy and troop withdrawal. Stories like "U.S.: Bush's Successor May Inherit Quagmire In Iraq," and "Kucinich: Iraq 'Progress Report' Acknowledges a No-Win Situation," used the political criticisms of President Bush's opponents to advance the quagmire narrative and counter both General Petraeus' testimony and the positive news reports on Iraq.[41] The *New York Times* printed a highly controversial MoveOn.org ad on the first day of the General's testimony titled "General Betrayus," asserting the General lied about progress in Iraq in a 2004 article, and argued that Iraq remained a quagmire.* The ad succeeded in stirring controversy, which drew attention away from the testimony and news of progress and kept it on the Iraq policy debates. A Google search on August 11, 2008 of "General Betrayus" produced 30,200 results, which all thirty of the first thirty results echoed the assertions that General Petraeus lied to Congress and that the favorable report was written by the White House.

Of the abundance of negative coverage overshadowing General Petraeus' testimony, Abu Ghraib and Haditha returned to the spotlight, though they had no connection to either current events in Iraq or General Petraeus' testimony. National Public Radio's (NPR) senior news analyst Daniel Schorr provided a predisposed report telling NPR's Liane Hansen:

---

* A review media visit logs during the author's Spring 2008 visit to al-Anbar Province, Iraq.

* *New York Times*, September 10, 2007.

> Haditha, Abu Ghraib, the very words make one wince. They are the titles of two shameful episodes in the history of American war making. In the Iraqi town of Haditha in 2005, four marine infantrymen killed 24 Iraqi civilians including women and children in a rampage through their homes. The Marines were apparently avenging the killing of a comrade.[42]

Such coverage, not only conveyed quagmire narrative, but also propagated Iraq War myths. By this time, however, charges against four of the eight originally charges had been dropped.[43]

A December 2007 PEJ study titled "The Portrait from Iraq - How the Press Has Covered Events on the Ground" reviewed 1,100 articles from forty news sources during the Surge period preceding General Petraeus' and Ambassador Crocker's testimony and concluded that:

> Through the first 10 months of the year, the portrait of Iraq that Americans have received from the news media has in considerable measure been a grim one. Roughly half of the reporting has consisted of accounts of daily violence. And stories that explicitly assessed the direction of the war have tended toward pessimism.[44]

Positive news, primarily U.S. troop morale and Iraqi views of U.S. presence, received only 1% of coverage (14 of 1,100 articles).[45]

While dangers inherit to directly reporting on events contributed significantly to deficient news coverage in Iraq, *The Project for Excellence in Journalism* found that market and industry changes continued to effect journalism. Media budgets continued to shrink as advertising revenue fell, which continued to leave even fewer journalists to cover news as new audience continued to fracture. Most interesting, however, amid the multitude of news sources across the Internet, traditional news sources gained online audiences as major providers of news—thus retaining their power to set the agenda and influence the public sphere.[46]

Following the Petraeus' September 2007 report to congress, news from Iraq as a whole began to wane as the media turned its attention to the 2008 presidential primaries, though the Iraq War policy debates continued to be a leading topic going into the 2008 presidential campaign season.[47] Indicative of this trend, the *New York Times'* article titled "With War in Senate Spotlight, Presidential Campaigns Converge in Washington," represented how the Iraq War policy debates dominated all news concerning Iraq.[48] As General Petraeus' and Ambassador Crocker's second report to congress neared, articles like "Protest Marks Fifth Anniversary of War" and "Rally to mark 4,000th American death in Iraq" saturated the media as the abundance of print and broadcast stories eclipsed positive news stories of Iraq.[49] *CNN* 's reported "Blast kills 4, raising U.S. toll in Iraq to 4,000," whereas *New York Times'* reported "Another Grim Milestone for the Military" on March 25, 2008 with a caption over a graphic as the paper marked 4,000 deaths in Iraq.[50]

Even al-Jazeera, which coverage remained skeptical of progress and suspicious of the U.S. involvement in Iraq, warmed to the Awakening. Articles like "Sunni tribes seek unity" described both the new tribal cooperation and new cooperation with U.S. forces against al-Qaeda, whereas an article titled "Iraq's Sunnis face new conflict" described the decline in violence reporting "tribesmen in Iraq's al-Anbar province are increasingly turning their guns on al-Qaeda."[51] Nonetheless, much like the Western media, headlines, stories, photos, and captions constantly remained the Arab public about the war's death and destructions, as well as reminding them who was to blame.

In the first half of 2008, fewer Western journalists traveled to al-Anbar Province than the previous year, and those who did usually embedded for brief periods. While most journalists followed embedding rules, some such as freelance photographer Zoriah Miller violated embedding policies by providing graphic photographs of death to news sources.[52] The *New York Times* published Miller's photos in a multimedia report along with an article titled "4,000 U.S. Deaths, and a Handful of Images," which also included Miller's distasteful image of dead U.S. Marines.[53] Meanwhile, the *Miami Herald's* March 2008 story titled "Pentagon Institute Calls Iraq War 'A Major Debacle' With Outcome 'In Doubt'," implied that respected strategic analyst Joseph Collins' paper "Choosing War: The Decision to Invade Iraq" and its Aftermath" was a timely assessment of the war at that time.[54] However, contrary to the *Miami Herald's* politically timed distortion of facts, Collin's paper was neither a Pentagon study or a timely assessment of the recent conflict, but rather an occasional paper for the National Defense University that assessed events between 2002-2004.[55] Nonetheless, many other publications either followed the *Herald's* erroneous assertions uncritically, reprinted the article, of linked to it.[56]

Examples of misinformation, speculation, and unfounded assertion to make assessments of Iraq's situation similarly abound. CNN's Nic Robertson, who allegedly fabricated information during a visit to Western Iraq, cited information from a previous year's trip to make an assessment of Iraq in 2008, making the unfounded assertion that Iraq's militias were "rearming" and were "better trained."[57] He also baselessly speculated that:

> The surge gave the narrowest of margins for improvement. Look at Mosul: when the surge in the south left them short, al Qaeda regrouped there and is re-emerging. The country is still on a knife

> edge, possibly slightly blunter but a fall on either side is nonetheless deadly.

As Robertson filed his report, however, the Iraqi Army, working with U.S. soldiers and Marines were shaping events leading to Operation Lion's Roar in May 2008.[58]

In another example of questionable journalists performance, Washington Post Baghdad Bureau Chief, Sudarsan Raghavan, was expelled for embedding with U.S. Marines in Fallujah under the false pretenses, violating embed policy, and lying to soldiers and Marines to get material for highly partisan stories. Marines suspected he also gave information on U.S. military facilities to insurgents. Raghavan then went to Basra and provided one-side reported favoring the Shiite insurgency.[*]

The *New York Times'* a front-page, above-the-fold story titled "Iraqi Unit Flees Post, Despite America's Plea," claimed that a whole company of Iraqi soldiers deserted during the April 2008 battle between the Iraqi Army and Moqtada al-Sadr's Iranian supported Jaysh al-Mahdi Militia Iraq.[59] However, the claim proved greatly exaggerated as a superior Iraqi Army force routed al-Sadr's Militia in Basra leading to a cease-fire and a major setback for the Iranian backed movement. The incident was more the result of Iraqi President Nouri al-Maliki' hasty, unilateral decision to send an unprepared unit into the fray with against an entrenched militia. Similarly, a CBS report titled "Reconciliation in Iraq 'Isn't Happening'" falsely claimed that "the gains made by agreements with militias (including from Sunni tribes and some Shiite tribes) to work with the Americans have almost disappeared in the face of the recent violence which spreads so quickly from Basra in the south of Iraq."[60] The claim was without merit, as al-Sadr's defeat in Basra solidified Iraqi unity.

Meanwhile, some reports in the United States used creative angles to diminish news of U.S. progress coming from Iraq. The *New York Times* published what it called "War Torn: A series of articles and multimedia about veterans of the wars in Iraq and Afghanistan who have committed killings, or been charged with them, after coming home."[61] However, the series misused statistics or used sketchy or statistically insignificant data to make the dubious claim that violent crimes committed by U.S. veterans of Iraq and Afghanistan are a rampant problem, and that U.S. service members are largely criminals or troubled individuals made more so by combat.[62] Filled with speculation, the reports also dismissed or downplayed other mitigating circumstances that contributed to the incidents reported on.[63]

---

[*] The author learned of Sudarsan Raghavan' activities along with concerns about CNN's Nic Robertson from I MEF Public Affairs officials while in Iraq in early 2008.

By mid-2008, trickles of positive news on Iraq began to soften the Iraq War debate and change U.S. public opinion, and as a result Iraq received less coverage and became less a campaign issue.[64] The July 1, 2008 report that fifteen of eighteen benchmarks of progress in Iraq were met, nearly double as the previous year, received little coverage and short media life.[65] All three network news channels, CBS Evening News, NBC Nightly News, and ABC's World News ignored the news.[66] Likewise, the July 31, 2008 report that U.S. casualties had the lowest monthly toll since the 2003 invasion received little attention.[67] The *New York Times* sought to downplay the decreased casualty rates, casting a pessimistic shadow over the trend by contending that "There have been troughs in American casualty rates before, only to be followed by increases. Just on Sunday, an American soldier was killed by a roadside bomb in Baghdad."[68]

Like the Western media, al-Jazeera also reported the reduced violence and improved security with suspicion. In its August 2008 report titled "Iraq between fear and hope," al-Jazeera began with an argument discrediting the Bush Administration's contention that Iraq posed and imminent threat, and that as a result of the U.S. invasion asserted that "first time in Iraq's history, Islamic fanaticism would rear its ugly head thanks to the constant stream of terrorists pouring across Iraq's poorly defended borders from countries known to be US allies."[69] Then, in a change of direction concluded:

> Nevertheless, Iraqis today still pin their hopes that the worst is over. In some areas of Baghdad, families are picking up the pieces, returning home and reopening their shops and businesses. With fragmented progress reported in some provinces - Al-Anbar's economy is thriving as the guns fall silent in Fallujah and Ramadi - Iraqis are looking forward to the elections planned for 2009.[70]

Such mixed reporting was not unlike the Western media, and although these articles reported progress and some sense of optimism, they continually reminded the public who was ultimately to blame for the Iraq War's devastation.

Importantly, in June 2008 the U.S. government concluded that the alleged Haditha "scandal," was neither "cold-blooded murder" nor "covered-up," and dropped the charges against all but one of the U.S. Marines involved, but the media largely overlooked this.[71] In fact, the *New York Times* printed only two brief reports exonerating the Marines compared to thirty-six sensationalized reports it published on the alleged "Haditha massacre," four of which compared the alleged incident to the My Lai incident in Vietnam.[72] Such lopsided coverage not only demonstrated the media's ability to try and convict the Marines in the media, but also threaten to deny the accused a fair trial.

With Iraq's success emerging as the dominant narrative, headlines such as the *New York Times*' "Deadly U.S. Milestone in Afghan War" reflected the media's turn toward Afghanistan and news of 500 U.S. deaths, applying the same quagmire perspective that it did to every 1,000 deaths in Iraq, emphasizing that U.S. fatalities in Afghanistan exceeded those in Iraq for the month of June 2008.[73]

The Iraq Syndrome: Amplifying Iraq's Quagmire Narrative

As happened during the months preceding the 2006 U.S. mid-term elections, a number of books attempting to influence the public debate on the Iraq War policy became available in 2007. Former U.S. diplomat Peter Galbraith's *The End of Iraq: How American Incompetence Created a War Without End* attempted to make a meaningful contribution to the Iraq policy debate based on his observations an diplomatic experience. However, Charles H Ferguson's *No End In Sight: Iraq's Descent Into Chaos* and Jonathan Steele's *Defeat: Why America and Britain Lost Iraq* were little more than partisan political tirades advancing the quagmire narrative an Iraq War mythology. Importantly, several books attempted to connect U.S. involvement in Iraq to that of Vietnam covered a spectrum of both perspectives and qualified scholarship. Jeffrey Record's and W. Andrew Terrill's *Iraq and Vietnam: Differences, Similarities, and Insights* provided a thoughtful examination comparing and contrasting U.S. involvement. Conversely, Kenneth J. Campbell's *A Tale of Two Quagmires: Iraq, Vietnam, and the Hard Lessons of War* offered a schizophrenic combination of thoughtful analysis and angry diatribe. Similarly, books such *Iraq and the Lessons of Vietnam: Or, How Not to Learn from the Past, Is Iraq Another Vietnam?* and *Vietnam in Iraq: Lessons, Legacies and Ghosts* provided premature examinations of a yet to be decided war through the narrow lens of Vietnam—built on a shaky foundation of Iraq War mythology and the media's quagmire narrative. Still, other books were more obvious in partisanship and political timing in their attempts to influence the public sphere. Philippe Sands' *Torture Team: Rumsfeld's Memo and the Betrayal of American Values* and Philip Gourevitch's and Errol Morris' *Standard Operating Procedure* aimed to keep the legacy of Abu Ghraib alive into the 2008 U.S. presidential elections. There were also a number of picture books showed the war through vivid imagery, but like Eddie Adams' famous picture of Nguyen Ngoc Loan in Vietnam only told part of the story and added to the quagmire narrative of the war. These included *Iraq War*, *Whiskey Tango Foxtrot*, *Iraq: The Space Between*, and *Courage*.

While books such as these attempted to add legitimacy to the quagmire narrative told in the news, films debuting in 2007 and 2008 also propagated the quagmire narrative and added a to Iraq War mythology, intending to affect U.S. public opinion during the 2008 Presidential election year. Writer and Director Nick Broomfield's "Battle for Haditha," highlighted underscored the media "abuses" and "atrocities" frames, and debuted before the government completed it investigation.[74] Like his book, Errol Morris' *Standard Operating Procedure* presented a highly subjective and very questionable film that added powerful images to his partisan commentary on Abu Ghraib and U.S. policy. Like erroneous and misleading news reports, these books and films only reinforced media myths and ingrained them into popular memory.

The Counter-Media Narrative Grows

While the media continued to provide an abundance of incomplete, inaccurate, and misleading reports in the months before the 2008 U.S. Presidential elections, some journalists also became bloggers and used the medium to tell the stories often neglected by the big media. Bill Roggio provided a mix of original, accurate reporting and analysis to counter the mainstream media's erroneous and deficient reporting in his *The Long War Journal*, as did David Dilegge and Bill Nagle on their Small Wars Journal.[75] Independent journalist Michael Totten has spent significant time with U.S. forces on the front lines in Iraq and provided honest, objective, and compelling reports far superior to those in the mainstream media.[76] Commenting on the disparity between reality in Iraq and media created perceptions, Totten wrote:

> Iraq is a tragic, unhappy, and often disturbing place, but it's less sinister and frightening up close than it is from a distance. That's because it's a country striving for normality, whose normal aspects rarely make their way into media reports that highlight violence, mayhem, and failure. On TV, Iraq looks like a nation of masked, gun-toting fanatics, but in person, one finds friendliness, solidarity, and reasonableness amid the chaos.[77]

Similarly, Michael Yon, an independent journalist with considerable time in Iraq as an embedded journalist, wrote in his online magazine *Michael Yon Online*:

> Looking back on the Iraq war, for all the attention the media paid, their reporting was anything but balanced. The outcome of the war was being negatively affected by irresponsible journalism, some of which was intentionally misleading. We truly could have lost the Iraq war due in large part to journalistic travesties. That

> we won the war despite the media demonstrates just how great our soldiers are.[78]

Yon 's also provided a scathing condemnation of the mainstream media, in his book *Moment of Truth in Iraq: How a New 'Greatest Generation' of American Soldiers is Turning Defeat and Disaster into Victory and Hope*, while also providing a compelling, detailed, first-hand accounts of the U.S. efforts in Iraq from 2005 to 2008. According to Communication Professor Stephen D. Cooper, bloggers like Roggio, Totten, and Yon not only supplied a richer story of events, but frequently challenged the media's accuracy, analysis, and framing conventions, sometimes forcing it to run corrections or admit mistakes.[79]

Meanwhile, other critics of the media's deficient reporting, such as former U.S. Army First Lieutenant Pete Hegseth and former U.S. Marine Lieutenant Wade Zirkle, have taken their criticism beyond mere Internet commentary, or *blogasphere.* Under the title Veterans for Freedom (VFF), Hegseth and Zirkle launched a counter-media effort to confront the media and provide a different view, even sending their own embedded journalists to Iraq, explaining:

> It's essential for the American people to know the facts about what is happening in Iraq. Some media outlets, and certain politicians, still fail to assess the situation objectively; so *Vets for Freedom* is heading Back to Iraq to let them know what has been accomplished, what still needs to be done, and how we should proceed in order to attain sustainable security in Iraq.[80]

Importantly, everyday Iraqi's benefiting from satellite television, the Internet, and other forms of information denied them by Saddam Hussein also witnessed the disparity in media reporting and provided their own counter-media narrative. In an interview with journalist Bill Roggio, Iraqi Army soldier Mohamed N. expressed similar sentiment about the U.S. media reports and their influence on waning U.S. public opinion, imploring Roggio to "Tell the American people we need the US Army here. We want to work with them for a longer time. And in the future we can say that we have built the Iraqi Army together."[81] Similarly, embedded journalist Franklin Raff explains:

> Non-English speaking Iraqis are distressed and disheartened by American media bias. Many feel personally offended by what they read in translation and hear of in the foreign press. I am not talking about press information and public affairs officers. I am not talking about coalition soldiers (though every one I spoke with on the subject was equally frustrated.) I am talking about Arabic-speaking Iraqis. They see a difference between what we're

> seeing and what we're saying. What does that tell you about the extent of our problem? [82]

Other Iraqis benefiting from new technology similarly provided their own eyewitness perspectives through the blogasphere, which often sharply contradicted the journalists' negative reports of events, while others took their message to the mainstream media.[83] Concerned about the prevalence of the quagmire narrative and its effect on U.S. public opinion, Iraq's Vice-president Tariq al-Hashimi was one of several leading Iraqis providing a counter-media narrative in late 2006 and 2007. Responding to the U.S. public's growing pessimism and call for withdraw of U.S. forces, al-Hashimi made a passionate call for continued support, outlining progress while acknowledging that Iraq needs more time to develop self-government.[84] Central to his concern was his observation that Americans had become weary of the bad news and cynicism carried by the media.[85] Despite al-Hashimi's efforts, his story received little media attention.

Cause and Effect II

Much like the collective media's abundant pessimistic Iraq war coverage and emphasis on the quagmire narrative adversely influenced public opinion in the months preceding the 2006 mid-term elections and resulting in the election of anti-war candidates, the media's continued deficient reporting in Iraq and concentration on the Iraq policy debate in the United States resulted in the suppression of good news about the Awakening and U.S. and Iraqi progress, which continued to adversely influence public opinion and not only led to more gains in the U.S. Congress for anti-war candidates, such as comedian Al Franken, but also the election of outspoken Iraq War opponent Barrack Obama to the presidency of the United States on a platform of withdrawing U.S. troops from Iraq and reversing many of President George W. Bush's Global War on Terror policies. Ironically, despite a plethora of news stories highlighting critics advocating withdraw, calls for U.S. withdrawal from Iraq were replaced with stories titled, "Soldiering On After The Election: Obama's Victory Is Not An Automatic Trip Home For Troops," and "US/IRAQ: Obama Likely To Choose Continuity Over Change."[86] What is more, in a few stories like "Jihadi Leader in Iraq Says Radicals Share in Obama Victory," some journalists noted what Obama's election to the presidency meant to al-Qaeda and other enemies of the United States.[87]

With the U.S. presidential election over, some journalists began to report the changes taking place in Iraq, catching up on what had largely received very little coverage over the previous two years, especially in al-Anbar Province. Many traveled to al-Anbar interviewing Iraqis involved in the

Awakening, hoping to be the first to break the full Awakening story. However, many of these journalists would get the story wrong because they interviewed Iraqis who claimed some participation in the Awakening but reported hearsay, or interviewed U.S. military or civilian officials who did not understand the history of engagement and operations surrounding it.* Though much of Iraq's news continued to receive short media attention, in headline titled "Dramatic Advances Sweep Iraq, Boosting Support for Democracy" and "Bush's 'Folly' is Ending in Victory," many journalists and observers began to acknowledge success in Iraq, though such stories were few.[88] Nonetheless, around the sixth anniversary of the Iraq War, stories titled "US military deaths in Iraq war at 4,278," reminded the American public of the quagmire narrative.[89] On New Year's Day, 2010, an *Associated Press* headline reported that "December 1st Month without US combat death in Iraq," but qualified the news with file photo of a flag-draped coffin being escorted by U.S. soldiers, which overshadowed the brief report.[90]

Chapter Conclusion

During the Iraq War, the war of ideas for the hearts and minds of the Iraqi people was the most important part of the war, and was waged largely through a plethora of highly partisan and highly competitively Arab and Western media outlets. Iraq's emerging insurgent groups became additional political actors who made effective use of propaganda and the sympathetic Arab media to shape public opinion toward their political aims. At the geopolitical and strategic levels, they sought to garner sympathetic international support while eroding both international support for the war and domestic U.S. public support believing the United States could be convinced to abandon its efforts in Iraq. At the operational and tactical levels, Iraq's insurgent groups used a combination of clever propaganda, media manipulation, and coercion to inflame the population against the Coalition, embolden insurgent groups, and deter cooperation. They also kidnapped and murdered Western journalists, as well as Arab and Iraqi journalists working with the Western media, in an effort to control the narratives of the Iraq War. At the same time, the Western and Arab media outlets reported the war with varying degrees of objectivity and partisanship and provided starkly different accounts of the fighting.

Meanwhile, the Coalition embarked on an ineffective effort to "win the hearts and minds" of the population to bring peace and stability to Iraq in

* The author interviewed a number of Iraqi sheikhs, government officials, police, soldiers, and former Baath Party regime members along with many U.S. military and civilians in 2008 and 2009 who gave accurate accounts of the insurgency and Awakening, and pointed out misrepresentations in the media.

preparation for establishing a democratic government. This effort was further hindered by misleading statements made by Bush Administration officials that inflated media skepticism and caused a decline in U.S. government credibility in the eyes of journalists. As a result, the U.S. government and military surrendered the information initiative to the insurgents, and lost numerous battles and engagements in the wars of ideas that accompanied the conflict. These tactical and operational losses in the arenas of ideas later had dramatic strategic and geopolitical consequences. Eventually, the U.S. military employed both a new military strategy and a new information strategy intended to defeat Iraq's insurgent groups and regain its information advantage. This combination helped enable the Iraqi people's turn from al-Qaeda and violence.

CHAPTER TWELVE

AFGHANISTAN AND BEYOND

Navigating Afghanistan's Complex Cultural and Political Landscape

As Coalition Forces toppled the Baath Party regime and fought a protracted insurgency in Iraq, Afghanistan remained relatively stable under NATO control until 2006 when it experienced a resurgence of the Taliban, which sought to destabilize the Afghan government and regain power. Although U.S. and Coalition Forces routed al-Qaeda and the oppressive Taliban in 2001 and 2002, the United States and its NATO allies did little to build on these gains in the years following, especially in the arena of ideas where winning hearts and minds was critical to long-term success. United States and NATO forces provided insufficient resources to maintain security, develop a functional Afghan police and military, and foster economic and social development. As a result, they failed to secure the population from the Taliban and win popular support for their mission. In 2008, the Bush administration began to increase the U.S. presence Afghanistan as it had in Iraq to counter the renewed Taliban threat, beginning with sending U.S. Marines to Helmand and Farah Provinces of Southern Afghanistan. This marked the beginning of a larger U.S. presence and expanded U.S. role in Afghanistan that would continue under President Barrack H. Obama in 2009 and 2010. As part of this buildup, U.S. military sought to apply the lessons of counterinsurgency and information operations learned from Iraq. However, Afghanistan's cultural and political landscape is much more complex than Iraq, and perhaps more indicative of future conflicts.

While a 2009 Asia Foundation poll showed that many Afghans were interested in the benefits of freedom and peace that democracy would bring, a 2010 Afghan public opinion poll revealed that despite some gains in the arena of ideas, United States and its NATO allies continued to lose popular support from the Taliban after more than eight years of conflict.[1] Moreover, a 2010 PEW Global attitudes poll found that despite President Obama's outreach to Muslim nations, Muslims worldwide still possess an unfavorable view of the United States, along with "fear of America's power and distrust of its intentions."[2]

Recognizing this, U.S. military forces sought to improve strategic communication efforts with their surge in forces, however, four factors would hinder the renewed engagement and strategic communication efforts. First, Afghanistan presented a much greater challenge to Coalition Forces than Iraq because of the population's greater diversity and its isolation from both the outside world and other communities within Afghanistan. Much of the country is very mountainous, which makes travel and communication difficult. This mountainous terrain has not only isolated these groups from each other, but also from Afghanistan's central government. While the majority of Afghans are Sunni Muslims, they are divided into several ethnic groups, each with different languages, whose first alliances are to their family, tribe, and ethnic group. They are largely poor and illiterate. Some villages have not seen outsiders for decades. For example, when U.S. Marine mentors entered on village with Afghan soldiers in 2009, some of the villagers thought the Marines were Soviet troops.[3] The complexity of Afghanistan's political, social, religious, and cultural environment, coupled with its history and isolation have created an environment that has cultivated fundamental Islam, the Taliban, and the nation's illicit drug trade. In the arena of ideas, the rugged terrain, isolated population, illiteracy, and language variance prohibits the use of most means of mass communication. As a result, coalition efforts are largely village-by-village and valley-by-valley efforts centered on shura councils, key leader engagement, flyers, posters, and radio receivers* combined with economic and social development programs. These efforts attempt to help Afghans economically, socially, and politically.

Second, unlike al-Qaeda in Iraq, the Taliban are a part of Afghanistan's population and not only have an identity with it, but also exercise influence and varying levels of control. They understand both the methods and messages to effectively influence local populations. They are also well adept at using and manipulating the world media and influencing world opinion, inviting journalists to accompany them and report for their side. The Taliban's effectiveness in using journalists prompted the Afghan government to "ban live coverage of suicide attacks and firefights," and "threatened to arrest reporters and confiscate their equipment if they cover such event without official sanction."[4] Nonetheless, the Taliban continues to make effective use of technology to influence domestic and foreign audiences, recruit fighters, and gain sympathetic financial support while banning these modern means of communication from the population under its control. This includes the use of web sites, Facebook, Twitter, and You Tube to post propaganda and sensational videos of suicide attacks. It also includes sending

* Coalition forces distribute these hand-crank powered "radios in a box" to the population.

journalists SMS text messages, pictures and videos, as well as to other insurgents and sympathetic subscribers to distribute through their social networks.[5] According to the editor-in-chief of *Al-Emarah*, an official Taliban website:

> Wars today cannot be won without media. Media aims at the heart rather than the body, [and] if the heart is defeated, the battle is won.[6]

This telling statement echoes what other adversaries have similarly observed about the wars of ideas and images that accompany conflicts. *Al-Emarah*, by the way, is presented in the Internet in English, Pashto, Dari, Urdu, and Arabic.[7]

Moreover, like al-Qaeda in Iraq, the Taliban are often very effective in countering Coalition efforts with murder and intimidation, to include delivering threatening "night letters" to people suspected of cooperating with the NATO coalition.[8] Typical of the Taliban's counter efforts, after U.S. Marines quickly defeated the Taliban in their Helmand Province stronghold of Marjah, the Taliban killed a number of Afghans who had cooperated with the Americans, along with three USAID workers.[9] Finally, despite U.S. efforts aimed at gaining the information initiative from the Taliban, the United States is still very slow to respond to events with the first truth than the enemy.

Third, Afghanistan has several regional neighbors vying to influence internal affairs inside the country. Iran not only actively seeks to undermine Coalition efforts in Afghanistan, but also cultivate Afghanistan's Shiite minority through humanitarian aid and goodwill projects and satellite broadcasts that penetrate as far as the capital of Kabul. As part of this effort, Iran is spearheading a Tajik-Afghan-Iranian television station to spread its influence throughout the region.[10] Likewise, Pakistan, Afghanistan's longstanding regional rival, seeks to both influence Afghanistan's affairs and limit its power. Both Pakistan and Iran have aided the Taliban to varying degrees. Meanwhile, India and China both have commercial interests in Afghanistan, as well as political interests as they compete for regional hegemony. Russia, Uzbekistan, Turkistan, and Tajikistan all have interest in Afghani affairs.[11]

Fourth, the change in U.S. administrations from President George W. Bush to brought a change in diplomatic and strategic communication efforts. Amid this complex environment, the NATO alliance has proven to be its own obstacle in winning Afghan hearts of minds. Without unity of effort, NATO forces provide an uneven effort with varying rules of engagement, competing messages, and significantly different approaches all based on varying degrees of support from their home nations. Even the United States, with a change of presidential administrations, has demonstrated the lack of unity of effort between the Department of State and Department of Defense, and with it the lack of effective strategic communication, leaving forces on the ground to operate at the tactical and operational levels in a strategic information void.† Moreover, mixed messages carried in the media's coverage of domestic U.S. political debates carry hints of questionable U.S. resolve, which further undermine the U.S. efforts.[12]

While a full assessment of the renewed U.S. civil-military and strategic communication efforts in Afghanistan is premature, early indications show that despite the increase in troops and resources, the United States was largely unprepared for the wars of ideas and images in Afghanistan, and struggled with delivering the right messages in a timely manner. In a telling statement of what is at stake in Afghanistan and the Global War on Terror as a whole, professor Carnes Lord keenly observes:

> In the language of strategic analysis, the "center of gravity" of Islamist terrorism lie not in its organizational structure but in its ideological inspiration—the real source of fresh recruits who continue to flock to the terrorist banner.[13]

Therefore, as the United States seeks to reach the Afghan population, the implications of U.S. strategic communication efforts in Afghanistan and beyond illustrate that the United States needs a strong public diplomacy and strategic communication program and consistent strategic messages that transcends political administrations if the United States is going to seriously compete in the international arena of ideas. This proactive approach to current and unforeseen future international crisis and conflicts requires unity of effort between the U.S. Department of State and the U.S. military, and continuity across all lines of operation and strategic, operational, and tactical levels. Importantly, this public diplomacy and strategic communication program needs to respond faster to tactical and operational events with the "first truth" if the United States is going to gain and maintain the information initiative in the wars of ideas and images that accompany conflict.

The Media and the U.S. Surge in Afghanistan

Unlike Iraq, Afghanistan suffers from a lack of media attention and study. However, an assessment of news articles reveals that, like Iraq, the phenomenon of incomplete, inaccurate, and misleading reporting began to duplicate itself in Afghanistan for much the same reasons. First, Western

† The author's experience in Afghanistan.

journalists covered the U.S. efforts with U.S. forces, and those who did often had considerable difficulties gaining access to places and events and forced to file reports with little or no first-hand knowledge. Those who did get out often had a very narrow picture of the U.S. effort and were often colored by the hardships, danger, and violence they experienced, while some clearly reported along the quagmire narrative of U.S. involvement in foreign affairs.

Second, as described above, the Taliban has proved itself to be very adept at using the international media to its advantage by inviting journalists to witness preplanned attacks on NATO and Afghan government targets, which include IEDs and suicide bombings. Like the international media's coverage of the 2006 Israel-Lebanon War, the Taliban has manipulated journalist by showing them the aftermath of "alleged" Coalition attacks to achieve their political aims. This includes killing Afghan civilians with grenades and then showing journalists the carnage from an alleged unmanned Predator attack on innocent civilians to sway international public opinion against the United States' use of these very effective means of eliminating Taliban command and control centers.[14]

Third, the whole U.S.-NATO and effort in Afghanistan has received uneven coverage from the international media, which grew increasing pessimistic coverage since 2006 and was often filled with hasty, unqualified journalistic analysis. As a result, reports of violence, casualties, Afghan corruption, or U.S. mistakes overshadowed reports of U.S. progress. Forth, the Western media not only reasserted itself in the U.S. Afghan policy debates, but also provided an abundance of coverage on the debates compared to actual coverage of U.S. efforts from Afghanistan. Articles such "POLITICS: OBSERVERS WONDER IF AFGHANISTAN IS NEXT U.S. QUAGMIRE" not only conveyed the Western media's pessimism, but also framed the U.S. Afghan policy debates as President Barrack Obama came into office.[15] Much like Iraq, coverage of the U.S. Efforts in Afghanistan were overshadowed by the ensuing and increasing heated political debates in the United States over U.S. role in Afghanistan, especially after U.S. commanders in Afghanistan asked for more troops.[16] Again, using sensational statements from prominent sources, such as U.S. Senator Harry Reid, numerous articles such as "Obama Tiptoeing Around Afghanistan Quagmire," "Is Afghanistan Obama's Vietnam?," "Afghanistan Is Vietnam: A Valid Analogy?," and "Obama's Vietnam: How to Salvage Afghanistan" conveyed the media's intention to shape public opinion and policy.[17] Like international media coverage of Iraq, the lack of media presence coupled with pessimistic reporting, hasty analysis, and coverage of highly partisan domestic debates over Afghanistan policy have adversely influenced the domestic resolve of NATO allies, and threatened U.S. resolve.[18]

Nonetheless, the lack of interest in media performance in Afghanistan compared to Iraq is troubling. It begs the question "why?" Perhaps media scholars and analysts, along with historians, will take an interest in media performance before the wars of ideas and images is lost.

Final Conclusion

The Global War on Terror that began following the September 11, 2001 terrorists' attacks was more a war of ideas than it was a military conflict. During the conflict, multiple wars of ideas played out on the geopolitical, strategic, operational, and tactical levels, as well as on the domestic U.S. political landscape for control of U.S. policy. Beginning long before military operations began on the ground in Iraq or Afghanistan, competing political interests used all available media to influence multiple public spheres toward their desired political goals. At the geopolitical and strategic levels, various Islamic based terrorists groups, including a-Qaeda, used terrorism and propaganda in concert with the media to challenge the West, especially the United States, and advance their political interests and ideology. This included clever propaganda and media manipulation to solicit international sympathy while deterring international support for the U.S. intervention in Middle East affairs, and forging solidarity among Muslims worldwide. Lacking a comprehensive strategic communication and public diplomacy program, the United States did little counter their adversary's ideological challenges at the geopolitical and strategic levels, and continued to rely on the free-media to communicate with the public sphere both domestically and abroad. As these various competing political interests used the media to influence public opinion and policy, the collective Western and Arab media, as independent political actors, also sought to frame the debates and shape public opinion and policy in the years before the war. Addressing the media's role in these wars of ideas, Kenneth Payne keenly observes:

> The media, in the modern era, are indisputably an instrument of war. This is because winning modern wars is as much dependent on carrying domestic and international public opinion as it is on defeating the enemy on the battlefield.[19]

This truth was clearly evident as the Iraq War unfolded.

The collective media's role as an independent political actor, its use as a weapon in the wars of ideas that accompanied the Iraq War, and its power to influence public opinion and policy are clear demonstrated in the Iraq War. In the twenty-four-hour news cycle dominated by satellite television, a small number of unilateral journalists in Iraq, facing unforgiving deadlines in a highly competitive environment that demanded a constant flow of information, provided only fragments of news based on hasty, superficial treatment of a developing story before all of the facts were known. What went unreported often told more. Moreover, affected by the extreme physical and emotional factors of a combat environment, along with the cultural complexities of reporting in a foreign land journalists operated in their own fog of war as they attempt to report on things they could not understand. Considering themselves, the watchdogs of democracy, the gatekeepers of information, and agents for social change, many journalists attempted to be influential in their reporting on Iraq. Despite the quality reporting of a few exceptional journalists, many blended facts with fiction, and often used questionable sources while dismissing U.S. government reports, and injected unqualified analysis and opinion into their reports. Based on a narrow perception of a much larger picture, many journalists often argued by assertion to support a claim in the absence of facts. Some journalists attempted to report the progress, and provide a richer account of Iraq's situation, but those reports either went unpublished, were given poor placement, received short media life, or appeared only on the Internet because they contradicted the media's quagmire narrative. Therefore, journalists did not provide a balanced portrayal of events in Iraq—instead conveying a pessimistic quagmire narrative that often narrowly defined and twisted perceptions of Iraq's complex realities. A 2009 PEW Research Center for People and the Press report titled "Press Accuracy Rating Hits Two Decade Low," though not directly addressing Iraq War media coverage, supports this conclusion by examining a broad 25-year trend in declining media accuracy.[20]

Without peer review or validating facts or sources, instantaneous mass communication in the forms of satellite television, and wire services, and the Internet carried journalists' perceptions to a wide global audience through thousands of media outlets around the world that reproduced their often incomplete, erroneous, and misleading stories uncritically. Like the Tet Offensive of 1968, these reports encouraged hasty, and often incorrect analysis that drew impulsive, half-informed conclusions, often amplified by popular "soft news" programs, which shaped initial perceptions and reactions that remained in public memory long after the event. Furthermore, the inaccurate, incomplete, or misleading coverage from Iraq influenced editors and producers who selected stories, images headlines and sound bites, and predisposed other journalists who covered the political scene and debates over U.S. policy in the United States.

This study concludes that, like the media's coverage of the Tet offensive in Vietnam, and despite the meaningful contributions of a few exceptional journalists, Americans, or the world for that matter, did not get the full story of Iraq. As with Tet, these sins of omission and commission gave a fuzzy and misleading picture of the political and military situation in Iraq—one that adversely influenced public opinion and policy. However, the media was not alone. Reminiscent of Vietnam, the U.S. government's misleading statements of inflated optimism amid continued conflict and violence during the early post Saddam conflict and its diminished relations with the media thereafter also contributed. This not only contributed to the loss of credibility in the media, but also over the course of time resulted in the loss of credibility among a significant segment of both the American and world population. These deficiencies have significant implications for the U.S. efforts in Afghanistan and future conflicts.

As demonstrated, war is more than combat. It is also a war of ideas that plays out at the tactical, operational, strategic, and geopolitical levels where the lines between fact and fiction are blurred, where intentionally shaped perceptions are often radically different than reality, and where the media not only plays a critical role in influencing public sentiment and public policy, but ultimately the course of events. This is most true in guerrilla wars and insurgencies where winning the population, not the terrain, is the goal. What is more, the media is never truly objective. The media's stand before and during the Iraq war greatly influenced its coverage, and through the conventions of priming, framing, and agenda setting, both journalists and the media industry sought to influence public opinion and policy throughout the conflict.

In Iraq, the dominance of the Arab media in covering events, with its partisan coverage, is a significant factor in the war of ideas that accompanies the war in Iraq and the War on Terror as a whole. Osama bin Laden, Saddam Hussein, Sheik Saleh, and Mohamad al-Janabi, referenced earlier in this study, all acknowledged the value of propaganda, and drew parallels to Vietnam in formulating their propaganda strategy. The inability of the Western media to provide a clear and accurate representation of events, coupled with its narrow and suspicious perspective of U.S. policy and presence, allowed the guerrillas and the partisan Arab media to shape public opinion and influence U.S. policy to achieve their political objectives in Iraq. Thus, while both sides of an issue or conflict have sought to use, manipulate, or control the media, in all of its forms, to influence the public, the media also served its own interests in reporting Iraq. In doing so, the media was often creator and purveyor of myths and a catalyst in historical events. The American mass media did not serve the U.S. democracy.

Likewise, the Taliban in Afghanistan have not only shown great understanding and sophistication in their media use, but also have revealed the wars of ideas and images of the future. As the U.S. government seeks to gain a voice in Afghanistan, the suspicious absence of uniform media coverage of U.S.-NATO efforts there indicates that the American mass media may again fail the American people.

While the shortcomings and criticisms of the media are plenty, it is important to note that the collective media cannot be blamed entirely as the U.S. government's ineffective communication and media handling at all levels, both domestically and internationally, as a result of its overreliance on the free media to convey its messages, deserves its share of the blame. As Iraq War veteran and author David J. Danelo astutely observed that:

> Leaders cannot anticipate using reporters or their mediums as avenues for sustaining the public's morale in a long, complex conflict. Nor can we place responsibility for the moral level of war on the shoulders of American writers. Blaming the press may be emotionally satisfying for a frustrated corps of officers and politicians, but it is not a truthful, useful, or intelligent course of action.[21]

Lessons for Historians and Scholars

Historians must be careful in relying on the media for a source of historical facts. They have an obligation to set the record straight. Like Herodotus in the fifth century B.C., historians must not only preserve important events for posterity, but separate truth from legend. This study illustrated some of the errors in the journalists' so-called "first draft" of history, though historians will continue to correct the record for decades. What is more, like Thucydides, historians must carefully analyze the political and military events to understand their true causes and influences. In regard to the Global War on Terror, just as there are multiple journalistic views of U.S. foreign involvement; there are multiples views of history. This study, to the best that available sources allowed, examined the complex factors contributing to the media's incomplete, inaccurate, or misleading reporting in Iraq—concentrating on the delimited and measurable events in 2004 Fallujah and 2005-2008 al-Anbar Province. As demonstrated to comparing the Western media's coverage of first weeks for the Iraq War to its coverage of the post-Saddam insurgency, reporters close to events provide a far more accurate and complete account of events than those who are not. This validates what General Anthony Zinni observes, "You'll never get a true picture of the battle that does not include that front-line perspective."[22]

SELECTED BIBLIOGRAPHY

Government Documents

Andrew, Rod. *The Battle of An-Nasiriyah.* Washington, DC: History Division, U.S. Marine Corps, 2009.

Fontenot, Gregory, E. J. Degen, and David Tohn. *On Point: The United States Army in Operation Iraqi Freedom.* Fort Leavenworth, Kan: Combat Studies Institute Press, 2004.

Groen, Michael S. *With the 1st Marine Division in Iraq, 2003: No Greater Friend, No Worse Enemy.* Quantico, VA: Marine Corps University, History Division, 2006.

Iraq Liberation Act of 1998, The Library of Congress, 1998

Joint Publication 3-13: Information Operations. Washington, DC: Department of Defense, 2006.

Kennedy, Christopher M. *U.S. Marines in Iraq, 2003: Anthology and Annotated Bibliography. U.S. Marines in the Global War on Terrorism.* Washington, DC: History Division, U.S. Marine Corps, 2006.

McWilliams, Timothy S. and Kurtis P. Wheeler, eds. *Al-Anbar Awakening Volume I. American Perspectives: From Insurgency to Counterinsurgency in Iraq, 2004-2009.* Quantico, VA: Marine Corps University Press, 2009.

Montgomery, Gary W. and Timothy S. McWilliams, eds. *Al-Anbar Awakening: Volume II: Iraqi Perspectives: From Insurgency to Counterinsurgency in Iraq, 2004-2009.* Quantico, VA: Marine Corps University Press, 2009.

Petraeus, General David H. Report to Congress on the Situation in Iraq, 10-11 September 2007.

Petraeus, General David H. Report to Congress on the Situation in Iraq, 8-9 April 2008.

Reynolds, Nicholas E. *U.S. Marines in Iraq, 2003: Basra, Baghdad and Beyond, U.S. Marines in the Global War on Terrorism*, Washington, DC: History Division, U.S. Marine Corps, 2007.

Todd, Lin et al., "Iraq Tribal Study—Al-Anbar Governorate: The Albu Fahd Tribe, the Albu Mahal Tribe, and the Albu Issa Tribe." Department of Defense Study. 18 June 2006.

Woods Kevin M., with Michael R. Pease, Mark E. Stout, Williamson Murray, and James G. Lacey. *Iraqi Perspectives Project: A View of Operation Iraqi Freedom from Saddam's Senior Leadership*. Joint Center for Operational Analysis, Washington, DC: 2006.

Wright, Donald P., and Timothy R. Reese. *On Point II : Transition to the New Campaign: The United States Army in Operation Iraqi Freedom*, May 2003-January 2005. Fort Leavenworth, KS: Combat Studies Institute Press, 2008.

The 9/11 Commission Report: Final Report of the National Commission on Terrorist Attacks Upon the United States (Authorized Edition). New York: W.W. Norton Company, 2004.

Books

Aburish, Said K. *Saddam Hussein: The Politics of Revenge*. New York: Bloomsbury Publishing, 2000.

Allard, Kenneth. *Warheads: Cable News and the Fog of War*. Annapolis: Naval Institute Press, 2006.

Allawi, Ali A. *The Occupation of Iraq: Winning the War, Losing the Peace*. New Haven, CT: Yale University Press, 2007.

Allen, Stuart and Barbie Zelizer, eds. *Reporting War: Journalism in Wartime*. New York: Routledge, 2004.

Armstrong, Karen, *Islam: A Short History*. New York: The Modern Library, 2002.

Artz, Lee and Yahya R. Kamalipour, eds. *Bring 'em On: Media and Politics in the Iraq War*. Lanham, MD: Rowman & Littlefield Publishers, 2005.

Arnett, Peter. *Live from the Battlefield: From Vietnam to Baghdad: 35 Years in the World's War Zones.* New York: Simon & Schuster, 1994.

Axelrod, Alan. *Political History of America's Wars.* Washington, DC: CQ Press, 2007

Bailyn, Bernard. *The Ideological Origins of the American Revolution.* Cambridge, MA: Belknap Press of Harvard Univ. Press, 1992.

Baum, Matthew A. *Soft News Goes to War: Public Opinion and American Foreign Policy in the New Media Age.* Princeton: Princeton University Press, 2003.

Benjamin, Daniel. *The Age of Sacred Terror.* New York: Random House, 2002.

Bennett, W. Lance and David L. Paletz, eds. *Taken by Storm: The Media, Public Opinion, and U.S. Foreign Policy in the Gulf War.* Chicago: University of Chicago Press, 1994.

Berenger, Ralph D. *Cybermedia Go to War: Role of Converging Media During and After the 2003 Iraq War.* Spokane, WA: Marquette Books, 2006.

Bernays, Edward L., and Mark Crispin Miller. *Propaganda.* Brooklyn, NY: Ig Publishing, 2005.

Blix, Hans. *Disarming Iraq.* New York: Pantheon Books, 2004.

Braestrup, Peter. *Big story: How The American Press And Television Reported and Interpreted the Crisis of Tet 1968 in Vietnam and Washington.* Boulder, CO: Westview Press, 1977.
------*Battle Lines: Report on the Twentieth Century Fund Task Force on the Military and Media.* New York: Priority Press Publications, 1985.

Briggs, Asa and Peter Burke. *A Social History of the Media: From Gutenberg to the Internet* Cambridge, UK: Polity Press, 2005.

Brigham, Robert K., *Is Iraq another Vietnam?.* New York: *Public Affairs*, 2006

Burden, Matthew Currier. *The Blog of War: Front-Line Dispatches from Soldiers in Iraq and Afghanistan.* New York: Simon & Schuster, 2006.

Chalberg, John. *Emma Goldman: American Individualist.* New York: HarperCollins, 1991.

Chehab, Zaki, *Inside the Resistance: The Iraqi Insurgency and the Future of the Middle East* New York: Nation Books, 2005.

Clausewitz, Carl von, Michael Howard, and Peter Paret. *On War.* Princeton, N.J.: Princeton University Press, 1976.

Combs, Cindy C. *Terror in the Twenty-First Century.* Upper Saddle River, NJ: Pearson/Prentice Hall, 2006.

Cooper, Stephen D. *Watching the Watchdog: Bloggers as the Fifth Estate.* Spokane, WA: Marquette Books, 2006.

Copeland, David A., and Daniel Schorr. *The Idea of a Free Press: The Enlightenment and Its Unruly Legacy. Visions of the American Press.* Evanston, Illinois: Northwestern University Press, 2006.

Coughlin, Con. *Saddam: King of Terror.* New York: Harper Collins, 2002.

Danelo, David J. *Blood Stripes: The Grunt's View of the War in Iraq.* Mechanicsburg, PA: Stackpole Books, 2006.

David, G. J., and T. R. McKeldin. *Ideas As Weapons: Influence and Perception in Modern Warfare.* Washington, D.C.: Potomac Books, 2009.

Davis, Donald E., and Eugene P. Trani. *The First Cold War: The Legacy of Woodrow Wilson U.S.-Soviet Relations.* Columbia: University of Missouri Press, 2002.

Dawisha, Adeed and Karen Dawisha, eds. *The Soviet Union in the Middle East: Policies and Perspectives.* New York: Holmes & Meier, 1982.

Debenedetti, Charles, and Charles Chatfield. *An American Ordeal: The Antiwar Movement of the Vietnam Era.* Syracuse, NY: Syracuse University Press, 1990.

Delong, Michael. *Inside CentCom: The Unvarnished Truth about the wars in Afghanistan and Iraq.* Washington, DC: Regnery Publishing, 2004.

Delong-Bas, Natana J. *Wahhabi Islam: From Revival and Reform to Global Jihad.* Oxford, UK: Oxford University Press, 2004.

Dodge, Toby. *Inventing Iraq: The Failure of Nation Building and a History Denied.* New York: Columbia University, 2003.

------*Iraq's Future: The Aftermath of Regime Change.* New York: Routledge, 2005.

Drinnon, Richard. *Rebel in Paradise: A Biography of Emma Goldman.* Chicago: University of Chicago Press, 1961.

Echevarria, Antulio Joseph. *Wars of Ideas and the War of Ideas.* Carlisle, PA: Strategic Studies Institute, U.S. Army War College, 2008.

Eickelman, Dale F. and Jon W. Anderson, eds. *New Media in the Muslim World: The Emerging Public Sphere.* Bloomington: Indiana University Press, 2003.

El-Nawawy, Mohammed and Abdel Iskandar. *Al-Jazeera: How the Free Arab News Network Scooped the World and Changed the Middle East.* Cambridge, MA: Westview Press, 2002.

Engel, Richard. *War Journal: My Five Years in Iraq.* New York: Simon & Schuster, 2008.

Entman, Robert M. *Projections of Power: Framing News, Public Opinion, and U.S. Foreign Policy.* Chicago : University of Chicago Press, 2004.

Ewen, Stuart. *PR!: A Social History of Spin.* New York: Basic Books, 1996.

Forbes, Edwin, *Thirty Years After: An Artist's Memoir of the Civil War.* Baton Rouge, LA: Louisiana State University Press, 1993.

Franklin, H. Bruce. *Vietnam and Other American Fantasies.* Culture, politics, and the Cold War. Amherst, Mass: University of Massachusetts Press, 2000.

Garfinkle, Adam M., *Telltale Hearts: The Origins and Impact of the Vietnam Antiwar Movement.* New York: St. Martin's Griffin, 1997.

Glubb, John Bagot. *A Short History of the Arab Peoples.* New York: Stein and Day, 1969.

Goldberg, Bernard. *Bias: A CBS Insider Exposes How the Media Distorts the News.* Washington, DC: Regnery Publishing, Inc., 2002.

Goldman, Emma. *Living My Life.* New York: Dover Publications, 1970.

Gordon, Michael R. and General Bernard Trainor. *Cobra II: The Inside Story of the Invasion and Occupation of Iraq.* New York: Pantheon Books, 2006.

Greenberg, Karen J., and Joshua L. Dratel. *The Torture Papers: The Road to Abu Ghraib.* New York: Cambridge University Press, 2005.

Halberstam, David. *The Making of a Quagmire.* New York: Random House, 1965.

Hall-Jamieson, Kathleen and Paul Waldman, *The Press Effect: Politicians, Journalists, and the Stories That Shape the Political World.* Oxford: Oxford University Press, 2007.

Hammel, Eric. *Fire in the Streets: The Battle for Hue: Tet, 1968.* New York: Dell, 1991.

Hamza, Khidhir and Jeff Stein. *Saddam's Bombmaker: The Daring Escape of the Man Who Built Iraq's Secret Weapon.* New York: Touchstone, 2001.

Hand, Richard J., *Terror on the Air!: Horror Radio in America, 1931-1952.* Jefferson, NC: Macfarlane & Company, 2006.

Harmon, Christopher, *Terrorism Today*, London & Portland: Frank Cass, 2002.

Hashim, Ahmed S. *Insurgency and Counter-Insurgency in Iraq.* Ithaca, NY: Cornell University Press, 2006

-----Iraq's Sunni Insurgency. Abingdon (Royaume-Uni): Routledge, 2009.

Hayden, Tom. *The Port Huron Statement: The Visionary Call of the 1960s Revolution.* New York: Thunder's Mouth Press, 2005.

Hayes, Stephen F. *The Connection : How al-Qaeda's Collaboration with Saddam Hussein Has Endangered America*, New York: Harper Collins, 2004.

Herman, Edward S. and Noam Chomsky, *Manufacturing Consent.* New York: Vintage, 2006.

Herz, Martin Florian, and Leslie Rider. *The Prestige Press and the Christmas Bombing, 1972: Images and Reality in Vietnam.* Washington, D.C.: Ethics and Public Policy Center, 1980.

Hess, Stephen and Marvin Kalb, ed. *The Media and the War on Terrorism.* Washington, DC: Brookings Institution Press, 2003.

Hirst, Martin, and Roger Patching. *Journalism Ethics: Arguments and Cases.* South Melbourne, Vic: Oxford University Press, 2005.

Hunt, Andrew E. *The Turning: A History of Vietnam Veterans Against the War.* New York: New York University Press, 1999.

Iggers, Jeremy. *Good News, Bad News: Journalism Ethics and the Public Interest.* Boulder, CO: Westview Press, 1998.

Jones, Charles. *Red, White, or Yellow?: The Media and the Military at War in Iraq.* Mechanicsburg, PA: Stackpole Books, 2008.

Juergensmeyer, Mark. *Terror In The Mind of God: The Global Rise Of Religious Violence.* Berkeley: University of California Press, 2000.

Kamalipour, Yahya R. *War, Media, and Propaganda.* Lanham, MD: Rowman & Littlefield, 2004.

Karabell, Zachary. *Parting the Desert: The Creation of the Suez Canal.* New York: A.A. Knopf, 2003.

Keane, John. *The Media and Democracy.* Cambridge, UK: Polity Press, 1991.

Kennedy, William V. *The Military and the Media: Why the Press Cannot Be Trusted to Cover a War.* Westport, CN: Praeger, 1993.

King, R. Alan. *Twice Armed.* St. Paul, MN: Zenith Press, 2006.

Kingseed, Cole C. Eisenhower and the Suez Crisis of 1956. Baton Rouge: Louisiana State University Press, 1995.

Klehr, Harvey, John Earl Haynes, and K. M. Anderson. *The Soviet World of American Communism.* Annals of Communism. New Haven: Yale University Press, 1998.

Knightly, Phillip. *The First Casualty: The War Correspondent as Hero and Myth-Maker from the Crimea to Iraq.* Baltimore: The Johns Hopkins University Press, 2004.

Kovach, Bill, and Tom Rosenstiel. *Warp Speed: America in the Age of Mixed Media.* New York: Century Foundation Press, 1999.

Kurlansky, Mark. *1968: The Year That Rocked the World.* New York: Ballantine, 2004.

Larson, Eric V. Casualties and Consensus: *The Historical Role of Casualties in Domestic Support for U.S. Military Operations.* Santa Monica, CA: RAND, 1996.

Laurie, B., and R. J. Del Vecchio. *Whitewash, Blackwash: Myths of the Viet Nam War.* [United States?]: Bill Laurie and R.J. Del Vecchio, 2005.

Lewis, Bernard. *The Crisis of Islam: Holy War and Unholy Terror.* New York: Modern Library, 2003.

Lewis, Justin, Rod Brookes, Nick Mosdell, and Terry Threadgold. *Shoot First and ask Questions Later: Media Coverage of the 2003 Iraq War.* New York: Peter Lang Publishing, Inc., 2006.

Lippmann, Walter. *Public opinion.* London: Allen & Unwin, 1922.

Litvak Meir, *Shi'i Scholars of Nineteenth-Century Iraq: The 'Ulama' of Najaf and Karbala.* New York: Cambridge University Press, 1998.

Livingston, Gary. *Fallujah, with Honor; First Battalion, Eighth Marine's Role in Operation Phantom Fury.* Caisson Press, 2006.

Lord, Carnes. Losing Hearts and Minds?: Public Diplomacy and Strategic Influence in the Age of Terror. Westport, CN: Praeger Security International, 2006.

Lynch, Marc. *Voices of the New Arab Public: Iraq, Al-Jazeera, and Middle East Politics Today.* New York: Columbia University Press, 2006.

Mackiewicz Wolfe, Wojtek. *Winning the War of Words: Selling the War on Terror from Afghanistan to Iraq.* Westport, CT: Praeger Security International, 2008.

Makiya, Kanan. *Republic of Fear: The Politics of Modern Iraq, Updated Edition.* Berkley and Los Angeles: University of California Press, 1998.

Marston, Daniel, and Carter Malkasian. *Counterinsurgency in Modern Warfare.* Oxford: Osprey, 2008.

Marszalek, John F. *Sherman's Other War: The General and the Civil War Press.* Memphis, TN: Memphis State University Press, 1981

McGeough, Paul. *Mission Impossible: The Sheikhs, the U.S. and the Future of Iraq.* Quarterly Essay, issue 14 2004. Melbourne, Victoria, AUS: Black Inc, 2004.

McLaughlin, Greg. *The War Correspondent.* London: Pluto Press, 2002

Marszalek, John F. *Sherman's Other War: The General and the Civil War Press.* Memphis [TN]: Memphis State University Press, 1981

Mellor, Noha. The Making of Arab News. Lanham, MD: Rowman & Littlefield Publishers, 2005.

Mermin, Jonathan. *Debating War and Peace: Media Coverage of U.S. Intervention in the Post-Vietnam Era.* Princeton, NJ: Princeton University Press, 1999.

Metz, Steven. *Iraq & the Evolution of American Strategy.* Washington, DC: Potomac Books, 2008.

Miles, Hugh. *Al-Jazeera: The Inside Story of the Arab News Channel that is Challenging the West.* New York: Grove Press, 2005.

Mockaitis, Thomas R. *Iraq and the Challenge of Counterinsurgency.* Westport, CT: Praeger Security International, 2008.

Morris, Mary E., *The Persistence of External Interest in the Middle East.* Santa Monica, CA: Rand, 1993.

Munson, Peter J. *Iraq in Transition: The Legacy of Dictatorship and the Prospects for Democracy.* Washington, DC: Potomac Books, 2009.

Mylroie, Laurie. *Study of Revenge: The First World Trade Center Attack and Saddam Hussein's War Against America.* Washington, DC: AEI Press, 2001.

Nakash, Yitzhak. *Reaching for Power: The Shi'a in the Modern Arab World.* Princeton: Princeton University Press, 2006.

Nixon, Richard M. *No More Vietnams.* New York: Arbor House, 1985

Noebel, David A. *Rhythm, Riots, and Revolution; An Analysis of the Communist Use of Music, the Communist Master Music Plan.* Tulsa, OK: Christian Crusade Publications, 1966.

Nolan, Keith William. *Battle for Hue: Tet, 1968.* New York: Dell, 1983.

Norris, Pippa, ed. *Politics and the Press: The News Media and their Influences*, Lynne Rienner Publishers, Inc.: Boulder, CO, 1997.

Oberdorfer, Don. *TET! The Turning Point in the Vietnam War.* New York: De Capo Press, 1984.

Obeidi, Mahdi, Kurt Pitzer. *The Bomb in My Garden: The Secrets of Saddam's Nuclear Mastermind.* Hoboken, NJ: John Wiley and Sons, 2004.

O'Donnell, Patrick K. *We Were One: Shoulder to Shoulder With the Marines Who Took Fallujah.* Cambridge, MA: De Capo Press, 2006.

Olsen, Kim. Iraq and Back: *Inside the War to Win the Peace.* Annapolis: Navy Institute Press, 2006.

Patai, Raphael. *The Arab Mind.* New York: Hatherleigh Press, 2002.
Pateman, Barry, and Alexander Berkman. *The Blast.* Edinburgh, Scotland: AK Press, 2005.

Paul, Christopher and James J. Kim. *Reporters on the Battlefield: The Embedded Press System in Historical Context.* Santa Monica: RAND Corporation, 2004.

Perone, James E. *Songs of the Vietnam Conflict.* Westport, Conn: Greenwood Press, 2001.

-----*Music of the Counterculture Era. American history through music.* Westport, CT: Greenwood Press, 2004.

Perry, Mark. *Talking to Terrorists: Why America Must Engage with Its Enemies.* New York: Basic Books, 2010.

Petrov, Jodie. *The Use of Music As Propaganda in the Consolidation of the Totalitarian States Under Hitler and Stalin.* Queensland Conservatorium of Music, Griffith University, 1993.

Phares, Walid. *The War of Ideas: Jihadism against Democracy.* New York: Palgrave Macmillan, 2008.

Pillar, Paul R. *Terrorism and U.S. Foreign Policy.* Washington, DC: Brookings Institute Press, 2001.

Post, Jerrold M. *The Psychological Assessment of Political Leaders: With Profiles of Saddam Hussein and Bill Clinton.* Ann Arbor: University of Michigan Press,

2005.

Prochnau, William W. *Once Upon a Distant War.* New York: Times Books, 1995

Purdum, Todd S. *A Time of Our Choosing: America's War in Iraq.* New York: Time Books, 2003.

Rajiva, Lila. *The Language of Empire: Abu Ghraib and the American Media.* New York: Monthly Review Press, 2005

Ricks, Thomas E. *Fiasco: The American Military Adventure in Iraq.* New York: The Penguin Press, 2006.

Rid, Thomas, and Marc Hecker. *War 2.0: Irregular Warfare in the Information Age.* Westport, CT: Praeger Security International, 2009.

Robinson, Piers. *The Myth CNN Effect: The Myth of News Media, Foreign Policy and Intervention.* New York: Routledge, 2002.

Romerstein, Herbert, and Eric Breindel. *The Venona Secrets: Exposing Soviet Espionage and America's Traitors.* Washington, DC: Regnery Publishing, 2000.

Rosenkranz, Keith. *Vipers in the Storm.* New York: Mc Graw Hill, 2002.

Roussel, Violaine, and Bleuwenn Lechaux. *Voicing Dissent: American Artists and the War on Iraq.* New York: Routledge, 2010.

Rugh, William A. ed. *Engaging the Arab and Islamic Worlds through Public Diplomacy: A Report and Action Recommendations.* Washington, DC: Public Diplomacy Council, 2004.

Rubin, Bernard. *Media, Politics, and Democracy.* Reconstruction of society series. New York: Oxford University Press, 1977

Sageman, Marc. *Understanding Terror Networks.* Philadelphia: University of Pennsylvania Press, 2004.

Safer, Morley. *Flashbacks: On Returning to Vietnam.* New York: Random House, 1990.

Satloff, Robert. *The Battle for Ideas in the War on Terror: Essays on U.S. Public Diplomacy in the Middle East.* Washington, DC: Washington Institute for Near East Policy, 2004.

Schechter, Danny. *Embedded: Weapons of Mass Deception: How the Media Failed to Cover the War on Iraq.* New York: Prometheus Books, 2003.

Scheuer, Michael. *Through Our Enemies' Eyes: Osama Bin Laden, Radical Islam & the Future of America.* Dulles, VA: Potomac Book, 2003.

Schmitz, David F. *The Tet Offensive: Politics, War, and Public Opinion.* Lanham, MD: Rowman & Littlefield Publishers, 2005.

Schudson, Michael. *The Sociology of News.* New York: W.W. Norton, 2003.

Schwarz, Benjamin C. *Casualties, Public Opinion, and U.S. Military Intervention: Implications for U.S. Regional Deterrence Strategies.* Santa Monica, CA: RAND, 1994.

Sciolino, Elaine. *The Outlaw State: Saddam Hussein's Quest For Power And The Gulf Crisis.* New York: Wiley, 1991.

Secunda, Eugene, and Terence P. Moran. *Selling War to America: From the Spanish American War to the Global War on Terror.* Westport, CT: Praeger Security International, 2007.

Seib, Philip M. *The Al Jazeera Effect: How the New Global Media Are Reshaping World Politics.* Washington, DC: Potomac Books, 2008.

Shoemaker, Pamela J., and Tim P. Vos. *Gatekeeping Theory.* New York: Routledge, 2009.

Skiba, Katherine M. *Sister in the Band of Brothers: Embedded with the 101st Airborne in Iraq.* Lawrence, KS: University Press of Kansas, 2005.

Small, Melvin. *Antiwarriors: The Vietnam War and the Battle for America's Hearts and Minds.* Vietnam--America in the War Years, v. 1. Lanham, MD: SR Books, 2004.

Snepp, Frank. *Decent Interval: An Insider's Account of Saigon's Indecent End Told by the CIA's Chief Strategy Analyst in Vietnam,* Lawrence, KS: University Press of Kansas, 1977.

Steinman, Ron. Inside Television's First War: A Saigon Journal. Columbia, MO: University of Missouri Press, 2002.

Sweeney, Michael S. *The Military and the Press: An Uneasy Truce. Visions of the American Press.* Evanston, Ill: Medill School of Journalism, Northwestern University Press, 2006.

Taleb, B.A.. *The Bewildered Herd: Media Coverage of International Conflict s & Public Opinion.* New York & Lincoln: iUniverse, Inc., August 19, 2004.

Tatham, Steve. *Losing Arab Hearts And Minds: The Coalition, Al Jazeera And Muslim Public Opinion.* Rockville Centre, NY: Front Street Press, 2006.

Thomas, Helen. *Watchdogs Of Democracy?: The Waning Washington Press Corps And How It Has Failed The Public.* New York: Scribner, 2006.

Tocqueville, Alexis de, Phillips Bradley, Henry Reeve, and Francis Bowen. *Democracy in America.* New York: A.A. Knopf, 1945.

Tripp, Charles. *A History of Iraq.* Cambridge, UK: Cambridge University Press, 2000.

Unger, Irwin, and Debi Unger. *Turning Point, 1968.* New York: Scribner, 1988

Varon, Jeremy. *Bringing the War Home: The Weather Underground, the Red Army Faction, and Revolutionary Violence in the Sixties and Seventies.* Berkeley: University of California Press, 2004

Venzke, Ben, and Aimee Ibrahim, *Al-Qaeda's Advice for Mujahideen in Iraq: Lessons Learned in Afghanistan v1.0 – 14 April 2003.* Alexandria, VA: Tempest Publishing, LLC, 2003.

Wallach, Janet. *Desert Queen: The Extraordinary Life of Gertrude Bell, Adventurer, Adviser to Kings, Ally of Lawrence of Arabia.* New York: Nan A. Talese/Doubleday, 1996.

Waller, J. Michael. *Fighting the War of Ideas Like a Real War: Messages to Defeat the Terrorists.* Washington, DC: Institute of World Politics Press, 2007.

Walton, C. Dale. *The Myth of Inevitable US Defeat in Vietnam.* Cass series--strategy and history, 3. London: F. Cass, 2002.

West, Bing. *No True Glory: A Frontline Account of the Battle for Fallujah*. New York: Bantam, 2005.

-----*The Strongest Tribe: War, Politics, and the Endgame in Iraq*. New York: Random House, 2008

Wexler, Alice. *Emma Goldman: An Intimate Life*. New York: Pantheon Books, 1984.

Willbanks, James H. *The Tet Offensive: A Concise History*. New York: Columbia University Press, 2007.

Wyatt, Clarence R. *Paper Soldiers: The American Press and the Vietnam War*. New York: W.W. Norton, 1993.

Yon, Michael. *Moment of truth in Iraq: How a New "Greatest Generation" of American Soldiers is Turning Defeat and Disaster Into Victory and Hope.* Minneapolis: Richard Vigilante Books, 2008.

Young, Peter R., and Peter Jesser. *The Media and the Military: From the Crimea to Desert Strike*. Basingstoke: Macmillan, 1997.

Zayani, Mohamed, ed. The *Al Jazeera Phenomenon: Critical Perspectives on New Arab Media*. Boulder, Co: Paradigm Publishers, 2005

Zinni, Anthony. *The Battle for Peace: A Frontline Vision of America's Power and Purpose*. New York: Palgrave MacMillan, 2006.

Zogby, James J. *Arab Voices: What They Are Saying to Us, and Why It Matters.* New York: Palgrave Macmillan, 2010.

NOTES

1. Asa Briggs and Peter Burke, *A Social History of the Media: From Gutenberg to the Internet*, (Cambridge, UK 2005), 1, 13-18, 42-49; David A. Copeland and Daniel Schorr, *The Idea of a Free Press: The Enlightenment and Its Unruly Legacy. Visions of the American press*, (Evanston, Illinois: Northwestern University Press, 2006), 8-10, 62, 63, 69.
2. John Keane, *The Media and Democracy*, (Cambridge, UK: Polity Press, 1991), 10-20; Copeland et al, *The Idea of a Free Press*, 4-10; Briggs et al, *A Social History of the Media*, 21-23, 30-32, 37; Bernard Bailyn, *The Ideological Origins of the American Revolution*, (Cambridge, MA: Belknap Press of Harvard Univ. Press, 1992), 12, 18-21.
3. Bailyn, *The Ideological Origins of the American Revolution.*
4. Ibid., 1.
5. Martin Hirst and Roger Patching,. *Journalism Ethics: Arguments and Cases*, (South Melbourne, Vic: Oxford University Press, 2005), 105.
6. Alexis de Tocqueville, Phillips Bradley, Henry Reeve, and Francis Bowen. *Democracy in America*, (New York: A.A. Knopf, 1945), 517-18.
7. Briggs et al, *A Social History of the Media*, 155; *The Advertising Cenury*, AdAge.com. (http://adage.com/century/index.html; accessed Nov 24, 2009).
8. From the companion piece accompanying the film, *The Time of the Lincolns.* (http://www.pbs.org/wgbh/amex/lincolns/index.html; accessed Dec 19, 2008).
9. Pippa Norris, ed., *Politics and the Press: The News Media and Their Influences*, (Lynne Rienner Publishers, Inc., 1997), 267.
10. Edwin Forbes, *Thirty Years After: An Artist's Memoir of the Civil War*, (Baton Bouge, LA: Lousianna State University Press, 1993), 1-2, 82, 133-135
11. John F. Marszalek, *Sherman's Other War: The General and the Civil War Press*, (Memphis [TN]: Memphis State University Press, 1981).
12. Ibid.; Briggs et al, *A Social History of the Media*, 155.
13. Idid.
14. Alan Axelrod, *Political History of America's Wars*, (Washington, DC: CQ Press, 2007), 314-315.
15. Michael S. Sweeney, *The Military and the Press: An Uneasy Truce.* Visions of the American press, (Evanston, Ill: Medill School of Journalism, Northwestern University Press, 2006), 1.
16. Alice Wexler, *Emma Goldman: An Intimate Life*, (New York: Pantheon Books, 1984), 52-58, 61-66, 73-76, 84-87; Richard Drinnon, *Rebel in Paradise: A Biography of Emma Goldman*, (Chicago: University of Chicago Press, 1961), 45, 57-60, 68-74; John Chalberg, *Emma Goldman: American Individualist*, (New York: HarperCollins Publishers Inc., 1991), 81; Goldman, Emma. *Living My Life.* New York: Dover Publications, 1970.
17. John Chalberg, *Emma Goldman: American Individualist*, (New York: HarperCollins Publishers Inc., 1991), 81.
18. Mark Twain, "The Greatest American Humorist, Returning Home," *New York World*, London, Oct 6, 1900.
19. Chalberg, *Emma Goldman*, 88–91; Wexler, *Emma Goldman*, 121–130; Chalberg, Emma Goldman, 88–91; Wexler, Emma Goldman, 121–130; Barry Pateman and Alexander Berkman. The Blast, (Edinburgh, Scotland: AK Press, 2005).
20. *Filmsite.* (http://www.filmsite.org/warfilms.html and http://www.worldfilm.about.com/od/toppicks/tp/antiwar.htm; accessed Jan 6, 2010).
21. Sweeney, *The Military and the Press*, 36.
22. Ibid. 45-50; Axelrod, *Political History*, 362-363.
23. Walter Lippmann, *Public opinion*, (London: Allen & Unwin, 1922).

---

24. Edward L. Bernays and Mark Crispin Miller, *Propaganda*, (Brooklyn, NY: Ig Publishing, 2005), 71.
25. Donald E. Davis and Eugene P. Trani, *The First Cold War: The Legacy of Woodrow Wilson U.S.-Soviet Relations*, (Columbia, Missouri: University of Missouri Press, 2002); Axelrod, *Political History*, 363-5.
26. Richard J. Hand, *Terror on the Air!: Horror Radio in America, 1931-1952*, (Jefferson, NC: Macfarlane & Company, 2006), 7.
27. "Zeppelin Explodes Scores Dead," Universal Studios, May 10, 1937. (http://www.archive.org/details/1937-05-10_Special_Release_Zeppelin_Explodes; accessed Dec 20, 2008); "Roosevelt Asked To Ban On Strikes," Sep 30, 1934. (http://www.archive.org/details/Roosevelt_Asked_To_Ban_On_Strikes; accessed Dec 20, 2008); Sweeney, *The Military and the Press*, 94.
28. Ibid., 64-65; Randall Rothenberg, "The Advertising Century," AdAge.com, (http://adage.com/century/rothenberg.html; accessed Dec 15, 2008).
29. Harvey Klehr, John Earl Haynes, and K. M. Anderson, *The Soviet World of American Communism*, (New Haven: Yale University Press, 1998), xiii.
30. Ibid. xiii, xxxv, 49.
31. Ronald Grigor Suny, *The Soviet Experiment: Russia, the USSR, and the Successor States.* New York and Oxford: Oxford University Press, 1998.
32. Davis and Trani, *The First Cold War.*
33. Stuart Ewen, *PR! A Social History of Spin*, (New York, NY: Basic Books, 1996), 6.
34. Sweeney, *The Military and the Press*, 65.
35. Ibid., 65.
36. Axelrod, *Political History*, 400.
37. Phillip Knightley, *The First Casualty: The War Correspondent as Hero and Myth-Maker from the Crimea to Iraq,* (Baltimore: The Johns Hopkins University Press, 2004), 336, 357-8.
38. John Hersey, "Hiroshima," *The New Yorker*, Aug 31 1946.
39. Klehr, Haynes, and Anderson, *The Soviet World of American Communism*, xiii; , xxvi, 138-140, 147-152; Herbert Romerstein and Eric Breindel. *The Venona Secrets: Exposing Soviet Espionage and America's Traitors*, (Washington, DC: Regnery, 2000), 12, 29-40,429, 450.
40. Sweeney, *The Military and the Press*, 123-125; Klehr, Haynes, and Anderson, *The Soviet World of American Communism*, xiii; Romerstein and Breindel. *The Venona Secrets*, 29-40.
41. Jeremy Iggers, *Good News, Bad News: Journalism Ethics and the Public Interest*, (Boulder, CO: Westview Press, 1998), 68.
42. Sweeney, *The Military and the Press*, 127.
43. The Museum of Broadcast Communications, (http://www.museum.tv/archives/etv/K/htmlK/kennedy-nixon/kennedy-nixon.htm; accessed Nov 23, 2008); Michael Schudson, *The Sociology of News*, (New York: W.W. Norton, 2003), 2, 13; Iggers, *Good News, Bad News*, 110, 111; Robert M. Entman, *Projections of Power: Framing News, Public Opinion, And U.S. Foreign Policy*, (New York: Pantheon Books, 2004), 93; Iggers, *Good News, Bad News*, 68, 69.
44. Melvin Small, *Antiwarriors: The Vietnam War and the Battle for America's Hearts and Minds. Vietnam--America in the War Years, v. 1*, (Lanham, MD: SR Books, 2004), 7-8; Charles Debenedetti and Charles Chatfield, *An American Ordeal: The Antiwar Movement of the Vietnam Era*, (Syracuse,NY: Syracuse University Press, 1990), 125, 134-6; Mark Kurlansky, *1968: The Year That Rocked the World*, (New York: Ballantine, 2004), 82-83; Varon, *Bringing the War Home*, 1; Tom Hayden, *Reunion: A memoir*, (New York: Random House, 1988); Tom Hayden; Students for a Democratic Society, *The Port Huron Statement: The Visionary Call of the 1960s Revolution*, (New York: Thunder's Mouth Press, 2005).
45. Prochnau, *Once Upon a Distant War*, 350.
46. David Halberstam, *The Making of a Quagmire*, (New York: Random House, 1965).

47. Dexter Filkins, "A Skeptical Vietnam Voice Still Echoes in the Fog of Iraq," *New York Times*, Apr 25, 2007. (http://www.nytimes.com/2007/04/25/world/middleeast/25halberstam.html; accessed Jan 15, 2010).
48. Daniel C. Hallin, *The "Uncensored War": The Media and Vietnam*, (New York, NY: Oxford University Press, 1986), 6; William M. Hammond, *Reporting Vietnam: Media and Military at War*, (Lawrence, KS: University Press of Kansas, 1998), 291.
49. Small, *Antiwarriors*, 7-8; Debenedetti et al, *An American Ordeal*, 125, 134-6; Kurlansky, *1968*, 82-83; Varon, *Bringing the War Home*, 1; Tom Hayden, *Reunion: A memoir*, (New York: Random House, 1988); Hayden, *The Port Huron Statement*; Andrew E. Hunt, *The Turning: A History of Vietnam Veterans Against the War*, (New York: New York University Press, 1999); H. Bruce Franklin, *Vietnam and other American Fantasies*, 90-91.
50. Adam Garfinkle, *Telltale Hearts: The Origins and Impact of the Vietnam Antiwar Movement*, (New York: St. Martin's Griffin, 1997), 13-14.
51. Axelrod, *Political History*, 434, 436.
52. Ibid., 436.
53. Walton, *The Myth of Inevitable US Defeat*, 37.
54. Irwin Unger and Debi Unger. *Turning Point, 1968* (New York: Scribner, 1988), 106.
55. James E. Perone, *Songs of the Vietnam Conflict*. (Westport, Conn: Greenwood Press, 2001), 6; David A. Noebel, *Rhythm, Riots, and Revolution; An Analysis of the Communist Use of Music, the Communist Master Music Plan*, (Tulsa, OK: Christian Crusade Publications, 1966); Petrov, Jodie. *The Use of Music As Propaganda in the Consolidation of the Totalitarian States Under Hitler and Stalin*, Queensland Conservatorium of Music, Griffith University, 1993.
56. Perone, *Songs of the Vietnam Conflict*, 6; Noebel, *Rhythm, Riots, and Revolution*, 6-7.
57. Perone, *Songs of the Vietnam Conflict*, 7.
58. Ibid., 6, 13-14; James E. Perone, *Music of the Counterculture Era. American history through music*, (Westport, CT: Greenwood Press, 2004), 33.
59. Matthew A. Baum, *Soft News Goes to War: Public Opinion and American Foreign Policy in the New Media Age*, (Princeton: Princeton University Press, 2003), 8.
60. Norris, ed., *Politics and the Press*, 291.
61. Entman, *Projections of Power*, 9, 10, 26, 31, 44; Schudson, *The Sociology of News*, 21. Hall-Jamieson, Kathleen and Paul Waldman, *The Press Effect: Politicians, Journalists, and the Stories That Shape the Political World*, (Oxford: Oxford University Press, 2007), 4.
62. "Framing the News: The Triggers, Frames, and Messages in Newspaper Coverage Frame," *The Project of Excellence in Journalism*, Jul 13, 1998. (http://www.journalism.org/node/445; accessed Jul 18, 2007).
63. Ibid; Pamela J. Shoemaker and Tim P. Vos, *Gatekeeping Theory*, (New York: Routledge, 2009).
64. Taleb, *The Bewildered Herd*, 466.
65. Helen Thomas, *Watchdogs of Democracy?: The Waning Washington Press Corps and How It Has Failed The Public*, (New York: Scribner, 2006), xiii.

Chapter Two

1. Don Oberdorfer, *TET! The Turning Point in the Vietnam War*, (New York: De Capo Press, 1984), 159.
2. Ibid., 20, 159.
3. Ron Steinman, *Inside Television's First War: A Saigon Journal*, (Columbia, MO: University of Missouri Press, 2002), 197.
4. Ibid., ix.
5. Ibid., x.

6. Peter Braestrup, *Big story: How The American Press And Television Reported and Interpreted the Crisis of Tet 1968 in Vietnam and Washington*, (Boulder, CO: Westview Press, 1977), 706.
7. Ibid., xxi.
8. Oberdorfer, *TET!*, 43-44, 78, 111, 163; Braestrup, *Big Story*, p. 53, 61-63; Sweeney, *The Military and the Press*, 144.
9. Peter R.Young and Peter Jesser, *The Media and the Military: From the Crimea to Desert Strike*, (Basingstoke: Macmillan, 1997), 80, 91-92.
10. Oberdorfer, *TET!*. 86.
11. Braestrup, *Big Story*, p. xix, 2, 4.
12. Sweeney, *The Military and the Press*, 139-140.
13. Richard Pyle, "From Tonkin Gulf to Persian Gulf: Veteran AP correspondent considers how war reporting has changed," CNN http://www.cnn.com/SPECIALS/cold.war/episodes/11/then.now/; accessed Oct 13, 2007).
14. Braestrup, *Big Story*, xxviii, 3, 4.
15. Ibid., 255.
16. Ibid., 140.
17. Ibid.
18. Oberdorfer, *TET!*, v.
19. Braestrup, *Big Story*, 172; Unger and Unger. *Turning Point, 1968*, 102.
20. Oberdorfer, *TET!*, 252.
21. Braestrup, *Big Story*, 172.
22. Oberdorfer, *TET!*, 254.
23. Ibid., 252.
24. Ibid., 241.
25. Braestrup, *Big Story*, xxviii.
26. Oberdorfer, *TET!*, 175.
27. Ibid., 162.
28. Ibid., 275.
29. Ibid., 258.
30 Braestrup, *Big Story*, 11, 12.
31. Steinman, *Inside Television's First War*, 197-199.
32. Ibid., 3-6.
33. William W. Prochnau, *Once Upon a Distant War*, (New York: Times Books, 1995), 92.
34. Ibid., 92.
35. Peter Arnett, *Live from the Battlefield: From Vietnam to Baghdad: 35 Years in the World's War Zones*, (New York: Simon & Schuster, 1994), 239-242.
36. Ibid., 8, 33; Braestrup, *Big Story*, 86.
37. Oberdorfer, *TET!*, 22.
38. Braestrup, *Big Story*, 93.
39. Ibid., xxvi; Oberdorfer, *TET!*, 31.
40. Oberdorfer, *TET!*, 33; Braestrup, *Big Story*, 715.
41. Oberdorder *TET!*, 33.
42. Braestrup, *Big Story*, 53, 54.
43. Steinman, *Inside Television's First War, 208.*
44. Braestrup, *Big Story*, 96-98.
45. Ibid., 96.
46. Ibid., 138.
47. Oberdorfer, *TET!*, 163.
48. Ibid., xii, 158.
49. Ibid., 166.

50. Ibid., 170.
51. Ibid., 170.
52. Eddie Adams, "Eulogy," *Time*, Jul 27, 1998. Available online at http://www.time.com/time/magazine/article/0,9171,988783,00.html; accessed Oct 17, 2007); Eddie Adams, *PBS*. Quicktime or Windows Media Video. (http://www.newseum.org/warstories/interviews/mov/journalists/journalistmovie.asp?id=22&anecdotenum=1&filename=bio_adams_1; accessed Oct 17, 2006).
53. Braestrup, *Big Story*, 138, 229, 713-4; Oberdorfer, *TET!*, 241, 243-44.
54. Oberdorfer, *TET!*, 243.
55. Braestrup, *Big Story*, 212, 213, 229
56. Oberdorfer, *TET!*, 244.
57. Braestrup, *Big Story*, 170.
58. Ibid., 138.
59. "Hanoi Attacks and Scores a Major Psychological Blow," *Newsweek*, Feb 12, 1968; "Shaken Assumptions About the War," *Life*, Feb 16, 1968; "Why the U.S. Isn't Winning a 'Little War'," *U.S. News and World Report*, Apr 1, 1968.
60. Oberdorfer, *TET!*, 183.
61. Braestrup, *Big Story*, 49.
62. Ibid., 14.
63. Ibid., 712.
64. Oberdorfer, *TET!*, 183.
65. Ibid.; Braestrup, *Big Story*, xix, 2, 4, 14, 49.
66. Braestrup, *Big Story*, 13, 15, 25, 287.
67. Oberdorfer, *TET!*, 183.
68. Braestrup, *Big Story*, 232.
69. Oberdorfer, *TET!*, 37, 38.
70. William V. Kennedy, *The Military and the Media: Why the Press Cannot Be Trusted to Cover a War*, (Westport, CT: Praeger, 1993), 88.
71. Ibid.
72. Braestrup, *Big Story*, 191, 204, 219.
73. Ibid., 204.
74. Braestrup, *Big Story*, 206.
75. Oberdorfer, *TET!*, 184.
76. Braestrup, *Big Story*, 286.
77. Eric Hammel, *Fire in the Streets: The Battle for Hue: Tet, 1968*, (New York: Dell, 1991), 167-8; and Keith William Nolan, *Battle for Hue: Tet, 1968*, 268, (New York: Dell, 1983).
78. "Battle of Hue," *Time*, Feb 16, 1968, 34; "Death of a Monument," *Newsweek*, Feb 26, 1968, 34; "Fight for a Citadel: Hue," *Time*, Mar 1, 1968, 20-21; John Olsen, "The Battle that Regained and Ruined Hue," *Life*, Mar 8, 1968, 24-29.
79. Ibid. 240-241.
80. Oberdorfer, *TET!*, 241.
81. Braestrup, *Big Story*, 337, 442.
82. Ibid., xxx, 444.
83. Ibid., 446.
84. Ibid., 572.
85. Ibid., 571.
86. B. Laurie and R. J. Del Vecchio, *Whitewash, Blackwash: Myths of the Viet Nam War*, ([United States?]: Bill Laurie and R.J. Del Vecchio), 2005, 18; Braestrup, *Big Story*, 142-43, 196-197.
87. Oberdorfer, *TET!*, 164.
88. Braestrup, *Big Story*, 706.
89. Prochnau, *Once Upon a Distant War*, 350.

90. Braestrup, *Big Story*, 23.
91. Steinman, *Inside Television's First War*, 223, 225-235.
92. Braestrup, *Big Story*, 13.
93. Ibid., 13.
94. Ibid., 287.
95. Ibid., 32.
96. Ibid., 33.
97. Ibid., 25.
98. Ibid., 32.
99. Ibid., 714.
100. Ibid., 713-4.
101. Ibid., xxix.
102. Ibid., 185.
103. Ibid., 13.
104. Ibid., 23.
105. Ibid., 161.
106. "Cronkite Speaks Out on Vietnam," *Newseum*, Feb 22, 2007. (http://www.newseum.org/news/news.aspx?item=nh_CRO070222&style=f; accessed Sep 20, 2009)
107. Laurie and Del Vecchio, *Whitewash, Blackwash*, 18.
108. "Cronkite Speaks Out on Vietnam," *Newseum*, Feb 22, 2007. (http://www.newseum.org/news/news.aspx?item=nh_CRO070222&style=f; accessed Sep 20, 2009).
109. Ibid., 287, 334.
110. Ibid., 715.
111. Ibid., xxv.
112. Ibid., xxxiii.
113. Oberdorfer, *TET!*, 331.
114. Ibid., 242.
115. Braestrup, *Big Story*, 727.
116. Ibid., 51.
117. Oberdorfer, *TET!*. 246.
118. C. Dale Walton, *The Myth of Inevitable US Defeat in Vietnam*, (London: Cass, 2002), 35.
119. General Creighton Abrams, Jr. (http://www.arlingtoncemetery.net/abrams.htm; accessed May 16, 2009)
120. Walton, *The Myth of Inevitable US Defeat*, 37.
121. Franklin, *Vietnam and other American Fantasies*, 92, 100; Walton, *The Myth of Inevitable US Defeat*, 37.
122. Melvin Small, *Antiwarriors: The Vietnam War and the Battle for America's Hearts and Minds*. (Lanham, MD: SR Books, 2004), 3.
123. Walton, *The Myth of Inevitable US Defeat*, 37.
124. Jeremy Varon, *Bringing the War Home: The Weather Underground, the Red Army Faction, and Revolutionary Violence in the Sixties and Seventies*, (Berkeley: University of California Press, 2004), 1, 54.
125. Ibid., 38, 84-86.
126. Vietnam Online, The American Experience, *PBS*, Mar 29, 2005. (http://www.pbs.org/wgbh/amex/vietnam/trenches/my_lai.html; accessed May 16, 2009); Creighton Williams Abrams Jr. (http://www.arlingtoncemetery.net/abrams.htm; accessed May 16, 2009).
127. General Creighton Abrams, Jr. (http://www.arlingtoncemetery.net/abrams.htm; accessed May 16, 2009)

128. Sweeney, *The Military and the Press*, 145
129. Walton, *The Myth of Inevitable US Defeat*, 37.
130. Martin Florian Herz and Leslie Rider, *The Prestige Press and the Christmas Bombing, 1972: Images and Reality in Vietnam*, (Washington, DC: Ethics and Public Policy Center, 1980), vii.
131. Herz and Rider Ibid., vii-viii, 15, 45-57.
132. Richard M. Nixon, *No More Vietnams*, (New York: Arbor House, 1985), 161-2).
133. Frank Snepp, *Decent Interval: An Insider's Account of Saigon's Indecent End Told by the CIA's Chief Strategy Analyst in Vietnam*, (Lawrence, KS: University Press of Kansas, 1977).
134. Morley Safer, *Flashbacks: On Returning to Vietnam*, (New York: Random House, 1990), 15.
135. Perone, *Songs of the Vietnam Conflict*, 6-7, 13-14; James E. Perone, *Music of the Counterculture Era*, 33-34.
136. *Internet Movie Database*. (http://www.imdb.com/title/tt0066026/; accessed Jan 19, 2010)
137. Stanley Kubrick, *Full Metal Jacket*, Warner Bros., 1987.
138. See Bill Laurie and R. J. Del Vecchio. *Whitewash, Blackwash: Myths of the Viet Nam War.* (Bill Laurie and R.J. Del Vecchio, 2005); Dale C. Walton, *The Myth of Inevitable US Defeat in Vietnam*, (London: F. Cass, 2002).
139. Sweeney, *The Military and the Press*, 147; Greg McLaughlin, *The War Correspondent*, (London: Pluto Press, 2002), 73-78.
140. Clarence R. Wyatt, *Paper Soldiers: The American Press and the Vietnam War*, (New York: W.W. Norton, 1993). 7, 216-17.
141. David F. Schmitz, *The Tet Offensive: Politics, War, and Public Opinion*, (Lanham, MD: Rowman & Littlefield Publishers, 2005), xiii-xvi, 157-162.
142. James H. Willbanks, *The Tet Offensive: A Concise History*, (New York: Columbia University Press, 2007), 110-117; Walton, *The Myth of Inevitable US Defeat*, 35.
143. Willbanks, *The Tet Offensive*, 110-117.
144. Benjamin C. Schwarz, *Casualties, Public Opinion, and U.S. Military Intervention: Implications for U.S. Regional Deterrence Strategies.* Santa Monica, CA: Rand, 1994; Eric V. Larson, *Casualties and Consensus: The Historical Role of Casualties in Domestic Support for U.S. Military Operations.* Santa Monica, CA: RAND, 1996.
145. Schudson, *The Sociology of News*, 13.
146. Norris, ed., *Politics and the Press*, 288.
147. Thomas, *Watchdogs of Democracy?*, 72, 73; Braestrup, *Battle Lines*, 12.

Chapter Three

1. "State of the News Media 2004: An Annual Report on American Journalism," *Project for Excellence in Journalism*, 2007. (http://www.stateofthenewsmedia.com/2004/; accessed Jul 18, 2007); "State of the News Media 2008: An Annual Report on American Journalism," *Project for Excellence in Journalism*, 2008. http://www.stateofthenewsmedia.com/2008/; accessed Jan 27, 2009).
2. Ibid.; Baum, *Soft News Goes to War*, 58.
3. Norris, ed., *Politics and the Press*, 1-6, 45; Baum, *Soft News Goes to War*, 4, 57-58, 99, 279; Kenneth Allard, *Warheads: Cable News and the Fog of War*, (Annapolis: Naval Institute Press, 2006), 40, 47.
4. Matthew A. Baum, *Soft News Goes to War*, 5, 58.
5. Briggs, *A Social History of the Media*, 249.
6. Lance W. Bennett and David L. Paletz, eds., *Taken by Storm: The Media, Public Opinion, and U.S. Foreign Policy in the Gulf War*, (Chicago: University of Chicago Press, 1994), 12.
7. Peter Braestrup, *Battle Lines: Report on the Twentieth Century Fund Task Force on the Military and the Media*, (New York: Priority Press Publications, 1985), 3, 4, 8.
8. Ibid., 3, 4, 8.
9. Ibid., 4.

---

10. Ibid., 96.
11. Keith Rosenkranz, *Vipers in the Storm*, (New York: Mc Graw Hill, 2002), 200, 231, 299.
12. CIA World Fact Book. (https://www.cia.gov/library/publications/the-world-factbook/geos/iz.html; accessed Jan 31, 2009)
13. Noha Mellor, *The Making of Arab News*, (Lanham, MD, 2005), 8; Marc Lynch, *Voices of the New Arab Public: Iraq, Al-Jazeera, and Middle East Politics Today*, (New York: Columbia University Press, 2006), 170; Hugh Miles, *Al-Jazeera: The Inside Story of the Arab News Channel that is Challenging The West*, (New York: Grove Press, 2005), 221; Mohamed Zayani, ed., *The Al Jazeera Phenomenon: Critical Perspectives on New Arab Media*, (Boulder, CO: Paradigm Publishers, 2005), 3, 23; Lynch, *Voices of the New Arab Public*, 6-7.
14. Piers Robinson, *The Myth CNN Effect: The Myth of News Media, Foreign Policy and Intervention*, (New York: Routledge, 2002), 2-3; Norris, ed., *Politics and the Press*, 293.
15. Anthony Zinni, *The Battle for Peace: A Frontline Vision of America's Power and Purpose*, (New York: Palgrave MacMillan, 2006), 30; Robinson, *The Myth CNN Effect*, 17, 25.
16. Ibid., 30.
17. Ibid.
18. Norris, ed., 293.
19. Taleb, *The Bewildered Herd*, 467; Entman, *Projections of Power*, 4, 100, 107.
20. Ibid., 101-104.
21. Jonathan Mermin, *Debating War and Peace: Media Coverage of U.S. Intervention in the Post-Vietnam Era*, (Princeton, NJ: Princeton University Press, 1999), 120.
22. "Trapped in Somalia," *Newsweek*, Oct 18, 1993, 32.
23. *The 9/11 Commission Report*, 97.
24. Jonathan Mermin, *Debating War and Peace: Media Coverage of U.S. Intervention in the Post-Vietnam Era.* (Princeton, NJ: Princeton University Press, 1999), 120.
25. "What was USIA?," *Public Diplomacy Web Site*, (www.publicdiplomacy.org/2.htm; accessed Aug 13, 2008); U.S. Information Agency Web Site. (http://dosfan.lib.uic.edu/usia/; accessed Aug 13, 2008).
26. "The State of the Media 2004: An Annual Report on American Journalism," *The Project of Excellence in Journalism*, 2004. (http://www.stateofthenewsmedia.com/2004/; accessed Jul 18, 2007).
27. Baum, *Soft News Goes to War*, 4, 57-58, 99, 279; Allard, *Warheads*, 40, 47.
28. "State of the News Media 2004: An Annual Report on American Journalism," *Project for Excellence in Journalism*, 2007. (http://www.stateofthenewsmedia.com/2004/; accessed Jul 18, 2007); Iggers, *Good News, Bad News*, 7.
29. "The State of the News Media 2004: An Annual Report on American Journalism," *The Project of Excellence in Journalism*, 2004. (http://www.stateofthenewsmedia.com/2004; accessed Jul 18, 2007).
30. "The State of the News Media 2005: An Annual Report on American Journalism," *The Project of Excellence in Journalism*, 2005. (http://www.stateofthenewsmedia.com/2005/; accessed Jul 18, 2007).
31. "The State of the News Media 2005: An Annual Report on American Journalism," *The Project of Excellence in Journalism*, 2005. (http://www.stateofthenewsmedia.com/2005/; accessed Jul 18, 2007).
32. "The State of the Media 2004: An Annual Report on American Journalism," *The Project of Excellence in Journalism*, 2004. (http://www.stateofthenewsmedia.com/2004/; accessed Jul 18, 2007).

33. Bill Kovach and Tom Rosenstiel, *Warp Speed: America in the Age of Mixed Media*, (New York: Century Foundation Press, 1999); "Embedded Reporters: What Are Americans Getting?" *Project for Excellence in Journalism*, Apr 3, 2003. (http://www.journalism.org; accessed Jul 18, 2007); Bill Kovach and Tom Rosenstiel, "Campaign Lite: Why Reporters Won't Tell Us What We Need to Know," *The Washington Monthly*, Jan 1, 2001. (http://www.journalism.org/node/348; accessed Jul 18, 2007).
34. Bill Kovach and Tom Rosenstiel, "Campaign Lite: Why Reporters Won't Tell Us What We Need to Know," *The Washington Monthly*, Jan 1, 2001. (http://www.journalism.org/node/348; accessed Jul 18, 2007).
35. Bill Kovach and Tom Rosenstiel, *Warp Speed: America in the Age of Mixed Media*, (New York: Century Foundation Press, 1999).
36. Bill Kovach and Tom Rosenstiel, *Warp Speed*; Howard Kurtz, "Hear No Lichtblau, See No Lichtblau," *The Washington Post*, C1, Jun 28, 2004. (from LexisNexis® Academic; accessed Feb 20, 2007; Edward S. Herman and Noam Chomsky, *Manufacturing Consent*, (New York: Pantheon Books, 1988), 4, 14.
37. Stephen D. Cooper, *Watching the Watchdog: Bloggers as the Fifth Estate*, (Spokane, WA: Marquette Books, 2006), 17-19.
38. "The State of the News Media 2007: An Annual Report on American Journalism," *The Project of Excellence in Journalism*, 2007. (http://www.stateofthenewsmedia.com/2007/; accessed Jul 18, 2007).
39. Bernard Goldberg, *Bias: A CBS Insider Exposes How the Media Distorts the News*, (Washington, DC: Regnery Publishing, Inc., 2002), 92-93.
40. Dexter Filkins, "A Skeptical Vietnam Voice Still Echoes in the Fog of Iraq," *New York Times*, Apr 25, 2007. (http://www.nytimes.com/2007/04/25/world/middleeast/25halberstam.html; accessed Jan 15, 2010).
41. Ibid.

Chapter Four

1. Elaine Sciolino, *The Outlaw State: Saddam Hussein's Quest For Power And The Gulf Crisis*, (New York: Wiley, 1991), 40, 42; Lewis, *The Crisis of Islam*, 130-2.
2. Karen Armstrong, *Islam: A Short History*, (New York: The Modern Library, 2002), 3.
3. Ibid., 4, 5, 17, 18, 20, 21, 29-32; Lewis, *The Crisis of Islam*, 34, 48, 50-51.
4. Armstrong, *Islam*, 20, 25, 33, 43; Yitzhak Nakash, *Reaching for Power: The Shi'a in the Modern Arab World*, (Princeton: Princeton University Press, 2006), 5.
5. Christopher Harmon, *Terrorism Today*, (London and Portland: Frank Cass, 2002), 27; Armstrong, *Islam*, 69-70, 85-87,93, 95-97.; Cindy Combs, *Terror in the Twenty-First Century*, (Upper Saddle River, NJ, 2006), 22, 23; Lewis, *The Crisis of Islam*, 144.
6. Lewis, *The Crisis of Islam*, 51-2.
7. Raphael Patai, *The Arab Mind*, (New York: Hatherleigh Press, 2002), 286-288, 305-307.
8. Cole C. Kingseed, *Eisenhower and the Suez Crisis of 1956*, 41; Zachary Karabell, *Parting the Desert: The Creation of the Suez Canal*, (New York: A.A. Knopf, 2003), 4, 266-7.
9. Patai, *The Arab Mind*, 295-304.
10. Ahmed S. Hashim, *Insurgency and Counter-Insurgency in Iraq*, (Ithaca, NY: Cornell University Press, 2006), 25; Marc Sageman, *Understanding Terror Networks*, (Philadelphia: University of Pennsylvania Press, 2004), 1; Lewis, *The Crisis of Islam*, 57.
11. Natana J. Delong-Bas, *Wahhabi Islam: From Revival and Reform to Global Jihad*, (Oxford, UK: Oxford University Press, 2004), 9.
12. Sageman, *Understanding Terror Networks*, 8.
13. Lewis, *The Crisis of Islam*, 121.
14. Sageman, *Understanding Terror Networks*, 8.

15. Lewis, *The Crisis of Islam*, 124, 128; Nakash, *Reaching for Power*, 20-28; Meir Litvak, *Shi'i Scholars of Nineteenth-Century Iraq: The 'Ulama' of Najaf and Karbala*, (New York: Cambridge University Press, 1998), 121, 122, 123, 131, 142.
16. Lewis, *The Crisis of Islam*, 160.
17. Hashim, *Insurgency and Counter-Insurgency*, 24-25.
18. Lewis, *The Crisis of Islam*, xvii-xvii.
19. The Investigative Project on Terrorism. (http://www.investigativeproject.org/documents/misc/135.pdf; accessed Dec 5, 2009)
20. Fereydoun Hoveryda, *The Broken Crescent*, (Westport, CT: Praegar Publishers, 2002), 56.
21. The Investigative Project on Terrorism. (http://www.investigativeproject.org/documents/misc/135.pdf; accessed Dec 5, 2009)
22. Lewis, *The Crisis of Islam*, 60-61, 72, 78.
23. Ibid., 60, 61.
24. Kingseed, *Eisenhower and the Suez*, 27-32.
25. Ibid., 28.
26. Ibid.
27. Ibid., 27-32, 126.
28. Lewis, *The Crisis of Islam*, 76-81.
29. Sayyid Qutb, *Milestones*, 1964; Marc Sageman, *Understanding Terror Networks*, (Philadelphia, PA 2004). Pp. vii, 1.
30. Sageman, *Understanding Terror Networks*, 17, 16.
31. Ibid., 17, 18.
32. Sayyid Qutb, *Milestones*. Sageman, *Understanding Terror Networks*, 1; Armstrong, *Islam*, 69-70, 85-87, 93, 95-97; Lewis, *The Crisis of Islam*, 48, 144, 157; Cindy C. Combs, *Terror in the Twenty-First Century*, (Upper Saddle River, NJ: Pearson/Prentice Hall, 2006), 22, 23; Christopher Harmon, *Terrorism Today*, (London, UK and Portland, OR: Frank Cass, 2002), 27.
33. *The 9/11 Commission Report: Final Report of the National Commission on Terrorist Attacks Upon the United States (Authorized Edition)*. (New York: W.W. Norton Company, 2004), 376.
34. Lewis p. 113.; Benjamin, p. 116.
35. Mark Juergensmeyer, *Terror In The Mind of God: The Global Rise of Religious Violence*, (Berkeley: University of California Press, 2000), 181; Kingseed, *Eisenhower*, 27, 28, 41; Lewis, *The Crisis of Islam*, 73.
36. Noha Mellor, *The Making of Arab News*, (Lanham, MD: Rowman & Littlefield Publishers, 2005), 39.
37. Lewis, *The Crisis of Islam*, 128.
38. Ibid., 113, 119; Daniel Benjamin, *The Age of Sacred Terror*, (New York: Random House, 2002), 116.
39. Sageman, *Understanding Terror Networks*, 18.
40. Armstrong, 20, 25, 69-70, 85-87, 93, 95-97; Lewis, *The Crisis of Islam*, 48, 50, 86, 138, 144, 157; Combs, *Terror*, 22, 23; Harmon, *Terrorism Today*, 27; Sageman, *Understanding Terror Networks*, 1-24, 38; *National Commission on Terrorist Attacks upon the United States. The 9/11 Commission Report: Final Report of the National Commission on Terrorist Attacks Upon the United States*. (New York: Norton, 2004), 55-60; Natana J. Delong-Bas, *Wahhabi Islam: From Revival and Reform to Global Jihad*, (Oxford, UK: Oxford University Press, 2004), 278; The Investigative Project on Terrorism. (http://www.investigativeproject.org/documents/misc/135.pdf; accessed Dec 5, 2009).
41. Lewis, *The Crisis of Islam*, 29, 30, 31.
42. Ibid., 31, 32.
43. Sageman, *Understanding Terror Networks*, 17; Lewis, *The Crisis of Islam*, 33, 39.
44. Combs, *Terror*, 161.

45. Harmon, *Terrorism Today*, 53, 63,70.
46. "Violent Islamist Extremism, The Internet, and the Homegrown Terrorist Threat," *United States Senate Committee on Homeland Security and Governmental Affairs*, May 8, 2008. (http://hsgac.senate.gov/public/_files/IslamistReport.pdf; accessed Jul 19, 2008); Daniel Kimmage, "The Al-Qaeda Media Nexus ," *Radio Free Europe/Radio Liberty, Mar 2008.* (http://docs.rferl.org/en-US/AQ_Media_Nexus.pdf; accessed Jul 19, 2008); Ben Venzke and Aimee Ibrahim, *Al-Qaeda's Advice for Mujahideen in Iraq: Lessons Learned in Afghanistan*, (Alexandria, VA: Tempest Publishing, LLC, 2003),
47. *The 9/11 Commission Report*, 55-60.
48. Mark Dubowitz, "Terrorist TV in Eurabia," *inFocus*, Dec 22, 2007. (http://www.defenddemocracy.org/index.php?option=com_content&task=view&id=11780863&Itemid=0; accessed Apr 29, 2009.)
49. Lewis, *The Crisis of Islam*, 83, 86.
50. Ibid., 83.
51. Nakash, *Reaching for Power*, 3, 4.
52. Said K. Aburish, *Saddam Hussein: The Politics of Revenge*, (New York: Bloomsbury Publishing, 2000), 6; Sciolino, *The Outlaw State*, 46.
53. Sciolino, *The Outlaw State*, 47.
54. Con Coughlin, *Saddam: King of Terror*, (New York, 2002), 23-25, 27-30.
55. Ibid., 39-40.
56. Ibid., 28, 43; Aburish, *Saddam Hussein*, 61; Sciolino, *The Outlaw State*, 63.
57. Sciolino, *The Outlaw State*, 62; Coughlin, *Saddam*, 48, 66.
58. Coughlin, *Saddam*, 73, 77; Sciolino, *The Outlaw State*, 49, 82, 93, 94, 95; Aburish, *Saddam Hussein*, 122.
59. Coughlin, *Saddam*, 112, 123.
60. Ibid., 2, 167; Aburish, *Saddam Hussein*, 124, 233; Kanan Makiya, *Republic of Fear: The Politics of Modern Iraq, Updated Edition*, (Berkley and Los Angeles: University of California Press, 1998), 66-67; Sciolino, *The Outlaw State*, 81.
61. Coughlin, *Saddam*, 142-145.
62. Hashim, *Insurgency and Counter-Insurgency*, 12.
63. Coughlin, *Saddam*, 78, 140-41; Harmon, *Terrorism Today*, 261.
64. Aburish, *Saddam Hussein*, 100; Adeed Dawisha and Karen Dawisha, eds. *The Soviet Union in the Middle East: Policies and Perspectives*, (New York: Holmes & Meier, 1982), 14, 16, 99, 108.
65. Dawisha, *The Soviet Union*, 67, 75; Coughlin, *Saddam*, 107.
66. Coughlin, *Saddam*, 126, 132, 133; Sciolino, *The Outlaw State*, 143, 146.
67. Coughlin, *Saddam*, 126-132.
68. Ibid., 132-6; Mahdi Obeidi and Kurt Pitzer. *The Bomb in My Garden: The Secrets of Saddam's Nuclear Mastermind*, (Hoboken, NJ: John Wiley and Sons, 2004), 49.
69. Sciolino, *The Outlaw State*, 83-83; Aburish, *Saddam Hussein*, 97, 124, 126.
70. Coughlin, *Saddam*, 124; Sciolino, *The Outlaw State*, 63.
71. Charles Tripp, *A History of Iraq*, Cambridge, UK: Cambridge University Press, 2000), 222, 224, 226; Sciolino, *The Outlaw State*, 50, 64-65.
72. Tripp, *A History of Iraq*, 238; Sciolino, *The Outlaw State*, 105, 112-116.
73. Dawisha 17, 153.
74. Paul R. Pillar, *Terrorism and U.S. Foreign Policy*, (Washington, DC 2001). 170.
75. Sciolino, *The Outlaw State*, 29, 146.
76. Ibid., 154.

Chapter Five

1. Lewis, *The Crisis of Islam*, 100.

2. Michael Delong, *Inside CentCom: The Unvarnished Truth about the wars in Afghanistan and Iraq.* (Washington, DC: Regnery Publishing, 2004), 11, 64-65.
3. Mary E. Morris, *The Persistence of External Interest in the Middle East,* (Santa Monica, CA 1993), 18, 19; Zayani, *The Al Jazeera Phenomenon,* 2, 5, 8, 168.
4. Osama bin Laden, "Full text: bin Laden's 'letter to America'," *The Observer,* Nov 24, 2002, http://observer.guardian.co.uk/print/0,,4552895-110490,00.html; accessed Sep 19, 2007).
5. *The 9/11 Commission Report,* 63-65.
6. Ibid., 69-70.
7. Rahimullah Yusufzai, "Conversation with Terror," *Time,* Jan 11, 1999. http://www.time.com/time/magazine/article/0,9171,989958,00.html; accessed Oct 17, 2007).
8. Ibid., 153.
9. Mohammed El-Nawawy and Abdel Iskandar, *Al-Jazeera: How the Free Arab News Network Scooped the World and Changed the Middle East,* (Cambridge, MA: Westview Press 2002), 8, 10, 69.
10. Zayani, *The Al Jazeera Phenomenon,* 2, 5, 8.
11. El-Nawawy and Iskandar, *Al-Jazeera,* 20.
12. Ibid., 51.
13. Ibid.; Steve Tatham, *Loosing Arab Hearts and Minds: the Coalition, Al-Jazeera and Muslim Public Opinion,* (Rockville Centre, NY: Front Street Press, 2006), 4.
14. Walid Phares, *The War of Ideas: Jihad against Democracy,* (Basingstoke, England: Palgrave Macmillan, 2008), x.
15. Ahmed S. Hashim, *Insurgency and Counter-Insurgency,* 26.
16. Scheherezade Faramarzi, "Saddam Invitees Believed Behind Insurgency," *Associated Press Online,* Jan 5, 2005. (LexisNexis® Academic; accessed Feb 20, 2007).
17. Sayed Mahdi Almodarresi, "Horrors of Iraq's mass graves," *ShiaNews.com,* 24 Jun 2003. http://www.shianews.com/; accessed 24 Jul 2006).
18. The author's collective experiences in Iraq interviewing both Iraqis and U.S. military officials.
19. Lin Todd et al., *Iraq Tribal Study—Al-Anbar Governorate: The Albu Fahd Tribe, the Albu Mahal Tribe, and the Albu Issa Tribe,* (Department of Defense, 18 Jun 2006).
20. Coughlin, *Saddam,* 143-144; Aburish, *Saddam Hussein,* 126; Harmon, *Terrorism Today,* 33.
21. Stephen F. Hayes, *The Connection : How al-Qaeda's Collaboration with Saddam Hussein Has Endangered America,* (New York, Harper Collins, 2004), 6, 50; Laurie Mylroie. *Study of Revenge: The First World Trade Center Attack and Saddam Hussein's War Against America,* (Washington, DC: AEI Press, 2001), xxiii, 40-41, 102-103, 111-115.
22. Laurie Mylroie, *Study of Revenge,* 260; William Kristol and Robert Kagan, "Bombing Iraq Isn't Enough," *The New York Times,* Jan 30, 1998. 17. (from LexisNexis® Academic; accessed Feb 4, 2007); "Endgame on Iraq," *The New York Times,* Jan 27, 1998, 18. (from LexisNexis® Academic; accessed Feb 4, 2007).
23. Entman, *Projections of Power,* 108; Robinson, *The Myth CNN Effect,* 4.
24. James Bennet, "U.S. Cruise Missiles Strike Sudan and Afghan Targets Tied to Terrorist Network," *The New York Times,* Aug, 1998. (LexisNexis® Academic; accessed Oct 4, 2007).
25. "Speech by President on Iraq to Pentagon Personnel," CNN, Feb 17, 1998; (www.cnn.com/ALLPOLITICS/1998/02/17/transcripts/clinton.iraq/; accessed Aug 13, 2008).
26. President Bill Clinton, Message to the Joint Chiefs of Staff, Feb 17, 1998.
27. Iraq Liberation Act of 1998, The Library of Congress, (http://thomas.loc.gov/cgi-bin/query/z?c105:H.R.4655.ENR:; accessed Aug 13, 2008).
28. Gordon, 66.

29. Delong, *Inside CentCom,* 11, 64-65; "Signs of Iraqi Arms Buildup Bedevil U.S. Administration," *The New York Times*, Feb 1, 2000, A1; (LexisNexis® Academic; accessed Feb 4, 2007).
30. "Post-Saddam Iraq: The War Game," National Security Archive. (http://www.gwu.edu/~nsarchiv/NSAEBB/NSAEBB207/index.htm#documents)
31. Entman, *Projections of Power*, 108; Robinson, *The Myth CNN Effect*, 4.
32. Ibid., 108.
33. Ibid.; R.W. Apple, "A Military Quagmire Remembered: Afghanistan as Vietnam," *The New York Times*, Oct 31, 2001. (LexisNexis® Academic; accessed Oct 4, 2007).
34. Delong, *Inside CentCom*,11, 64-65.
35. Ibid., 63-66, 79.
36. George W. Bush, *State of the Union Address*, Jan 29, 2002. (http://www.whitehouse.gov/news/releases/2002/01/20020129-11.html; accessed Feb 4, 2007); *National Security Strategy* of the United States of America, Sep 2002. (http://www.whitehouse.gov/nsc/nss.pdf; accessed Feb 4, 2007).
37. Ed Vulliamy, "Will Saddam really risk a fight?" *The Observer*, Dec 22, 2002. Available at: www.guardian.co.uk/world/2002/dec/22/iraq1 ; accessed Feb 4, 2007).
38. Entman, *Projections of Power*, 111-115.
39. Ibid., 108, 115.
40. Violaine Roussel and Bleuwenn Lechaux, *Voicing Dissent: American Artists and the War on Iraq*, (New York: Routledge, 2010), 2-6, 8.
41. Charles Jones, *Red, White, or Yellow?: The Media and the Military at War in Iraq*, (Mechanicsburg, PA: Stackpole Books, 2008), 20-22.
42. Entman, *Projections of Power*, 107-8, 112.
43. Eugene Secunda and Terence P. Moran. *Selling War to America: From the Spanish American War to the Global War on Terror*, (Westport, CT: Praeger Security International, 2007), 149,169.
44. Wojtek Mackiewicz Wolfe, *Winning the War of Words: Selling the War on Terror from Afghanistan to Iraq*, (Westport, CT: Praeger Security International, 2008), 57-58, 62-71.
45. Ibid., 112, 119.
46. Ibid. 109.
47. "Violent Islamist Extremism, The Internet, and the Homegrown Terrorist Threat," *United States Senate Committee on Homeland Security and Governmental Affairs*, May 8, 2008. (http://hsgac.senate.gov/public/_files/IslamistReport.pdf; accessed Jul 19, 2008); Daniel Kimmage, "The Al-Qaeda Media Nexus ," *Radio Free Europe/Radio Liberty, Mar 2008*. (http://docs.rferl.org/en-US/AQ_Media_Nexus.pdf; accessed Jul 19, 2008); Ben Venzke and Aimee Ibrahim, *Al-Qaeda's Advice for Mujahideen in Iraq: Lessons Learned in Afghanistan*, (Alexandria, VA: Tempest Publishing, LLC, 2003),
48. El-Nawawy, 158, 190; Zayani, *The Al Jazeera Phenomenon*, 83.
49. Zayani, *The Al Jazeera Phenomenon*, 168.
50. Ibid., 153.
51. "Violent Islamist Extremism, The Internet, and the Homegrown Terrorist Threat," *United States Senate Committee on Homeland Security and Governmental Affairs*, May 8, 2008. (http://hsgac.senate.gov/public/_files/IslamistReport.pdf; accessed Jul 19, 2008); Daniel Kimmage, "The Al-Qaeda Media Nexus ," *Radio Free Europe/Radio Liberty, Mar 2008*. (http://docs.rferl.org/en-US/AQ_Media_Nexus.pdf; accessed Jul 19, 2008); Ben Venzke and Aimee Ibrahim, *Al-Qaeda's Advice for Mujahideen in Iraq: Lessons Learned in Afghanistan*, (Alexandria, VA: Tempest Publishing, LLC, 2003),
52. Ben Venzke and Aimee Ibrahim, *Al-Qaeda's Advice for Mujahideen in Iraq: Lessons Learned in Afghanistan*, (Alexandria, VA: Tempest Publishing, LLC, 2003), 16.
53. Miles, *Al-Jazeera*, 135.

54. Lynch, *Voices of the New Arab Public*, 19.
55. Ibid., 151.
56. Ibid., 157, 170.

Chapter Six
1. John Otis, "Critics Accuse Arab Media of War Bias," Knight Ridder Tribune Business News, Apr 5, 2003. (http://www.ProQuest LLC.com/. ; accessed Dec 13, 2009).
2. Montgomery et al, *Al-Anbar Awakening Volume II*, 194.
3. Toby Dodge, *Iraq's Future: The Aftermath of Regime Change*, (New York and London: Routledge, 2005), 18, 61; Hashim, *Insurgency and Counter-Insurgency*, 139-140; Montgomery et al, *Al-Anbar Awakening Volume II*, 194; Hashim, *Insurgency and Counter-Insurgency*, 139-140.
4. Donald P.Wright and Timothy R. Reese. *On Point II: Transition to the New Campaign: The United States Army in Operation Iraqi Freedom, May 2003-Jan 2005*, (Fort Leavenworth, KS: Combat Studies Institute Press, 2008), 268, 621; Dodge, *Iraq's Future*, 12, 14-15, 20, 67; Delong, *Inside CentCom*, 117
5. Hashim, *Insurgency and Counter-Insurgency*, 12.
6. Zaki Chehab, *Inside the Resistance: The Iraqi Insurgency and the Future of the Middle East*, (New York: Nation Books, 2005), 8.
7. Hashim, *Insurgency and Counter-Insurgency*, 147.
8. Delong, *Inside CentCom*, 87.
9. Knightley, *The First Casualty*, 528.
10. Ibid., 528.
11. Richard Engel, *War Journal: My Five Years in Iraq*, (New York: Simon & Schuster, 2008), 132.
12. Steve Tatham, *Losing Arab Hearts And Minds*, 127, 138; Miles, *Al-Jazeera*, 127, 138, 241-243, 290-293; Lynch, *Voices of the New Arab Public*, 23; Marine Colvin, "Focus: How Saddam's agents targeted Al-Jazeera" *The Sunday Times*, May 11, 2003, 20. [Online]; (LexisNexis® Academic; accessed Feb 4, 2007; "Report: Saddam's spies infiltrated al-Jazeera," *Worldnetdaily.com*, May 11, 2003. (http://www.worldnetdaily.com/news/article.asp?ARTICLE_ID=32513; accessed Feb 4, 2007); Stephen F. Hayes, "Al Jazeera: 'Fair,' 'Balanced,' and Bought'," *The Daily Standard*, May 28, 2003. (http://www.weeklystandard.com/Content/Public/Articles/000/000/002/736nibie.asp; accessed Feb 4, 2007); "Opposition Leader Claims Iraqi Intelligence Infiltrated Al-Jazeera," *Fox News*, Apr 29, 3003. (http://www.foxnews.com/story/0,2933,85538,00.html; accessed Feb 4, 2007).
13. Gordon, *Cobra II*, 145, 165.
14. John F. Burns, "Threats And Responses: Baghdad; In Iraqi Capital, People Prepare As War Looms," New York Times, Mar 18, 2003. Available at: http://www.nytimes.com/2003/03/18/world/threats-and-responses-baghdad-in-iraqi-capital-people-prepare-as-war-looms.html?pagewanted=1; accessed 31 Mar 2010).
15. Fontenot, *On Point*, 88-89, 101, 154-59, 210; Nicholas E. Reynolds, *U.S. Marines in Iraq, 2003: Basra, Baghdad and Beyond, U.S. Marines in the Global War on Terrorism*, (Washington, DC: History Division, U.S. Marine Corps, 2007), 65- 77; 65- 77; Rod Andrew, *The Battle of An-Nasiriyah*, (Washington, DC: History Division, U.S. Marine Corps, 2009), 6-42; Hashim, *Insurgency and Counter-Insurgency*, 14; Delong, *Inside CentCom*, 109.
16. Ibid., 3, 9-13, 82; Kevin M. Woods, with Michael R. Pease, Mark E. Stout, Williamson Murray, and James G. Lacey, *Iraqi Perspectives Project: A View of Operation Iraqi Freedom from Saddam's Senior Leadership*, (Washington, DC, 2006), 125-126.
17. Miles, *Al-Jazeera*, 245; Tracy Connor, "Iraqis Forced to Fight or See Children Killed," *Daily News* (New York), Mar 28, 2003, 6. (LexisNexis® Academic; accessed Feb 4, 2007).

18. Gregory Fontenot, E. J. Degen, and David Tohn. *On Point: The United States Army in Operation Iraqi Freedom*, (Fort Leavenworth, KS: Combat Studies Institute Press, 2004), 88-89, 101, 154-59, 210; Reynolds, *U.S. Marines in Iraq, 2003*, 65- 77; Andrew, *The Battle of An-Nasiriyah*, 6-42; Hashim, *Insurgency and Counter-Insurgency*, 14; Delong, *Inside CentCom*, 109.
19. Fontenot, *On-Point*, 88-89, 101, 154-59, 210.
20. Accumulation of the author's formal military training and independent study. The descriptions of terrorist organization can be corroborated through numerous sources.
21. Hashim, *Insurgency and Counter-Insurgency*, 14.
22. Delong, *Inside CentCom*, 107.
23. Ibid., 103.
24. Hashim, *Insurgency and Counter-Insurgency*, 56-57.
25. McWilliams, *Insight into the Awakening*, Draft.
26. Howard Kurtz, "Unembedded Journalist's Report Provokes Military Ire," *The Washington Post*, Mar 27, 2003. (LexisNexis® Academic; accessed Jun 7, 2007); Rupert Cornwell, "The Iraq Conflict: In Bed With The Army: Why The Media Is A Hit With The Military," *The Independent*, Mar 29, 2003. (LexisNexis® Academic; accessed Jun 7, 2007).
27. Katherine M. Skiba, *Sister In The Band Of Brothers: Embedded With The 101st Airborne In Iraq*, (Lawrence, KA: University Press of Kansas, 2005), 233.
28. Charles Jones, *Red, White, or Yellow?: The Media and the Military at War in Iraq*, (Mechanicsburg, PA: Stackpole Books, 2008), 37-38, 41.
29. Ibid., 103.
30. Delong, *Inside CentCom*, 105.
31. "Stahl Frets Over War Problems, Powell Dismisses Her 'Nonsense,' Media Research Center, Mar 27, 2003. (http://www.mediaresearch.org/cyberalerts/2003/cyb20030327.asp; accessed Dec 13, 2009); *48 Hours*, Mar 25, 2003.
32. "Jennings and Stahl Raise Vietnam 'Are You...Feeling Deja Vu?,' Media Research Center, Mar 27, 2003. (http://www.mediaresearch.org/cyberalerts/2003/cyb20030327.asp; accessed Dec 13, 2009); *48 Hours*, Mar 25, 2003.
33. Greg Mitchell, "From quick war to quagmire?" *Editor & Publisher*, Mar 31, 2003, 10-12. (http://www.ProQuest LLC.com/; accessed Dec 13, 2009).
34. Ibid.
35. Trevor Kavanagh, "BBC's own man blasts his bosses over 'bias'," *The Sun*, Mar 26, 2003. (http://www.thesun.co.uk/sol/homepage/news/article157659.ece; accessed Dec 13, 2009).
36. Delong, *Inside CentCom*, 105.
37. Allard, *Warheads*, 2-3.
38. James Lacey, "Who's Responsible for Losing the Media War in Iraq?," *U.S. Navy Proceedings*, Oct 2004. (http://www.military.com/NewContent/0,13190,NI_1004_Media-P1,00.html; accessed Sep 14, 2009).
39. Miles, *Al-Jazeera*, 242; Delong, *Inside CentCom*, 109.
40. Miles, *Al-Jazeera*, 241.
41. John Otis, "Critics Accuse Arab Media of War Bias," Knight Ridder Tribune Business News, Apr 5, 2003. (http://www.ProQuest LLC.com/. ; accessed Dec 13, 2009).
42. Ibid.
43. Miles, *Al-Jazeera*, 242; Hashim, *Insurgency and Counter-Insurgency*, 12.
44. Christopher Paul and James J Kim, *Reporters on the Battlefield: The Embedded Press System in Historical Context*, (Santa Monica: RAND Corporation, 2004), 55; Frank Rich, "Iraq Around The Clock," *The New York Times*, Mar 30, 2003. (LexisNexis® Academic; accessed Feb 20, 2007).
45. Tatham, *Losing Arab Hearts And Minds*, 175; Miles, *Al-Jazeera*, 272, 273.

46. Tatham, *Losing Arab Hearts And Minds*, 175.
47. John F. Burns, "The Iraqi Capital: Hussein Rallies Iraqi Defenders To Hold Capital, *The New York Times*, Mar 25, 2003. (LexisNexis® Academic; accessed Feb 20, 2007); Anthony Shadid, "Iraqi officials welcome attack on Baghdad: U.S., British forces drawn into a quagmire that 'they will never get out of'," *The Vancouver Sun*,"Mar 24, 2003. (LexisNexis® Academic; accessed Feb 20, 2007); Eric Schmitt, "Key to Baghdad: How Hard Will Republican Guard Fight?," *The New York Times*, Mar 25, 2003. (LexisNexis® Academic; accessed Feb 20, 2007).
48. "WAR'S QUAGMIRE," *Philippine Daily Inquirer*, Mar 29, 2003. (LexisNexis® Academic; accessed Feb 20, 2007); David E. Sanger, "As a Quick Victory Grows Less Likely, Doubts Are Quietly Voiced in Washington, *The New York Times*, Mar 30, 2003. (LexisNexis® Academic; accessed Feb 20, 2007); R. W. APPLE Jr. "Bush Peril: Shifting Sand and Fickle Opinion," *The New York Times*, Mar 30, 2003. (LexisNexis® Academic; accessed Feb 20, 2007).
49. "NBC's Couric & Miklaszewski Refute Arnett's Baghdad Reporting," Media Research Center, Mar 27, 2003. (http://www.mediaresearch.org/cyberalerts/2003/cyb20030327.asp; accessed Dec 13, 2009); *Today*, Mar 25, 2003.
50. "Embedded Reporters: What Are Americans Getting?"*Project for Excellence in Journalism*, Apr 3, 2003. http://www.journalism.org/; accessed Jul 18, 2007).
51. Richard Engel, *War Journal*, 63.
52. Delong, *Inside CentCom*, 120.
53. Paul Stanway, "All Quagmires Should Go This Well," *Edmonton Sun*, Apr 5, 2003. (LexisNexis® Academic; accessed Feb 20, 2007).
54. Andy Geller, "'Monumental' Day Of Victory - * Mob Destroys Saddam Statue * Iraqi U.N. Diplo: Hussein Who? * Looting In Streets Of Baghdad," *The New York Post*, Apr 10, 2003. (LexisNexis® Academic; accessed Feb 20, 2007).
55. Tatham, *Losing Arab Hearts And Minds*, 138.
56. Ibid.
57. Mellor, *The Making of Arab News*, 2.
58. Lynch, *Voices of the New Arab Public*, 23; Miles, *Al-Jazeera*, 258.
59. "The Vanishing Embedded Reporter in Iraq," *The Project of Excellence in Journalism*, Oct 26, 2006. http://www.journalism.org; accessed Jul 18, 2007); Joe Strupp, "Only 185 journalists remain 'embedded'," *Editor and Publisher*, Apr 24, 2003. http://www.editorandpublisher.com/; accessed Feb 4, 2007); Thomas E. Ricks, *Fiasco: The American Military Adventure in Iraq*, (New York, 2006), 360.
60. Kim Olsen, *Iraq and Back: Inside the War to Win the Peace*, (Annapolis: Navy Institute Press, 2006), 10; "The Vanishing Embedded Reporter in Iraq," *The Project of Excellence in Journalism*, Oct 26, 2006. http://www.journalism.org/; accessed Jul 18, 2007).
61. Thomas E. Ricks, *Fiasco: The American Military Adventure in Iraq*, (New York: The Penguin Press, 2006), 360; "The Vanishing Embedded Reporter in Iraq," *The Project of Excellence in Journalism*, Oct 26, 2006. http://www.journalism.org/; accessed Jul 18, 2007).
62. Chehab, *Inside the Resistance*, 1-3; James Glanz, "The Twilight World of the Iraqi News Stringer," *The New York Times*, Sep 25, 2005. (LexisNexis® Academic; accessed Jun 7, 2007); David Jones, *The Washington Times*, Sep 14, 2003, A08. (LexisNexis® Academic; accessed Feb 20, 2007); Philip Bennett, "The Press: Too Far From the Story?,"*The Washington Post*, Jun 6, 2004, B01. (LexisNexis® Academic; accessed Jun 7, 2007).
63. Miles, *Al-Jazeera*, 279.
64. Ibid., 283, 289; Munson, *Iraq in Transition*, 71.
65. Peter J. Munson, *Iraq in Transition: The Legacy of Dictatorship and the Prospects for Democracy*, (Washington, DC: Potomac Books, 2009), 236.

66. Cora Sol Goldstein, "A Strategic Failure American Information Control Policy," Military Review, Mar-Apr 2008, 58-63.
67. Munson, *Iraq in Transition*, 71.
68. Ibid, 58.
69. Marines in Iraq, 2003 Anthology, Tikrit, South to Babylon, BGen John Kelly, Feb 2004, pg 223; Groen, Michael S. *With the 1st Marine Division in Iraq, 2003: No Greater Friend, No Worse Enemy*. Quantico, VA: Marine Corps University, History Division, 2006; Reynolds, Nicholas E. *U.S. Marines in Iraq, 2003: Basra, Baghdad and Beyond, U.S. Marines in the Global War on Terrorism*, Washington, DC: History Division, U.S. Marine Corps, 2007.
70. Wright. *On Point II*, 13, 70, 72, 88-89.
71. Christopher M. Kennedy, *U.S. Marines in Iraq, 2003: Anthology and Annotated Bibliography. U.S. Marines in the Global War on terrorism*, (Washington, DC: History Division, U.S. Marine Corps, 2006), 223-225; McWilliams, *Insight into the Awakening*, Draft.
72. Ibid.
73. Groen, *With the 1st Marine Division in Iraq*, 369.
74. Gary W. Montgomery and Timothy S. McWilliams, *Al-Anbar Awakening Volume II: Iraqi Perspectives From Insurgency to Counterinsurgency in Iraq, 2004-2009*, (Quantico, VA: Marine Corps University, History Division, 2009), vii.
75. Timothy S. McWilliams, Insight into the Awakening, Draft; Bing West, *No True Glory: A Frontline Account of the Battle for Fallujah*, (New York: Bantam, 2005), 12.
76. Dodge, Iraq's Future, 14, 67; *Al-Anbar Awakening Volume II*; Delong, *Inside CentCom*, 117; Dodge, *Iraq's Future*, 12. 15, 20; Eric Schmitt and Thom Shanker, "Estimates by US See more Rebels with Funds," *The Guardian*, 23 Oct 2004. (LexisNexis® Academic; accessed Feb 20, 2007).
77. Delong, *Inside CentCom*, 117; Dodge, *Iraq's Future*, 12. 15, 20; Eric Schmitt and Thom Shanker, "Estimates by US See more Rebels with Funds," *The Guardian*, 23 Oct 2004. (LexisNexis® Academic; accessed Feb 20, 2007)
78. Montgomery et al, *Al-Anbar Awakening Volume II*, viii, 12.
79. Dodge, *Iraq's Future*, 14, 67.
80. Hashim, *Insurgency and Counter-Insurgency*, 19.
81. Alan R. King, *Twice Armed*, (St. Paul, MN: Zenith Press, 2006), 66.
82. Wright, *On-Point II*, 13, 70, 72, 88-89.
83. Olsen, *Iraq and Back*, 17.
84. Ibid., 94.
85. Hashim, *Insurgency and Counter-Insurgency*, xv, 17; Dodge, *Iraq's Future*, 9.
86. King, *Twice Armed*, 56; Trudy Rubin, "The Quagmire that is Iraq," *The Record*, Jun 3, 2003. (LexisNexis® Academic; accessed Feb 20, 2007).
87. Delong, *Inside CentCom*, 123-124; Olsen, *Iraq and Back*, 151.
88. Wright, *On-Point II*, 27, 94-95.
89. Ibid., 18, 21; Chehab, *Inside the Resistance*, 29.
90. Hashim, *Insurgency and Counter-Insurgency*, 33, 89, 98, 103, 122.
91. "Iraqi Government releases '41 Most Wanted' list," Multinational Forces-Iraq, Jul 2, 2006. (http://www.mnf-iraq.com/index.php?option=com_content&task=view&id=572&Itemid=128. accessed Dec 13, 2009.
92. Ibid., 20.
93. Ibid., 20, 28; King, *Twice Armed*, 115; Chehab, *Inside the Resistance*, 8.
94. Richard Engel, *War Journal*, 62.
95. Ibid.
96. "Into The Abyss - Reporting Iraq, 2003-2006: An Oral History." *Columbia Journalism Review*, Nov/Dec 2006. Vol. 45, Iss. 4.

97. Wright, *On Point II*, 30, 624.
98. Hashim, *Insurgency and Counter-Insurgency*, 29.
99. Wright, *On Point II*, 322.
100. Hashim, *Insurgency and Counter-Insurgency*, 21-23, 29.
101. Dodge, *Iraq's Future*, 18.
102. Hashim, *Insurgency and Counter-Insurgency*, 136; Dexter Filkins, "Memo Urges Qaeda to Wage War in Iraq," *International Herald Tribune*, Feb 10, 2004. (LexisNexis® Academic; accessed Feb 20, 2007); Justin Huggler, "Is this man the Mastermind of Massacres?" *Independent*, Mar 7, 2004. (LexisNexis® Academic; accessed Feb 20, 2007).
103. Hashim, *Insurgency and Counter-Insurgency*, 33, 39; Chehab, *Inside the Resistance*, 9; Dodge, *Iraq's Future*, 11.
104. Chehab, *Inside the Resistance*, 13.
105. Montgomery et al, *Al-Anbar Awakening Volume II*, 20-22, 45-46; Munson, *Iraq in Transition*, 237.
106. Dodge, *Iraq's Future*, 17, 18; Hashim, *Insurgency and Counter-Insurgency*, 259.
107. Nakash, *Reaching for Power*, 7.
108. Hashim, *Insurgency and Counter-Insurgency*, 249; Dodge, *Iraq's Future*, 20.
109. Montgomery et al, *Al-Anbar Awakening Volume II*, 242, 284-295.
110. McWilliams, *Insight into the Awakening*, Draft.
111. Delong, *Inside CentCom*, 121.
112. "US occupation forces kill 11 Iraqis," Al-Jazeera, Apr 7, 2003. (http://english.aljazeera.net/archive/2003/07/2008410134816898152.html; accessed Jan 12, 2010).
113. "Resistance attacks continue in Iraq," Al-Jazeera, Apr 9, 2003. (http://english.aljazeera.net/archive/2003/09/200849161732362821.html; accessed Jan 12, 2010); "Resistance bomb adds to US deaths," Al-Jazeera, Jul 16, 2003. (http://english.aljazeera.net/archive/2003/07/200841012116889203.html; accessed Jan 12, 2010); "Resistance ambush kills US soldiers," Al-Jazeera, Aug 27, 2003. (http://english.aljazeera.net/archive/2003/08/20084914574121308.html; accessed Jan 12, 2010); "Iraqis fighting US seen as 'martyrs'," Al-Jazeera, Oct 11, 2003. (http://english.aljazeera.net/archive/2003/10/20084916288450806.html; accessed Jan 12, 2010).
114. "US troop morale in Iraq plummets," Al-Jazeera, Jul 16, 2003. (http://english.aljazeera.net/archive/2003/07/20084109261546324.html; accessed Jan 12, 2010).
115. Zayani, *The Al Jazeera Phenomenon*, 18.
116. Chehab, *Inside the Resistance*, 9, 21.
117. Ibid, 10.
118. David Miller, *Tell Me Lies: Propaganda and Media Distortion in the Attack on Iraq*, (London: Pluto, 2004), 6-7.
119. Ibid.
120. Entman, *Projections of Power*, 119.
121. Alex Belida, "Rumsfeld Denies US Seeks Access to Military Bases in Iraq," *Voice of America News*, Apr 21, 2003. (LexisNexis® Academic; accessed Feb 20, 2007); Pauline Jelinek, "Rumsfeld Downplays Resistance in Iraq," Associated Press Online, Jun 18, 2003. (LexisNexis® Academic; accessed Feb 20, 2007).
122. Entman, *Projections of Power*, 115.
123. Gwynne Dyer, "Friendless: The U.S. is lost and alone in Iraq Quagmire, UN Members Unlikely to Agree to Help," Sudbury Star, Sep 4, 2003. (LexisNexis® Academic; accessed Feb 20, 2007).

124. Howard Fineman, "Living Politics: Echoes of Vietnam Grow Louder," *Newsweek*, Oct 29, 2003. (LexisNexis® Academic; accessed Feb 20, 2007); Patrick Healy, "Kennedy Gives Kerry Campaign a Lift in Iowa," *The Boston Globe*, Sep 28, 2003. (LexisNexis® Academic; accessed Feb 20, 2007).
125. King, *Twice Armed*, 242.
126. James Lacey, "Who's Responsible for Losing the Media War in Iraq?," *U.S. Navy Proceedings*, Oct 2004. (http://www.military.com/NewContent/0,13190,NI_1004_Media-P1,00.html; accessed Sep 14, 2009).
127. Joseph C. Wilson 4th, "What I Didn't Find in Africa," *New York Times*, Jul 6, 2003. (LexisNexis® Academic; accessed Jul 18, 2007)
128. Dexter Filkins, "A Skeptical Vietnam Voice Still Echoes in the Fog of Iraq," *New York Times*, Apr 25, 2007. (http://www.nytimes.com/2007/04/25/world/middleeast/25halberstam.html; accessed Jan 15, 2010).
129. Ibid.
130. James Lacey, "Who's Responsible for Losing the Media War in Iraq?," *U.S. Navy Proceedings*, Oct 2004. (http://www.military.com/NewContent/0,13190,NI_1004_Media-P1,00.html; accessed Sep 14, 2009).
131. Captain Joseph M. Plenzer, "Conducting Expeditionary Public Affairs" *Marine Corps Gazette*, Feb 2004, 29.
132. James Lacey, "Who's Responsible for Losing the Media War in Iraq?," *U.S. Navy Proceedings*, Oct 2004. (http://www.military.com/NewContent/0,13190,NI_1004_Media-P1,00.html; accessed Sep 14, 2009).
133. Walter Cronkite, *Reuters*, Apr 22, 2003.
134. Phillip Knightley, *The First Casualty*, 531, 533.
135. Danny Schechter, *Embedded: Weapons of Mass Deception: How the Media Failed to Cover the War on Iraq*, (New York: Prometheus Books, 2003), 19, 40.
136. Ibid., 19.
137. Justin Lewis, Rod Brookes, Nick Mosdell, and Terry Threadgold, *Shoot First and Ask Questions Later: Media Coverage of the 2003 Iraq War*, (New York: Peter Lang Publishing, Inc., 2006), 92, 95; Allen, Stuart and Barbie Zelizer, eds. *Reporting War: Journalism in Wartime*, (New York: Routledge, 2004), 294.
138. "Embedded Reporters: What Are Americans Getting?" *Project for Excellence in Journalism*, Apr 3, 2003. (http://www.journalism.org; accessed Jul 18, 2007.
139. "Iraq War," *The Project of Excellence in Journalism*, May 25, 2007. (http://www.journalism.org (accessedJul 18, 2007); Are the Media Opting for "Civil War?" *The Project of Excellence in Journalism*, Nov 30, 2006. (http://www.journalism.org; accessed Jul 18, 2007); David Carr, "A 'Civil War' Puts Words On Trial," *The New York Times*, Dec 4, 2006, 1. (LexisNexis® Academic; accessed Jul 18, 2007); Tariq al-Hashimi, "Don't Give Up On Iraq Yet" *The Washington Post*, Jan 10, 2007; A13. (LexisNexis® Academic; accessed Jun 7, 2007); Tariq al-Hashimi, "No, America, Iraq is not a lost cause," *The Star Ledger*, Jan 11, 2007, 19. (LexisNexis® Academic; accessed Jun 7, 2007).
140. Larry Kaplow, "Why Reporters Are Still Here, And How We're Staying Alive," *Austin American-Statesman*, Apr 18, 2004. (LexisNexis® Academic; accessed Aug 13, 2007).
141. Larry Kaplow, "Dangers Grow For Those Of Us Who Report From Iraq: Baghdad More Hazardous Now Then It Ever Was During The Height Of The War," *Edmond Journal*, Apr 15, 2004. (LexisNexis® Academic; accessed Aug 13, 2007).
142. "The Vanishing Embedded Reporter in Iraq," *The Project of Excellence in Journalism*, Oct 26, 2006. http://www.journalism.org; accessed Jul 18, 2007).
143. Lynch, *Voices of the New Arab Public*, 6.

144. Entman, *Projections of Power*, 115. Cathy Young, "A Flood Of Bad News On Iraq," The Boston Globe, Apr 5, 2004. (LexisNexis® Academic; accessed Feb 20, 2007).
145. Entman, *Projections of Power*, 115.
146. Thomas Rid and Marc Hecker. *War 2.0: Irregular Warfare in the Information Age*, (Westport, CT: Praeger Security International, 2009) 1-2.

Chapter Seven

1. *Al-Anbar Awakening Volume II*, 11, 107, 121.
2. Ibid.; Lin Todd et al., *Iraq Tribal Study—Al-Anbar Governorate: The Albu Fahd Tribe, the Albu Mahal Tribe, and the Albu Issa Tribe*, (Department of Defense, 18 Jun 2006); Also see John Bagot Glubb, *A Short History of the Arab Peoples*, (New York: Stein and Day, 1969); and Janet Wallach, *Desert Queen: The Extraordinary Life of Gertrude Bell, Adventurer, Adviser to Kings, Ally of Lawrence of Arabia*, (New York: Nan A. Talese/Doubleday), 1996.
3. Lin Todd et al., *Iraq Tribal Study*, 5-54; Montgomery et al, *Al-Anbar Awakening Volume II*, 11, 107, 121.
4. Allawi, Ali A., *The Occupation of Iraq: Winning the War, Losing the Peace*, Yale University Press: (New Haven, 2007), 90; Paul McGeough, *Mission Impossible: The Sheikhs, the U.S. and the Future of Iraq.* Quarterly Essay, issue 14, 2004, (Melbourne, Vic: Black Inc, 2004); Montgomery et al, *Al-Anbar Awakening Volume II*, 121-126.
5. Gregory Fontenot, E. J. Degen, and David Tohn, *On Point: The United States Army in Operation Iraqi Freedom*, (Fort Leavenworth, Kan: Combat Studies Institute Press, 2004), 252-254; Montgomery et al, *Al-Anbar Awakening Volume II*, 7-8, 107, 121-131; Allawi, Ali A., *The Occupation of Iraq: Winning the War, Losing the Peace*, Yale University Press: (New Haven, 2007), 90; Lin Todd et al., *Iraq Tribal Study.*
6. Fontenot, Degen, and Tohn, *On Point*, 252-254; Gavrilis, James A. "The Mayor of Ar Rutbah." *Foreign Policy*, Nov/Dec 2005. http://www.foreignpolicy.com/articles/2006/01/03/the_mayor_of_ar_rutbah; accessed 26 Feb 2010)
7. Ibid.; Montgomery et al, *Al-Anbar Awakening Volume II*, 33, 45, 86-87, 121-136.
8. John McCary, presentation, working paper, Jan 22, 2009.
9. Paul McGeough, *Mission Impossible: The Sheikhs, the U.S. and the Future of Iraq.* Quarterly Essay, issue 14, 2004, (Melbourne, Vic: Black Inc, 2004).
10. John McCary, presentation, working paper, Jan 22, 2009.
11. Montgomery et al, *Al-Anbar Awakening Volume II*, 13, 90-91, 201, 207, 265-266.
12. Montgomery et al, *Al-Anbar Awakening Volume II*, 33, 45, 86-87, 121-136.
13. Ibid.
14. Major General Najim Abed al-Jabouri, presentation, working paper, Jan 22, 2009.
15. Ali A. Allawi, *The Occupation of Iraq: Winning the War, Losing the Peace*, (New Haven, CT: Yale University Press, 2007), 158.
16. Major General Najim Abed al-Jabouri, presentation, working paper, Jan 22, 2009.
17. McWilliams, *Insight into the Awakening*, Draft; John McCary, presentation, working paper, Jan 22, 2009.
18. Hashim, *Insurgency and Counter-Insurgency*, 24-25; Lieutenant General John F. Sattler and Lieutenant Colonel Daniel H. Wilson, "Operation Al FAJR: The Battle of Fallujah—Part II," *Marine Corps Gazette*, Jul 2005.
19. Ibid., 24-26.
20. Sandra Mackey, "A City That Lives for Revenge," *The New York Times*, Apr 29, 2004. (LexisNexis® Academic; accessed Feb 20, 2007).
21. Hashim, *Insurgency and Counter-Insurgency*, 25.
22. West, *No True Glory*, 12.
23. Ibid., 34.

24. Larry Kaplow, "Why Reporters Are Still Here, And How We're Staying Alive," *Austin American-Statesman*, Apr 18, 2004. (LexisNexis® Academic; accessed Aug 13, 2007).
25. Hashim, *Insurgency and Counter-Insurgency*, 33, 39; Chehab, *Inside the Resistance*, 9; Dodge, *Iraq's Future*, 11.
26. West, *No True Glory*, 17, 26; Hashim, *Insurgency and Counter-Insurgency*, 23-29.
27. Timothy S. McWilliams and Kurtis P. Wheeler, *Al-Anbar Awakening Volume I*: American Perspective, (Quantico, VA: Marine Corps University Press, 2009), 48; McWilliams, *Insight into the Awakening*, Draft; Donald P. Wright, and Timothy R. Reese, *On Point II : Transition to the New Campaign: The United States Army in Operation Iraqi Freedom, May 2003-Jan 2005*, (Fort Leavenworth, KS: Combat Studies Institute Press, 2008).
28. McWilliams et al, *Al-Anbar Awakening Volume I*, viii, 127-9, 146; Montgomery et al, *Al-Anbar Awakening Volume II*, 20-22, 45-46.
29. McWilliams et al, *Al-Anbar Awakening Volume I*; McWilliams, *Insight into the Awakening*, Draft; Montgomery et al, *Al-Anbar Awakening Volume II*..
30. West, *No True Glory*, 50.
31. Ibid.
32. McWilliams et al, *Al-Anbar Awakening Volume I* , 23.
33. Ibid, xi, 108, 125-28, 136; McWilliams, *Insight into the Awakening*, Draft.
34. Ricks, Fiasco, 318.
35. *Iraq: Journalists in Danger*, Committee to Protect Journalists. (http://www.cpj.org/reports/2008/07/journalists-killed-in-iraq.php
36. Larry Kaplow, "Dangers Grow For Those Of Us Who Report From Iraq: Baghdad More Hazardous Now Then It Ever Was During The Height Of The War," *Edmond Journal*, Apr 15, 2004. (LexisNexis® Academic; accessed Aug 13, 2007).
37. Larry Kaplow, "Why Reporters Are Still Here, And How We're Staying Alive," *Austin American-Statesman*, Apr 18, 2004. (LexisNexis® Academic; accessed Aug 13, 2007).
38. Ian Fisher, "Reporting, and Surviving, Iraq's Dangers," *The New York Times*, Jul 18, 2004. (LexisNexis® Academic; accessed Jul 7, 2007).
39. James Lacey, "Who's Responsible for Losing the Media War in Iraq?," *U.S. Navy Proceedings*, Oct 2004. (http://www.military.com/NewContent/0,13190,NI_1004_Media-P1,00.html; accessed Sep 14, 2009).
40. "Iraqi Police Say Four Foreigners Killed In Al-Fallujah Attack - Al-Jazeera," *BBC Monitoring International Reports*, Mar 31, 2004. (LexisNexis® Academic; accessed Feb 20, 2007).
41. West, *No True Glory*, 2.
42. Jack Fairweather, "Falluja becomes Iraq's Mogadishu: Iraqi mob kills four Americans, hangs their bodies up 'like slaughtered sheep," *National Post* (Canada), Apr 1, 2004. (LexisNexis® Academic; accessed Feb 20, 2007); Monica Davey, "Americans Are Jolted By Gruesome Reminders Of the Day in Mogadishu," *The New York Times*, Apr 1, 2004, 13. (LexisNexis® Academic (accessedFeb 20, 2007).
43. Richard Gwyn, "Time for U.S. to Cut and Run," *The Toronto Star*, Apr 4, 2004. (LexisNexis® Academic; accessed Feb 20, 2007).
44. McWilliams et al, *Al-Anbar Awakening Volume I*, 29, 50-52; McWilliams, *Insight into the Awakening*, Draft.
45. Montgomery et al, *Al-Anbar Awakening Volume II*, 90-91.
46. McWilliams et al, *Al-Anbar Awakening Volume I*, 33-36, 50-54.
47. Jeffrey Gettleman, "Mix of Pride and Shame Follows Killings and Mutilation by Iraqis," *The New York Times*, Apr 2, 2004. A1. (LexisNexis® Academic; accessed Feb 20, 2007).
48. McWilliams et al, *Al-Anbar Awakening Volume I*, 33-36.
49. Ibid.
50. McWilliams et al, *U.S. Marines in Battle: Al-Fallujah, 2004* (DRAFT).

51. Ibid., 33-36, 50-54.
52. Ibid., 55.
53. Scott Peterson, "Marines Poised for Fallujah Offensive," *Christian Science Monitor*, Apr 23, 2004. (LexisNexis® Academic; accessed Feb 20, 2007).
54. "Arab Press Compares US Fallujah Assault To Jenin "Massacre" By Israel," *ONASA News Agency*, Apr 10, 2004. (LexisNexis® Academic; accessed Feb 20, 2007); Patrick Cockburn, "Iraq: The Descent Into Chaos: US Has Killed 280 In Fallujah This Week, Says Hospital Doctor," *The Independent*, Apr 9, 2004. (LexisNexis® Academic; accessed Feb 20, 2007).
55. McWilliams et al, *Al-Anbar Awakening Volume I*, 51-53; "Signaling Resolve, Democratization, and the First Battle of Fallujah," Carter Malkasian, *Journal of Strategic Studies*, Vol. 29, No. 3, 423-452, Jun 2006.
56. Scott Peterson, "Marines Poised for Fallujah Offensive," *Christian Science Monitor*, Apr 23, 2004. (LexisNexis® Academic; accessed Feb 20, 2007); Abdul-Qader Saadi And Lourdes Navarro, "Cease-Fire Holds In An Iraqi City Where 600 Died," *The Star-Ledger*, Apr 12, 2004. (LexisNexis® Academic; accessed Feb 20, 2007).
57. "US: Fierce Falluja fighting recalls Vietnam," Al-Jazeera, Apr 7, 2003. (http://english.aljazeera.net/archive/2004/04/2008410142330912439.html; accessed Jan 12, 2010); "Fighting resumes in Falluja," Al-Jazeera, Apr 7, 2003. (http://english.aljazeera.net/archive/2004/04/200841014318891656.html; accessed Jan 12, 2010).
58. Gary W. Anderson, "Fallujah and the Future of Urban Operations," *Marine Corps Gazette*, Nov 2004, 52.
59. West, *No True Glory*, 63.
60. "TV Networks Pool Resources in Iraq," Pittsburgh Post-Gazette, Apr 14, 2004. (LexisNexis® Academic; accessed Feb 20, 2007).
61. "Al-Jazeera Reports 52 Killed in US Bombing of Iraq's Al-Fallujah," *BBC Monitoring International Reports*, Apr 7, 2004. (LexisNexis® Academic; accessed Feb 20, 2007).
62. "Al-Fallujah Hospital Director Puts This Week's Iraqi Toll At 280," *BBC Monitoring International Reports*, Apr 8, 2004. (LexisNexis® Academic; accessed Feb 20, 2007); "Al-Jazeera Reports US Use of Cluster Bombs in Al-Fallujah, Iraq," *BBC Monitoring International Reports*, Apr 9, 2004. (LexisNexis® Academic; accessed Feb 20, 2007).
63. "Massacre in Fallujah: Over 600 Dead, 1,000 Injured, 60,000 Refugees," democracynow.org, Apr 12, 2004, (http://www.democracynow.org/2004/4/12/massacre_in_fallujah_over_600_dead; accessed March 30, 2011).
64. "Al-Fallujah Battalion 'Commander' Says Five US Planes Downed 7 Apr," *BBC Monitoring International Reports*, Apr 8, 2004 (LexisNexis® Academic; accessed Feb 20, 2007).
65. David, G. J., and T. R. McKeldin, *Ideas As Weapons: Influence and Perception in Modern Warfare*, (Washington, D.C.: Potomac Books, 2009), 341-2.
66. Ibid., 342.
67. Ibid., 343; "U.S. Bombards Mosques Complex," *BBC*, 7 Apr, 2004. (http://news.bbc.co.uk/2/hi/3609665.stm; accessed Jan 11, 2010); Bassem Mroue and Abdul-Qader Saadi, "US Bombs Fallujah Mosque; More Than 40 Worshippers Killed," *Associated Press*, Apr 7, 2004. (http://www.commondreams.org/headlines04/0407-06.htm; accessed Jan 11, 2010).
68. Ibid., 344-45.
69. Gwen Ifill, "Deadly Day," PBS, Apr 7, 2004. (http://www.pbs.org/newshour/bb/middle_east/jan-Jun04/day_04-07.html; accessed Jan 11, 2010).

70. Pam Belluck, "The Struggle for Iraq: The Nation's Mood," *The New York Times*, Apr 8, 2004. (LexisNexis® Academic; accessed Feb 20, 2007).
71. Eric Schmitt, "Troops in Iraq Strain to Hold Lines of Supply" *The New York Times*, Apr 13, 2004. (LexisNexis® Academic; accessed Feb 20, 2007).
72. West, *No True Glory*, 92.
73. Ibid, 144.
74. Ibid.
75. "Into The Abyss - Reporting Iraq, 2003-2006: An Oral History." *Columbia Journalism Review*, Nov/Dec 2006. Vol. 45, Iss. 4.
76. West, *No True Glory*, 119-120.
77. Ibid; Ralph Peters, "War and the Media," *Arm Chair General*, Mar 2007, 84.
78. McWilliams et al, *Al-Anbar Awakening Volume I*, 56.
79. Ibid.
80. Lynch, *Voices of the New Arab Public*, 6.
81. The Story Line in Iraq, *The New York Times*, Apr 11, 2004. (LexisNexis® Academic; accessed Feb 20, 2007).
82. West, *No True Glory*, 92.
83. Ralph Peters, "Kill Faster!" *The New York Post*, May 20, 2004 (LexisNexis® Academic; accessed Feb 20, 2007).
84. "Abuse Of Iraqi POWs By GIs Probed," *CBS News*, Apr 28, 2004. (http://www.cbsnews.com/stories/2004/04/27/60II/main614063.shtml; accessed Aug 14, 2008), Thom Shanker, "Horrific Scenes From Abu Ghraib," *New York Times*, May 2, 2004. p. 4.2. (ProQuest LLC; accessed Aug 14, 2008).
85. Allard, *Warheads*, 119.
86. Pamela Hess, "An American in Sparta," *UPI*, Aug 2, 2004. (LexisNexis® Academic; accessed Feb 20, 2007).
87. Pamela Hess, "An American in Sparta," *UPI*, Aug 2, 2004. (LexisNexis® Academic; accessed Feb 20, 2007).
88. Allard, *Warheads*, 114.
89. Thanassis Cambanis, "Iraqi Detentions Fuel Anti-Us Sentiment," *The Boston Globe*, Mar 28, 2004. (LexisNexis® Academic; accessed Feb 20, 2007).
90. King, *Twice Armed*, 195.
91. Ibid.
92. Timothy S. McWilliams and Robert Yarnell, *U.S. Marines in Battle: Al-Fallujah, 2004* (DRAFT). Washington, DC: History Division, U.S. Marine Corps, 2011.
93. Jones, *Red, White, or Yellow?, 109.*
94. Woods, *Iraqi Perspectives Project*, viii-x, 16, 32.
95. Robert D. Kaplan, The Real Story Of Fallujah, *Wall Street Journal*, May 24, 2004. (LexisNexis® Academic; accessed Jun 7, 2007).
96. Ralph Peters, "War and the Media," *Arm Chair General*, Mar 2007, 86.
97. Mockaitis, *Iraq and the Challenge of Counterinsurgency*, 122.
98. The Story Line in Iraq, *The New York Times*, Apr 11, 2004. (LexisNexis® Academic; accessed Jun 7, 2007).

Chapter Eight

1. West, *No True Glory*, 144.
2. Andy Geller, "Thugs' Human Shields - Women & Kids Used In Fallujah," *The New York Post*, Apr 29, 2004. (LexisNexis® Academic; accessed Feb 20 2007).
3. Hashim, *Insurgency and Counter-Insurgency*, 43.
4. Chehab, *Inside the Resistance*, 8.
5. Sattler et al, "Operation Al FAJR,"12.

---

6. "Iraqi: Al-Fallujah Preacher Says 'Monkey Cannot Rule Us'," BBC Monitoring International Reports, Jun 25, 2004. (LexisNexis® Academic; accessed Feb 20, 2007).
7. Hashim, *Insurgency and Counter-Insurgency*, 41.
8. Montgomery et al, *Al-Anbar Awakening Volume II*, 103.
9. Ibid. 36-37, 181, 264.
10. Montgomery et al, *Al-Anbar Awakening Volume II*, viii, 21, 22.
11. David Kilcullen, "Anatomy of a Tribal Revolt," *Small Wars Journal*, Aug 29, 2007, (http://www.smallwarsjournal.com/blog/2007/08/anatomy-of-a-tribal-revolt,; accessed Oct 17, 2009).
12. Jeffery Gettlemen, "The Re-Baathification of Falluja," New York Times Sunday Magazine, Jun 24, 2004, 55.
13. McWilliams et al, *Al-Anbar Awakening Volume I*, viii, 127-9, 146; Montgomery et al, *Al-Anbar Awakening Volume II*, 13, 20-22, 45-46, 90-91, 201, 207, 265-266; Sattler et al, "Operation Al FAJR,".
14. Hashim, *Insurgency and Counter-Insurgency*, 44.
15. Operational Environment- Iraq: Critical Events Assessment OIF, 20 Sep 04; West, *No True Glory*, 241.
16. Karl Vick, "Fallujah Group Comes to Table," Washington Post, Oct 7, 2004, A14. (LexisNexis® Academic; accessed Feb 20, 2007).
17. John Hughes, "In battle for hearts and minds, Iraqi insurgents are doing well," Christian Science Monitor, Jun 20, 2007. (http://www.csmonitor.com/2007/0620/p09s01-cojh.html; accessed Aug 14, 2008).
18. Peter Brookes, "Flashpoint: As the Terror Turns Al-Qaida Is Shifting Its Tactics and Finding New Followers, *Armed Forces Journal*, (http://www.afji.com/2008/08/3609397; accessed Aug 14, 2008).
19. Major General Najim Abed al-Jabouri, presentation, working paper, Jan 22, 2009.
20. Montgomery et al, *Al-Anbar Awakening Volume II*, 64-67.
21. Ibid.
22. McWilliams et al, *Al-Anbar Awakening Volume I* , 58, 118, 144, 155-156, 227-229, 261; Montgomery et al, *Al-Anbar Awakening Volume II*, 11, 56, 129, 303.
23. David Rose, "Heads in the Sand," *Vanity Fair*, May 12, 2009. (http://www.vanityfair.com/politics/features/2009/05/iraqi-insurgents200905; accessed Apr 17, 2010); Mark Perry. *Talking to Terrorists: Why America Must Engage with Its Enemies*, (New York: Basic Books, 2010).
24. Hashim, *Insurgency and Counter-Insurgency*, 36, 44-45.
25. Beth Gardiner, "Iraq Won't Allow Falluja to Remain in Insurgent Control," Associated Press, Sep 30, 2004. (LexisNexis® Academic; accessed Feb 20, 2007).
26. Monica Davey, "For 1,000 Troops, There Is No Going Home," *The New York Times*, Sep 9, 2004. (http://www.nytimes.com/2004/09/09/national/09deaths.html; accessed Oct 17, 2008); "A Grim Milestone: 1000 U.S. Dead," *The New York Times*, Sep 9, 2004.
27. McWilliams et al, *Al-Anbar Awakening Volume I* , 73-73.
28. Miles, *Al-Jazeera*, 325; Mellor, *The Making of Arab News*, 85; Sabrina Tavernise, "Iraqi Leader Orders Temporary Closing of Al Jazeera's Bureau in Baghdad," *The New York Times*, Aug 8, 2004. (LexisNexis® Academic; accessed Feb 20, 2007).
29. Ibid.
30. Donald P. Wright, and Timothy R. Reese, *On Point II : Transition to the New Campaign: The United States Army in Operation Iraqi Freedom, May 2003-Jan 2005*, (Fort Leavenworth, KS: Combat Studies Institute Press, 2008), 43-44.
31. Scott Baldauf, "Militia's Other Weapon: Videos," *Christian Science Monitor*, Aug 25, 2004. (LexisNexis® Academic; accessed Jul 7, 2007).

32. Donald P. Wright, and Timothy R. Reese, *On Point II : Transition to the New Campaign: The United States Army in Operation Iraqi Freedom, May 2003-Jan 2005*, (Fort Leavenworth, KS: Combat Studies Institute Press, 2008), 43-44.
33. Sattler et al, "Operation Al FAJR," 12.
34. Ibid., 14.
35. Ibid.; Luke Baker, "U.S. Spies on Iraq's Insurgency Through Eagle Eyes," *Reuters*, Aug, 2, 2004. (LexisNexis® Academic; accessed Feb 20, 2007).
36. McWilliams et al, *Al-Anbar Awakening Volume I*, 82-82, 91-92; Sattler et al, "Operation Al FAJR," 14.
37. Sattler et al, "Operation Al FAJR," 13-14.
38. McWilliams, *Insight into the Awakening*, Draft.
39. Donald P. Wright, and Timothy R. Reese, *On Point II : Transition to the New Campaign: The United States Army in Operation Iraqi Freedom, May 2003-Jan 2005*, (Fort Leavenworth, KS: Combat Studies Institute Press, 2008), 43-44.
40. McWilliams et al, *Al-Anbar Awakening Volume I*, 77-80; Lieutenant General Thomas F. Metz, Lieutenant Colonel Mark W. Garrett, Lieutenant Colonel James E. Hutton, and Lieutenant Colonel Timothy W. Bush, U.S. Army, "Massing Effects in the Information Domain: A Case Study of Aggressive Information Operations" *Military Review*, May-Jun 2006.
(http://www.army.mil/professionalwriting/volumes/volume4/Jul_2006/7_06_2.html; accessed Aug 14, 2008).
41. McWilliams, *Insight into the Awakening*, Draft.
42. Metz, Garrett, Hutton, and Bush, "Massing Effects."
43. Sattler et al, "Operation Al FAJR," 13-14.
44. McWilliams et al, *Al-Anbar Awakening Volume I*, 77-80.
45. Metz, Garrett, Hutton, and Bush, "Massing Effects."
46. McWilliams et al, *Al-Anbar Awakening Volume I*, 82; Sattler et al, "Operation Al FAJR,"16.
47. McWilliams et al, *Al-Anbar Awakening Volume I*, 81-85.
48. McWilliams, *Insight into the Awakening*, Draft.
49. Ibid., 80, 90.
50. Sattler et al, "Operation Al FAJR," 14.
51. Ibid., 12; McWilliams et al, *Al-Anbar Awakening Volume I*, 90.
52. Roussel et al, *Voicing Dissent*, 2-6, 8, 55, 58.
53. "Private's plea doesn't take higher-ups off the hook"; *USA TODAY*. May 3, 2005. (ProQuest LLC®; accessed Jun 27, 2008).
54. Lila Rajiva, *The Language of Empire: Abu Ghraib and the American Media*, (New York: Monthly Review Press, 2005), 70.
55. Monica Davey, "Where to Catch a Rising Political Star? Try Illinois," *New York Times*, Oct 27, 2004. pg. A.12. (ProQuest LLC®; accessed Jul 14, 2008); Monica Davey, "A Surprise Senate Contender Reaches His Biggest Stage Yet," *New York Times*, Jul 26, 2004. pg. A.1. (ProQuest LLC®; accessed Jul 14, 2008); Robin Toner and Katharine Q. Seelye, "Republicans Add Seats in South; Obama Wins," *New York Times*, Nov 3, 2004. pg. A.1.
56. McWilliams et al, *Al-Anbar Awakening Volume I*, 8, 81; Sattler et al, "Operation Al FAJR," 20.
57. McWilliams et al, *U.S. Marines in Battle: Al-Fallujah* (DRAFT).
58. Ibid.; McWilliams et al, *Al-Anbar Awakening Volume I*, 77-80; Sattler et al, "Operation Al FAJR," 20.
59. McWilliams et al, *U.S. Marines in Battle: Al-Fallujah* (DRAFT).
60. McWilliams et al, *U.S. Marines in Battle: Al-Fallujah* (DRAFT).
61. Ibid.; Sattler et al, "Operation Al FAJR," 20-21.

62. McWilliams et al, *U.S. Marines in Battle: Al-Fallujah* (DRAFT); Patrick K. O'Donnell, *We Were One: Shoulder to Shoulder With the Marines Who Took Fallujah*, (Cambridge, MA: De Capo Press, 2006), 148; Sattler et al, "Operation Al FAJR," 20-21; West, *No True Glory*, 275.
63. Ibid..
64. Sattler et al, "Operation Al FAJR," 24.
65. Sattler et al, "Operation Al FAJR," 23-24.
66. "In Falluja's Ruins, Big Plans and a Risk of Chaos," *New York Times*, Dec 1, 2004. p. A.1. (ProQuest LLC; accessed Aug 14, 2008); "No Victory in Falluja," *The Nation*, Dec 6, 2004. Vol. 279, Iss. 19; pg. 3, 2. (ProQuest LLC; accessed Aug 14, 2008).
67. McWilliams et al, *U.S. Marines in Battle: Al-Fallujah* (DRAFT).
68. Dahr Jamail, "IRAQ: CIVILIAN DEATHS CAST DOUBTS ON U.S. 'SUCCESS' IN FALLUJAH," Global Information Network, Nov 15, 2004. p. 1. (ProQuest LLC; accessed Aug 14, 2008).
69. McWilliams et al, *U.S. Marines in Battle: Al-Fallujah* (DRAFT).
70. "Something Was Not Right': Cameraman Goes Public on Video Footage of Marines," *The Independent*, Nov 23, 2004. (LexisNexis® Academic; accessed Jun 7, 2007).
71. McWilliams, *Insight into the Awakening*, Draft.
72. Robert F. Worth, "Newsman Who Taped Marine Shooting Captive Keeps Silent," *The New York Times*," Nov 18, 2004. (LexisNexis® Academic; accessed Jun 7, 2007).
73. As described to the author by another Marine from the battalion.
74. Mahbub Husain Khan, "The Falluja Tragedy," *The Independent*, Nov 22, 2004. (LexisNexis® Academic; accessed Jun 7, 2007).
75. Robert F. Worth, "Newsman Who Taped Marine Shooting Captive Keeps Silent," *The New York Times*," Nov 18, 2004. (LexisNexis® Academic; accessed Jun 7, 2007).
76. "Into The Abyss - Reporting Iraq, 2003-2006: An Oral History." *Columbia Journalism Review*, Nov/Dec 2006. Vol. 45, Iss. 4.
77. Ibid.

Chapter Nine

1. Steven Komarow, "More bombs as Iraq voting nears," *USA TODAY*. Jan 20, 2005. p. A.1. (ProQuest LLC®; accessed Jun 27, 2008).
2. Bill Powell, "Can Iraq's Election Be Saved?," *Time*. Jan 24, 2005. Vol. 165, Iss. 4; p. 32. (ProQuest LLC®; accessed Jun 27, 2008); "The Calm Before The Storm," Economist.com, Jan 25, 2005. pg. 1. (ProQuest LLC®; accessed Jun 27, 2008).
3. "Iraqis provide lesson in courage,"USA TODAY, Feb 2, 2005. p. A.12. (ProQuest LLC®; accessed Jul 9, 2008).
4. "Optimism After Iraq Election, But Views on War Remain," *The New York Times*. New York, Feb 1, 2005. p. A.10. (ProQuest LLC®; accessed Jul 9, 2008);
5. "The Vanishing Embedded Reporter in Iraq," *The Project of Excellence in Journalism*, Oct 26, 2006. http://www.journalism.org; accessed Jul 18, 2007). The Project for Excellence in Journalism obtained their material from the Department of Defense. The Public Affairs Office of the Multi-National Forces Iraq reports higher embedded numbers, however, their data was insufficient at the time of this writing.
6. Ibid.
7. Michael Yon, "Censoring Iraq: Why are there so few reporters with American troops in combat? Don't blame the media," *The Weekly Standard*, Oct 30, 2006. (http://www.weeklystandard.com/Content/Public/Articles/000/000/012/844nigml.asp; accessed Aug 7, 2008).

8. P. Mitchell Prothero, "Letter from Iraq," *Center to Protect Journalists.* http://www.cpj.org/Briefings/2004/DA_fall04/Iraq_Prothero_DA_fall04.html; accessed Oct 17, 2007).
9. Ralph Peters, "War and the Media," *Arm Chair General*, Mar 2007, 84.
10. Franklin Raff, "I have seen the enemy…," *WorldNetDaily*, Apr 14, 2006. http://www.worldnetdaily.com/news/article.asp?ARTICLE_ID=49739; accessed Feb 20, 2007).
11. Ibid.
12. "Journalists Killed in 2007," *Center to Protect Journalists.* http://www.cpj.org/killed/killed07.html; accessed Oct 17, 2007); Paul von Ziebauer and Andrew E. Kramer, "Iraqi Journalists is Shot and Killed in Baghdad," *The New York Times*, Oct 14, 2007. http:///www.newyorktimes.com/2007/10/15/world/middleeast/15iraq.html; accessed Oct 17, 2007). "Iraq: Journalists in Danger," *Center to Protect Journalists.* http://www.cpj.org/Briefings/Iraq/Iraq_danger.html; accessed Oct 17, 2007); "Iraq Snapshot," *Center to Protect Journalists.* (http://cpj.org/Briefings/2006/DA_spring_06/bassam/bassam_DA.html; accessed Oct 17, 2007).
13. "Journalists in Iraq - A Survey of Reporters on the Front Lines," *The Project of Excellence in Journalism*, Nov 28, 2007. (http://www.journalism.org; accessed Jul 18, 2007).
14. Cooper, *Watching the Watchdog*, 160-175; Miles, *Al-Jazeera*, 283, 289.
15. "Violent Islamist Extremism, The Internet, and the Homegrown Terrorist Threat," *United States Senate Committee on Homeland Security and Governmental Affairs*, May 8, 2008. (http://hsgac.senate.gov/public/_files/IslamistReport.pdf; accessed Jul 19, 2008); Daniel Kimmage, "The Al-Qaeda Media Nexus ," *Radio Free Europe/Radio Liberty, Mar 2008.* (http://docs.rferl.org/en-US/AQ_Media_Nexus.pdf; accessed Jul 19, 2008).
16. David Danello and Andrew Lubin, "False Stories abound in Chaos of Iraq," *On Point*, Mar 1, 2007. http://uscavonpoint.com/articles2/Article.aspx?id=1840; accessed Mar 3, 2007).
17. Cooper, *Watching the Watchdog*, 160-175.
18. John Hughes, "In Battle for Hearts and Minds, Iraqi Insurgents Are Doing Well," Christian Science Monitor, Jun 20, 2007. (http://www.csmonitor.com/2007/0620/p09s01-cojh.html; accessed Aug 20, 2008).
19. Lieutenant General Thomas F. Metz, Lieutenant Colonel Mark W. Garrett, Lieutenant Colonel James E. Hutton, and Lieutenant Colonel Timothy W. Bush, "Massing Effects in the Information Domain: A Case Study of Aggressive Information Operations" *Military Review*, May-Jun 2006. (http://usacac.leavenworth.army.mil/CAC/milreview/English/MayJun06/webpdf/Metz.pdf; accessed Jul 29, 2008); "Violent Islamist Extremism, The Internet, and the Homegrown Terrorist Threat," *United States Senate Committee on Homeland Security and Governmental Affairs*, May 8, 2008. (http://hsgac.senate.gov/public/_files/IslamistReport.pdf; accessed Jul 19, 2008).
20. Daniel Kimmage, "The Al-Qaeda Media Nexus ," *Radio Free Europe/Radio Liberty, Mar 2008.* (http://docs.rferl.org/en-US/AQ_Media_Nexus.pdf; accessed Jul 19, 2008); "Violent Islamist Extremism, The Internet, and the Homegrown Terrorist Threat," *United States Senate Committee on Homeland Security and Governmental Affairs*, May 8, 2008. (http://hsgac.senate.gov/public/_files/IslamistReport.pdf; accessed Jul 19, 2008); "Journalists in Iraq - A Survey of Reporters on the Front Lines," *The Project of Excellence in Journalism*, Nov 28, 2007. (http://www.journalism.org; accessed Jul 18, 2007).

21. Sudarsan Raghavan and Joshua Partlow, "5 Die in Ambush of U.S. Patrol in Iraq: Massive Search Launched for 3 Missing After 'Coordinated' Attack'," *The Washington Post*, May 13, 2007. (http://www.washingtonpost.com/wp-dyn/content/article/2007/05/12/AR2007051200388_pf.html; accessed Oct 30, 2007).
22. Sudarsan Raghavan and Joshua Partlow, "5 Die in Ambush of U.S. Patrol in Iraq: Massive Search Launched for 3 Missing After 'Coordinated' Attack," May 13, 2007. (http://www.washingtonpost.com/wp-dyn/content/article/2007/05/12/AR2007051200388.html; accessed March 30, 2011).
23. McWilliams, *Insight into the Awakening*, Draft.
24. John A. McCary, "The Anbar Awakening: An Alliance of Incentives, *The Washington Quarterly*, Jan 2009, 43-59.
25. Maher Al-Jasem, "Tribal rivalries undermine security," Al-Jazeera, Aug 15, 2006. (http://english.aljazeera.net/archive/2006/08/200849145723650592.html; accessed Jan 13, 2010).
26. McWilliams et al, *Al-Anbar Awakening Volume I*, viii, 3, 10.
27. David Kilcullen, "Anatomy of a Tribal Revolt," *Small Wars Journal*, Aug 29, 2007, (http://www.smallwarsjournal.com/blog/2007/08/anatomy-of-a-tribal-revolt,; accessed Oct 17, 2009).
28. Ibid.
29. McWilliams, *Insight into the Awakening*, Draft; McWilliams et al, *Al-Anbar Awakening Volume I*, 240; Andrew Lubin, "Ramadi From Caliphate to Capitalism," *Proceedings*, Apr 2008.
30. Montgomery et al, *Al-Anbar Awakening Volume II*, 20-22.
31. "15 executed near Falluja, police say," Al-Jazeera, Aug 29, 2005. (http://english.aljazeera.net/archive/2005/08/200849143243661837.html. ; accessed Jan 13, 2010).
32. Francis J West, *The Strongest Tribe: War, Politics, and the Endgame in Iraq*, (New York: Random House, 2008), 131-32.
33. "Corpses of slain Iraqi soldiers found,"Al-Jazeera, Jan 1, 2005. (http://english.aljazeera.net/archive/2005/01/200849154450473428.html. ; accessed Jan 13, 2010); "Iraqi troops find headless corpses," Al-Jazeera, Mar 5, 2005. (http://english.aljazeera.net/archive/2005/03/200849153634755931.html; accessed Jan 13, 2010)
34. "Many die in Samarra, Ramadi attacks," Al-Jazeera, Jun 25, 2005. (http://english.aljazeera.net/archive/2005/06/200841012123773743.html. ; accessed Jan 13, 2010).
35. Ibid. 20-22, 45-46; McWilliams et al, *Al-Anbar Awakening Volume I*, viii, 127-9, 146; Andrew Lubin, "Ramadi From Caliphate to Capitalism," *Proceedings*, Apr 2008.
36. Andrew Lubin, "Ramadi From Caliphate to Capitalism," *Proceedings*, Apr 2008.
37. Ibid; McWilliams et al, *Al-Anbar Awakening Volume I*, 274; Montgomery et al, *Al-Anbar Awakening Volume II*, 48, 141, 175.
38. John A. McCary, "The Anbar Awakening: An Alliance of Incentives, *The Washington Quarterly*, Jan 2009, 43-59; Carter Malkasian, "Did the Coalition Need More Forces in Iraq? Evidence for Al Anbar," *Joint Forces Quarterly*, Issue 46, 3rd quarter 2007.
39. Fred Kagan, "Kaboom!: How to enrage Iraq's Sunnis," Slate, May 18, 2005. (; accessed Nov 4, 2009); Hannah Allam and Mohammed al Dulaimy, "Iraqis Lament a Call for Help," *Philadelphia Inquirer*, May 17, 2005.

40. Ibid.; Mariam Fam, "More Iraqis Tipping Off Security Forces," *Associated Press*, Apr 3, 2005. ((from LexisNexis® Academic; accessed Jun 1, 2006); Edward Wong and Dexter Filkins, "In and About-Face, Sunnis Want U.S. to Remain in Iraq," New York Times, Jul 17, 2006. (from LexisNexis® Academic; accessed Jul 17, 2006); "U.S. Reclaims Baghdad Neighborhood," Military.com, Jun 1, 2007. http://www.military.com/NewsContent/0,13319,137768,00.html; accessed Jun 1, 2007).
41. Munson, *Iraq in Transition*, 214.
42. McWilliams et al, *Al-Anbar Awakening Volume I*, 24, 27, 32, 34, 50, 130, 185, 231, 244, 280.
43. McWilliams et al, *Al-Anbar Awakening Volume I*, 105-108, 117; McWilliams, *Insight into the Awakening*, Draft.
44. Ibid.
45. Elliot Blair Smith, "Pa. native thwarts car-bomb attack," *USA TODAY*, Apr 17, 2005. (http://www.usatoday.com/news/world/iraq/2005-04-17-iraq-hero_x.htm. accessed Nov 9, 2009; Steve Fainaru, "The Grim Reaper, Riding a Firetruck in Iraq, Marines Recount Dramatic Assault At Base Near Syria," *Washington Post*, Apr 19, 2005, (http://www.washingtonpost.com/wp-dyn/articles/A64291-2005Apr18.html; accessed Nov 9, 2009).
46. McWilliams et al, *Al-Anbar Awakening Volume I*, 10-12, 274-76, 279, 301; Montgomery et al, *Al-Anbar Awakening Volume II*, 108, 135-36, 139, 14-42, 144, 154, 168, 204, 265.
47. McWilliams, *Insight into the Awakening*, Draft.
48. McWilliams et al, *Al-Anbar Awakening Volume I*, 24, 27, 32, 34, 50, 130, 185, 231, 244, 280; McWilliams, *Insight into the Awakening*, Draft.
49. Ellen Knickmeyer and Othman Mohammed, "Governor in Iraq Is Found Dead Abducted Anbar Official Apparently Died As U.S. Tanks Battled Foreign Fighters," *Washington Post*, Jun 1, 2005. (http://www.washingtonpost.com/wp-dyn/content/article/2005/05/31/AR2005053100204.html accessed Apr 23, 2009).
50. Ibid.; McWilliams, *Insight into the Awakening*, Draft.
51. Montgomery et al, *Al-Anbar Awakening Volume II*, 161,164.
52. Ibid. 132.
53. Ibid. 2, 181, 197,
54. Ibid., 24, 27, 32, 34, 50, 130, 185, 231, 244, 280; McWilliams, *Insight into the Awakening*, Draft.
55. McWilliams et al, *Al-Anbar Awakening Volume I*, 9, 105; U.S. Marine Corps Operations in Iraq, 2003-2006, Kenneth W. Estes, (Marine Corps History Division, 2009), 100-101.
56. McWilliams et al, *Al-Anbar Awakening Volume I*, 2.
57. Ibid., 106-108; McWilliams, *Insight into the Awakening*, Draft.
58. Ibid.
59. Montgomery et al, *Al-Anbar Awakening Volume II*, 142.
60. "Operation Steel Curtain Concludes Along Iraq-Syria Border," American Forces Press Service, Nov 22, 2005. (http://www.defenselink.mil/news/newsarticle.aspx?id=18236. accessed Nov 9, 2009.
61. McWilliams et al, *Al-Anbar Awakening Volume I*, 9-10, 105.
62. Center for Strategic and International Studies, *Iraqi Force Development: A Current Status Report Jul 2005-Feb 2006, Working Draft*, Feb 14, 2006.
63. McWilliams et al, *Al-Anbar Awakening Volume I*, 9, 101, 105, 107, 125-126, 150.
64. Ibid., xi, 108, 125-28, 136.
65. James Soriano and Brigadier General John Allen, *Briefing on Reconstruction Progress in Iraq*, (http://merln.ndu.edu/archivepdf/iraq/State/94575.pdf.
66. McWilliams et al, *Al-Anbar Awakening Volume I*, 9, 101, 105, 107, 125-126, 150.
67. Ibid., 130-133.

68. Ahmad Janabi, "Zarqawi v Iraqis: Conflict of interest?," Al-Jazeera, Dec 15, 2005. (http://english.aljazeera.net/archive/2005/12/20084913111872624.html; accessed Jan 13, 2010).
69. "Former Baathists urge Sunnis to vote," Al-Jazeera, Dec 12, 2005. (http://english.aljazeera.net/archive/2005/12/20084913251346332.html; accessed Jan 13, 2010).
70. "15 executed near Falluja, police say," Al-Jazeera, Aug 29, 2005. (http://english.aljazeera.net/archive/2005/08/200849143243661837.html. ; accessed Jan 13, 2010).
71. McWilliams, *Insight into the Awakening*, Draft.
72. Ellen Knickmeyer and Othman Mohammed, "Governor in Iraq Is Found Dead Abducted Anbar Official Apparently Died As U.S. Tanks Battled Foreign Fighters," *Washington Post Foreign Service*, Jun 1, 2005; Page A16. (http://www.washingtonpost.com/wp-dyn/content/article/2005/05/31/AR2005053100204.html accessed Apr 23, 2009).
73. McWilliams, *Insight into the Awakening*, Draft.
74. Ibid.
75. McWilliams, *Insight into the Awakening*, Draft.
76. Dexter Filkins and Khalid al-Ansary, "Demonstrators In Iraq Demand That U.S. Leave," New York Times, Apr 10, 2005. p. 1.1. (ProQuest LLC®; accessed Jul 14, 2008).
77. "Hundreds of Rallies Held Across U.S. to Protest Iraq War," *The New York Times*, New York, Mar 20, 2005. p. 1.35. (ProQuest LLC®; accessed Jul 9, 2008); Marc Santora, "Mother Who Lost Son in Iraq Continues Fight Against War," New York Times. New York, N.Y.: Sep 19, 2005. p. B.2. (ProQuest LLC®; accessed Jul 14, 2008).
78. Richard W. Stevenson, "Of Many Deaths in Iraq, One Mother's Loss Becomes a Protest of the President's Policy," *New York Times*, Aug 8, 2005. (ProQuest LLC®; accessed Jul 14, 2008).
79. Charlie Savage, "Rank and file have taken heat for Abu Ghraib," Knight Ridder Tribune Business News, Apr 28, 2005. p. 1. (ProQuest LLC®; accessed Jul14, 2008).
80. Karen J.Greenberg and Joshua L. Dratel. *The Torture Papers: The Road to Abu Ghraib*, (New York: Cambridge University Press, 2005).
81. "Periscope,"*Newsweek*, May 9, 2005. p. 4. (ProQuest LLC®; accessed Jul 9, 2008).
82. Evan Thomas, "How A Fire Broke Out," *Newsweek*, May 23, 2005. (http://www.newsweek.com/id/52117; accessed Jul 9, 2008); "Interview: Carlotta Gall discusses anti-American protests in Afghanistan following a story in Newsweek which said US personnel at Guantanamo desecrated the Koran," *NPR: All Things Considered*, May 12, 2005. p 60. 1. (ProQuest LLC®; accessed Jun 27, 2008); Richard Lacayo, "When a Story Goes Terribly Wrong," *Time*, Vol 165. May 30, 2005. P. 60. (ProQuest LLC®; accessed Jun 27, 2008).
83. John N. Frank, "'Newsweek' Article Fallout Could Echo Through the Media," PRweek, Volume 8 Issue 22, May 30, 2005. p. 7 (ProQuest LLC®; accessed Jun 27, 2008); Liz Halloran, "A Burning Issue for Journalism; An erroneous report fuels anti-American protests--and debate over 'sources,' U.S. News and World Report, May 30, 2005. p 34. (ProQuest LLC®; accessed Jun 27, 2008).
84. Richard M. Smith, "A Letter to Our Readers," *Newsweek*, May 30, 2005. (http://www.newsweek.com/id/52169; accessed Jul 9, 2008); Ken Waine "The Editor's Desk," *Newsweek*, May 30, 2005. (http://www.newsweek.com/id/52170; accessed Jul 9, 2008); Christopher Dickey, "Shadowland: The Road to Rendition," *Newsweek*, Jun 16, 2005. (http://www.newsweek.com/id/49884; accessed Jul 9, 2008)
85. Vicky Ward, "Double Exposure," Vanity Fair, Jan 2004. (http://www.vanityfair.com/politics/features/2004/01/plame200401; accessed

Dec 16, 2009); Edward T. Pound, Silla Brush, Kevin Whitelaw, Jennifer Jack, "A Case of Trouble; The Charges Against A Top Aide Could Be Just The Beginning," *U.S. News & World Report*, Nov 7, 2005. Vol. 139, Iss. 17; p. 38; Jonathan Kennedy, "America Turns On Bush As All The President's Staff Face Integrity Test," *Knight Ridder Tribune Business News*, Oct 30, 2005. p. 1; "UNITED STATES: Bush Faces Challenge Regaining Trust," *Oxford Analytica Daily Brief Service*, Nov 30, 2005. p. 1.

86. "Iraq War," *The Project of Excellence in Journalism*, May 25, 2007. (http://www.journalism.org; accessed Jul 18, 2007).
87. James Dao, "2000 Dead: As Iraq Tours Stretch On, a Grim Mark," *New York Times*, Oct 26, 2005. (http://www.nytimes.com/2005/10/26/international/middleeast/26deaths.html; accessed Aug 15, 2008).
88. Rick Klein, "Democrats struggle to find one voice on Iraq,"*Knight Ridder Tribune Business News*. Jun 30, 2005. p. 1. (ProQuest LLC®; accessed Jul 14, 2008).
89. Karlyn H. Bowman, *Public Opinion on the War with Iraq*, American Enterprise Institute. (Last updated Jun 20, 2008). p. 36. (http://www.aei.org/publicopinion2; accessed Jul 12, 2008).
90. Mark Silva, "Bush officials scramble to overcome rising opposition to war in Iraq," *Knight Ridder Tribune Business News*, Jun 24, 2005. p. 1. (ProQuest LLC®; accessed Jul 14, 2008).
91. Susan Page, "Poll: USA is losing patience on Iraq; 59% support troop cuts -- a new high," *USA TODAY*, Jun 13, 2005. p. A.1. (ProQuest LLC®; accessed Jul 14, 2008); Neil Abercrombie and Dennis J. Kucinich, "Time for U.S. to withdraw," USA *TODAY*, May 17, 2005. p. A.12. (ProQuest LLC®; accessed Jul 14, 2008).
92. "TV's Bad News Brigade: ABC, CBS and NBC's Defeatist Coverage of the War in Iraq," Media Research Council, Oct 2005. (http://www.mrc.org/SpecialReports/2005/pdf/TVs_Depressing_Iraq_News.pdf; accessed Aug 7, 2008).

Chapter Ten

1. McWilliams et al, *Al-Anbar Awakening Volume I*, 130-133; McWilliams, *Insight into the Awakening*, Draft.
2. Radha Iyengar and Jonathan Monten, *Is There an "Emboldenment' Effect?" Evidence from the Insurgency in Iraq*, Belfer Center for Science and International Affairs, Kennedy School of Government, Harvard University: Cambridge, MA. May 2008. (http://people.rwj.harvard.edu/~riyengar/insurgency.pdf; accessed Jul 10, 2008).
3. "Analysis: Iraq violence kills more than 200 in a week," *NPR*, Jan 11, 2006; "Iraq's Bloodiest Day in Months Includes 11 U.S. Deaths," *New York Times* Jan 7, 2006. (ProQuest LLC. accessed Dec 17, 2009.
4. Author's observations reviewing ProQuest LLC and LexisNexis® Academic.
5. Lieutenant Colonel John M. Kanaley, "Unreported History in Baghdad," *RealClearPolitics.com*, Feb 13, 2006. (http://www.realclearpolitics.com/Commentary/com-2_13_06_JMK.html; accessed Aug 19, 2008).
6. "From Iraq Shrine's Rubble, Civil War Threat Emerges," *USA TODAY*, Feb 24, 2006. p. A.12. (ProQuest LLC®; accessed Jul 9, 2008); Julian E. Barnes, "Sliding Toward an Uncivil War," *U.S. News & World Report*, Mar 6, 2006. Vol. 140, Iss. 8; p. 14-15;Karlyn H. Bowman, *Public Opinion on the War with Iraq*, American Enterprise Institute. (Last updated Jun 20, 2008). (http://www.aei.org/publicopinion2; accessed Jul 12, 2008). p. 178.
7. "85 Bodies Found in Baghdad in Sectarian Strife," *New York Times*, Mar 15, 2006. p. A.1; Daniel Marston and Carter Malkasian, *Counterinsurgency in Modern Warfare*, (Oxford: Osprey, 2008), 258; Carter Malkasian, "Did Coalition Forces Need More Forces in Iraq? Evidence from Al Anbar," *Joint Forces Quarterly*, Issue 46, 3rd Quarter, 2007, 124.

8. Tim McGirk, "Collateral Damage or Civilian Massacre in Haditha?," *Time.* Mar 19, 2006. (http://www.time.com/time/world/article/0,8599,1174649,00.html. accessed Jun 27, 2008; Tim McGirk, "One Morning in Haditha," *Time.* Mar 27, 2006. Vol. 167, Iss. 13; p. 34. (ProQuest LLC®; accessed Jul 9, 2008).
9. Hearing of the House Foreign Affairs Committee, Mar 18, 2009; Tim McGirk, "Collateral Damage or Civilian Massacre in Haditha?," *Time.* Mar 19, 2006. (http://www.time.com/time/world/article/0,8599,1174649,00.html. accessed Jun 27, 2008; Tim McGirk, "One Morning in Haditha," *Time.* Mar 27, 2006. Vol. 167, Iss. 13; p. 34. (ProQuest LLC®; accessed Jul 9, 2008).
10. Fred Barnes, "The My Lai Lie," *The Weekly Standard,* Jul 3-Jul 10, 2006. Vol. 11, Iss. 40; p. 9. (ProQuest LLC®; accessed Jul 9, 2008); Demetri Sevastopulo, "Haditha revives memory of US abuses," *Financial Times.* Jun 1, 2006. p. 6. (ProQuest LLC®; accessed Jul 9, 2008). (ProQuest LLC®; accessed Jul 15, 2008).
11. Your World Today, *CNN*, May 30, 2006 (http://transcripts.cnn.com/TRANSCRIPTS/0605/30/ywt.01.html; accessed Aug 7, 2008).
12. Wolf Blitzer, *CNN*, May 19, 2006. (http://transcripts.cnn.com/TRANSCRIPTS/0605/19/sitroom.03.html; accessed Jul 15, 2008).
13. Ibid.
14. Kimberly Kagan, "How They Did it: Executing the Winning Strategy in Iraq," The Weekly Standard, Volume 013, Issue 10, Nov 11, 2007. http://www.weeklystandard.com/Content/Public/Articles/000/000/014/346ydlgo.asp; accessed Nov 13, 2007); "U.S. Pursuing Diplomacy With Iran," *Associated Press Online*, Sep 16, 2007. (LexisNexis® Academic; accessed Sep 18, 2007).
15. "Iraq War," *The Project of Excellence in Journalism*, http://www.journalism.org, May 25, 2007; Are the Media Opting for "Civil War?" *The Project of Excellence in Journalism*, http://www.journalism.org, Nov 30, 2006; David Carr, "A 'Civil War' Puts Words On Trial," *The New York Times*, Dec 4, 2006, Pg. 1; Tariq al-Hashimi, "Don't Give Up On Iraq Yet" *The Washington Post*, Jan 10, 2007; Page A13, Tariq al-Hashimi, "No, America, Iraq is not a lost cause," *The Star Ledger*, Jan 11, 2007 , Pg. 19. Associated Press, "Head of Marines Sees Vietnam Parallels," *Military.com*, Jul 11, 2007.
16. Franklin Raff, "I have seen the enemy…," *WorldNetDaily*, Apr 14, 2006. http://www.worldnetdaily.com/news/article.asp?ARTICLE_ID=49739; accessed Feb 20, 2007).
17. "Iraq War," *The Project of Excellence in Journalism*, May 25, 2007. http://www.journalism.org; accessed Jul 18, 2007).
18. "Rep. Cardin Calls For President To Submit Strategy To Withdraw U.S. Troops From Iraq," *US Fed News Service*, May 11, 2006. (ProQuest LLC®; accessed Jul 9, 2008); Jill Zuckman, "Capitol Hill Showdown on Iraq: GOP Crafts Resolution In Support Of War; Democrats Call For Timetable To Withdraw Troops," Knight Ridder Tribune Business News. Jun 13, 2006. p. 1. (ProQuest LLC®; accessed Jul 9, 2008)
19. "Rep. Cardin Calls For President To Submit Strategy To Withdraw U.S. Troops From Iraq," *US Fed News Service*, May 11, 2006. (ProQuest LLC®; accessed Jul 9, 2008); Jill Zuckman, "Capitol Hill Showdown on Iraq: GOP Crafts Resolution In Support Of War; Democrats Call For Timetable To Withdraw Troops," Knight Ridder Tribune Business News. Jun 13, 2006. p. 1. (ProQuest LLC®; accessed Jul 9, 2008)
20. William Neikirk, "GOP Defeats Democrats On Pullout," *Knight Ridder Tribune Business News*, Jun 23, 2006. pg. 1. (ProQuest LLC®; accessed Jul 9, 2008)
21. McWilliams et al, *Al-Anbar Awakening Volume I*, 130-133; McWilliams, *Insight into the Awakening*, Draft.

22. McWilliams et al, *Al-Anbar Awakening Volume I*, 24, 27, 32, 34, 50, 130, 185, 231, 244, 280; Montgomery et al, *Al-Anbar Awakening Volume II*, viii, 12, 19-23, 108, 152-55, 265-66.
23. McWilliams et al, *Al-Anbar Awakening Volume I*,; Montgomery et al, *Al-Anbar Awakening Volume II*, 129; "Iraqi tribal leaders responding to U.S. overtures draw insurgent retaliation," *Iraqi News*, Feb 19, 2006. (http://www.iraqinews.com/politics/iraqi-tribal-leaders-responding-to-u.s.-overtures-draw-insurgent-retaliation.html?Itemid=126#top. accessed Nov 6, 2009.
24. McWilliams et al, *Al-Anbar Awakening Volume I*, 143, 156, 170, 1780182, 184, 279.
25. McWilliams et al, *Al-Anbar Awakening Volume I*, 129; Montgomery et al, *Al-Anbar Awakening Volume II*, viii, 21; "Iraqi tribal leaders responding to U.S. overtures draw insurgent retaliation," *Iraqi News*, Feb 19, 2006. (http://www.iraqinews.com/politics/iraqi-tribal-leaders-responding-to-u.s.-overtures-draw-insurgent-retaliation.html?Itemid=126#top. accessed Nov 6, 2009.
26. McWilliams et al, *Al-Anbar Awakening Volume I*, 218; Montgomery et al, *Al-Anbar Awakening Volume II*, 151.
27. James Soriano and Brigadier General John Allen, *Briefing on Reconstruction Progress in Iraq*, (http://merln.ndu.edu/archivepdf/iraq/State/94575.pdf.
28. Andrew Lubin, "Ramadi From Caliphate to Capitalism," *Proceedings*, Apr 2008.
29. McWilliams, *Insight into the Awakening*, Draft; Neil Smith and Sean MacFarland, "Anbar Awakens: The Tipping Point," *Military Review*, Mar-Apr 2008, 43.
30. McWilliams et al, *Al-Anbar Awakening Volume I*, 114-116; "Iraqi tribal leaders responding to U.S. overtures draw insurgent retaliation," *Iraqi News*, Feb 19, 2006. (http://www.iraqinews.com/politics/iraqi-tribal-leaders-responding-to-u.s.-overtures-draw-insurgent-retaliation.html?Itemid=126#top. accessed Nov 6, 2009.
31. McWilliams et al, *Al-Anbar Awakening Volume I*, 129-130; Neil Smith and Sean MacFarland, "Anbar Awakens: The Tipping Point," *Military Review*, Mar-Apr 2008, 43.
32. Daniel Marston and Carter Malkasian, *Counterinsurgency in Modern Warfare*, (Oxford: Osprey, 2008), 258; Carter Malkasian, "Did Coalition Forces Need More Forces in Iraq? Evidence from Al Anbar," *Joint Forces Quarterly*, Issue 46, 3rd Quarter, 2007, 124.
33. McWilliams et al, *Al-Anbar Awakening Volume I*, 130, 141-142, 146.
34. Ibid.; Daniel Marston and Carter Malkasian, *Counterinsurgency in Modern Warfare*, (Oxford: Osprey, 2008), 255-258; Carter Malkasian, "Did Coalition Forces Need More Forces in Iraq? Evidence from Al Anbar," *Joint Forces Quarterly*, Issue 46, 3rd Quarter, 2007, 123-124.
35. McWilliams et al, *Al-Anbar Awakening Volume I*, 141-142, 146.
36. Ibid.,131-132,
37. Smith and MacFarland, "Anbar Awakens," 41-42.
38. McWilliams et al, *Al-Anbar Awakening Volume I*,131-132; McWilliams, *Insight into the Awakening*, Draft.
39. Ibid.
40. West, *The Strongest Tribe*, 132-133.
41. McWilliams et al, *Al-Anbar Awakening Volume I*, 130-132.
42. Ibid.,134.
43. Neil Smith and Sean MacFarland, "Anbar Awakens: The Tipping Point," *Military Review*, Mar-Apr 2008; Sean MacFarland, "Addendum Anbar Awakens," *Military Review*, May-Jun 2008, 42-44; McWilliams et al, *Al-Anbar Awakening Volume I*, 177-178.
44. Ibid.
45. Ibid.; McWilliams, *Insight into the Awakening*, Draft.
46. Anthony Dean, "Providing Security Force Assistance in an Economy of Force Battle," *Military Review*, Jan-Feb 2010, 80.

---

47. Neil Smith and Sean MacFarland, "Anbar Awakens: The Tipping Point," *Military Review*, Mar-Apr 2008; Sean MacFarland, "Addendum Anbar Awakens," *Military Review*, May-Jun 2008, 42-44; McWilliams et al, *Al-Anbar Awakening Volume I*, 177-178; McWilliams, *Insight into the Awakening*, Draft.
48. Ibid.
49. McWilliams et al, *Al-Anbar Awakening Volume I*, 33, 223-224; Neil Smith and Sean MacFarland, "Anbar Awakens: The Tipping Point," *Military Review*, Mar-Apr 2008; Sean MacFarland, "Addendum Anbar Awakens," *Military Review*, May-Jun 2008, 44.
50. McWilliams et al, *Al-Anbar Awakening Volume I*, 244; Montgomery et al, *Al-Anbar Awakening Volume II*, 187-90; Andrew Lubin, "Ramadi From Caliphate to Capitalism," *Proceedings*, Apr 2008. P. 54-55. (http://www.usni.org/magazines/proceedings/story.asp?STORY_ID=1420; accessed Jul 31, 2008).
51. Andrew Lubin, "Ramadi From Caliphate to Capitalism," *Proceedings*, Apr 2008. (http://www.usni.org/magazines/proceedings/story.asp?STORY_ID=1420; accessed Jul 31, 2008).
52. McWilliams et al, *Al-Anbar Awakening Volume I*, 236; Andrew Lubin, "Ramadi From Caliphate to Capitalism," *Proceedings*, Apr 2008. (http://www.usni.org/magazines/proceedings/story.asp?STORY_ID=1420; accessed Jul 31, 2008).
53. Ibid., 234; Andrew Lubin, "Ramadi From Caliphate to Capitalism," *Proceedings*, Apr 2008. (http://www.usni.org/magazines/proceedings/story.asp?STORY_ID=1420; accessed Jul 31, 2008).
54. Montgomery et al, *Al-Anbar Awakening Volume II*, 56-57; Andrew Lubin, "Ramadi From Caliphate to Capitalism," *Proceedings*, Apr 2008. (http://www.usni.org/magazines/proceedings/story.asp?STORY_ID=1420; accessed Jul 31, 2008)..
55. McWilliams et al, *Al-Anbar Awakening Volume I*, 179-80, 198, 202; Anthony Dean, "Providing Security Force Assistance in an Economy of Force Battle," *Military Review*, Jan-Feb 2010, 80-84; Andrew Lubin, "Ramadi From Caliphate to Capitalism," *Proceedings*, Apr 2008. 54-55. (http://www.usni.org/magazines/proceedings/story.asp?STORY_ID=1420; accessed Jul 31, 2008).
56. Montgomery et al, *Al-Anbar Awakening Volume II*, 187-90; Andrew Lubin, "Ramadi From Caliphate to Capitalism," *Proceedings*, Apr 2008. P. 54-55. (http://www.usni.org/magazines/proceedings/story.asp?STORY_ID=1420; accessed Jul 31, 2008).
57. McWilliams et al, *Al-Anbar Awakening Volume I*, 271-283.
58. Ibid., 146, 163-68, 178-80; Montgomery et al, *Al-Anbar Awakening Volume II*, 187-90; Andrew Lubin, "Ramadi From Caliphate to Capitalism," *Proceedings*, Apr 2008. P. 54-55. (http://www.usni.org/magazines/proceedings/story.asp?STORY_ID=1420; accessed Jul 31, 2008).
59. Farook Ahmed, "Backgrounder #23: Sons of Iraq and Awakening Forces," Institute for the Study of War, Feb 21, 2008. (http://www.understandingwar.org/files/reports/Backgrounder%2023%20Sons%20of%20Iraq%20and%20Awakening%20Forces.pdf ; accessed Jul 31, 2008).
60. Ibid.; Michael J. Totten, Hope for Iraq's Meanest City: How the surge brought order to Fallujah," *City Journal*, Spring 2008. (http://www.city-journal.org/2008/18_2_fallujah.html; accessed Aug 18, 2008).

---

61. Edward Wong and Dexter Filkins, "In an About-Face, Sunnis Want U.S. to Remain in Iraq," New York Times, Jul 17, 2006. (www.nytimes.com/2006/07/17/world/middleeast/17sunnis.html; accessed Jul 31, 2008).
62. "Sunni fighters claim Ramadi," Al-Jazeera, Oct 19, 2006. (http://english.aljazeera.net/archive/2006/10/200849125327298882.html; accessed Jan 13, 2010).
63. McWilliams et al, *Al-Anbar Awakening Volume I*, 182; Montgomery et al, *Al-Anbar Awakening Volume II*, 65-69.
64. McWilliams et al, *Al-Anbar Awakening Volume I*, ix, 135-36, 171, 173, 198-99, 203-04.
65. Anthony Dean, "Providing Security Force Assistance in an Economy of Force Battle," *Military Review*, Jan-Feb 2010.
66. *Counterinsurgency: Field Manual (FM) 3-24*, Headquarters, Department of the Army, Washington, DC, 15 Dec 2006, the final draft signed by LtGen James F. Amos in lieu of LtGen Mattis; David S. Cloud and Thom Shanker, "Pentagon Widens Its Battle To Shape News of Iraq War," *New York* Times, Nov 3, 2006. pg. A.17. Available on ProQuest LLC; accessed Aug 18, 2008)
67. *Joint Publication 3-13: Information Operations.* Washington, DC: 2006.
68. Karen Hughes, *Strategic Communication and Public Diplomacy: Interagency Coordination*, Remarks at Department of Defense Conference on Strategic Communication, Jul 11, 2007. (http://www.state.gov/r/us/2007/88630.htm; accessed Jul 30, 2008).
69. Marston and Malkasian, *Counterinsurgency*, 255.
70. Thomas Ricks, "Situation Called Dire in West Iraq," *The Washington Post*, Sep 11, 2006.
71. McWilliams et al, *Al-Anbar Awakening Volume I*, 134-135.
72. Ibid., 183.
73. Ibid.
74. Ibid., 171.
75. Ibid, 173.
76. "One Hundred Too Many," *Broadcasting & Cable*, Apr 30, 2007. Vol. 137, Iss. 18; pg. 32. (ProQuest LLC; accessed Aug 7, 2008).
77. "Fresh Iraq violence claims 135 lives," Nov 13, 2006. (http://english.aljazeera.net/archive/2006/11/2008410131457554673.html; accessed Jan 13, 2010).
78. "Zarqawi video vows defeat for US," Al-Jazeera, Apr 26, 2006. (http://english.aljazeera.net/archive/2006/04/200849152737760645.html; accessed Jan 13, 2010); "Transcript: Bin Laden accuses West," Al-Jazeera, Apr 23, 2006. (http://english.aljazeera.net/archive/2006/04/2008410162648212577.html; accessed Jan 13, 2010).
79. "Sunni fighters claim Ramadi," Al-Jazeera, Oct 19, 2006. (http://english.aljazeera.net/archive/2006/10/200849125327298882.html; accessed Jan 13, 2010).
80. "Many killed in US raid on Ramadi," Al-Jazeera, Nov 16, 2006. (http://english.aljazeera.net/archive/2006/11/200841011196187645.html; accessed Jan 13, 2010).
81. John M. Broder, "In Call for More Troops, McCain Places His Bet on Iraq," *New York Times*, Nov 14, 2006. pg. A.18; Pete Hegseth, "More Troops, Please," *Wall Street Journal*, Oct 3, 2006. pg. A.26; Michael R. Gordon, "Grim Outlook Seen in West Iraq Without More Troops and Aid," Sep 12, 2006. pg. A.1; Susan Page, "Most in poll want plan for pullout from Iraq," *USA Today*, Jun 27, 2006. pg. A.8. (from ProQuest LLC; accessed May 5, 2009).

82. "The Iraq War on Cable TV: CNN and MSNBC vs. The Fox News Channel," Media Research Council, Dec 2006. (http://www.mrc.org/SpecialReports/2006/IraqWarCableTV/IraqCable.pdf; accessed Aug 7, 2008).
83. Ibid.
84. Karlyn H. Bowman, *Public Opinion on the War with Iraq*, American Enterprise Institute. (Last updated Jun 20, 2008). pp. 27, 129. (http://www.aei.org/publicopinion2; accessed Jul 12, 2008).
85. Shaila DeWan, "The Impetus for Changes: Voters Display Frustrations and Dissatisfactions," *New York Times*, Nov 8, 2006. pg. P.8. (from ProQuest LLC; accessed May 5, 2009); Jackie Calmes and David Rogers, "Power Shift: Democrats Take Control of House; Divided Government Looms As Voters Seek Change; Senate Outcome Close; Crucial Role of Hispanics," *Wall Street Journal*, Nov 8, 2006. pg. A.1. (from ProQuest LLC; accessed May 5, 2009).
86. Roussel et al, *Voicing Dissent*, 30, 32, 171, 204, 223.
87. Radha Iyengar and Jonathan Monten, *Is There an "Emboldenment' Effect?" Evidence from the Insurgency in Iraq*, Belfer Center for Science and International Affairs, Kennedy School of Government, Harvard University: Cambridge, MA. May 2008. (http://people.rwj.harvard.edu/~riyengar/insurgency.pdf; accessed Jul 10, 2008).
88. Ibid.
89. McWilliams et al, *Al-Anbar Awakening Volume I*, 195.
90. Jim Rutenberg, Sheryl Gay Stolberg, "Removal of Rumsfeld Dates Back to Summer," New York Times, Nov 10, 2006. pg. A.22. (from ProQuest LLC; accessed May 5, 2009); John M. Broder, "In Call for More Troops, McCain Places His Bet on Iraq," *New York Times*, Nov 14, 2006. pg. A.18. (from ProQuest LLC; accessed May 5, 2009); Pete Hegseth, "More Troops, Please," *Wall Street Journal*, Oct 3, 2006. pg. A.26. (from ProQuest LLC; accessed May 5, 2009); Michael R. Gordon, "Grim Outlook Seen in West Iraq Without More Troops and Aid," Sep 12, 2006. pg. A.1. (from ProQuest LLC; accessed May 5, 2009).
91. Associated Press, "Head of Marines Sees Vietnam Parallels," Jul 11, 2007. (http://www.military.com; accessed Aug 13, 2007).
92. Ricks, 426.
93. Delong, *Inside CentCom*, xiii.
94. The MudVille Gazette Web Site, http://www.mudvillegazette.com/milblogs/; accessed Jun 7, 2007); Milblogging Web Site, http://www.milblogging.com/; accessed Jun 7, 2007).
95. Tim Sumner, "NY Times Names WOT's Dead; Tosses Their Heroism," web site *9/11 Families for a Safe & Strong America*, http://www.911familiesforamerica.org/?p=554 Oct 30, 2007; accessed Oct 30, 2007).
96. Clay Waters, "Medal of Honor Winner's Story Unfit to Print?," *Timeswatch*, Oct, 15, 2007. (http://www.timeswatch.org/articles/2007/20071015120146.aspx; accessed Aug 17, 2008); Clay Waters, "Times Again Almost Ignores Medal of Honor Recipient," *Timeswatch*, Apr 4, 2008. (http://www.timeswatch.org/articles/2008/20080404151525.aspx; accessed Aug 17, 2008);
97. Anderson Copper 360 Degrees, "Inside Hezbollah," *CNN*, Jul 24, 2006. (http://transcripts.cnn.com/TRANSCRIPTS/0607/24/acd.02.html; accessed Apr 29, 2009.)
98. Anderson Copper 360 Degrees, "Crisis in the Middle East, Day Seven; *CNN*, Jul 18, 2006. (http://transcripts.cnn.com/TRANSCRIPTS/0607/18/acd.02.html; accessed Apr 29, 2009.)

99. Reliable Sources, "Coverage of Mideast Conflict," *CNN*, Jul 23, 2006. (http://transcripts.cnn.com/TRANSCRIPTS/0607/23/rs.01.html; accessed Apr 29, 2009.)
100. Ibid.
101. Jonathan L. Snow, Using Mickey Mouse to Incite Terror, *The Providence Journal*, May 26, 2007. (http://www.defenddemocracy.org/index.php?option=com_content&task=view&id=11779748&Itemid=0; accessed Apr 29, 2009.)
102. Mark Dubowitz, Roberta Bonazzi, "Jihad TV in Europe," Wall Street Journal, Feb 18, 2009. (http://online.wsj.com/article/SB123490878778903321.html; accessed Apr 29, 2009.)
103. Ibid.
104. Mark Dubowitz, "Terrorist TV in Eurabia," *inFocus*, Dec 22, 2007. (http://www.defenddemocracy.org/index.php?option=com_content&task=view&id=11780863&Itemid=0; accessed Apr 29, 2009.)
105. Islamic Terrorism briefing at Marine Corps University, 2009.
106. Author's review of Arab media while traveling the Middle East in Feb, 2009.
107. Richard Engel, *War Journal*, 62.

Chapter Eleven

1. "Kimberly Kagan, "How They Did it: Executing the Winning Strategy in Iraq," The Weekly Standard, Volume 013, Issue 10, Nov 11, 2007. (http://www.weeklystandard.com/Content/Public/Articles/000/000/014/346ydlgo.asp; accessed Nov 13, 2007); General David H. Petraeus, Report to Congress on the Situation in Iraq, 10-11 Sep, 2007. http://www.foreignaffairs.house.gov/110/pet091007.pdf; accessed Oct 17, 2007).
2. McWilliams et al, *Al-Anbar Awakening Volume I*, 248.
3. Bill Roggio, "The Long War Journal: Al Qaeda, the Anbar SalvationCouncil and the Amiriya Battles," *The Long War Journal*, Match 20, 2007. (http://www.longwarjournal.org.archives/2007/03/al_qaedathe_anbar_s-print.php; accessed Apr 26, 2009).
4. General David H. Petraeus, "Hope has been rekindled," Dec 28, 2007. (http://www.weeklystandard.com/Content/Public/Articles/000/000/014/535mehzn.asp; accessed Apr 26, 2009).
5. Ibid.; Michael Yon, "Maysan: A Small Battle in the Media War," *Michael Yon: Online Magazine*, Apr 18, 2007. (http://www.michaelyon-online.com/wp/maysan.htm; accessed Oct 17, 2007); "Iraq Resumes Control of Karbala," *United Press International*, Oct 29, 2007. http://www.upi.com/NewsTrack/Top_News/2007/10/29/iraq_resumes_control_of_karbala/6355/; accessed Oct 29, 2007).
6. William Selby, "Al Qaeda Leader's Diary Reveals Organization's Decline," *American Forces Press Service*, Feb 9, 2008. (http://www.defense.gov/news/newsarticle.aspx?id=48914; accessed Dec 21, 2009).
7. Martin, Fletcher, "Al-Qaeda leaders admit: 'We are in crisis. There is panic and fear'," *The Times*, Feb 11, 2008. (http://www.timesonline.co.uk/tol/news/world/iraq/article3346386.ece; accessed Dec 21, 2009).
8. Michael Totten, *New York Daily News* "What I See Every Day in Iraq: Locals Turning Against the Insurgents, Dec 2nd 2007. (http://www.nydailynews.com/opinions/2007/12/02/2007-12-02_what_i_see_every_day_in_iraq_locals_turn.html; accessed Aug 16, 2008).
9. Ibid.

10. Oliver North, "Iraq: The Real Story Friday," *Townhall.com*, Mar 21, 2008. (*http://townhall.com/columnists/olivernorth/2008/03/21/iraq_the_real_*story; accessed Aug 18, 2008); Kimberly Kagan and Frederick W. Kagan, "How Prime Minister Maliki Pacified Iraq," *Wall Street Journal*, Jun 10, 2008. p. A.17. Available on ProQuest LLC; accessed Aug 18, 2008); Gina Chon, "Iraqi Forces Arrest al-Qaeda Leader," *Wall Street Journal*, May 9, 2008. p. A.12 Available on ProQuest LLC; accessed Aug 18, 2008); Ernesto Londoño and Sudarsan Raghavan, "Iraqi Troops Welcomed In Sadr City: U.S. Absence Seems To Make Difference," *Washington Post*, May 22, 2008; Page A01. Available on http://www.washingtonpost.com/wp-dyn/content/article/2008/05/21/AR2008052103056.html; accessed Aug 18, 2008); Marie Colvin, "Iraqis Lead Final Purge Of Al-Qaeda In Mosul," *The Sunday Times*, Jul 6, 2008. Available on http://www.timesonline.co.uk/tol/news/world/iraq/article4276486.ece; accessed Aug 18, 2008).
11. General David H. Petraeus, "General Petraeus' Report to Congress on Situation in Iraq," Apr 8, 2008. (http://www.america.gov/st/texttrans-english/2008/Apr/20080408125259eaifas0.9614984.html; accessed Aug 6, 2008.)
12. Ibid.; Iraq Coalition Casualty Count. Aug 7, 2008. (http://icasualties.org/oif/; accessed Jul 31, 2008); Khalid al-Ansary, "Iraq Begins Crackdown In Restive Diyala Province," *Reuters*, Jul 29, 2008. (http://www.breitbart.com/article.php?id=080731124350.si8k6wlc&show_article=1; accessed Jul 31, 2008); Michael Yon, "As Iraqis Stop Living In Fear, End Of Iraq War Is At Hand," *New York Daily News*, Jul 20th 2008. (http://www.nydailynews.com/opinions/2008/07/20/2008-07-20_as_iraqis_stop_living_in_fear_end_of_ira.html; accessed Aug 11, 2008).
13. Michael Yon, "As Iraqis Stop Living In Fear, End Of Iraq War Is At Hand," *New York Daily News*, Jul 20th 2008. (http://www.nydailynews.com/opinions/2008/07/20/2008-07-20_as_iraqis_stop_living_in_fear_end_of_ira.html; accessed Aug 11, 2008).
14. Ibid.
15. Ibid.
16. Robert Burns and Robert H. Reid, "Analysis: US Now Winning Iraq War That Seemed Lost," Associated Press, Jul 26, 2008. (http://news.yahoo.com/s/ap/20080726/ap_on_an/iraq_winning_the_war; accessed Jul 31, 2008).
17. Kimberly Kagan and Frederick W. Kagan, "Iraq's Remarkable Election," The Wall Street Journal, Feb 4, 2009. (http://online.wsj.com/article/SB123380162010450689.html; accessed May 6, 2009).
18. Ibid.
19. Samir Sumaida'ie, "The Promise In Iraq's Rebirth," *Washington Post*, Feb 7, 2009, Page A13. (http://www.washingtonpost.com/wp-dyn/content/article/2009/02/06/AR2009020602748.html?referrer=emailarticle; accessed May 6, 2009).
20. Before Saddam Hussein's invasion of Kuwait in 1990, most Iraqis drove Toyota Coronas or Brazilian-made Volkswagen Passats, which the government imported in early 1980s as part of an arms deals between Iraq and Brazil. However, the flow of new cars was cut as a result on UN sanctions following the 1991 Gulf War, leaving many aged and constantly repaired vehicles. Sameer N. Yacoub, "In Baghdad, a big craze for new cars," *Associated Press*, Apr 9, 2009. (http://hosted.ap.org/dynamic/stories/m/ml_iraq_new_car_craze?site=ap§ion=home&template=default&ctime=2009-04-09-14-40-48; accessed Apr 30, 2009).

21. Gary Langer, "Dramatic Advances Sweep Iraq, Boosting Support for Democracy," ABC News/BBC/NHK National Survey of Iraq, Mar 16, 2009. (http://abcnews.go.com/PollingUnit/story?id=7058272&page=1; accessed Apr 30, 2009).
22. Navy Petty Officer 3rd Class William Selby, "U.S. Forces Continue to Transfer Responsibilities to Iraqis," *American Forces Press Service*, Apr 9, 2009. (http://www.defenselink.mil/news/newsarticle.aspx?id=53861; accessed Apr 30, 2009).
23. Middle East Institue Annual Conference. Transcripts available online at: http://www.mei.edu/Portals/0/Content%20Edition%20C&O/MEI%202009%20Conference%20Transcripts.pdf ; accessed Dec 22, 2009).
24. Adam Schreck, "US Marines end role in Iraq; Biden in Baghdad," *MyWay*, Jan 23, 2010. Available online at: http://apnews.myway.com/article/20100123/D9DDEHH00.html;; accessed Jan 24, 2010).
25. "Iraq War," *The Project of Excellence in Journalism*, May 25, 2007. (http://www.journalism.org; accessed Jul 18, 2007).
26. Jones, *Red, White, or Yellow?*, 4-5.
27. Ibid., 4.
28. "Iraq War," *The Project of Excellence in Journalism*, May 25, 2007. http://www.journalism.org; accessed Jul 18, 2007).
29. Ibid.
30. Ibid.
31. "Surge is the Word," *The Project of Excellence in Journalism*, Jan 17, 2007. http://www.journalism.org; accessed Jul 18, 2007).
32. Lizette Alvarez and Andrew Lehren, "3,000 Deaths in Iraq, Countless Tears at Home," New York Times, Jan 1, 2007. (http://www.nytimes.com/2007/01/01/us/01deaths.html?_r=1&sq=Another%20Grim%20Milestone%20for%20the%20Military&st=cse&adxnnl=1&oref=slogin&scp=1&adxnnlx=1218830676-/wtlevFtjxeXGZM2gdWiXQ&pagewanted=print; accessed Aug 15, 2008).
33. Michael Weisskopf, "A Grim Milestone: 500 Amputees," *Time*, Jan 18, 2007. Available online at: http://www.time.com/time/nation/article/0,8599,1580531,00.html?cnn=yes (accessedAug 15, 2008).
34. Karlyn H. Bowman, *Public Opinion on the War with Iraq*, American Enterprise Institute. (Last updated Jun 20, 2008). (http://www.aei.org/publicopinion2; accessed Jul 12, 2008). p. 107.
35. "Why News of Iraq Dropped," *Project for Excellence in Journalism*, Mar 26, 2008. (http://www.journalism.org/print/10365 ; accessed Jul 18, 2007).
36. Michael Yon, "Maysan: A Small Battle in the Media War," *Michael Yon: Online Magazine*, Apr 18, 2007. (http://www.michaelyon-online.com/wp/maysan.htm; accessed Oct 17, 2007).
37. "Anti-U.S. Mar Marks Fourth Anniversary of Iraq Occupation," *The New American*, Apr 30, 2007. Vol. 23, Iss. 9; p. 8 (1 page). (ProQuest LLC®; accessed Aug 8, 2008); Jane Stancill, Marti Maguire and Josh Shaffer, "Students Mark War's Anniversary: Protests Across Nation Recall 1960s," *Knight Ridder Tribune Business News*. Mar 21, 2007. p. 1. (ProQuest LLC®; accessed Aug 8, 2008); Haider Rizvi, "Politics-U.S.: Thousands Protest On Fourth Anniversary Of War," *Global Information Network*, Mar 20, 2007. p. 1. (ProQuest LLC®; accessed Aug 8, 2008); Emma Graves Fitzsimmons and Nancy Ryan "Anger Over War In Iraq Has Thousands On Mar," *Knight Ridder Tribune Business News*, Mar 21, 2007. p. 1. (ProQuest LLC®; accessed Aug 8, 2008).
38. "Fighting about the war America and Iraq," *Economist.com/Global Agenda*, Apr 30, 2007. pg. 1. (ProQuest LLC®; accessed Aug 8, 2008).

39. Michael E. O'Hanlon and Kenneth M. Pollack, "A War We Just Might Win," *New York Times*," Jul 30, 2007. (LexisNexis® Academic; accessed Aug 7, 2007); Petraeus, General David H. Report to Congress on the Situation in Iraq, 10-11 Sep, 2007. http://www.foreignaffairs.house.gov/110/pet091007.pdf; accessed Oct 17, 2007).
40. "Couric: 'Real Progress In Iraq," *WCSBTV.com*, Sep 5, 2007. http://www.wcbstv.com; accessed Sep 5, 2007).
41. Jim Lobe, "U.S.: Bush's Successor May Inherit Quagmire In Iraq," *Global Information Network*, Sep 13, 2007. pg. 1. (ProQuest LLC; accessed Aug 8, 2008); "Kucinich: Iraq 'Progress Report' Acknowledges a No-Win Situation," *PR Newswire*, Sep 10, 2007. (ProQuest LLC; accessed Aug 8, 2008)
42. Liane Hansen, "War Crimes in Iraq: Haditha and Abu Ghraib," National Public Radio. Sep 2, 2007. p. 1. (ProQuest LLC®; accessed Jul 9, 2008).
43. "Highest-ranking officer cleared in Haditha deaths," CNN, Jun 17, 2008. (http://www.cnn.com/2008/US/06/17/haditha.charges/index.html; accessed Aug 19, 2008); Dan Whitcomb, "Haditha charges dropped against top Marine," *Reuters*, Jun 18, 2008. (http://uk.reuters.com/article/idUKN1737326520080617; accessed Dec 22, 2009).
44. "The Portrait from Iraq - How the Press Has Covered Events on the Ground," *Project for Excellence in Journalism*, Dec 19, 2007. (http://www.journalism.org/node/8996; accessed Aug 11, 2008).
45. Ibid.
46. "The State of the News Media 2008: An Annual Report on American Journalism," *The Project of Excellence in Journalism*, 2007. (http://www.stateofthenewsmedia.com/2008/; accessed Aug 18, 2008).
47. "The Portrait from Iraq - How the Press Has Covered Events on the Ground," *Project for Excellence in Journalism*, Dec 19, 2007. (http://www.journalism.org/node/8996; accessed Aug 11, 2008).
48. Elisabeth Bumiller, "With War in Senate Spotlight, Presidential Campaigns Converge in Washington," *The New York Times*, Apr 8, 2008. Section A; Pg. 10. (Lexis-Nexis Academic®; accessed Aug 9, 2008).
49. Rhoda Amon, "Rally to mark 4,000th American death in Iraq," *McClatchy - Tribune Business News*, Mar 27, 2008. (ProQuest LLC®; accessed Aug 8, 2008); Edith Brady-Lunny, "Protest Marks Fifth Anniversary of War," *McClatchy - Tribune Business News*, Mar 23, 2008. (ProQuest LLC®; accessed Aug 8, 2008).
50. "Blast kills 4, raising U.S. toll in Iraq to 4,000," *CNN*, Mar 24, 2008. (http://www.cnn.com/2008/WORLD/meast/03/23/iraq.main/index.html; accessed Aug 16, 2008); Clay Waters, "NYT Can't Wait: 'Deadly U.S. Milestone' of 500 Deaths in Afghanistan," Timeswatch, Aug 7, 2008. (http://www.timeswatch.org/articles/2008/20080807120040.aspx; accessed Aug 17, 2008).
51. Maher Al-Jasem "Sunni tribes seek unity," Al-Jazeera, Sep 19, 2007. (http://english.aljazeera.net/news/middleeast/2007/09/2008525141728481550.html; accessed Jan 13, 2010); Maher Al-Jasem "Iraq's Sunnis face new conflict," Al-Jazeera, Jun 24, 2007. (http://english.aljazeera.net/news/middleeast/2006/11/2008525185224282143.html; accessed Jan 13, 2010).
52. Michael Kamber and Tim Arango, *New York Times*, "4,000 U.S. Deaths, and a Handful of Images, Jul 26, 2008. (http://www.nytimes.com/2008/07/26/world/middleeast/26censor.html; accessed Aug 17, 2008).

53. Michael Kamber and Tim Arango, *New York Times*, "4,000 U.S. Deaths, and a Handful of Images, Jul 26, 2008. (http://www.nytimes.com/2008/07/26/world/middleeast/26censor.html; accessed Aug 17, 2008).
54. Reprinted on the Web as: Jonathan S. Landay and John Walcott, "Pentagon institute calls Iraq war 'a major debacle' with outcome 'in doubt,'" *McClatchy Newspapers*, Apr 17, 2008. (http://www.mcclatchydc.com/103/story/34101.html; accessed Aug 10, 2008). *Small Wars Journal*, Apr 18, 2008. (http://smallwarsjournal.com/blog/2008/04/pentagon-study-current-events/; accessed Aug 10, 2008).
55. *Small Wars Journal*, Apr 18, 2008. (http://smallwarsjournal.com/blog/2008/04/pentagon-study-current-events/; accessed Aug 10, 2008).
56. Peter Goodspeed, "U.S. Military School Calls Iraq War A Debacle; Outcome Remains In Doubt, Study Says," National Post, Apr 22, 2008. (Lexis-Nexis Academic®; accessed Aug 10, 2008); *The Huffington Post*, Apr 17, 2008. (http://www.huffingtonpost.com/2008/04/18/pentagon-institute-iraq-w_n_97407.html; accessed Aug 10, 2008); Mother Jones, (http://www.motherjones.com/mojoblog/archives/2008/04/8006_iraq_war_a_majo.html; accessed Aug 10, 2008)
57. Nic Robertson, "Behind The Scenes: Surge Helping, But Iraq Still on Knife's Edge," CNN, Apr 8, 2008. (http://www.cnn.com/2008/WORLD/meast/04/08/surge.status/index.html?iref=newssearch; accessed Aug 17, 2008).
58. Eric Hamilton, "Operation Lion's Roar," *Institute for the Study of War*, May 12, 2008. (http://www.understandingwar.org/commentary/operation-lion's-roar; accessed Aug 17, 2008); Eric Hamilton, "The Fight for Mosul: Iraq Report #8," *Institute for the Study of War*, Jun 4, 2008. (http://www.understandingwar.org/report/the-fight-for-mosul; accessed Aug 17, 2008).
59. Michael R. Gordon, "Iraqi Unit Flees Post, Despite American's Plea," *New York Times*, Apr 16, 2008. (http://www.nytimes.com/2008/04/16/world/middleeast/16sadr.htm; accessed Aug 18, 2008).
60. "Reconciliation In Iraq 'Isn't Happening:' In Advance of Gen. Petraeus' Report To Congress This Week, Reporters Discuss What Recent Violence In Iraq Means," *CBS News*, Apr 6, 2008. (http://www.cbsnews.com/stories/2008/04/06/ftn/main3996674.shtml; accessed Aug 17, 2008).
61. Deborah Sontag and Lizette Alvarez, "Across America, Deadly Echoes of Foreign Battles," *New York Times*, Jan 13, 2008. (http://www.nytimes.com/2008/01/13/us/13vets.html; accessed Aug 17, 2008).
62. Ibid.
63. Lizette Alvarez, "Army and Marine Corps Grant More Felony Waivers," *New York Times*, Apr 22, 2008. (http://www.nytimes.com/2008/04/22/washington/22waiver.html ; accessed Aug 17, 2008), Lizette Alvarez, "After the Battle, Fighting the Bottle at Home," *New York Times*, Jul 8, 2008. (http://www.nytimes.com/2008/07/08/us/08vets.html; accessed Aug 17, 2008).
64. Andrew Kohut, "The Iraq Challenge," Pew Research Center Special to the New York Times, Jun 2, 2008. (http://pewresearch.org/pubs/856/the-iraq-challenge; accessed Jul 31, 2008). "Increasing Optimism About Iraq: Obama Has The Lead, But Potential Problems Too," (http://people-press.org/report/?pageid=1258 ; accessed Aug 11, 2008); John D. McKinnon, "Sentiment On Iraq Is Changing," *Wall Street Journal*, Mar 5, 2008. (http://www.pewtrusts.org/news_room_detail.aspx?id=37160; accessed Aug 19, 2008).

65. "ABC, CBS, NBC Skip Report of Benchmarks Met in Iraq," *Media Research Center*, Jul 9, 2008. (http://www.mrc.org/cyberalerts/2008/cyb20080702.asp#; accessed Aug 17, 2008).
66. Ibid.
67. (http://icasualties.org/oif/; accessed Jul 31, 2008). Khalid al-Ansary, "Iraq Begins Crackdown In Restive Diyala Province," *Reuters*, Jul 29, 2008. (http://www.breitbart.com/article.php?id=080731124350.si8k6wlc&show_article=1; accessed Jul 31, 2008).
68. Andrew E. Kramer, "U.S. Deaths in Iraq Fell Sharply in May," *New York Times*, Jun 2, 2008. (http://www.nytimes.com/2008/06/02/world/middleeast/02iraq.html; accessed Aug 17, 2008).
69. Firas Al-Atraqchi, "Iraq between fear and hope," Al-Jazeera, Aug 18, 2008. (http://english.aljazeera.net/focus/theiraqinvasionfiveyearson/2008/03/200861516573600242.html; accessed Jan 13, 2010).
70. Ibid.
71. "Highest-ranking officer cleared in Haditha deaths," CNN, Jun 17, 2008. (http://www.cnn.com/2008/US/06/17/haditha.charges/index.html; accessed Aug 19, 2008).
72. Clay Waters, "Times Maintains Near Silence as Haditha 'Massacre' Case Crumbles," Timeswatch, Jun 18, 2003. (http://www.timeswatch.org/articles/2008/20080618114909.aspx; accessed Aug 17, 2008).
73. Kirk Semple and Andrew W. Lehren, "Deadly U.S. Milestone in Afghan War," *New York Times*, Aug 6, 2008. (http://www.nytimes.com/2008/08/07/us/07afghan.html Academic; accessed Aug 15, 2008).
74. " 'Battle for Haditha' Stars Vets, Iraqi Refugees," *National Public Radio*, May 3, 2008. (ProQuest LLC®; accessed Jul 9, 2008); Rafer Guzman, "Battle for Haditha," *McClatchy - Tribune Business News*. May 9, 2008. (ProQuest LLC®; accessed Jul 9, 2008), "For the Record," *New York Times*. May 16, 2008. p. A.4. (ProQuest LLC®; accessed Jul 9, 2008)
75. http://longwarjournal.com; http://smallwarsjournal.com.
76. http://michaeltotten.com.
77. Michael J. Totten, "The Real Iraq," *City Journal*, 16 May 2008. (http://www.city-journal.org/2008/bc0516mt.html; accessed Aug 19, 2008).
78. Michael Yon, "Af-Pak Reporting," *Michael Yon Online Magazine*, Aug 19, 2008. (http://www.michaelyon-online.com/index.php?option=com_content&view=article&id=1819:af-pak-reporting&catid=34:dispatches&Itemid=55; accessed Aug 19, 2008).
79. Cooper, *Watching the Watchdog*, 21, 26-33, 86-87, 93, 105-107, 116-117, 125, 157, 175, 201-202, 253-254.
80. "Vets for Freedom is headed 'Back to Iraq'," *Veterans for Freedom*. http://www.vetsforfreedom.org/fourmonths/backtoiraq.aspx; accessed Aug 20, 2008).
81. Bill Roggio, " 'Tell the American people we need the U.S. Army here:' An Interview with the Jundi," *In DC Journal*, Feb 20, 2007. http://www.indcjournal.com/archives/002948.php; accessed Feb 22, 2007.
82. Franklin Raff, "I have seen the enemy…," *WorldNetDaily*, Apr 14, 2006. http://www.worldnetdaily.com/news/article.asp?ARTICLE_ID=49739; accessed Feb 20, 2007).
83. Cooper, *Watching the Watchdog*, 17-19.

84. Tariq al-Hashimi, "Don't Give Up On Iraq Yet" *The Washington Post*, Jan 10, 2007; A13. (LexisNexis® Academic; accessed Jun 7, 2007); Tariq al-Hashimi, "No, America, Iraq is not a lost cause," *The Star Ledger* (Newark, New Jersey), Jan 11, 2007, 19. (LexisNexis® Academic; accessed Jun 7, 2007).
85. Ibid.
86. Brian Callaway, Scott Kraus, "Soldiering On After The Election: Obama's Victory Is Not An Automatic Trip Home For Troops," *McClatchy - Tribune Business News*, Nov 11, 2008. (ProQuest LLC; accessed Dec 22, 2009); "US/IRAQ: Obama Likely To Choose Continuity Over Change," *OxResearch*, Nov 12, 2008. p. 1. (ProQuest LLC; accessed Dec 22, 2009).
87. Michael Slackman and Souad Mekhennet, "Jihadi Leader in Iraq Says Radicals Share in Obama Victory," *New York Times*, Nov 8, 2008. pg. A.6. (ProQuest LLC; accessed Dec 22, 2009).
88. Gary Langer, "Dramatic Advances Sweep Iraq, Boosting Support for Democracy," ABC News/BBC/NHK National Survey of Iraq, Mar 16, 2009. (http://abcnews.go.com/PollingUnit/story?id=7058272&page=1; accessed Apr 30, 2009); Jeff Jacoby, "Bush's 'folly' is ending in victory," The Boston Globe, Mar 25, 2009. (http://www.boston.com/bostonglobe/editorial_opinion/oped/articles/2009/03/25/bushs_folly_is_ending_in_victory/; accessed Apr 30, 2009).
89. "US military deaths in Iraq war at 4,278," *Associated Press*, Apr 30, 2009. (http://hosted.ap.org/dynamic/stories/U/US_IRAQ_US_DEATHS?SITE=AP&SECTION=HOME&TEMPLATE=DEFAULT&CTIME=2009-04-30-19-56-10; accessed Apr 30, 2009).
90. "Dec 1st Month without US combat death in Iraq,"*Associated Press*, Jan 1, 2010. (http://news.yahoo.com/s/ap/20100101/ap_on_re_mi_ea/ml_iraq_us_casualties; accessed Jan 19, 2010).

Chapter Twelve

1. Galston, William A. "A Question of Life and Death: U.S. Policy in Afghanistan," The Brookings Institution, June 2010, (http://www.brookings.edu/opinions/2010/0615_afghanistan_galston.aspx; accessed July 19, 2010); "Afghanistan in 2009: A Survey of the Afghan People." The Asia Foundation, 2009, (http://www.asiafoundation.org/resources/pdfs/Afghanistanin2009.pdf; accessed Jul 10, 2010), 99.
2. Wike, Richard. "Repairing the U.S. Image in Muslim World" The Pew Charitable Trusts, July 29, 2009, (http://www.pewtrusts.org/news_room_detail.aspx?id=54398; accessed June 23, 2010).
3. A story conveyed to the Marine Corps History Division.
4. Mudaqiq, Mohammad Amin, "Afghan Reporters Caught in the Crossfire." *Radio Free Europe*, Mar 5, 2010, (http://www.rferl.org/content/Afghan_Reporters_Caught_In_The_Crossfire/1975677.html; accessed Jun 28, 2010).
5. Bashir Ahmad Gwakh, "Taliban Employs Modern Weapons In 'War of Words'." *Radio Free Europe*, Mar 16, 2011, (http://www.rferl.org/articleprintview/2340644.html; accessed Mar 16, 2011).
6. Ibid.
7. Ibid.
8. Phares, *The War of Ideas*, 36-44; Central Intelligence Agency. *The World Factbook*. (https://www.cia.gov/library/publications/the-world-factbook/; accessed Mar 16, 2011).
9. Joe Klein, "Barack Obama's Big Fat Afghan Dilemma." *Time*, June 17, 2010, (http://www.time.com/time/nation/article/0,8599,1997241,00.html; accessed Mar 16, 2011).

10. "Iran Ready To Set Up Joint TV Station With Tajikistan, Afghanistan." *Radio Free Europe*, Feb 11, 2011, (http://www.rferl.org/content/iran_afghanistan_tajikistan_tv_station/2305842.html; accessed Mar 16, 2011).
11. Shanthie Mariet D'Souza. "India's Tripartite Plan for Afghanistan" *WSJ.com.* (http://online.wsj.com/article/SB10001424052748704388504575418570882789914.html; accessed Aug 9, 2010); Karen Brulliard and Karen De Young. "Pakistan, Afghanistan begin talks about dealing with insurgents" *WashingtonPost.com*, Jun 19, 2010. (http://www.washingtonpost.com/wp-dyn/content/article/2010/06/18/AR2010061805638.html; accessed Jun 19, 2010); Greg Bruno and Lionel Beehner. "Iran and the Future of Afghanistan." Council on Foreign Relations, Mar 30, 2009. (http://www.cfr.org/publication/13578/iran_and_the_future_of_afghanistan.html; accessed on Jun 23, 2010); Anthony Kuhn, "China Becomes a Player in Afghanistan's Future". NPR, Oct 21, 2009, (http://www.npr.org/templates/story/story.php?storyId=113967842; accessed Jun 23, 2010); Lee, Jesse. "A New Strategy for Afghanistan and Pakistan" The White House Blog, Mar 27, 2009, (http://www.whitehouse.gov/blog/09/03/27/A-New-Strategy-for-Afghanistan-and-Pakistan/; accessed Jun 24, 2010).
12. Helle Dale, "Public Diplomacy 2.0: Where the U.S. Government Meets 'New Media,'" *The Heritage Foundation*, Dec 8, 2009, (http://www.heritage.org/Research/Reports/2009/12/Public-Diplomacy-2-0-Where-the-US-Government-Meets-New-Media; accessed on Jun 29, 2010). Judith A. McHale, "Future of U.S. Public Diplomacy." U.S. Department of State, Mar 10, 2010, (http://www.state.gov/r/remarks/138283.htm; accessed June 24, 2010); J. Michael Waller, *Fighting the War of Ideas Like a Real War: Messages to Defeat the Terrorists.* Washington, DC: Institute of World Politics Press, 2007; "Public Opinion on the War with Iraq." *AEI Public Opinion Studies.* Mar 19, 2009, (http://www.aei.org/publicopinion2; accessed Mar 16, 2011); Joseph S. Nye Jr, 2004. "Comments - The Decline of America's Soft Power - The Bush Administration May Dismiss the Relevance of Soft Power, but It Does so at Great Peril. Success in the War on Terrorism Depends on Washington's Capacity to Persuade Others Without Force, and That Capacity Is in Dangerous Decline". Foreign Affairs. 83, no. 3: 16.
13. Carnes Lord, *Losing Hearts and Minds?: Public Diplomacy and Strategic Influence in the Age of Terror.* Westport, Conn: Praeger Security International, 2006, 4.
14. Joshua Partlow, "U.S. uses Predator drone to hit suspected insurgents in Afghanistan; 13 killed," The Washington Post, Jan 13, 2010. (http://www.washingtonpost.com/wp-dyn/content/article/2010/01/12/AR2010011201644.html; accessed Mar 16, 2011); Noah Shachtman, "General: Blame Taliban, Media for Furor Over Afghan Civilian Deaths," Wired, Dec 10, 2009. (http://www.wired.com/dangerroom/2009/12/us-general-blame-taliban-media-for-afghan-civilian-deaths/#; accessed Mar 16, 2011).
15. Thalif Deen, "POLITICS: OBSERVERS WONDER IF AFGHANISTAN IS NEXT U.S. QUAGMIRE," *Global Information Network*, Feb 20, 2009. (ProQuest LLC; accessed Dec 22, 2009).
16. Mark Jurkowitz, "Afghanistan Dominates While Two Scandals Fascinate," *The Project of Excellence in Journalism*, Dec 2009. http://www.journalism.org; accessed Dec 22, 2009).
17. "Obama Tiptoeing Around Afghanistan Quagmire," *All Things Considered* (NPR), Sep 2, 2009. (ProQuest LLC; accessed Dec 22, 2009); James G. Blight, "Is Afghanistan Obama's Vietnam?," *The Chronicle of Higher Education*, Feb 27, 2009. (ProQuest LLC; accessed Dec 22, 2009); "Afghanistan Is Vietnam: A Valid Analogy?," *Newsweek*, Feb 23, 2009. (ProQuest LLC; accessed Dec 22, 2009); "Obama's Vietnam: How to Salvage Afghanistan," *Newsweek*, Feb 9, 2009. (ProQuest LLC; accessed Dec 22, 2009).

18. Elisabeth Bumiller, "Gates Faults U.S. Allies on Afghan War," The New York Times, Mar 11, 2011. (http://www.nytimes.com/2011/03/12/world/europe/12gates.html; accessed Mar 16, 2011).
19. Kenneth Payne, "The Media as an Instrument of War," *Parameters*, Spring 2005. (http://www.usamhi.army.mil/USAWC/Parameters/05spring/payne.htm; accessed Jan 16, 2010).
20. "Press Accuracy Rating Hits Two Decade Low: Public Evaluations of the News Media: 1985-2009," PEW Research Center for People and the Press, Sep 13, 2009. (http://people-press.org/report/543/; accessed Jan 19, 2010)
21. David J. Danelo, "Stop Blaming the Press," *U.S. Naval Institute Proceedings*; January 2008.
22. Anthony Zinni, *The Battle for Peace,* 33.

8202752R0

Made in the USA
Charleston, SC
17 May 2011